Building the 21st Century Home

The sustainable urban neighbourhood

Building the 21st Century Home
The sustainable urban neighbourhood

David Rudlin & Nicholas Falk
URBED (The Urban and Economic Development Group)

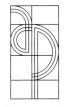

Architectural Press

Oxford   Auckland   Boston   Johannesburg   Melbourne   New Delhi

Architectural Press
An imprint of Butterworth-Heinemann
Linacre House, Jordan Hill, Oxford OX2 8DP
225 Wildwood Avenue, Woburn, MA 01801-2041
A division of Reed Educational and Professional Publishing Ltd.

 A member of the Reed Elsevier plc group

First published 1999

British Library Cataloguing in Publication Data
A catalogue record for this book is available from the British Library
Library of Congress Cataloguing in Publication Data
A catalogue record for this book is available from the Library of Congress

ISBN 0 7506 2528 7

Designed by David Rudlin
Printed and bound in Great Britain

FOR EVERY TITLE THAT WE PUBLISH, BUTTERWORTH-HEINEMANN
WILL PAY FOR BTCV TO PLANT AND CARE FOR A TREE.

Title sheet illustration: A proposed mixed-use development
in Smithfield Manchester (see page 225)

Contents

Case studies

The book is dedicated to Luca and Jonah
and the city in which they will grow up

The authors

Both David Rudlin and Nicholas Falk are directors of URBED (the Urban and Economic Development Group). URBED is a not-for-profit urban regeneration consultancy which for twenty-two years has pioneered many of the regeneration techniques which are now commonplace. They are currently focusing on how the threats to town centres can be tackled and on models for sustainable urban development. The latter has been developed through the Sustainable Urban Neighbourhood Initiative, a project with funding from the Department of the Environment, Transport and the Regions.

URBED has always combined research with consultancy and has published a wide range of reports. This however is the first time that the ideas and the philosophy of the company have been set out in a book. While the book focuses mainly on the Sustainable Urban Neighbourhood it draws upon many aspects of URBED's work as well, of course, as over twenty years of experience working on the frontline of urban regeneration in the UK.

David Rudlin BA MTP: A planner and urban designer who joined URBED in 1990 to head up the Little Germany Action project in Bradford which was subsequently to receive a BURA best practice award. He studied planning at Manchester University and prior to joining URBED was a senior planner with Manchester City Council. He has worked on numerous projects including town centre urban design projects in Bristol, Bracknell, Swansea and Coventry, strategies for housing estates in Stoke, Wythenshawe and Moss Side as well as regeneration projects in Liverpool, Manchester and Hackney. He currently manages the Sustainable Urban Neighbourhood Initiative.

He is the author of a report *Valuing the value added* on Housing Plus for the Housing Corporation and has recently completed a report, *Tomorrow: a peaceful path to urban reform* published by Friends of the Earth. He was responsible for the *21st Century Homes* report for the Joseph Rowntree Foundation, was a co-author of the *Hulme Guide to Development* and a member of the expert panel responsible for the *Manchester Guide to Development*. He is also a founder member of the Homes for Change Housing Co-op.

Dr. Nicholas Falk BA MBA: An economist and strategic planner with over twenty years experience of urban regeneration and local and economic development. He has degrees from Oxford, Stanford Business School and the London School of Economics and worked in marketing for Ford Motor Company before founding URBED in 1976 in Covent Garden. He was the principal author of two reports on town centres for the Government, *Vital and Viable Town Centres* and *Town Centre Partnerships*. He has been responsible for many major studies, from large cities such as Birmingham and Bristol to smaller towns such as Cirencester and Bexleyheath. Area regeneration studies have included award winning schemes for Exeter Riverside, and Birmingham's Jewellery Quarter. He was a member of the Department of the Environment's Property Advisory Group from 1979 to 1988 and the Planning Research Advisory Group from 1993 to 1994.

Acknowledgements

This book draws upon the ideas of many people too numerous to mention here. It draws upon our research and consultancy work over many years and we are grateful for everyone who has contributed.

Worthy of particular mention are our colleagues at URBED including Christopher Cadell, Francesca King, Kate Johnson, Kieran Yates and Khoria Steward. The book draws heavily on our previous work for the Joseph Rowntree Foundation, Friends of the Earth as well as for Hulme Regeneration and through the DETR's Environmental Action Fund. Particularly important roles have been played either as clients or associates by Esther Caplin, Richard Best and John Low of the Joseph Rowntree Foundation, Simon Festing of Friends of the Earth, Charlie Baker and Sarah Hughes of Build for Change, George Mills and Ian Beaumont of MBLC Architects, Jon Rowland, David Levitt, John Doggart, Joe Ravetz, David Lunts and Barbara McLoughlin.

Direct inputs have also been made by David Malcolm and Christina Swensson helped develop the case studies. We are also indebted to the knowledge and passion of sustainability brought by Nick Dodd although we no doubt still fall short of his high standards.

Help with design has come from Jason Crouch of M15 Design, additional illustrations have been provided by Vibeke Fussing and many of the drawings are based on photography by Anne Worthington or Charlie Baker.

Thanks also go to Cecile and Vincent in Périgueux for providing a refuge and a source of inspiration for the completion of the final part of the book. Most important of all has been the role played by Hélène as a critic and confidante without whom very little would have been written.

Preface

David Rudlin

My first experience of the city was as a child in Birmingham. I grew up in Hall Green, a respectable suburb in the south of the city, and could look out of my bedroom window across treetops and rooftops to the city centre on the far horizon. My earliest memories of Birmingham were of peering through rain splattered bus windows at the lights of a city as we travelled home on dark winter evenings along the Stratford Road. Indeed much of our life seemed to revolve around the Stratford Road. My family lived near the Stratford Road, as had my grandparents; my dad worked at a factory and my mum in a shop both also on the Stratford Road. It was where we did our shopping, where the family went to church, where the library, swimming baths, police station and cinema were to be found and where my sisters and I were to go to school. To me it represented the city far more than the distant city centre.

Millions of people will know the Stratford Road. It runs from Digbeth on the southern edge of the city centre through Sparkhill and Sparkbrook, Moseley, Hall Green and Shirley to the countryside on the edge of the city, a distance of some twelve miles. It is lined almost continuously by shops, public buildings, pubs, cinemas (now sadly closed) and churches. When I go home to visit my parents I still travel

along the road. When I do I am pleased to see that it remains largely intact and indeed is thriving with activity and life when ten years ago it seemed to be on the brink of terminal decline. To a small child it seemed to be the essence of the cosmopolitan city with its Asian shops and Irish pubs and side streets which led into a warren of terraced housing with corner shops and more pubs. I was not to know that I was travelling along a tenuous thread of urban activity running through largely dull and lifeless residential areas. To me the city seemed to go on forever in all directions and was at once frightening and exciting. This part-imagined city was the territory that I populated in my dreams and which provided the setting for the stories of my childhood, be it Oliver Twist or Mary Poppins. This mixture of fear and excitement seems to me a typical reaction to the urban life.

My other main memory of growing up in Birmingham was the fact that it was being transformed. The city centre was a perpetual building site with the construction of the inner ring road, the Bull Ring and the maze of flyovers and underpasses which were to encircle the city. It was all so modern and confident, and my parents and their friends seemed to agree that it was a change for the better. I am too young to remember the Birmingham which predated this great trans-formation – the Victorian city of a thousand trades – and find it difficult to mourn its loss. However I do remember the pride of Birmingham people in the new city that was emerging. Visiting friends and relations would be taken to see the Rotunda and the other modern buildings just as today they are taken to see Chamberlain Square and the new conven-tion centre. It is less easy to remember when disillusionment set in but set in it did. It did not take long for the concrete and steel of the flyovers and high-rise buildings to lose their shine. We seemed to go less and less into the centre of town, preferring to go to Solihull which itself had not entirely escaped the attention of the planners. Somewhere in the early 1970s the municipal planners and architects fell from grace and nowhere was this more obvious than in the pages of the local paper, the *Birmingham Evening Mail*, which revelled in holding the city and the council up to ridicule.

It seems to me now that what happened to Birmingham is a microcosm of what has happened to all cities in Britain to a greater or lesser extent over the last forty years. The city fathers along with their planners, architects and engineers who transformed Birmingham in the 1960s did not do so out of malice or spite. They believed passionately in what they were doing just as those of us who seek to shape cities today believe that what we are doing is right. They were also, on the whole, supported by the community to a degree which is often forgotten. However something went horribly wrong. The areas that they created, which looked so appealing bathed in sunlight and populated with contented people in the artists' impressions, looked so different on wet grimy winter evenings, strewn with the litter of shoppers and clogged with traffic. The public esteem of the urban professions has never really recovered from this sorry period of our history. A bond of trust has been broken and we are no longer confident that we have all the answers. If we are to regain this trust and confidence we must understand what it was that went wrong, which is what we try and do in the first part of this book.

In the late 1970s I moved to Manchester to study town planning. It is the city where I have made my home and which has provided a constant source of material and examples for this book. Manchester is a city which was fortunate enough to experience its boom in the Victorian period when at least they built decent buildings. The plans of Manchester's city fathers in the 1950s were no less radical than those in Birmingham. Manchester however was in decline. The city has lost a third of its population since 1961 and its industrial base has been decimated. It therefore lacked the resources to realise its dreams so that, with the exception of Piccadilly Plaza and the Arndale Centre, its centre, at least, came through the 1950s, 60s and 70s largely unscathed.

Jane Jacobs in her book *The Economy of Cities* has a section entitled 'efficient Manchester, inefficient Birmingham'. In this she contrasts the great mills of the former with their large compliant workforces with the thousands of small inefficient workshops in Birmingham. She suggests however that this diversity of economic activity was the basis for Birmingham's growth as a great city in the twentieth century at a time when northern cities like Manchester were declining. It is in such small enterprises, Jacobs argues, that innovation and new business is generated. This is what made Birmingham such an ideal location for the car industry with its need for large numbers of component manufacturers. One need only compare the engineering sections of the Birmingham and Manchester Yellow Pages to see that there are still vastly more small manufacturing firms in the former.

However to me as a young student Manchester was so much more exciting and inviting as a city. You could walk around on real streets thronging with people rather than being forced underground in dark subways which felt, and often were, dangerous. This may explain why in the 1990s Manchester has managed to reinvent itself. It is now service and knowledge based industries rather than manufacturing which are becoming the backbone of urban economies and these creative industries seem to thrive more in the lively traditional streets of Manchester. The city may not be booming but it has managed to reverse its decline and to find a new confidence. It is significant that an important part of this renaissance is based upon an urban vision for the planning of the city.

I started studying planning at a time of great uncertainty, an interregnum when the certainties of the 1960s were being questioned but nothing had emerged to take their place. We knew that system-built estates such as Hulme, where many of us as students lived, had been a mistake but were still taught many of the principles which lay behind such developments. Indeed we were taken on a field trip to admire the Southgate Estate in Runcorn which has since been demolished as a failure. It still amazes me that I spent five years studying planning and was never required to read the *Death and Life of Great American Cities*. It is true that we were taught urban design and studied the great medieval cities of Europe, but only as history, these seemed to have no connection to the practical projects that we were set to design housing estates or town centres. Here the driving force was logic, the zoning of uses, the separation of vehicles and pedestrians and the promotion of open space. If any of us had dared to suggest a layout based on Siena or even Bath we would certainly have been failed.

I nevertheless left university a committed urbanist and got a job in the City Planning Department in Manchester. This was a large well-resourced department with a good reputation but was no place for an urbanist, at least outside the city centre. Urban design meant listed buildings, conservation areas and street furniture. It was not the concern of a frontline planning officer dealing with planning applications. Indeed, like my university projects, the planning system left no room for the urban design principles that I had learnt in the pages of Bacon's *Design of Cities* or Kevin Lynch's *Townscape*. Issues such as density, permeability, enclosure and a mix of uses, far from being promoted were the reasons we used to refuse planning applications. Of course we used different names – density became overdevelopment, mixed uses became incompatible uses, and enclosure became overlooking. It was however inescapable that the planning orthodoxies that we worked by, which in themselves were perfectly logical, when taken together were profoundly anti-urban. At first I thought that I had been naïve in wanting to promote urban principles as a planner and set about changing my ways. However I soon became disillusioned and came to believe that planning was the enemy of the city not its saviour. I effectively left the profession by joining my co-author Nicholas Falk at the urban regeneration consultants URBED where I still work.

It was not until the early 1990s that my interest in planning and to some extent my faith in the profession were restored. A friend of mine, Charlie Baker, had been asked to prepare an urban design code as part of the City Challenge sponsored redevelopment of the Hulme estate in Manchester where he and I lived. He asked me to help and we started by going back to all of our half-forgotten urban design text books. We were emboldened by the emerging Urban Villages movement and stories that were starting to emerge about the New Urbanism movement in America. We soon realised that while urbanism had seemed dead from the coalface of planning and architectural practice it lived on elsewhere and even seemed to be making a comeback. We assembled our own set of urban principles for the rebuilding of Hulme based partly on our reading but mostly on our experience of what we liked about urban areas.

Our research cannot have been that thorough because, I am ashamed to say, at the time we were not aware of the work coming out of what was then Oxford Polytechnic. It was therefore with a mixture of relief and disappointment that we realised that the urban framework that we have developed for Hulme and thought so original had been published in an almost identical form and a great deal more detail by Bentley a few years earlier. However while our principles for Hulme were nothing new or radical, what was new was the fact that they were taken seriously by politicians and council officers. We can take no credit for this. It was, after all, the council which had commissioned us to write an urban design guide and we did little more than put meat on an urban vision that had already been adopted. The *Hulme Guide to Development* was adopted by the council and subsequently revised for adoption as supplementary planning guidance covering the whole of the city, a process that we describe in Chapter 13.

The process of developing the urban design guide for Hulme and watching its subsequent application to the redevelopment of the area and the planning of the wider city has been the impetus for this book. What started with the politicians' wish to make Manchester more like the European cities that they had visited as part of the city's bid to stage the Olympics seemed to end up questioning some very fundamental assumptions behind the way that we plan and build within cities. Urban design principles which had been accepted for years, in theory at least, were being applied to the messy business of planning a city and everything was turned on its head. Everyone involved seemed to support the principles but when it came to implementation the resistance from developers, housebuilders, the police, investors, planners and engineers was concerted and fierce. This caused many of us to question why ideas that had such a wide currency, like permeability, were so threatening and radical when put into practice. This book is an attempt to provide some answers and to develop a rationale for the further development of these ideas in the twenty-first century.

This book will no doubt be seen as part of the new urbanism movement, as indeed it should be. But it is hopefully more than this. It is based on experience of living and working in cities and from a frustration at the harm that has been done and how, with the best of intentions, we seem to have created the worst of all worlds. My co-author, Nicholas Falk has been dealing with these issues for far longer than I. Together we wanted to get to the root of why things have gone wrong and to look at how they can change. This book is therefore about far more than a new aesthetic for urban areas – it is about a new vision for urban Britain.

David Rudlin
June 1998

Introduction

If the typical nineteenth century home was the urban terrace and the twentieth century home was the suburban semi, where will we be living in the twenty-first century? Places that one generation regard as normal and even inevitable can very quickly be seen as inappropriate for subsequent generations with different needs. It is the contention of this book that just such a change is taking place at present and the housing which has dominated our towns and cities in the twentieth century will fail to meet our future needs. We argue that a revolution will take place, is already taking place, which is comparable to the switch from the predominantly urban society of the Victorian age to the suburban society which has dominated the twentieth century.

There is something remarkable about a century. We characterise history as if revolutions in technology and values take place as one century passes into the next when in practice development is much more complex. The Industrial Revolution, for example, is seen as a nineteenth century phenomenon whereas, in reality, the key developments took place in the eighteenth century and many of the practices, such as the use of machinery and the employment of large numbers of people in one building, could be found in some places centuries earlier still. The advent of a new century is, however, a time for reflection and a reassessment of values and priorities. Such was the case at the beginning of the twentieth century when the garden city pioneers succeeded in transforming the British view of the ideal home. At the turn of the century people tend to look forward and New Year resolutions are writ large on the national consciousness. If this is the case at the end of a century, how much more should it be the case at the end of a millennium.

When we plan our towns and cities, when we build housing, we should be thinking at least 100 years ahead, something that we have manifestly failed to do in the recent past. Successful places are those that stand the test of time, that are built to last. It is ironic that prefabs built as a temporary solution to housing short-

What will be the twenty-first century home?
A change as radical as that from the nineteenth century terrace to this century's suburban close is likely to take place in the twenty-first century

ages after the war remained popular for many years and some have recently been listed, yet council housing built in the 1960s and 1970s has been demolished. Huge mistakes have been made in the way that we have planned our towns and cities and built public housing. This represents a profligate waste of resources, not only in terms of the loans which are still being paid off, or indeed the materials and energy which have been wasted, but, most importantly, in terms of the blighted lives of thousands of people forced to live in someone else's flawed Utopia. Those who care about housing need to follow Ruskin's advice: 'When we build let us think that we build for ever'. This is a test that we have too often failed in the twentieth century, a failure that we must not repeat in the future.

At the start of the nineteenth century the population of the UK was booming and dwellings were required in huge numbers to house the expanding industrial workforce. At the start of the twentieth century there was also a major housing shortage due to the stagnation of private building. More significantly there was an overwhelming feeling after the First World War that standards had to be improved to provide 'homes fit for heroes'. This was translated not only into a huge increase in output and the creation of mass council housing, it also

led to a major rethink in the way that these houses were built. At the end of the twentieth century the debate is also about housing numbers, as a result not of population growth but household growth. Yet while the debate rages about where new housing should be built and the balance between green field and urban development there is much less debate about what we should be building and the sort of towns and cities that we should be creating. Having had our fingers burnt badly when we last addressed these issues there is little appetite for innovation and a feeling that housing design should be left to the market. Yet if we are to accommodate more housing in urban areas to protect the countryside we must rethink the way that housing is built just as the garden city reformers did at the end of the last century. This is both an enormous challenge and an important opportunity to reshape our towns and cities for the new millennium.

The pressure for change

In order to understand the nature of this challenge we must understand the significant changes that are taking place in the population profile of Britain. Demographic change is causing household size to fall and the increase in household numbers to outstrip population growth. There can be few people who are not aware of the 4.4 million extra households that have been projected by government by 2016[1] since the issue has spilled out from the pages of the professional press into the national media. The scale of this figure is enormous. There are, for example only 2.8 million households living in Greater London, the entire new town programme after the war only accommodated around 1 million households and to accommodate household growth through new town building we would have to build more than forty cities the size of Milton Keynes.

However even these projections may be an underestimate. Government statisticians have warned that actual rates of household growth are outstripping the projections – partly as a result of inward migration from the Euro-

Flawed Utopias: Never again should we force people with no other choices to live in someone else's flawed Utopia

pean Union – and that the estimates may be raised by as much as a million households in the next round of projections. The Joseph Rowntree Foundation has also estimated that there is a need to provide a further 480 000 homes to meet the backlog of unmet housing need[2] suggesting that household growth could be as much as 6 million between 1991 and 2016. If we discount from this the 850 000 homes already built since 1991 we are left with a need to accommodate just over 5.1 million households in the next 17 years. This represents 300 000 homes a year which would mean a doubling of current housing output.

The accommodation of this household growth has become the great planning issue of our time. The prospect of house building covering England's green and pleasant land has led to demonstrations on the streets of London and the eco-campaigners, who were so effective in causing government to reassess its road building policy, are now turning their attention to the housebuilding industry. While the rate of household growth today is not greater than it has been for much of the century, there is a feeling that enough is enough and we can no longer continue to sacrifice our countryside to the relentless sprawl of urban areas. To this have been added concerns about the fact that urban sprawl is fuelling car use leading to a build-up of pressure for change.

We review these pressures for change in this book and suggest where and how the homes of the twenty-first century should be built. The reform of urban Britain may seem a vast and daunting task but decisions we take now could have a far-reaching effect on our towns and cities. If we were to assume that household growth in the next century continued at the same pace as it has done in the twentieth century and that this was accommodated with new housebuilding, we will have built 19 million new homes by 2100. If we were to assume that, in addition to this, we will replace 15 000 existing homes a year, the total housing stock in the year 2100 will be just over 38 million, more than half of which are yet to be built.

Decisions that we make at the turn of the millennium about the future shape of housing will therefore have a fundamental effect on the future of our towns and cities and the wellbeing of a large proportion of the population.

If we choose to accept existing trends of dispersal and population drift to the south, we will face the continuing and perhaps irreversible decline of urban areas, the loss of valued green belt and agricultural land, as well as a huge growth in car use. If we do not we must rethink, almost from first principles, UK planning policy. It is our contention that we must do the latter and in doing this must rediscover the town and the city as the most natural and civilised form of human settlement.

Rediscovering the city

The potential to accommodate household growth in existing settlements has received increasing attention over recent years. This raises a number of issues about the ethics and practicality of government dictating where people should live. Should housing allocations be based on demand or do they distort demand? Should they be used as a tool for social engineering by shifting population back to urban areas which have been losing population for much of this century? This may help to meet housing need, to address urban decline, and to create more sustainable transport patterns but it would mean forcing people to live where they clearly do not wish to. Such a policy has been described as 'Stalinist'[3] but a more realistic charge is that it is simply unrealistic. Population shifts are part of wider economic trends such as the increase of home ownership, the growth of the middle-classes and the decline of manufacturing industry. Jobs and economic activity have moved out of cities and those with resources to do so have followed. This has combined with a preference for the sort of physical environment that suburban areas offer to undermine the attraction of urban areas. The repopulation of cities will not therefore be achieved through regulation. This would have as much chance of success as King Canute did in turning the tide. If urban areas are to be repopulated it must be through attraction rather than coercion. We need to create urban environments able to attract people back to towns and cities. It is this task that we address in this book.

In building the twenty-first century home we are concerned not so much with the individual home, important as this is. What matters far more is the location of housing, its layout, its relationship to different uses, to transport systems and to open space. In short we are talking about the shape of our towns and cities. Housing is the predominant urban land use in the UK so that no discussion about the future of urban areas can ignore the issue of housing. The reverse is also true and no discussion of housing can ignore its effect on the wider health of urban areas. Yet this is just what hard-pressed housing developers in all sectors are doing. In catering for the short-term needs of the market and pressures to meet pressing housing needs they are producing housing which looks to the past rather than the future and reinforces trends which are no longer sustainable. They are taking the safest option, the lowest common denominator, rather than seeking to raise standards and cater for society's changing needs.

We must question this short-sighted approach. We must not allow social housing developers to create suburban 'sink' estates that will rival the council high-rise disasters of the 1960s and 1970s just as we must prevent private developers creating 'gated communities' cut of from society or places that add to already unsustainable levels of car use. We will show that the current pattern of housing development is inextricably linked to the growth in car use, to environmentally unsustainable patterns of life, to the increasing polarisation of society, and to the decline of large parts of our cities. We argue that housing needs to be viewed in this wider context to develop housing forms which will serve the needs of both residents and wider society by rediscovering the benefits of the city and creating attractive, *sustainable urban neighbourhoods* where people will want to live.

A divided society

For much of the twentieth century the housing debate has focused not on the wider impact of housing development but on improving conditions for the tenants of social housing. This has led professionals to postulate in bricks and mortar (and concrete and steel), what is good for people, what will promote their health, communities, family life and comfort. Over-simplistic theories and inappropriate values have been applied to housing and have blighted the lives of thousands of people least able to cope with the consequences. The operation of communities and the way people live does not yield easily to such logical analysis. The designation on a plan of a play area does not mean that children will play there. 'Defensible space' means little if it is not defended. Designers are constantly thwarted by 'difficult' residents who do not live their lives in the way that was intended and fail to share the middle-class values of the designer and developer.

Indeed the middle classes, able to choose where and how they live, have largely been able to avoid the attentions of the housing professions. Working through private developers they have created their own 'Bourgeois Utopias' as Robert Fishman has called them[4]. The middle-class suburb, which has changed little over the last 100 years, has many detractors but is undoubtedly the most enduring and successful housing form created in the twentieth century. The suburb with its curving tree-lined streets, semi-detached housing and gardens front and back has, more than any of the utopias developed by architects and housing thinkers in the last hundred years, been the real twentieth century housing success. While its origins can be traced back to the garden city pioneers, its success is based upon the extent to which it meets the concerns, and aspirations of a large part of the population.

Twentieth century housing has therefore given physical form to the divisions in society. Council housing, originally envisaged as providing for the affluent working classes[5], has, along with housing association development,

THE
THREE MAGNETS
FOR THE 21ST CENTURY

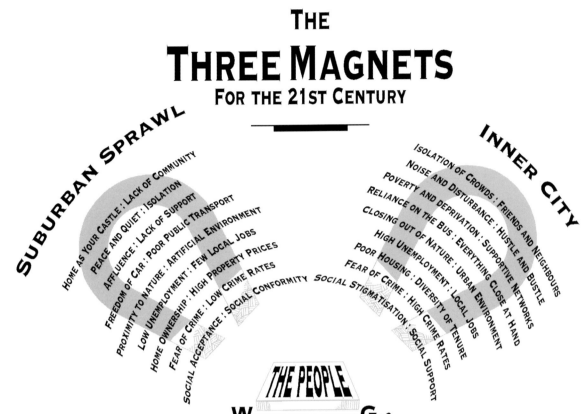

SUBURBAN SPRAWL

HOME AS YOUR CASTLE : LACK OF COMMUNITY
PEACE AND QUIET : ISOLATION
AFFLUENCE : LACK OF SUPPORT
FREEDOM OF CAR : POOR PUBLIC TRANSPORT
PROXIMITY TO NATURE : ARTIFICIAL ENVIRONMENT
LOW UNEMPLOYMENT : FEW LOCAL JOBS
HOME OWNERSHIP : HIGH PROPERTY PRICES
FEAR OF CRIME : LOW CRIME RATES
SOCIAL ACCEPTANCE : SOCIAL CONFORMITY

INNER CITY

ISOLATION OF CROWDS : FRIENDS AND NEIGHBOURS
NOISE AND DISTURBANCE : HUSTLE AND BUSTLE
POVERTY AND DEPRIVATION : SUPPORTIVE NETWORKS
RELIANCE ON THE BUS : EVERYTHING CLOSE AT HAND
CLOSING OUT OF NATURE : URBAN ENVIRONMENT
HIGH UNEMPLOYMENT : LOCAL JOBS
POOR HOUSING : DIVERSITY OF TENURE
FEAR OF CRIME : HIGH CRIME RATES
SOCIAL STIGMATISATION : SOCIAL SUPPORT

THE PEOPLE
WHERE WILL THEY GO?

THE URBAN NEIGHBOURHOOD

PRIVACY : COMMUNITY
URBAN VITALITY : SANCTUARY
A MIX OF CLASSES : CLOSE COMMUNITY
LOCAL SERVICES : EASE OF ACCESS
RICH ENVIRONMENT : URBAN ECOLOGY
MIX OF USES : ECONOMIC OPPORTUNITY
DIVERSITY OF TENURE : BALANCE OF CLASSES AND AGES
SECURE BY DESIGN : SOCIAL INTEGRATION
ENERGY EFFICIENCY : ENVIRONMENTAL AWARENESS

AFTER EBENEZER HOWARD'S THREE MAGNETS
FROM - TOMORROW: A PEACEFUL PATH TO REAL REFORM

Where will the people go in the 21st century? It is a hundred years since Ebenezer Howard published his three magnets in *Tomorrow — A peaceful path to real reform*. It has become one of the most potent symbols of twentieth century planning. However times have changed and we now need to reverse the polarity of the magnets by developing new models which will attract people back to cities in the twenty-first century.

become the stigmatised housing of last resort. The problems of social housing and urban areas have become synonymous and those with the means to do so have abandoned the city to the poor and socially excluded. Will Hutton[6] describes a 40:30:30 society based not on wealth but on security. He estimates that 40% of the population are privileged to feel secure, 30% are struggling and insecure and 30% are effectively excluded. The excluded live in a world of dependency and benefits, often on estates which are the legacy of failed housing ideals. Large parts of our cities are being abandoned to this excluded 30%. Unlike Disraeli's Two Nations who may have lived separately but at least mixed together on the city's streets, Hutton's three societies live increasingly separated lives. Today's middle classes shun the city not because of industry and pollution but through fear of crime and concerns about their children's education. This is not a recipe for a just or a healthy city or indeed a healthy society.

The only way to overcome these divisions is to reinvent urban areas as civilised places that can meet the residential aspirations of a much broader cross section of society. We are not suggesting that the suburb should be abandoned but that people should at least be given the option of urban living. This does not mean replacing one set of outdated dogmas with another. It requires jettisoning the ideological baggage of social housing and gentrification by the left and right. But most of all it means the developing of urban housing that will attract those able to choose where to live.

Structure of this book

The first part of this book is devoted to the forces which shape housing development and the pattern of settlements. Chapter 1 explores the way that towns and cities have developed in Britain and the effect that this has had on our perceptions of the type and location of housing that is valued. Chapter 2 deals with the influence of Utopian thinkers on the twentieth century home, both as the root of many current attitudes and as a case study of how change is brought

about. Chapter 3 describes the legacy of this thinking on the way that settlements have been planned and Chapter 4 shows how these forces have shaped housing over the last two centuries and have led to the housing that we build today. These factors must be understood by anyone seeking to influence future housing.

Part 2 of the book then sets out the four main influences which we believe will shape future housing, the *Four Cs* as we call them; conservation, choice, community and cost. These factors have, to a greater or lesser extent, always shaped housing. The change, for example, from the extended Victorian family to the self-sufficient nuclear family fundamentally affected housing choices and ideas of community. The predicted future growth in single and childless households may have an equally significant affect on housing preferences.

In Part 3 we describe the sort of housing and urban areas that could result from these trends. We argue that the Four Cs point to the need for housing which is denser, contains a mix of uses, house types and tenures, reduces car use and supports good public transport, is robust and safe, and promotes a sense of community. In short we argue that housing must become more urban and that the *sustainable urban neighbourhood* should be developed as a model that can compete with the attractions of the suburb.

Throughout the book we use the shorthand 'towns and cities' to describe settlements in the UK. Some of the people who looked through the early drafts assumed that we are talking solely about large cities. This is not the case. The processes and attitudes that we describe – which have led to the suburbanisation of urban areas – apply, to a greater or lesser extent, to the majority of settlements in the UK from the largest city to the smallest town. This is not to say, of course, that all towns are the same. Suburbanisation has taken place to a much lesser extent in traditional places such as market towns and even historic cities such as Oxford and Chester. However we believe that the conclusions and lessons that we draw are relevant to the majority of UK settlements.

We may be accused of putting forward our own Utopia, as unrealistic and unachievable as those of the past. We believe, however, that the ideas that we set out are nothing new; they have been advocated by the urban design profession for many years, if rarely put into practice on the ground. They are also reflected in government policy and some local authority plans (partly in response to the advocacy of the Urban Villages campaign). They are being built, as we write, in enlightened pockets throughout Britain, Europe and North America if not yet on a sufficient scale. What we have done is to draw these strands together within the context of the changing trends described in the first part of this book both to document and contribute to an emerging movement – 'New Urbanism' as it has been called in the US.

We are not prescriptive about where and how housing should be built. Chapter 9 explores the location of housing and argues that there is a place for suburban development and new settlements alongside urban consolidation and infill. We seek to promote the latter rather than criticise the former. Yet the design of housing must reflect its location. Currently when urban development takes place the resulting housing, for want of more appropriate models, often ends up aping its suburban cousins. In an over-reaction to the mistakes of the past the curving cul-de-sac and semi-detached starter home is starting to appear in the heart of towns and cities. We argue that this is damaging to the grain, diversity and heritage of urban areas. But these arguments alone will carry little weight against the cry of 'give the people what they want'. More important is the affect of such low density development on the economy of towns and cities, on their community life and sustainability, and their ability to meet the needs of new household types.

We therefore argue that there is a need for new models of urban development to stand alongside the tried and tested suburban models. We do not suggest that these new models should be imposed on the suburbs, any more than suburban models should be imposed on the city. There are already some good urban models emerging through the Urban Villages Forum in Britain, the European Sustainable Cities

The changing face of urban housing: For want of more appropriate models the suburban semi is colonising the very heart of our cities and is as inappropriate as much of the high-rise housing that it has replaced

Campaign and, in America, the Pedestrian Pocket movement. These models, whilst often developed for new settlements, are increasingly being applied to existing urban areas. They point to a rediscovery of the art of creating self-sustaining urban neighbourhoods. What we seek to do is to synthesise this emerging urban thinking into a new agenda for our towns and cities which can reverse the destructive dispersal of the last 150 years. Our aim is to create urban areas that rank alongside successful continental cities rather than following the sad decline of many American urban areas.

Over the last few years we have been closely involved in these issues, through consultancy work for local authorities throughout the UK. Through this work the ideas set out in this book have been discussed with local authorities, developers, professionals and residents across the country. The response has been illuminating. On the one hand when the ideas are discussed in general terms there is relatively little disagreement. They are seen as common sense or in some cases a statement of the obvious. This is due in part to the images that people conjure up when thinking about urban areas – the historic market town, Georgian Bath, or the vibrant continental towns that they visit on holiday. However, if you take the discussion to the next level of detail, the way in which these ideas affect what is built, the reaction is often very different and much more hostile. Private developers claim that it will never sell, housing associations say that it cannot be built within

cost limits, highway engineers complain that it is unsafe, planners argue that there will be conflicts of use or town cramming. Whilst everyone wants a better environment they object to restrictions on the unfettered right to use and park their car. The usual response is 'I have no objection to the principles but do have a number of detailed concerns'. Yet when you add up the detailed concerns they undermine the basic principles.

It has become clear to us that it is not sufficient to describe the physical form of the *Sustainable Urban Neighbourhood*. We must also explore the processes by which it can be built. Otherwise there will be a tendency for developers and authorities to accept the ideas but misapply them on the ground. In the concluding chapter we therefore explore the process by which urban areas are created and the way in which this can be used to create the *Sustainable Urban Neighbourhood* and to overcome the barriers to successful urban regeneration.

This book argues that housing and urban planning are about to go through another ice age, comparable to that induced by the industrial revolution. It is aimed at those who want to survive, the voles rather than the dinosaurs. We hope that it will be of interest to those who commission new housing, who influence its design and who want a return on their investment whether it be their money or their time. It sets an agenda for future urban housing and the development of towns and cities which should stand the test of time.

Part 1

THE ORIGINS

Any attempt to shape the future of housing must be based upon an understanding of how we have got where we are today. Our attitudes towards new development are shaped by perceptions of what has and has not worked in the past and the cultural baggage which has become associated with the home and its place in towns and cities. In the first part of this book we therefore seek to chart the way that social and economic trends along with Utopian theories and urban reformers have shaped the pattern of housing and the attitudes of developers and residents that we have today.

'If we would lay a new foundation for urban life, we must understand the historic nature of the city'

Lewis Mumford - *The City in History*, Secker and Warburg 1961

CHAPTER 1
The flight from the city

Why is it that in Britain and America there is such a deep enmity towards the city? Why is it that continental cities are celebrated whilst most British and US cities are reviled and even feared? If it is true that without cities we have no civilisation, what does our attitude towards our cities tell us about the state of our society? If we are to reinvent the city it is important to understand the reasons for the Anglo-American city's fall from grace and the domination of UK urban values by American rather than European approaches.

The golden age of cities

There was a time when the builders of cities were glorified. Cities were the centres of civilisation and the places where the arts, government and commerce thrived. The design of cities was a noble pursuit attracting leading creative minds, from Vitruvius to Michelangelo, Baron Haussmann to John Nash. The building of great cities was the concern of kings, from Pope Sixtus V's desire to remodel Rome as the capital of Christendom, Peter the Great's commissioning of St. Petersburg as his capital and Napoleon III's redevelopment of Paris as a city of boulevards and squares. It was in the cities of Mesopotamia and the Nile Valley that civilisation first flowered. It was in the cities of the Greek and Roman empires that European civilisation was shaped and in the cities of northern Italy where it was rediscovered through the renaissance. Cities have always been centres for religion, trade and culture lie at the foundation of modern society. Whilst academics may argue about which came first, whether cities gave birth to civilisation or whether civilisation necessitated the building of cities[1], the two are inextricably linked.

It is these cities which predate the industrial revolution and the motorcar which retain their appeal and have given rise to the urban qualities that we still prize today and on which much urban design thinking is founded. Perhaps the most enduring image of this pre-industrial city is the Italian hill town of Siena which has been endlessly analysed and plundered for inspiration. Indeed it is argued[2] that the Commission for the European Union's ideas for the 'compact city'[3] are based more upon the unattainable ideal of the Italian hill town than the rather messier urban realities of most European cities today.

The medieval city was typically small, mixed-use, and based upon travel by foot. At the height of its powers the city state of Florence had a population of just 50 000 which is little bigger than Barnsley or Basingstoke. Yet Florence was one of the largest cities of the renaissance and was almost twice the size of cities like Vienna, Prague and Barcelona[4]. The medieval city was also dense, covering a fraction of the land area of a modern town of similar size. This compactness of built form created the tight urban streets and crowded buildings that we enjoy in historic towns such as Chester and York. The density was partly the result of city walls which restrained growth. But as Hoskins[5] has shown, even unwalled towns and cities with no constraints on growth were remarkably dense. It has been suggested[6] that this density resulted from the needs of travel by foot which undoubtedly played a role in the compactness of great cities like London. It may also have been that compact development was driven by a need to conserve the surrounding agricultural land on which the city relied for its food. These arguments have all been explored at length but they do not hold the whole answer. Most pre-industrial cities were built at far greater densities than can be explained by physical constraints, the needs of travel by foot or the protection of agricultural land. There were other forces at play which go to the heart of the nature of cities and our inability to recapture their character today.

Why is it that the most remote farmhouse is built so that it abuts directly onto the only road for miles? Why is it that remote settlements surrounded by acres of seemingly unused land are built so that their houses almost fall over each other? It seems that historically there was something deep within the human consciousness which sought companionship and security. It may be that this dates back to the earliest encampments clustered around the communal campfire. Is it too far-fetched to imagine the tents becoming permanent shelters and the camp fire becoming the town square? Once the unseen dangers of the surrounding wilderness had been overcome the pattern of human settlement had been established.

However the need for human contact does not entirely explain the density of early settlements. Whilst fear of the wilderness may have been the initial motive this would soon have been combined with economic and political forces. It is likely that, in those early encampments, the tents nearest the fire would have been occupied by the chief and the most important members of the community. Here they would be close to the warmth of the fire

The ideal compact city? Siena is the archetypal compact city. Despite the fact that it was built entirely without the aid of planners and urban designers it has been mined for inspiration by generations of urban professionals

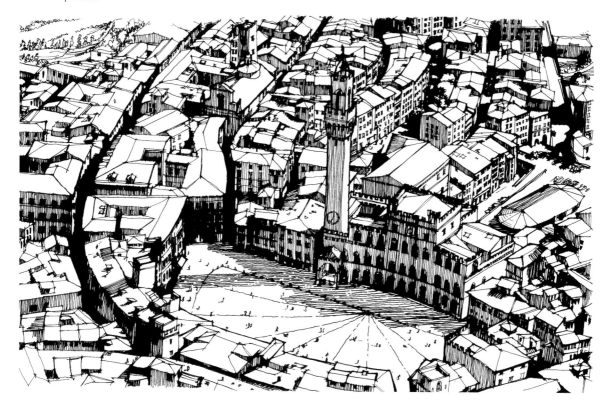

and to the focus of community life and decision making. The lower status members of the community would have been relegated to the outskirts of the camp, vulnerable to attack and cut off from the seat of power and status. Since humans have always aspired to improve themselves, it is reasonable to assume that the citizens of those early encampments would have aspired to be near the camp fire, both for the benefits that it would bring but also as a symbol of their status and position.

It is not hard to imagine this process transferred to the earliest cities. As Robert Fishman has described in *Bourgeois Utopia*[7], the dynamic of the pre-industrial city meant that the centre of the town was the place to be. The richer you were, and the more status and power you had, the nearer to the centre you sought to live and work. The elite of the town, the merchants, nobles, church men and administrators would jostle for the best locations at the centre of town, much as the prime retailers like Marks & Spencer do in modern shopping centres. Just as in a shopping centre, this demand for the best location would have increased land values

so that central areas also became the most expensive and the most profitable. The density of the pre-industrial city is the result of this demand for central sites. The competition for land meant that every available site would be developed to its maximum potential so that buildings became higher and more closely packed. Remember that in these early cities the merchants generally lived over their business, as indeed did many of their employees, so that pressures were intense. An extreme example of this can be seen in the 2 000 year old high-rise buildings in the Yemen.

In these ancient towns there was a gradation in social status as one moved away from the centre. The poorest people and the dirty or marginal uses were pushed to the edge of the town, often outside the protection of the city walls. Indeed the term 'suburb' was originally coined as a disparaging expression meaning literally 'less than urban'. However a dominant force within these cities was a desire to move closer to the centre of town and thus the centre of power and commerce. The poorest denizen of the suburb would covet the neighbourhoods

The UK compact city? Fine historic environments are not only to be found in Italy. Many UK market towns like Calne in Wiltshire have equally attractive and popular environments

The shatter zone:
A figure ground plan of Barnsley in Yorkshire today. This clearly shows the structure of a dense medieval town surrounded by a zone of ill-defined space which separates it from the surrounding residential development.

This is not to say that early suburban trends did not exist. As early as Elizabethan times there was concern about merchants moving out to the country, no doubt aping the landed gentry. However this was often based on single houses well beyond the poor suburbs and the houses tended to be used as weekend retreats. This is similar to the 'dacha' tradition still common in many eastern European countries. In some cases these weekend retreats would be transformed over time into the main family residence with the merchant commuting into town for business. This trend however remained relatively insignificant until the advent of the industrial revolution.

The industrial city

This picture of growth in the pre-industrial city is a mirror image of modern Anglo-American settlements. Fishman has described the way that the industrial revolution placed such intense pressures on the traditional city that it reversed the polarity of settlements. In the modern Anglo-American city, status is measured not by how close to the centre you live, but by the distance that you can put between yourself and the perceived squalor of urban life. In the modern Anglo-American city (we will turn to the continental experience in a short while) the pressure for development is not in the centre but at the periphery. This has been the case with housing development for many years but it is now true of all manner of activity. Town centre shopping has declined as we switch our allegiance to the suburban supermarket or out-of-town shopping centre. The newspaper industry has largely abandoned Fleet Street for Docklands. Staff in central office districts have been decanted to peripheral business parks and urban cinemas have succumbed in the face of the multiplex.

Many reasons have been put forward for this dispersal of activity. It has been attributed to increasing mobility, initially due to commuter railways but more recently and more potently to the private car. It has been put down to changing retail and business needs which cannot be

within the city walls. The artisans within the walls would covet the middle class areas nearer the centre and the middle classes would aspire to a location on or near the town square. What is more, this would happen in towns where one could walk from the centre to open countryside in less than twenty minutes.

In Manchester there is still a sign on a building on the southern edge of the city centre which proclaims the 'Boundary of the Township of Manchester'. Beyond this is the Gaythorne area, an old industrial quarter which is part of an arc of old industry which encircles much of the city centre. Such industrial areas can be found in many modern cities and can clearly be seen on the figure ground plan of Barnsley (above). They mark the line of the original poor suburbs and now lie sandwiched between the town centre and the inner city and yet have a quite different character. Indeed these are areas which have always been impoverished and have often been swept aside as the line of least resistance for ring roads.

accommodated in congested urban areas, to the workings of the land market, and to demographic change. All have played their part; however at its heart this trend of 'counterurbanization' is driven by the same forces which drove urbanisation in the early cities, it is just that today these forces are working in the opposite direction.

Fishman suggests that perhaps the first true suburb was Clapham in London where the Evangelicals, led by Wilberforce, sought to protect their families from the evil influence of the city in the latter half of the eighteenth century. Clapham was a development of the earlier 'dacha' trend but was conceived from the outset as a suburb around Clapham Common

intended to provide the main family residence for its occupants. It represents an important step in the separation of home and family from work and commerce. As such it was an influential model for Victorian family life which was to take such a hold later in the century, exemplified in satires such as *Diary of a Nobody* by the Grossmiths, with its focus on the trivia of maintaining a household rather than the delights of urban living.

The next step in Fishman's history of the suburb took place in Manchester. This is significant, because whereas the Evangelicals were escaping from the traditional city, in Manchester the traditional city was being swamped by the industrial revolution and something quite

The pre-industial city: Green's map of Manchester from 1794. This illustrates that the structure of the pre-industrial city in Britain was similar to the Italian cities that we admire today

different was happening. Before the industrial revolution the form of Manchester was similar to many medieval towns, as can be seen from Green's map of the city (above) published in 1794 . The dense form of pre-industrial Manchester was the result of the same forces of concentration which shaped the Italian hill town. For the early years of Manchester's industrialisation it maintained this traditional model of growth with densities increasing towards the centre and the most affluent merchants living in areas like Moseley Street, Fountain Street, King Street and St. Anne's Square in the very heart of the city. However the cotton mills which came to dominate the city required large workforces, and economic opportunity attracted rural migrants in vast numbers. As H. G. Wells said, this process turned cities like Manchester into 'great surging oceans' of humanity.

The conditions in the early industrial cities have been well documented elsewhere. Our concern here is the catalytic effect that the industrial revolution had on the British city. The phenomenal growth of population and industry in cities like Manchester, Leeds, Liverpool and Sheffield stretched the capacity of the traditional city beyond breaking point. The industrial city came to be seen not as the chalice of civilisation but as the receptacle for all that is

wrong with society. In the words of one commentator, 'Civilisation works its miracles, and civilised man is turned back almost into a savage'. Cities had limited sanitation, were overcrowded, dangerous and characterised by pollution, crime and congestion. In 1841 the average life expectancy in Manchester was just 24 years and thousands, from all classes, were killed in the great cholera epidemics of 1832, 1848 and 1866[8]. In the other great textile town, Bradford, conditions were, if anything, worse with life expectancies of 19 years and an environment described by one German visitor as 'like being lodged in no other place than with the devil incarnate'. These images of the industrial city have coloured our perception of the city ever since. The potent image of the dark, dangerous city described by Dickens and Conan Doyle along with the paintings of L. S. Lowry have created a stereotypical image of the city which has outlasted the conditions it portrayed.

The great escape

Even as the industrial city boomed an exodus was beginning. The first escapees may have been the London Evangelicals but in Manchester it was Samuel Brookes, a wealthy banker who first broke ranks, moving from his Moseley Street address and leapfrogging the poor suburbs to establish the city's first suburb on sixty acres of agricultural land three miles or so south of the city. He called the area Whalley Range after his home town in Lancashire. He laid out streets, built a college and a church, as well as a fine house for himself and his family. The remainder of the area was then marked out as plots for the development of substantial residences. There is in Manchester some dispute about whether Whalley Range was the first suburb, with some claiming that the much grander Victoria Park was built a few years earlier. However it is clear that both were being planned at around the same time and represented the start of an important trend. The great escape had begun. Throughout the country in areas like Manningham in Bradford, Edgbaston in Birmingham, Sefton in Liverpool or Stoke Newington and

Remnants of the early suburbs: Many inner city areas are characterised by large villas dating from the mid-nineteenth century when the areas were developed as early suburbs. Designed for large households with servants, many have been converted to bedsits or institutional uses

Islington to the north of London the merchants and factory owners were setting up residence away from the smoke and the teeming masses of the overcrowded city. These early suburbs provided the foundations for many of the attitudes which have shaped towns and cities ever since.

The first is the idea that the city is bad and the countryside is good so that people who can should move as far away as possible from the city. For Samuel Brooks, dependent upon the horse for transport, this distance may not have been great, but there was open countryside between Whalley Range and the city (a low boggy area known as Moss Side). With modern transport the quest to escape the city can strike deeper and deeper into the countryside until it penetrates the most isolated rural areas.

The second view is that high density is bad and low density is good so that people should not only distance themselves from the city but also from each other. As Muthesius[9] has described, this led many of the early suburbs to be surrounded by high walls and protected by toll gates. It also meant that houses were set within landscaped grounds with high walls and curving driveways to hide the house from the street and neighbours. Echoes of these elements of early suburbia can still be seen in the modern suburb.

The third trend has been the separation of home and work and the birth of the commuter as first seen in Clapham. This commuting was initially by horse-drawn carriage but subsequently, with the development of buses, trams and railways, travel became possible to ever more distant suburbs and urban dispersal became possible, if not inevitable. The difficulty and expense of commuting protected the early suburbs from the 'lower classes' even when they were very close to the centre of the town. However as public transport developed these suburbs became vulnerable and the middle classes were forced to move further away from the town to protect their tranquillity.

The fourth and possibly the most significant trend was a reversal in the polarity of cities. The richer and more successful people started to measure their status not by how close they lived to the town square but by the distance that they could put between themselves and the centre. In the twentieth century the suburban flight of the merchants was followed by the middle classes as public transport networks were established, and eventually even by the working classes as they were decanted from the urban 'slums' to overspill estates and new towns. Whether this migration was by choice or by coercion the reason was the same – the city is bad for you. The result was that the city's role as a home for a cross section of society was undermined and urban populations became dominated by those groups least able to escape. The predominant residential aspiration of British people became the leafy suburb. Negative perceptions of the city were thus reinforced as the problems of the urban poor came to be seen as one and the same as the problems of the city.

This desire of people to escape the city is well documented by market research[10]. Survey after survey has shown that for the majority of people the countryside is their desired place of residence and that urban areas are places from which they desire to escape. The main reasons were that towns were dirty, noisy, stressful and over-crowded. This again illustrates an interesting interplay of perceptions and reality. Census information shows that the central parts of most cities have been losing population for years and in relative terms are anything but overcrowded, yet in people's minds they clearly still appear that way. Many people who desire to live in the country end up in the suburbs. It is a matter of speculation whether they see the suburb as an option of second choice or whether suburban life is really able to offer the rural benefits which they desire.

The effects of these attitudes can be seen in the population distribution in England as charted by census data[11]. This shows a consistent movement of population since 1945 from London and other metropolitan areas to smaller urban areas and rural districts. Indeed the largest gains have been in the 'remote largely rural'

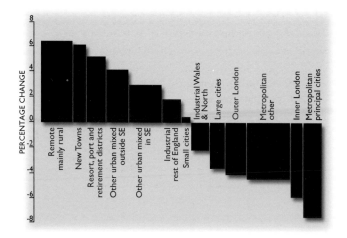

Above - Urban depopulation: This shows a clear correlation between the urbanity of different types of area and the rate of population loss. Source: OPCS 1992 from Blowers 1993.

Below - The lost urban jobs: The loss of employment from urban areas has taken an identical path. Source: NOMIS.

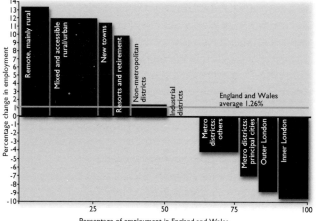

category. This suggests, as Peter Hall predicted, that the trend is more than suburbanisation but rather the counterurbanization of settlement patterns in Britain.

It is true that in the last decade this trend has slowed. Research for London Transport[12] has shown that between 1981 and 1991 inner London gained 77 000 people and suggests that this trend will accelerate in the future. Other metropolitan areas may still have been losing population in the 1980s (a fall of 100 000 people or 2.8% of their population) but the rate of decline was slowing. Indeed government household predictions foresee a modest increase in the population (and a greater increase in household numbers) in most UK urban areas.

In the second half of the twentieth century the exodus of people has been followed by an exodus of investment and jobs. The city always thrived on the need for proximity between people and activities. Indeed the growth of the early suburbs, based as they were on public transport, tended to reinforce town and city centres which remained the points of greatest accessibility. If you lived on a suburban railway line then you had little choice but to go into the centre for employment, shopping and other services. However with the growth in the private car this was no longer the case. As society has become more mobile and advances have been made in electronic communications, city locations have become seen as a hindrance rather than a necessity for commercial activity. Industry and warehousing were the first to leave to the new industrial estates and distribution parks. Offices followed to business parks, and retail activities to out-of-town shopping centres. Bustling cities became conurbations with sprawling commercial and residential suburbs surrounding a small city centre.

Research undertaken as part of URBED's *Vital and Viable Town Centres* report for the UK government[13] charted the loss of employment in cities. Manufacturing employment has declined generally, but to a much greater extent in cities. Factories have closed or relocated and major inward investors such as Japanese car plants will only consider out-of-town sites. However cities have also been losing jobs in the service sector where the main beneficiaries have been small towns and rural areas. The same is true of retail development as work by Hillier Parker as part of the same research illustrated. In the development boom of 1987–90, 66% of all new retail floor space was out-of-town of which 51% was in retail parks. Even committed town centre retailers like Marks & Spencer started to build out-of-town stores and the development of major out-of-town centres like Meadowhall in Sheffield posed a major threat to traditional town centres. It is estimated, for example that Sheffield City Centre lost 30% of its trade to Meadowhall and that many shops only remained because they were tied into leases. Similar trends can be seen in entertainment and leisure. Whilst cinema audiences are growing this is largely due to multi-screen out-of-town centres as urban cinemas continue to decline. Even pub and restaurant chains are tending to direct their new investment to out-of-town sites.

The inner city

Another consequence of dispersal and suburban growth has been inner city decline. As the suburbs have grown, large areas of our cities have been deserted by the middle classes, businesses and investors. These areas have become characterised by poverty, dereliction and a range of social problems. This has given rise to the classic form of the Anglo-American city with an embattled centre surrounded by decline and an outer ring of prosperous suburbs. Perhaps the most extreme example of this is Washington DC in the United States where the centre dominated by government buildings is surrounded by some of the worst deprivation in the country. Over the last 30 or so years the tendency has been for the inner city to expand at the expense of the city centre fringes and inner suburbs.

The recognition of these problems in Britain dates from the mid 1970s and in particular the Labour government's 1976 Inner City Act. A Fabian pamphlet in 1975, co-authored by Nicholas Falk[14], brought together available evidence to show that the problems of multiple deprivation could not be solved without widening economic opportunities in areas which had lost their traditional role. Since that time, a great deal has been written about problems of the inner city and a range of reasons have been put forward to explain the problem. This has given rise to an alphabet soup of initiatives to address the problem, particularly following the riots of the early 1980s. Work has been done to provide training, promote small businesses, tackle housing and environmental problems and improve access. However these initiatives have tended to address the symptoms of the problem rather than the root causes. As a result they have had little impact and in some cases have made

the problem worse. As research for the Department of the Environment by Brian Robson[15] has illustrated, despite all of the effort and expenditure on the inner city the numbers of unemployed and the indicators of deprivation and other social problems remain largely the same today as they were before all of the initiatives were started.

This is not, on the whole, because initiatives have failed. Many have been very successful in creating jobs, giving people skills, improving the environment and housing conditions and addressing social problems. But the result has been to empower certain people within the inner city to do what people with such power have been doing for a hundred years, namely to move out to the suburbs. Take the example of a major local employer in a deprived inner city area in one of Britain's larger cities. The company was given permission to expand onto council-owned land on the condition that the jobs created went to local people. This they did, but two years later a survey of the workforce showed that virtually none lived locally. To some this cast doubt on the reliability of local people or the commitment of the employer. However the reality was that the local employees had used their new-found earning power to move to a less stigmatised area, perhaps to buy a home, certainly to send their children to better schools. In another case the headteacher of an inner city school commented on the fact that an increasing number of Afro-Caribbean pupils were doing very well academically. The reason she suggested was that they saw education as a ticket out of the area. It could even be suggested that initiatives to improve access by building new roads in the inner city have conspired with this process. Far from improving access for businesses coming into the area they have made it easier for local people to live elsewhere and commute to local jobs.

A society where most of the people living in cities are those without the capacity to escape will always be a divided society. While this remains the case there will never be a solution to the inner city problem or to social exclusion no matter how much money is thrown at it. What is more, whilst the problem remains unsolved the real and perceived problems of the inner city will cast a shadow over attempts to revitalise cities. Yet the only real hope for the inner cities is the reversal of the forces of dispersal by creating attractive neighbourhoods where people will want to stay when they find work and which will persuade others to return to the city.

Inner city problems are not confined to run-down housing estates. Similar forces have been at work in commercial areas, as much of URBED's urban regeneration work has demonstrated. Most cities in Britain have traditional industrial and commercial areas which have declined as companies have closed or moved out to industrial estates. These include areas like

Little Germany in Bradford, the Lace Market in Nottingham, the Jewellery Quarter in Birmingham and Ancoats in Manchester. The issues here are quite different to housing estates. These industrial areas are often of significant architectural and historic importance, yet they have become anachronisms since the buildings and narrow streets which give them their character are unable to accommodate the modern needs of the industry for which they were built. Instead they have become home to a range of marginal businesses, attracted by the low rents but unable to maintain the built fabric. The importance of these areas means that their continued decline is not seen as an acceptable option. However if they are to be regenerated it is important to reverse the exodus of activity by developing new economic roles. The intrinsic quality of many industrial heritage areas is undoubtedly an asset in this process and it may be that recent improvements to the areas, like Little Germany and the Lace Market could show the way to the development of sustainable urban neighbourhoods elsewhere in the inner city.

American experience

Through these trends the modern Anglo-American city was born. Indeed the process in the UK may not have reached its natural conclusion. One needs only look at American towns and cities to see that, if these trends continue unchecked, the city centre itself can die. Even in successful American cities like Atlanta the percentage of retail sales attracted by the city

Inner city decline does not just affect housing areas: Commercial activity has also abandoned cities, leaving historic areas like Little Germany in Bradford without the economic activity to sustain its fine built fabric. Built by German worsted merchants in the last century, the area covers just 20 acres yet contains 53 listed buildings, a third of which were vacant by the mid 1980s. These areas have often been the subject of successful regeneration initiatives such as the project managed by URBED in Little Germany. This attracted commercial activity back into the area, promoted tourism and has eventually created a residential community. Such areas have an advantage because of their attractive environment, but they hold many lessons for those seeking to regenerate other urban areas.

centre fell from 26% in 1958 to just 7% in 1972, and many US city centres retain only a residual retail role.

The dispersal of many American cities has led to town centres which are little more than historic theme parks surrounded by desolate inner cities and an outer ring of peripheral growth characterised by Joel Jarreau as 'edge cities'[16]. Indeed younger American cities like Los Angeles have developed without a clearly defined centre. Such sprawling suburban cities based on the accessibility of the private car are the natural conclusion of suburban trends which started with the Evangelicals of Clapham.

There is widespread concern about the effects of this urban sprawl in the US. In March 1995 the Bank of America in conjunction with a range of other agencies released a manifesto entitled 'Beyond Sprawl'. This listed the social and economic costs of sprawl and argued for compact and efficient growth. It was followed by a *Newsweek* cover story suggesting a 'sprawl-busting' strategy based on retrofitting existing suburbs and 'new urbanism'[17].

However the condemnation of sprawl in the US is not universal. To some it represents not the destruction of the city but its evolution into new forms. Felson[18] has described the concept as 'Metroreefs', coral atolls of activities linked by networks of highways. This has echoes of the garden city and its attraction is that it balances large amounts of personal space with high levels of accessibility to services and facilities dispersed from traditional congested centres. These ideas are controversial in the US where there is at least the space for such dispersed settlements. In the UK, where land is more precious and we have a greater tradition of urban settlements it is even more difficult to envisage. However if it is to be avoided we need to break the Anglo-American mould of thinking about cities which has characterised British culture for much of the twentieth century. In doing this it is useful to look to continental cities which have been shaped by very different forces and which seem to be faring much better.

Continental experience

The troubles of the typical Anglo-American city can be vividly contrasted with experience on the continent. Here the industrial revolution created the same pressures as in England. In Paris this led to suburban growth in the early 1800s which, like London, was originally based on weekend retreats. It is likely that, given time, Paris would have followed the British experience. However this was not allowed to happen because of the transformation brought about by Hausemann's plans for the city. Olsen in *The City as a Work of Art* [19] describes Napoleon's vision for Paris, which Hausemann was charged with implementing. Napoleon saw Paris as the capital of a great empire and wanted the physical form of the city to reflect this. Hausemann achieved this by cutting great boulevards through the cramped medieval city. These boulevards were to be bounded by buildings of at least six storeys and the only use with the potential to

Europe at night: A satellite image of Europe showing the extent of urban spread. This illustrates a sharp contrast between the land covered by Paris, Madrid and Barcelona, for example, compared to the spraw-ling conurbations of Britain

fill the volume of buildings implied by this was housing. Indeed to fund the quality of building desired this had to be middle-class housing.

Yet the development of such large amounts of middle-class housing was inconceivable if the middle classes continued to move out of the city to the suburbs. Incentives were therefore introduced through the tax system to make the new apartment blocks financially attractive and the National Bank channelled national savings into the grand projects. This had the effect of stopping middle-class suburbanisation in its tracks. Within a remarkably short period the spacious urban apartment became established as the residential aspiration of the French middle classes at a time when their English equivalents were switching their aspirations to the suburban villa.

There are lessons here for the UK government in the 1990s which is also seeking to channel housing back into cities. Napoleon's great success was not to control suburbanisation but to make urban housing more financially attractive. French middle-class aspirations have survived the intervening 150 years more or less intact. True Paris now has affluent suburbs but it is still common for well-to-do families to live in the heart of the city. It is something of a culture shock to visit a busy street in Paris full of shops and cafés. A door between the shops will give access to a staircase and caged lift or perhaps a gateway leading to a secluded courtyard. On the first and second floors there are likely to be solicitors, dentists and other small businesses. On the top floor there may be small inexpensive flats but in between will be the apartments of middle-class families. These apartments are as spacious as many English villas and many would originally have had servant's quarters. However they are still lived in today by families with children who would be considered eccentric by their English counterparts but who are still seen as quite normal in France.

In Paris the suburb has a very different connotation to the English suburb. There are affluent suburbs, particularly in satellite towns like La Varenne St. Hilaire. However the term

suburb or 'banlieu' refers to the municipal housing estates and poor working-class areas on the edge of the city. Paris's inner city problems are on its periphery and are all the more intractable and divisive because of this. It does however mean that in general terms Paris has retained the traditional pre-industrial pattern of growth, dispersal has been far less pronounced and its character as a great city is intact enabling it to adopt a strategy to become the cultural capital of a unified Europe.

Paris is significant because it provided a model for the Emperor Franz Joseph's replanning of Vienna in the second half of the nineteenth century. Together Paris and Vienna provided a model for other continental cities and indeed for those of South America. This influence extended not only to architects and planners but also to the general public and the middle classes in particular who aspired to the Parisian ideal of the urban apartment. This is not just confined to major cities. It can be seen in towns of all types and sizes on the continent including industrial towns.

In terms of urban growth the developed world can therefore be divided into two traditions: the Anglo-American model which also characterises Australia, and the French model which characterises most of Europe, Latin America and to a lesser extent Canada.

This explains why continental towns have retained their form, density and vitality to a far greater extent than British cities. One need only look at similar cities such as Marseille and Liverpool or Milan and Birmingham to see the impact of these trends. This is not to say that continental towns have all the answers. They too suffer from urban problems and in recent years have not been immune from the dispersal of people and investment. However if we in Britain are seeking to rediscover the benefits of living in the heart of towns and cities there is much that we could learn from continental models. Yet it must be understood that the differences between British and continental towns are not superficial and cannot be overcome with a few street cafés. They go to the very heart of the urban forces which shape our towns and cities. It is unlikely that we can ever put the clock back 150 years to redirect these forces. The task instead is to draw upon continental and British models to create successful British urban models which can meet the needs of the next century.

The continental model: The grand boulevards of Paris as laid out by Hausemann (far left). The Ringstrasse, Vienna (above) which was modelled on Paris. The apartment block, often containing a mix of uses, became the predominant building type in continental cities

An urban renaissance? Cities like Manchester and Glasgow have undergone an unprecedented revival in recent years. It would once have been inconceivable that grey, wet northern cities would develop a thriving café culture

The urban renaissance

There have been times in the twentieth century when the city has seemed to be dying. Indeed when you visit a city like Liverpool which rattles around in the husk of a once great metropolis it is difficult to be optimistic. However the predictions of the death of the city have been greatly exaggerated. Over the last 10–15 years there has been a remarkable renaissance in many British cities. Whilst the decline of urban populations is yet to be entirely stemmed, and despite the advent of anti-urban trends such as home working, tele-shopping and computer conferencing, many British towns and cities seem to be finding new roles. The heavy industry and overcrowding which gave rise to the flight from the city no longer exist, even though they may live on in people's perceptions. Whilst there are problems of traffic pollution and urban crime it is clear that many British towns and cities could potentially provide attractive environments in which to live and work. The stage may be set for an 'urban renaissance' in Britain, a term first used in a Council of Europe Campaign and popularised in Britain through speeches by HRH The Prince of Wales.

Cities like Glasgow with its *Smiles Better* campaign have slowly overcome their poor image and a growing number of people are rediscovering the joys of city living. While the pronouncement of an urban renaissance in Britain may be somewhat premature, there are a number of trends which may bolster the role of towns and cities. The first is transport. Despite the fact that car-based transport has been responsible for urban depopulation, towns and cities remain important transport hubs with mainline railway stations, excellent motorway connections and, crucially, airports. They have also benefited from investment in public transport infrastructure such as the tram system in cities like Newcastle, Sheffield and Manchester.

Cities may also benefit from the growth of service industries such as financial services, and cultural or knowledge industries such as music, design and publishing. While these activities are based on modern telecommunication, they feed off face-to-face contact, the ability to attract talented people and the activity produced by dense urban populations. It is difficult to imagine a rural stock exchange, bank or national newspaper. It is equally hard to picture a thriving fashion or music industry which was not able to feed on the street life of a large city.

Linked to this is the importance of higher education both to the life of cities and to their economies. Whilst there are universities on isolated campuses, they are currently losing out to the urban universities with the culture and night life to attract students. In attractive cities students tend to stay on after their courses finish, so contributing their skills and energy to the town and its economy. This can be seen in cities as diverse as Liverpool and Sunderland which benefit greatly from high student stay-on rates. Former art students account for the fact that Sunderland, despite its size and location, was the Arts Council City of Visual Arts and is the base for the only national magazine for artists.

The 1980s have seen the emergence of a new urban middle class providing a fresh source of demand for services. As Peter Hall has noted[20] 'the arrival of the yuppies, those suburban-born children of the emigres from the city of the 1940s and 1950s, is creating a boom in consumer-led service employment and in associated construction, which may at last provide the basis for broad-based economic revival with jobs for a wide spectrum of skills and talents'. This process is particularly evident in the US in festival marketplaces like Quincey Market in Boston, and the Inner Harbour in Baltimore, and along the waterfronts of many cities which were declining until recently. Such American initiatives have exploited continental ideas about urban space. It is ironic that we in Britain have found it easier to import ideas like festival marketplaces second-hand from the US than to take them directly from our continental neighbours.

American cities have also started to recognise the economic potential of people in cities with time and money to spend, ranging from ethnic minorities and 'grey power' to the 'pink dollar'. This is also happening in Britain with the development of leisure attractions, the promotion of China Towns and even, in Manchester, a 'Gay Village' which has become a thriving commercial district. Hall argues that recognising and promoting these new urban economies will require 'new kinds of urban planning skills, hardly now taught at all in the planning schools'. It is no longer sufficient to sit back and rely on the control of development pressures since very often those pressures no longer exist. Planning in our cities must become far more pro-active, marketing the city as a product, seeking out and exploiting opportunities and developing new forms of economic activity.

This is what is happening in many British provincial cities which also have a new confidence about them. Glasgow, Leeds, Birmingham, Newcastle and Manchester have all succeeded in reinventing themselves and transforming their image. This, in turn, has stimulated their local rivals to respond. The provincial resurgence of the late 1980s was partly fuelled by the displacement of activity from the overheated London market during the property boom and the fact that cities in the North were less affected by the slump when it came. However it has outlasted this temporary effect and there is now a new sense of political leadership and partnership in these cities as witnessed by the success of the City Pride Partnerships in Manchester and Birmingham in 1994 which seem to have achieved more than in London. There is a feeling that cities should no longer be apologetic and defensive but should promote themselves on an international stage. This is not true of all cities. Sheffield, Liverpool and Bristol were slow to recognise the potential or have been distracted by other problems. However even here there are signs of new confidence with initiatives such as Sheffield's Cultural Industries Quarter, the resurgence of the Duke Street/Bold Street area in Liverpool and Bristol's Harbourside development.

It has also been argued that with the rise of the European Union and the declining power of the nation state, cities will become more important. Cities across Europe are already developing strong cross-border links and networks as they become powerful economic forces in their own right. Medieval Europe was domi-

nated by the City State and trading organisations such as the Hanseatic League. The same may be true in a future Europe where countries without strong cities will struggle to compete on the international stage.

We have yet to deal with London which raises very different issues. London is the only British city which would meet Jane Jacobs' criteria for a great city. It is a city of great contrasts, with pockets of deprivation as severe as anything in the north adjacent to areas of great wealth and intense demand. As with all great cities, it also draws people to itself to a far greater extent than any other British city. The population of inner London started to rise in the 1980s after years of decline, and is predicted to rise rapidly over the next twenty years, partly as a result of immigration from the European Union. Yet fifteen of the UK's twenty most deprived wards are to be found in London. It faces the problems of growth and congestion at the same time as the problems of decline and depopulation and is therefore a microcosm of the situation in the UK as a whole. Through the 1980s London experienced an unprecedented development boom and in its docklands gave birth to the 'yuppy' apartment which started to change British perceptions of the ideal home. However the recession of the late 1980s severely dented this boom and London has been held back by the lack of city-wide local government. It has been governed by a patchwork quilt of small authorities unable to muster the resources and capacity of the confident provincial city councils. However London is once again 'cool' according to *Newsweek Magazine* and is finding a new confidence. It is likely that, with the election of a London Mayor in the near future, London will once again lead the UK's urban renaissance.

The capacity to mobilise the skills and energies of large numbers of people is the factor which has always sustained cities. The city is like a magnifying glass, it focuses and concentrates human activity both positive and negative. It is no accident that cities house the worst excesses of crime and poverty, but the reverse side of this is that they also house the best of the arts, learning, sports and, even today, commerce. If cities did not exist we would not have great art galleries, libraries and theatres; we would not have a subculture to feed and sustain mainstream culture; we would not have a venue for great public events and a focus for regional power and even in the days of the electronic office we would lose the catalyst for economic growth. The magnifying glass works because of the concentration of people who live and work in cities. Human nature requires face-to-face interaction and it is the city, not the suburban close or the motorway service station, where the density of people exists to sustain the creativity of human contact. As Jane Jacobs argued in the *Economy of Cities*[21] it is only in cities that new work is added to existing activities. This, she suggests, is the engine for human and economic growth. It is this basic truth which has saved the city from extinction and which sustains and nourishes its renaissance. As more people are attracted back to the city, and despite the complaints of gentrification and colonisation, there are signs that the traditional role of the city as a marketplace is re-emerging.

Shaky as this role may seem today, further trends may emerge which reinforce the role of urban areas. It is possible that the need for more sustainable development patterns and the reduction in car use may reinforce this role in the future. The growing numbers of childless households may also place more value on the advantages that towns and cities can offer. It may be that a sea change in our attitude to the city is taking place, reversing trends which date back to the industrial revolution.

The historic structure of London:
London is the only UK city which would pass Jane Jacobs' test of a great city.

CHAPTER 2
Lost Utopias

In considering the form of housing for the twenty-first century it is important to understand the forces that have shaped the design of housing in previous centuries. The wider urban trends described in the last chapter help to explain the impetus behind different forms and locations of development. They do not however explain how the nineteenth century terrace evolved into the twentieth century semi-detached house or indeed the high-rise block and how this might transform into the twenty-first century home. This is what we will seek to do in this and the following two chapters. The first task is to trace the roots of the concepts of housing and its place within towns and cities which have dominated the twentieth century. In doing this we need to go back to the Utopians who shaped the twentieth century home.

An ancestor of the garden city:
Bournville Village in Birmingham developed by George Cadbury in 1879

The great shapers of the twentieth century home were the Utopian thinkers[1]. No book on the subject would be complete without Ebenezer Howard's three magnets or Le Corbusier's Ville Radieuse. These and other visionaries reacted against the evils of the industrial city whilst embracing the opportunities of the industrial age. Their ideas have had a lasting effect on modern town planning. At the end of the twentieth century new visions are required which respond not so much to the technological opportunity of the modern age but to the unsustainable patterns of development that technology has produced. In doing this it is important to learn from the twentieth century visionaries and the way that they have influenced housing and urban development.

The garden city pioneers

The early visionaries were the enlightened industrial philanthropists, people like Robert Owen who developed New Lanark in 1800 to provide better conditions for his workers and to defuse political unrest. He was followed by industrialists such as Titus Salt in Bradford (Saltaire 1853), George Cadbury in Birmingham (Bournville 1879), and William Hesketh Lever in Birkenhead (Port Sunlight 1888) as well as Joseph Rowntree's development of New Earswick in York (1902). These developments combined a genuine concern for the well-being of workers, with a degree of self aggrandisement, and sound commercial sense. They varied greatly in their form, structure, the degree of communal provision and common ownership that they incorporated. However together they provided many of the elements which crystallised at the turn of the century into the garden city movement.

It is 100 years since the garden city idea was developed by Ebenezer Howard in his book *Tomorrow: A peaceful path to real reform* in 1898[2], republished in 1902 as *Garden Cities of Tomorrow*. Howard recognised that the city had many advantages: social opportunity, employment, well-lit streets and 'palatial edifices'. However there were also many disadvantages such as the 'closing out of nature… the isolation of crowds… foul air and murky skies… slums and gin palaces'. He also saw the countryside as having a balance of advantages and disadvantages and proposed the garden city as a means of combining the advantages of both town and country without the disadvantages. This equation was illustrated with

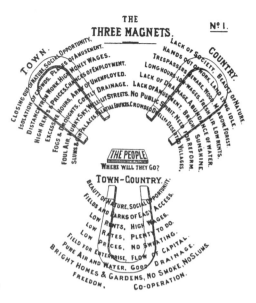

Above - The three magnets: Developed by Ebenezer Howard a century ago the diagram has taken on almost iconic status

Below - The Social City: A network of garden cities providing a framework of development encompassing both urban and rural uses

a picture of three magnets which has since featured in virtually every book written on town and country planning. Howard's vision was to reform the organisation of towns, the pattern of settlements and indeed the wider organisation of society. He advocated new towns with a population of 32 000 on 6 000 acres with the majority of land used for agriculture. These towns were to be part of a network of garden cities across the countryside which Howard called the 'Social City'. This abolished the distinction between town and country since agricultural and urban uses were incorporated within a common framework. Land was to be owned co-operatively with everyone paying rents to service debt and to generate a surplus to cover services, health care and pensions.

The form of the garden city was illustrated in a series of diagrams which are almost as famous as Howard's magnets. The garden city was to be organised in concentric rings around a central park surrounded by a covered glass arcade containing shops and services. Beyond this were rings of housing separated from

The suburban environment: The hedges and trees of Hampstead Garden Suburb still represent, to many people, the ideal suburban environment

the outer ring of industry by a grand avenue. Many of these features find echoes in modern towns, the covered glass-roofed shopping centres, the tree-lined avenues and the zoning of uses. Howard sought to build his utopia with the formation of the Garden City Pioneer Company in July 1902. The first true garden cities were Letchworth designed by Parker and Unwin in 1903, and then in 1919 Welwyn Garden City designed by Louis De Soissons.

The garden city movement gave birth to the British new town movement and still lies at the heart of the philosophy of the Town and Country Planning Association which Howard helped to start. However our interest here is in the wider influence that the garden city has had on housing development. Here it is not so much the concept of the garden city but the designs for the first developments which have had a lasting effect. The most influential designers at the time were Louis de Soissons who designed Welwyn Garden City and Barry Parker and Raymond Unwin who designed New Earswick, Letchworth and Hampstead Garden Suburb, the latter with Sir Edwin Lutyens. Through these schemes they developed the form of the garden city which was

subsequently to have such an influence on twentieth century suburban planning. Raymond Unwin described his philosophy in two influential books, *The Art of Building a Home* and *Town Planning in Practice*[3]. His vision was of wide frontaged semi-detached houses and short terraces at densities of twelve units to the acre in a landscaped setting with plenty of vistas – influenced by Sitte's street pictures. Another important influence was the revival of organic vernacular and Gothic forms through the arts and crafts movement and particularly the work of John Ruskin and William Morris. Parker and Unwin believed that the disposition of housing should be guided by the topography of the site rather than street patterns. This led to the use of 'closes' of houses set away from the road. In New Earswick these were initially served by footpaths. However with the growth in car use these closes evolved into cul-de-sacs which were first seen in Letchworth and Hampstead Garden Suburb. Hampstead which, due to Lutyens' influence, is more formal than the other garden cities, is probably the finest example of Parker and Unwin's work. However Victorian by-laws, designed to prevent the unwholesome yards which had characterised London slums, specified the development of wide through roads. The narrow roads, closes and cul-de-sacs of Hampstead therefore required a special Act of Parliament to make them possible. Concerns about traffic congestion led to a stipulation that housing densities be reduced to eight houses to the acre. Unwin argued that, with the growing number of cars, closes and cul-de-sacs would create a quiet residential environment as well as reducing the land area devoted to roads. However his main concern was to avoid the housing layout being dictated by the road network which, he felt, led to monotonous grids and ribbon development. The closes and cul-de-sac therefore allowed far greater variety of form which in Unwin's hands led to a streetscape of enduring quality. However as with many visionaries the concepts have not fared so well on the drawing boards of less talented designers where the results are more often clutter and confusion.

The first cul-de-sac?
Louis de Soissons' designs for Welwyn Garden City (below) one of the first to make extensive use of the cul-de-sac (above)

Some of the most enthusiastic exponents of the ideas of the garden city movement were the newly created council housing departments in the years after the First World War. One of the most influential departments was the Greater London Council which undertook developments such as the Old Oak Estate in Hammersmith. Another very influential development was Wythenshawe, developed by Manchester City Council on the outskirts of the city in 1930. This was designed by Barry Parker and has been described by Peter Hall[4] as the third garden city. However, unlike the other garden cities, Wythenshawe has remained a predominantly poor working-class area. It is tempting to look at somewhere like Letchworth or Hampstead Garden Suburb which remain popular and to believe that our problems would be less if only all housing were built like this. Yet Wythenshawe is almost identical in design and, as recent work by URBED[5] has shown, the social and economic problems of parts of Wythenshawe, such as Benchill, are as bad and in some cases worse than Manchester's most notorious inner city areas. How much this is due to the physical design of the area is unclear, but the isolation of the area from the city which is compounded by the disorientating nature of the street layout undoubtedly plays its part. There is a lesson here for those who would argue that the wholesale replacement of high-rise estates with suburban housing will solve the problems of the inner city.

Parker's designs for Wythenshawe incorporated two further ideas which were to have a lasting influence. The first was the concept of the neighbourhood unit served by local facilities and surrounded by arterial roads. The second was the parkway, an arterial road set within parkland which ran between these neighbourhoods. Princess Parkway, the southern part of which is now the M56 motorway, remains a major arterial route out of Manchester and the concept of setting the road within a linear park can be seen not just in Wythenshawe but also in the much later development of Hulme, of which we will hear more later. The concept of the neighbourhood unit and the parkway were subsequently

to coincide with the ideas of the modernist movement as we will see in the next chapter.

As with all visionaries Howard's ideas and the designs of Parker, Unwin and Louis de Soissons have suffered in less enlightened hands. Forgotten are the ideas for social reform and the organisation of uses and settlements. Lost is the respect for topography and the understanding of how housing can be arranged in a landscaped setting. In superficial terms the modern suburban housing estate owes much to the early garden city designs but rarely have they achieved the same level of quality and character.

The housing designs which emerged from the garden city movement have also become firmly embedded in the public consciousness. The suburban ideal has become an almost universal aspiration of UK households. It has exerted a powerful influence on municipal housing, alongside the modernist movement, and has be-come the stock-in-trade of private housebuilders who, for much of the century, have built little else. Ebenezer Howard would, no doubt, shudder to be called the father of the modern suburb but this is perhaps his greatest legacy.

The modernist reformers

The garden city pioneers were not the only utopians to influence the twentieth century home and town planning. Another group of visionaries were equally concerned to sweep away the worst excesses of urban squalor but sought to do this, not by turning to the countryside for inspiration, but to art and science. The modernist movement sought to bring order and logic to the confusion and muddle of the city. Tony Garnier and Le Corbusier in France and the Bauhaus in Germany were some of the leading exponents of these ideas and like Ebenezer Howard their aim was no less than to reinvent the city.

The Cité Industrielle: One of Tony Garnier's original illustrations

Tony Garnier first produced his plan for the ideal industrial town in 1904 just as Howard started to develop Letchworth. Garnier's ideas were published as *Une Cité Industrielle* [6] in 1917. He envisaged a town of segregated uses with a residential zone, a train station quarter and an industrial zone. The town was to promote social justice through common ownership and, so widespread would social harmony be, Garnier saw no need for the town to include a police station, courts or churches. In an echo of the issues which will concern us in the twenty-first century, the town was to be energy self-sufficient. Development was sited in relation to the sun and wind and would draw all of its energy from a hydro-electric dam. Residential quarters were to be laid out in east-west blocks allowing all housing to face south. Narrow streets were not to have trees, with wider streets only being allowed trees on the southern side to avoid shading. This is one of the first attempts at passive solar design although at the time the motivation was the health-giving properties of sunlight rather than energy efficiency.

Garnier's Cité Industrielle was never built although echoes of some of his ideas can be seen in the Tony Garnier Estate in Lyon, not least because in recent years a series of enormous murals of Garnier's drawings have been created on the gable ends of the blocks[7]. The architectural style of Garnier's buildings is remarkably contemporary and more accessible than the later proposals of Le

Corbusier largely because they are human in scale. His high-density residential quarters are similar to the urban development of the 1990s described later in this book. However in other respects Garnier's legacy is more damaging to the modern city. He was one of the first to develop the idea of zoning uses as well as the modernist concept of buildings as objects within a landscape rather than the 'walls of urban streets'. Garnier's other legacy is his influence on Le Corbusier and it is through Le Corbusier that the ideas were largely transferred to Britain and America.

Le Corbusier, born in 1887 as Charles Edouard Jeanneret, published his utopian vision in two books *The City of Tomorrow* in 1922 and *La Ville Radieuse* in 1933[8]. Whilst these were a development of Garnier's ideas they were less of a reaction to the problems of the industrial city and more of a response to the opportunities of the industrial age. Le Corbusier's vision was based on mechanisation and new technology. It exploited the potential of the car and aeroplane, as well as the new building technologies which allowed for high-rise building and mass production. However the influence of the machine went deeper still into Le Corbusier's vision. He believed that, just as science was ordering nature, so it could order the city. His city is rational, efficient and ordered. Its plan can be read as a diagram of its functions but it makes few if any concessions to the complexity of urban life.

Le Corbusier's aims in developing La Ville Radieuse are similar to those of Howard and to many subsequent planners in the twentieth century. He sought to decongest the centre of cities, increase mobility and increase the amount of parks and open space. However he differed in one important respect. Unlike the garden city builders and most of modern planning, he wanted to increase urban densities to around 1 200 inhabitants to the acre, almost ten times the average density of Paris at the time. The overcrowding of cities was seen at the time as one of the main problems requiring reform and much of modern planning has sought to address this by reducing densities. Le Corbusier however saw higher densities as a prerequisite for mechanised production

The city in landscape: Le Corbusier's vision of blocks built on stilts so as not to interrupt the flow of the landscape

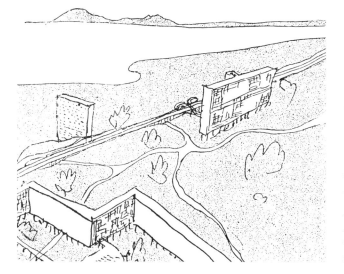

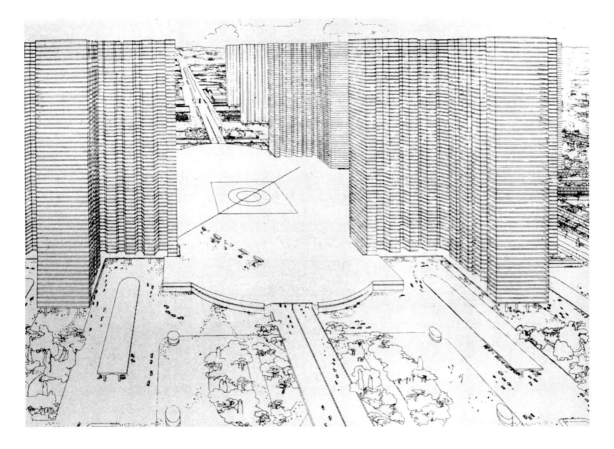

so that, far from reducing densities, he proposed technological solutions to overcome the problems that this creates. This he achieved by building upwards and proposing high-rise blocks accommodating not just housing but all of the services required for modern life: schools, shops, services and employment. This liberated 95% of the land area within the large urban blocks that he proposed for open space and parks.

Le Corbusier has been credited, or condemned, as the father of the high-rise blocks. Again, like all visionaries, this is largely due to the way in which his ideas have been interpreted by lesser architects. The schemes that he completed, most notably Unité d'Habitation in Marseilles, remain successful. But the influence of his ideas is equally significant in terms of the organisation of cities which, with the exception of Chandigarh in the Punjab, were never built. He condemned the traditional street thus: 'The corridor street should be tolerated no longer, for it poisons the houses that border it'. Such streets were seen as incapable of accommodating the swift movement of goods in the quantities required for industrial production. These sentiments reflected the thinking of Barry Parker in Wythenshawe and, as we will see, subsequent planners like Abercrombie with his concern to eliminate muddle. La Ville Radieuse was therefore the first city plan to include a hierarchy of roads. Subterranean routes were to be created for heavy traffic linked to a network of loading bays. Ground level streets would then be used for getting around the city and, above this, free flowing highways, the precursors of modern motorways, would cater for longer journeys. The streets would be straight and junctions spaced at 400 yards to reduce congestion. This distance determined the scale of urban blocks. However there is little mention of the pedestrian in Le Corbusier's writing and it is clear that the scale of his proposals is based around the needs of the car rather than travel by foot.

The Ville Radieuse: Le Corbusier's ordered and rational urban Utopia, dominated by technology as witnessed by the pride of place given to the airport

The influence of these ideas on post war commercial and residential development hardly needs spelling out. The vertical separation of uses and movement, with underground loading, elevated motorways and housing on streets in the sky, can be seen throughout the country and has blighted town centres and residential estates alike. The dominance of the motor car at the expense of the pedestrian who is relegated to the subway or elevated walkway, the use of mechanised production, and the infamous high-rise estates which in 1980 were estimated to house 1 in 4 UK households[9], can all be traced back in part at least to Le Corbusier. It is tempting to think that Le Corbusier's ideas are dead. However they are still being taught with reverence in many planning schools, appealing as they do to the planner's wish for control and order. His highway engineering ideas, transmuted as we will see through various reports and government guidance, still influence modern practice.

A further influence on housing design came from the Bauhaus in Germany. Here housing design was approached with the same systematic, functional discipline that the Bauhaus sought to apply to all elements of design. While this was on a much smaller scale than Garnier and Le Corbusier it shared a design philosophy focused on industrial production. The Bauhaus was concerned with art, product design and architecture rather than the planning of cities. However the ideas for residential design developed by the Bauhaus were to have a profound influence

The Bauhaus model: Ideas for a multi-storey housing settlement developed by Ludwig Hilberseimer at the Bauhaus around 1930

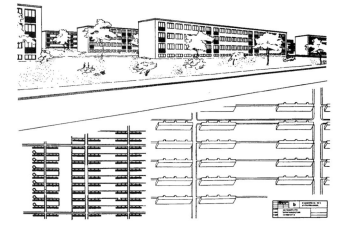

on the modernist movement. The experimental *Haus am Horn* built for the Bauhaus Exhibition in 1923 was intended as a showcase for modern household products and attracted considerable interest. It reflected the rejection by the Bauhaus of the arts and crafts philosophy that had dominated its earlier years and the embracing of technology to create a *Wohnmaschine* or living machine. The house was of steel frame and concrete construction and its design reflected this – form followed function. It was simple, sparse, and logical, perfectly matched to its function if not to the more traditional notions of home. As Walter Gropius, the director of the Bauhaus, said: 'To build means to shape the activities of human life. The organism of a house derives from the activities which take place within it... The shape of a building is not there for its own sake'[10]. There were plans to develop a Bauhaus housing estate. While these were dropped, work was done by Ludwig Hilberseimer at the Bauhaus on the design of estates where he advocated mixing high-rise and single-storey dwellings. This, he said, means that... 'a development would not only become freer but also achieve a spatial arrangement which results directly from the requirements and which... does not have to rely on decorative trimmings for its urban design'[11].

Paradise lost

The work of Garnier, Le Corbusier and the Bauhaus must be seen in the context of the emerging modernist movement. Just as Howard, Parker and Unwin drew upon the arts and crafts movement, the modernists interpreted the ideas emerging from painters like Mondrian and applied them to the development of housing and the organisation of cities. Both movements held a strong appeal to planners and architects in Britain. Opportunities to implement these ideas were created by the housing shortages and need for reconstruction after the two world wars which led to huge building programmes. After the First World War it was the garden city which held sway. But the modernists came to the fore in the 1920s and 30s and it was they who most swayed the hearts and minds of planners and architects after

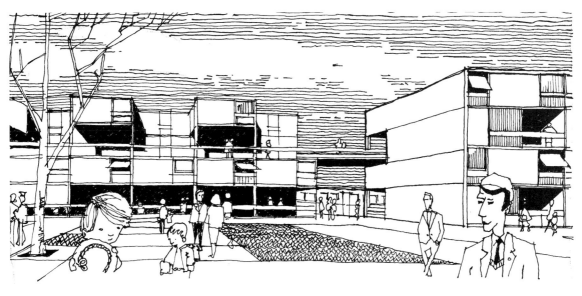

Utopia in practice: One of the early architect's illustrations of Hulme in Manchester illustrating how the planning ideas of the pioneers were put into practice

the Second World War. The modernists did not however supplant the ideas of the garden city pioneers and the two approaches have existed side by side for much of the century. Whilst the modernist school came to dominate planning in cities, the garden city movement's influence has thrived in the new town, the overspill estate and the suburb. What is more when it comes to the organisation of towns and cities, as we will see in the next chapter, the ideas of the two movements are very similar and have been mutually reinforcing.

As we approach the end of the century it is clear that the influence of the modernists is rapidly waning. The failure of many of the redevelopment schemes of the 1950s, 60s and early 70s is now apparent and there are few people who would hold up Le Corbusier as a model for future urban development. However with the fall of modernists we are left with only the garden city as a tried and tested philosophy for the design of cities. Whilst this may be appropriate for new settlements and suburbs it is of less value when considering the redevelopment and repopulation of urban areas. This leaves us with a void for those seeking solutions to our towns and cities and points up a pressing need for new urban models.

In seeking to develop such models we can learn a great deal from the twentieth century visionaries. They have shown that through published work, a small number of demonstration projects and, no doubt, a great deal of luck, it is possible to profoundly alter the course of housing development and town planning, if not always in the way that was originally envisaged. It may well be that as young professions, housing and planning in the twentieth century have been particularly susceptible to new ideas. The visionaries described in this chapter provided an ideological and philosophical base for these professions at a time when they needed to establish their identities. The same may be more difficult in the future. However the fact that so many local councils have jumped on the urban village band waggon suggests that new visions have not entirely lost their potency or their capacity for misinterpretation. The effective twenty-first century Utopians must understand the way in which their ideas are translated into practice by the planning and housing professions. It is this that we seek to do in the next two chapters.

CHAPTER 3
The taming of the city

The industrial revolution left a legacy of fear and mistrust towards the city in the minds of many people. This in turn fuelled the flight to the suburbs in both Britain and America. At the same time the Utopian visionaries in the early part of the century were busy developing alternatives to the city. In some cases, such as Le Corbusier, they were advocating the wholesale redevelopment of existing towns. Most however confined themselves to new settlements, blank canvases on which towns and cities could be reinvented free of the constraints of history. The planners and other urban professionals who took up these ideas did not have such freedom. They sought to apply Utopian ideas to the great task of reforming existing settlements and eliminating what in their eyes was the muddle and confusion of urban life. With the need for reconstruction and the introduction of the modern town planning system after the Second World War they were given the opportunity to put these ideas into practice. The context set by the Utopians in the early part of the century was largely anti-urban and this was reflected in the attitudes of postwar planners. It was not that they wanted to do away with the city, they sought instead to make it more efficient, equitable and healthy, in short to tame and control it. They undoubtedly saw themselves as the saviours of towns and cities but in reality they ended up destroying what they sought to protect. In this chapter we describe the nature of and justification for this destruction.

The ideas of the urban visionaries were transmitted into practice through a variety of routes. It is tempting to suggest that the garden city predominated in the interwar years but after the Second World War its influence was largely confined to new towns with the architectural modernists coming to the fore in urban areas. However the situation is more complex. In developing the intellectual foundation of modern town planning and postwar social housing practitioners drew heavily on both the garden city and modernist traditions. Whilst in terms of physical form the two traditions would seem to be poles apart, in terms of their underlying principles there were in fact many similarities. Both thought in terms of neighbourhood units, promoted the benefits of open space and sought to reorganise settlements to accommodate the motor car. Indeed to many, Le Corbusier's ideas were an application of garden city ideals to high-density urban living.

One of the most important organisations responsible for bringing these ideas together and applying them to the planning of cities was the Congrès International de l' Architecture Moderne (CIAM). Formed in 1928 and including people like Walter Gropius of the Bauhaus, this group was responsible for popularising and making practical the ideas of the visionaries. Through the Charter of Athens in 1933[1] CIAM created the other great foundation of modern planning to counterbalance Howard's *Peaceful path to real*

The rebuilding of Coventry: Before German bombing and British planning Coventry was a fine medieval city. It was originally seen as one of the great successes of postwar planning. Much of the design philosophy underlying its redevelopment has been discredited yet the quality of the original vision can still be seen in parts of the city centre

reform. The Charter of Athens developed Le Corbusier's ideas into a set of practical principles which could be applied to the problems of overcrowding and congestion which characterised the modern city.

An insight into the thinking of CIAM can be found in the report of the 1952 CIAM conference on the Heart of the City[2] which took place in England. The conference proceedings are full of statements such as: 'The study of past and present urban shapes, urban ecological process, and urban health will give material for the urbanist's vision'. The conference stressed diversity, and encouraged humanitarian cities

where spontaneity flourishes, the 'individual is king (and) the pedestrian is his own master'. The influences cited by the conference were also promising with references to the very Italian piazzas admired by many of today's urban designers. Yet the developments which the conference used to illustrate these ideas were the recently completed pedestrian precincts of Coventry and Stevenage. The City Architect of Coventry told the delegates that their plans represented 'the first time that a central area (had been) analysed in terms of its main uses and a plan drawn up which retained only those necessary to its correct functioning; both industry and housing were excluded'. Indeed, despite Coventry's problems, many of the positive aspects of the modernist vision can still be seen in the city. However in other areas the high ideals of CIAM and the visionaries from which they drew their inspiration turned into the soulless pedestrian precincts and the ghettoised high-rise council estates which have since so blighted our towns and cities. It is paradoxical that Coventry, one of Britain's greatest medieval cities, should have been so readily sacrificed whereas in Germany cities like Nuremberg have been painstakingly rebuilt on traditional lines. The reason for this lies in a number of principles developed by CIAM which became the foundations, some would say the dogma, on which modern planning was based.

Comprehensive redevelopment

One of CIAM's concerns between the wars was slum clearance because of the clear correlation between poor housing and ill health. CIAM believed that slum areas could not be improved since the building form was fundamentally flawed. They therefore advocated that areas of poor housing should be swept away to be replaced with modern blocks positioned to receive the sun and surrounded by open space. Whilst they were against overcrowding they viewed low densities as uneconomic. It was therefore logical to follow Le Corbusier's lead by advocating high-rise blocks. These were to be built in a landscape setting leaving no place for traditional streets. In this way CIAM was to establish a blue print which was to guide much of the slum clearance work in America and Britain. This contrasts sharply with the war-damaged sections of West German cities despite the German origins of many modernist ideas. German towns and cities were rebuilt with 4-5 storey blocks on traditional streets which accommodated rather than separated traffic and pedestrians. Germany and many other parts of Europe have therefore retained the vitality of their urban areas and modernist development, where it has taken place, is confined to the periphery of the town. The attitudes of postwar planners in Britain have therefore reinforced the historic differences between British and European towns.

BRACKNELL NEW TOWN

In 1950 Bracknell was a small town of 5 000 people spread out along a traditional high street with eight pubs, a cattle market, shops, a cinema and a garage. In 1944 Abercrombie's Plan for London identified the need to decentralise population to a series of new and expanded towns around the capital including Bracknell. These were to become the Mark One New Towns included in the 1949 New Towns Act.

Bracknell was originally designated as a new town with a population of up to 25 000 and plans were developed for a modest expansion to the town retaining the high street. However in 1961 the planned population was increased to 60 000. By then the philosophy of town building had changed radically and traffic was seen as much more of a problem. A series of principles were established for the new development, many of which are similar to those that would be put forward today. The vision was of a lively mixed-use centre to be achieved within an urban structure which was more logical and functional than traditional towns. The key element to this was traffic management and the new town plan stated: 'The needs of motor traffic in the Town Centre are quite different from those of pedestrians, whatever their purpose, each should be provided for separately. Cars and delivery vehicles should have a direct service approach to every building and from whatever direction the town centre is approached car parking should be obvious and adequate. Access for pedestrians from car parks and other approaches to the centre should be direct, safe and of constant interest'. This requirement alone fixed the development form of the centre since it required the use of different levels, the creation of two ring roads and extensive service yards.

The remnants of the original high street

Despite the aim of creating a mixed-use centre, the form of the new town has made this difficult to achieve. There are few restaurants and cafés, fewer pubs than there were on the original high street, and most of the leisure development has been concentrated in a leisure centre on the edge of the centre. In creating a functional centre, the planners overlooked many of the fundamentals which make a town work. The town would have worked well when its population had little option but to use the centre for shopping and other services. However a more mobile population with greater choice is turning its back on Bracknell as somewhere to shop. It lacks the range of uses envisaged in the original plan and does not even provide shopping for the town's population let alone a wider catchment.

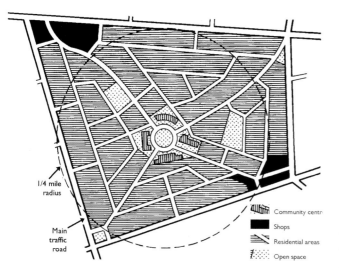

1/4 mile
radius

Main
traffic
road

Community centre

Shops

Residential areas

Open space

**The neighbour-
hood unit:**
Conceived by Clarence
Perry for the New York
Plan in the 1920s, the
neighbourhood unit is
delineated by major
routes with community
facilities in the centre.
However Perry posi-
tioned shops at the
junctions of the major
routes whereas in the
UK shops were placed
in the centre of the
neighbourhood and so
were deprived of
passing trade

The neighbourhood unit

CIAM also took on board the concept of the neighbourhood unit. As we have seen this played a role in Howard's ideas and was a central part of Barry Parker's proposals for Wythenshawe. It had also been central to Clarence Perry's plan for New York[3] in the 1920s which advocated neighbourhoods of 5 000 people based on the catchment of a primary school with major roads consigned to the edge of each neighbourhood. CIAM developed the neighbourhood unit into the idea of super blocks, each served by a range of local facilities – schools, shops, doctors – and with an allotted area of open space. These blocks were accessible only to the residents. There was however a crucial difference between this and Perry's ideas. Perry placed shopping areas at the junctions of the major roads dividing the neighbourhood units but retained their character as traditional streets. CIAM, by contrast, advocated small district centres at the heart of the neighbourhood keeping the major peripheral roads free of frontage development to ensure the free flow of traffic. This was a direct application of the parkway concept which Parker used in Wythenshawe. Industrial, shopping and commercial areas were similarly to be zoned into blocks to create industrial estates, shopping centres and commercial districts. These zones were to be separated by swathes of open space within which would run a fast and efficient transport system of roads and motorways.

The free flow of traffic

The great insight of Le Corbusier and the other great visionary not mentioned so far, Frank Lloyd Wright, was to foresee the growth of car use. They saw the car as a liberating force to be accommodated in towns and cities. If this meant that the whole city had to be redesigned then so be it, an attitude which characterised the approach of most postwar planning until recently. The streets which lay at the heart of traditional urban areas played the dual role of a transport artery and a focus for the surrounding community. They were, as a result, lined with shops and services and bustling with the sort of activity and diversity prized by writers like Jane Jacobs and the visitors to historic towns. However to the tidy mind of the modern planner this 'solified chaos' in the words of Lewis Mumford[4] was inefficient and was choking the commercial lifeblood of cities and undermining the quality of life of urban communities. Planners and highway engineers therefore sought to reform the system of roads in cities drawing inspiration from Le Corbusier's and Wright's freeways and Parker's parkways. These ideas were developed by H. Alker Tripp, an assistant commissioner in the Metropolitan Police responsible for traffic. In a book entitled *Town Planning and Traffic*[5], which was to influence Abercombie's plan for London, he advocated that the streets of London should be divided into arterial routes, subarterial routes and local roads. The higher order routes were to be segregated from the highway system, free of frontage development, with widely spaced junctions to reduce congestion.

By the 1960s the emphasis had changed from exploiting the potential of the car to coping with the challenges of congestion. The landmark report *Traffic in Towns* by a group chaired by Sir Colin Buchanan in 1963[6] stared into the abyss that we still face today: 'The potential increase in the number of vehicles is so great that unless something is done conditions are bound to become extremely serious within a comparatively short period of years. Either the utility of vehicles in towns will decline rapidly or the pleasantness and safety of surroundings will deteriorate catastrophically – in all probability both will happen together'. The report goes on to say that these problems concern the form and organisation of urban areas which will become the 'supreme social problem of the future'. To be fair to Buchanan, the arguments in the report are more sophisticated than their subsequent application would suggest. He suggested that in planning for future roads both the economic costs and the environmental costs should be taken into account. If the environmental costs were considered by the community to be unacceptable then traffic restraint rather than road building should be pursued. He therefore put forward maximal and minimal traffic solutions, although it was the maximal solutions which received most interest and which have had the lasting effect. Buchanan has therefore come to be associated with the network of motorways with grade separated junctions and pedestrian walkways and subways which were so close to the heart of the planners and highway engineers in the 1960s and 70s. While there is now an acceptance of the negative effects of these ideas, the damage has been done. Resources have been wasted, communities divided and isolated and town centres cut off from their hinterland by ring roads which have become the modern equivalent of city walls. Principles such as a hierarchy of distributor routes with frontage development only allowed on minor streets were enshrined in the government's *Design Bulletin 32 – Residential Roads and Footpaths*[7]. This has been a major influence on highway engineers and remains in force. Design guidance developed by Alan Baxter Associates (1998)[8] is intended to promote a more flexible interpretation of the guidelines. However we are still allowing the car to dominate urban development and to undermine the qualities which make urban living attractive.

The high street: Traditional streets such as the Stratford Road in Birmingham serve the dual function of a major traffic route and a community focus. Many of these routes have been transformed into free-flowing traffic arteries free of frontage development and devoid of urban character. However recent improvements to the Stratford Road show how traffic flow can be maintained while retaining vitality. This has been done by creating a single lane of traffic in each direction uninterrupted by parking or turning lanes. This has allowed pavements to actually be widened while traffic flow has been eased.

The benefits of open space

Underlying much of modern planning is the idea that open space is a good thing. One of the problems with the overcrowded industrial town was that people had little or no public or private open space. The by-law terraces may have been a great improvement on the earlier urban slums but they made little or no provision for recreation or indeed greenery of any kind. It was this which gave impetus to the development of Victorian parks which provided a valuable oasis of open space in areas where trees were rare, play areas unheard of and many people did not even have access to a back yard. However such was the belief in the quality of life-enhancing aspects of open space, that Le Corbusier's assertion that 95% of the land area should be given over to open space was accepted by many planners. Great deserts of grassland with lollipop trees and the occasional forlorn playground have therefore come to dominate many parts of our cities. Even in the 1970s and 80s large parts of the London Borough of Southwark were blighted by Abercrombie's vision of new parks and riverside walkways in pursuit of which the council continued to buy up and clear large areas of housing and workshops.

The development of buildings in a landscape is common to the garden city and modernist movements. In the garden city, however, most of the land was in gardens. The open space was therefore largely 'privatised' so that it was used and maintained by the residents. In the modernist vision, by contrast, open space was communal and part of the public domain. Some of it may have been used as playgrounds or sports pitches but most lacked any function other than providing a buffer to traffic noise and a 'pleasant' outlook to residents. However someone living on the tenth floor of a tower block has little use for the formless grassland in which the block is set. The reality was therefore that much of this space was unused, dangerous and a burden on public authorities responsible for maintenance.

Yet planners still insist on lavishing their plans with great swathes of open space while architects designate 'landscaping' with no discernible function or generator of activity. Indeed local plans today still often treat open space as a land use in its own right regardless of function or usefulness. They fail to recognise why the open space is spurned by ungrateful residents, has not created value and has harmed the vitality of surrounding areas. This can be seen with many areas of open space such as Burgess Park in Southwark or Mile End Park in Tower Hamlets. Far from being great assets for the community these have quickly come to be seen as problems, little used by local people and with a reputation for crime.

The curse of overcrowding

One of the issues to have sowed most confusion in postwar planning is the issue of density. This is linked to the issue of open space but has more commonly been driven by concern about overcrowding, something which had been recognised as the curse of working-class areas since Victorian times. Overcrowding has been linked to ill-health, poverty and crime and was one of the main targets of slum clearance programmes. However the issue of overcrowding – the number of people per room – has consistently been confused with the issue of density – the number of dwellings or people per acre. High-density areas need not be overcrowded and conversely it is quite possible to have a low-density area in which overcrowding is a problem if houses are overoccupied. The visionaries discussed in the previous chapter sought to reduce overcrowding; however, with the exception of Le Corbusier, they failed to recognise this point and their objective became the reduction of densities.

The concern to lower densities can perhaps be traced back to Raymond Unwin's book, *Nothing gained by overcrowding* published in 1912[9]. This argued that if sufficient open space was provided the savings in land area to be gained from higher densities were marginal and outweighed by the benefits of lower density development. He suggested an ideal density of twelve houses to the acre, a target which became the norm for garden city development even though it was lower than the fifteen homes to the acre suggested by Ebenezer Howard. This target was also adopted by the influential Tudor-Walters

The density myth: It is often believed that the problem of many of the redevelopments undertaken in the 1960s was that densities were too high. However as these plans of Hulme illustrate, this was far from the case. The plan on the left is from the 1930s when the area was built to 150 dwellings/hectare. The plan below is the redevelopment of the 1960s and was built at only 37 dwellings to the hectare (15 dwellings to the acre) which is the density proposed by Ebenezer Howard for the garden city. The problem is that the high-rise nature of the redevelopment made it feel very dense as illustrated on the following page.

report of 1918[10] and became the standard density of most interwar development in both the public and private sectors.

In the more recent past the prejudice against density was reinforced by research on rats by Calhoun published as the *Behavioural Sink* in 1962[11]. Indeed this research was quoted in questions by members of the House of Commons Environment Select Committee in 1998 as part of their enquiry into housing! Calhoun showed that if a rat colony becomes too large its social structure breaks down. This was equated to the problems in high-density housing areas. However subsequent work has shown that social breakdown is a result of the size of the colony not its density and the situation is not improved by making the enclosure larger. Yet problems are avoided if the colony is fenced off into smaller enclosures even if densities are not reduced.

With the redevelopment of tightly packed urban areas after the Second World War it was felt

that the garden city density targets were unrealistic even with the decanting of a large part of the population to overspill estates. The emphasis therefore switched to accommodating higher densities whilst avoiding the problems of overcrowding. Following Le Corbusier's lead this was achieved by building upwards to allow for generous amounts of open space. There was also a trend in the 1970s to develop high-density low-rise estates based around a warren of alleyways.

However even at these higher densities these new developments were built at substantially lower densities than the terraced areas that the new development replaced. Indeed, as Alice

Coleman[12] has pointed out, the scale of high-rise estates gives the impression of high densities, an impression often shared by residents who feel that the area is overcrowded. Yet in terms of the number of houses to the acre, these estates were often built to relatively low densities. They therefore achieved the worst of both worlds – the impression of high density without any of the benefits. The Hulme area in Manchester, for example, was once home to 130 000 people not to mention countless small factories, pubs, shops and public buildings. The redevelopment of the 1960s swept this away to create 5 000 flats in six deck-access estates housing around 12 000 people. Similarly the Five Estates in Peckham were developed at a fraction of the density that had once existed in the area. This however was achieved by building at relatively high densities on part of the site and using the rest to create Burgess Park which, as we have seen, became a vast and poorly-used area of open space. It also resulted in many of the local shops on Rye Lane which was once known as the 'Golden Mile' closing for lack of trade. Yet consultants' reports continued to suggest that one of the area's problems was the fact that it was too dense. The Five Estates are currently the subject of a massive redevelopment programme which is likely to further reduce densities. Yet such is the hold that the benefits of lower densities and open space have on professionals and politicians that no one would dare suggest the obvious solution of building on part of the park to reduce its scale, increase numbers of potential users and provide passive surveillance and boost the local economy.

Jane Jacobs reports a conversation that she had with a planner about the West End in Boston[13] in the 1960s. The planner was ashamed to admit that an area with 275 dwellings to the acre still existed in the city and indicated that, when resources allowed, it would be redeveloped. However he also admitted that the area scored well on indices such as delinquency, disease and infant mortality and even confessed that he enjoyed the street life of the area. The West End may have been unique and there were certainly many dense working-class areas where disease, poverty and crime were severe problems. The point however is that the blanket use of density as an indicator of such problems is rarely justified.

Unlike many of the orthodoxies of modern planning the concern with densities is as strong today as it ever was. Despite the continued depopulation of our cities, increasing homelessness and lack of housing sites in many areas, there is still a drive to reduce urban densities. As many high-rise estates are redeveloped densities are being further reduced at huge public expense in a forlorn attempt to overcome the areas' problems. In reality the loss of density in the original redevelopment was one of the causes of the problems. The challenge now is to increase densities rather than to exacerbate these problems with further reductions.

Postwar plan making

These various influences came together in the rash of town and city plans developed after the Second World War. The most influential was the plan for the postwar reconstruction of London developed by Patrick Abercrombie with J. H. Forshaw, the chief architect for London County Council, produced in 1944[14] and published as a Penguin special edited by Arno Goldfinger. This plan brought together many of the ideas described in this chapter. London's arterial routes were to become parkways through landscaped strips, bounding inward-looking neighbourhoods arranged around pedestrianised shopping precincts. Much of the development was to be new with the Victorian housing areas which survived the blitz being cleared to create modern, zoned areas of development.

Even at a time of postwar reconstruction, the structure of London's local government, financial constraints and the complexity of the city largely defeated the planners so that Abercrombie's plan was only partly realised. This was not the case in the provincial cities, in small towns due for expansion and of course in the rash of new towns planned after the war. The plans which emerged for these towns took a lead from Abercrombie and what is more strong provincial councils were far more able to put them into practice. The 1949 plan for Manchester[15] conceded to the

Planned and organic towns: Figure ground plans of Devizes (above right) and Yate (above left). The towns are roughly the same size and the plans are approximately the same scale. They show a stark contrast between a dense traditional town and one developed in the 1950s applying the principles of postwar planning

retention of only a handful of city centre buildings. Even Waterhouse's town hall was to be demolished! The radial routes were to be replanned as parkways, the results of which can be seen along Oldham Road and Rochdale Road to the North of the city. Even greater 'progress' was made in places like Birmingham, Coventry and Stevenage, and even quite small towns like Yate to the north of Bristol or Hemel Hempstead to the north of London. Here existing centres were razed or new towns built to create comprehensively planned centres surrounded by a wilderness of ring roads and parking.

The lost urban vision

The effect of these policies on the vitality and life of cities is best summed up by Jane Jacobs in her tirade in the introduction to the *Death and Life of Great American Cities*. She summarises the ideas which are taken for granted in orthodox planning thus: 'The street is bad as an environment for humans; houses should be turned away from it and faced inward, towards sheltered greens. Frequent streets are wasteful, of advantage only to real estate speculators who measure value by the front foot. The basic unit of city design is not the street but the block, and more particularly the super-block. Commerce should be segregated from residences and greens. A neighbourhood's demand for goods should be calculated "scientifically", and this much and no more commercial space allocated. The presence of many other people is, at best, a necessary evil and good city planning must aim for at least an illusion of isolation and suburban privacy.'

It is hard to better this and the eloquence of Jacobs' argument for the importance of cities. The visionaries and their followers described in this and the previous chapter made the mistake of thinking that towns, cities and the human society that they accommodate are like machines, that they can be described entirely in terms of uses, functions, movement and systems. True such concepts have an analytical value in describing existing settlement patterns. They are however fatally flawed as tools for future planning. First of all towns and cities exist in all of their complex glory. Ordering this complexity requires resources far beyond that which was available even in the building boom after the war. Simplistic Utopias applied to existing urban areas are therefore bound to be compromised and undermined. Thus compromised they are unlikely to work as envisaged and are destined to fail.

However even when there is not the complexity of an existing town to deal with, the application of Utopian visions to a new town is fraught with difficulties. It is almost impossible for a master planner to conceive, on paper, a town which works as well as a traditional town, which is the result of centuries of evolution. This is not unlike the attempts in robotics to replicate the complexity of the human body. Artificial towns, like robots, may be more efficient and many businesses and residents may find this attractive, but they lack the diversity, vitality and character of their older cousins. Also as Jacobs said in the conclusion to *the Economy of Cities*[16]: '...bureaucratised, simplified cities, so dear to present-day city planners and urban designers, and familiar also to readers of science fiction and Utopian proposals, run

counter to the processes of city growth and economic development. Conformity and monotony, even when they are embellished with a froth of novelty, are not attributes of developing and economically vigorous cities'. This is why town planning at its best is essentially an art rather than a science and why successful urban development is organic rather than mechanistic.

Of course artificial towns can still work. It is instructive to be asked, as we were[17], to advise on the revitalisation of the centre of a new town like Milton Keynes, which incorporates many of the principles of modern town planning. Milton Keynes remains the fastest-growing city in the UK and is based upon a 'supergrid' of streets bounding neighbourhood units with a town centre based around boulevards and a covered shopping centre. It is generally popular with residents even if they do sometimes yearn for areas like Covent Garden where people can be seen throughout the day. However most recognise that the town is convenient and meets their every need. Milton Keynes remains probably the best example in Britain of the sort of urban environment envisaged by post war planners. However for

Milton Keynes: An illustrative section of the masterplan for Milton Keynes showing the supergrid of major routes which are free of frontage development and the neighbourhood developments within the grid. The city is perhaps the purest expression of much of the philosophy of post-war planning

The suburban conspiracy: Modern planning policies would no longer allow the creation of historic urban areas such as Bradford upon Avon (above). Instead a suburban conspiracy is overtaking our cities in which inappropriate housing turns its back on to the streets to which they should be giving life as in Moss Side, Manchester (below right)

and planners to justify development which the visionaries and early planners would have abhorred. However a philosophy which has destroyed the life of large parts of our cities must be questioned in terms of its conception rather than just its implementation. In the twenty-first century as in the 1990s we will continue to struggle with the momentous task of reforming our cities. We are however increasingly dealing not with the exhausted fabric of the Victorian city but with the legacy of twentieth century mistakes. Yet can we be sure that we are not repeating the same mistakes? It is true that we have overthrown many of the most damaging dogmas of the twentieth century. The question is, have we done this only to replace them with an equally inappropriate dogma, which we have called the suburban conspiracy?

The suburban conspiracy

It is clear that enmity towards the city is shared by many of those involved with the planning and development of housing and urban areas. In an effort to sanitise and tame the city we have managed to throw out the baby with the bath water and destroyed what we sought to preserve. The underlying ethos of most professions and investors concerned with the urban environment has been, and largely still is, anti-urban. Indeed all of the urban professions (with the exception of urban

every Milton Keynes there are countless examples of areas where the application of this conventional wisdom has created not popular environments, but alienating places devoid of identity, character and life. Once people have satisfied their basic needs for food and shelter they yearn for higher things such as human contact, cultural expression, community, hustle and bustle, and a sense of continuity. People do not miss these things until they are deprived of them, a loss which may be manifested as 'new town blues' or the alienation of people on peripheral estates. Older towns may be less efficient but they undoubtedly meet these human needs more effectively than many modern settlements and the evidence can be seen in the values placed on property.

Much of the legacy of twentieth century visionaries is therefore negative and over the last twenty years or so has increasingly been recognised as such, particularly in the case of the modernists. Some may argue that this is because many of the ideas have been 'bastardised' by lesser architects

design) have been brought into existence to tame the city and to regulate human activities. There is no Anglo-American equivalent of the European 'urbaniste'.

Many of these negative attitudes live on in the minutiae of urban policy today. The planning system which seeks to protect housing and other development from noise and traffic, ends up making houses turn their backs on the very streets to which they should reiate. Rather than creating a sense of enclosure and streets which are attractive places to be, buildings are set back behind a landscape buffer and streets become little more than desolate traffic routes. Privacy distances, parking standards, building lines, fear of 'over development', the zoning of uses and landscaping requirements all remain central parts of planning ideology. Similarly highway engineering is based upon the eradication of congestion and the reduction of accidents. Who can argue against a policy which saves the lives of children, even if it does make life miserable for pedestrians who are isolated on pavements dominated by traffic noise, pedestrian bridges and underpasses? Road hierarchies (with limited access from distributor roads), parking requirements, turning heads, visibility splays, curb radii and opposition to crossroads make it impossible to recreate today many of the historic urban environments that we so prize. Such are the constraints imposed by modern highway

engineers that it is no longer possible to build the medieval streets of York, the Georgian crescents of Bath or even the early twentieth century developments like Hampstead Garden Suburb.

So whilst many of the tenets of twentieth century planning theory may appear to have been discredited the tenacity of their hold over the urban professions should not be underestimated. Indeed with the fall from grace of the modernists it is possible to argue that our towns and cities today are threatened by a suburban conspiracy. The conspirators include planners, highway engineers, investors, and, as we will see in the next chapter, the housebuilding industry and residents who have bought into the suburban ideal. The extent to which the current urban professions are equipped to create places which can stand the test of time is therefore open to question.

New planning disasters

There is perhaps another lesson that we can learn from the twentieth century attempts to tame the city. In this chapter we have questioned the philosophy of twentieth century planning but it may also be that there is something inherently flawed with the idea of imposing a conventional land-use plan on the complexity of urban life. The best and most enduring of places seem to have grown organically over time within a planning framework rather than to have sprung from the inspired hand of a single master planner. Yet in Britain we have been obsessed with grandiose end-state plans. The town centres and housing estates conceived on the drawing boards of the 1960s looked fine on the architect's blue prints. But these bore little relation to the situation on the ground within a few short years. This is a lesson that we have not learned. Architects are once more producing plans for the redevelopment of housing estates to sweep away the mistakes of the past. Is there any more chance that they will get it right this time or is the very process of conceiving a neighbourhood on paper and building it over a few short years a recipe for failure?

However the people with the real power to undertake comprehensive development at the end of the twentieth century are not weak underfunded councils but private developers. Far from being able to impose its will on the city the modern planning system struggles to control a market in which sprawling supermarkets, out-of-town shopping centres and business parks bring the greatest profits. Canary Wharf may have been the product of the over-inflated market of the 1980s but in conception and planning it bears many similarities to the comprehensive developments of the 1960s and 70s. The same is true of Meadowhall in Sheffield, the Metro Centre in Gateshead and numerous retail, leisure and business parks that leach the life from towns and cities. These developments also seek to tame the city by recreating it in safe, comfortable, sanitised environments. They attract car-borne customers and create large profits for the financial institutions which fund them. Is the logical conclusion of twentieth century urban trends for Britain to follow the shopping mall culture of the United States? If unchecked there is little hope for our towns and cities, for environmental sustainability or for the ability of communities to respond to future needs.

Is this the future city?
The shopping developments of the 1980s and 90s based upon American models such as this are creating new sanitised environments to tame the rough edges of the city

CHAPTER 4
The shaping of the English home

How have the forces of urban decentralisation, Utopian thinking and town planning shaped the sort of housing that we have built over the last 200 years? As we approach the end of the millennium the predominant type of housing being built in Britain appears, at least, to have changed little since the great suburban boom of the 1920s. In terms of its form, structure, and internal layout the new home of the 1990s could be compared to a Model T Ford. It is tempting to believe that this type of low density, detached and semi-detached development is somehow a natural or even an inevitable part of British life which is unlikely to change in the future. However the history of housing over the last two centuries illustrates that major design changes can take place over relatively short periods of time, prompted by social and economic trends, legislative change and the influence of reformers. It seems reasonable to suggest that such trends will continue to have an influence on the housing of the future. In this chapter we therefore seek to chart the development of housing through the nineteenth and twentieth centuries.

The nineteenth century home

The traditional image of the nineteenth century home is of drab uniform rows of terraced housing in the shadow of 'dark satanic mills'. Such housing is associated with the subjugation and exploitation of the working classes by the unfettered growth of capitalism after the industrial revolution, and the concentration of most of Britain's population in metropolitan centres. This image has been fuelled by the accounts of the nineteenth century reformers such as Peter Gaskell's *Manufacturing Population of England* (1833)[1] which states: 'The housing of great numbers of the labouring community in the manufacturing districts present many of the traces of a savage life. Filthy, unfurnished, deprived of all the accessories to decency or comfort, they are indeed but too truly an index of the vicious and depraved lives of their inmates.'

The true picture is however somewhat more complicated than this. As John Burnett[2] has pointed out, such accounts describe the worst housing of the time as if it were the average. In actual fact as Freidrich Engels wrote in 1844; 'Houses of three or four rooms and a kitchen form throughout England, some parts of London excepted, the general dwellings of the working

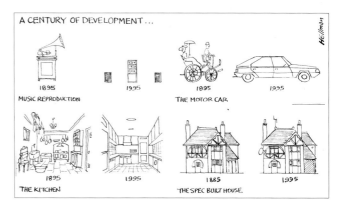

A CENTURY OF DEVELOPMENT...

1895   1995
MUSIC REPRODUCTION

1895   1995
THE MOTOR CAR

1895   1995
THE KITCHEN

1885   1995
THE SPEC BUILT HOUSE

class'[3]. The worst housing conditions were largely confined to overcrowded cellars, lodging houses and older tenements graphically described in books such as Jack London's *Edge of the Abyss*. The back-to-back terrace, so universally condemned from the mid-nineteenth century onwards, was in fact relatively desirable since it was self-contained and afforded a degree of privacy to a family.

The development of the 'through' terrace represented even greater progress. This allowed

for a back yard with an individual privy which could be cleared by night soil men from the back alley. The greater size of dwellings enabled the separation of living, cooking and sleeping activities as well as meeting those great concerns of reformers for ventilation and day light. Most importantly the terrace started to change the nature of urban life. The early residents of the industrial city, out of necessity if not choice, had lived a very communal life, sharing space, sanitation, and services. This life had taken place in back courts largely hidden from the rest of the city. The Victorians viewed this communal life as a breeding ground for vice, dirt and disease and sought to counter this by promoting the nuclear rather than the extended family. The through terrace allowed the separation of private family life from the public life of the street. The lace curtained parlour and the polished front step created an impenetrable barrier for all but invited guests. This also marked the beginning of the separation of the sexes in which women became housewives responsible for the respectability of the home whilst men went out to work. The through terrace can therefore be seen as the birth place of a number of trends, the natural result of which was the suburbia of the 1900s.

By the second half of the nineteenth century the through terrace had become the norm.

This was spurred not so much by changes in the housing market but by public health reforms, in particular the by-laws which were introduced locally from 1840 onwards and nationally in 1877. By-law terraces have been widely condemned for their monotony of row upon row of treeless streets with little or no open space. Builders may have built to the lowest standards allowable but these standards were considerably higher than those of earlier decades. By-law terraces were more sanitary, less dense, more airy and light, and internally they were better built, with larger windows, higher ceilings and improved materials. In terms of layout the effect was to create the familiar gridiron layout with regularly spaced streets and occasional cross streets. This however was far more open and easy to understand and police than the warren of yards and back courts of the early part of the century. Whilst large areas of bylaw terracing were demolished in the slum clearance programmes of the twentieth century, the areas which have survived have generally fared well. Indeed many areas have out-survived the twentieth century redevelopment schemes which were meant to replace them. The passage of time has often seen them develop into desirable areas that have become 'gentrified' by owner-occupation.

Middle-class suburbs

Another equally significant trend in the middle of the nineteenth century was the emergence of the middle-class suburbs. Censuses of the time show that perhaps three million out of a population of eighteen million could be considered as middle-class. As we saw from Chapter 1, whilst this class was the product of the wealth generated by the industrial revolution it was also repelled by the conditions that it created, and sought to construct a way of life which was insulated from the 'evils' of the industrial city. This life centred around Christian values, polite behaviour, privacy, order, and taste. These were the sentiments of Mr. Bulstrode in *Middlemarch* and a far cry from the urban lifestyle of Charles Dicken's characters. The

Middle-class housing: The housing of the middle classes was also terraced and high-density although on a much grander scale

symbol of this way of life was the middle-class home or villa.

As Stefan Muthesius[4] has described, for much of the nineteenth century these middle-class aspirations were achieved in terraced housing. This housing was grander, in some cases far grander, that the homes of the working classes but the form was essentially the same. Indeed Muthesius has described how the frontage width of even the grandest terraces was not vastly greater than its more modest cousins. Larger houses were built upwards, sometimes to six storeys, and plots became deeper with coach houses and servants' quarters facing onto the rear alley. Terraces of such houses were made to look like palaces particularly in areas like Grosvenor Square in London and Bath with classical columns and central pediments. Often these urban houses served as second homes for families 'up for the season' who also had country houses from which they derived their status and sense of identity.

In the early part of the nineteenth century these middle-class terraces became so popular that they were favoured over the detached villa. However as the century progressed the middle-class aspirations for privacy, order and godliness found increasing expression in more suburban housing forms. Donald Olsen[5] convincingly argues that

MIDDLE-CLASS HOUSING IN LONDON

The development of middle-class housing in London is illustrated by looking at four estates as chronicled by Olsen[6], in Primrose Hill, Dyos[7], in Camberwell, Gillian Tyndall[8] in Kentish Town and most recently Linda Clarke[9] in Somers Town. The precarious nature of residential development at the time meant that Primrose Hill and Camberwell remained 'desirable' while, Somers Town became a slum.

These areas were developed speculatively with four-storey housing. A plan would be commissioned by the owner showing the roads, the class of houses to be erected together with amenities such as churches, shops and public houses. This was controlled through the London Building Act of 1774 which divided houses into four 'rates', and stipulated their height in relation to the width of roads as well as the details of their construction.

The four rates of house specified in the 1774 London Building Act

Thus the Eton Estate, which owned Primrose Hill, limited the number of mews, because it knew these frequently degenerated into slums, and sought a balance between the 'higher class' houses along Regent's Park Road and the 'lower class' behind them.

Once approved, leases were sold to small builders so that streets developed incrementally. The builders in turn, sold the houses to small tradesmen who rented them out to provide an income before the days of pensions. The Paving Commissioners laid out the pavements and infrastructures. There was however a major difference between landowners like the Bedford Estate, who thought in terms of long-term value, and those who went in for short-term gains, as in Somers Town.

Somers Town was started in 1773 by the architect Leroux under an agreement with Lord Somers. Leroux's finance came from brick making rather than development values and the 'ring of fire' from brick making put off investors. Pressure to build quickly caused standards to fall and the houses were small, or were tenements dressed up to look like Georgian houses.

By contrast on the neighbouring estate Lord Southampton's direct control meant that a generous layout was retained without 'back streets nor any of so retired a kind as to be liable on that account to be improperly occupied and to injure the reputation of the district'. The development was protected by gates and designed to 'have as few communications as possible with Somers Town'.

By 1800 Somers Town was characterised by dust hills and dung heaps and proximity to the canal encouraged industry. The tenements became overcrowded and the gardens were built upon, further increasing densities. When the estate was sold in 1802, control was further fragmented. By 1831 it was 'dingy with smoke and deprived almost entirely of gardens and fields'. With 8.4 persons per house it was not surprising that cholera broke out. Many of the houses were demolished as the railways were cut through the worst parts of the area, the remainder being replaced by public housing in the 1930s.

Why is it that such places deteriorate into slums whilst others which outwardly appear very similar succeed? The factors include short-term profiteering from land sales, insufficient public space, air pollution, the loss of social balance, overcrowding, poor standards and neglected maintenance. The lesson is that developers need to retain control and to take a long-term view otherwise grand plans can end up as slums.

Middle-class sanctuary:
Many cities retain districts of
spacious housing dating from the
middle of the nineteenth century
like Whalley Range in
Manchester

the physical form of Victorian development was
a deliberate response to what were seen as immoral
Georgian values. These had emphasised street life
(the promenade) and public pleasures (the spa
and the subscription rooms where dances were
held). They were less concerned with the need to
separate classes or to celebrate the family. Georgian
towns like Bath or Cheltenham excelled in what
we now think of as a continental way of life. Early
precursors of the Victorian era like Belgravia in
London and Victoria Park in Manchester
represented a very different view of civic life. They
erected walls and gates to protect them from
'lower-class' districts but as time went on gates
were not enough and the middle classes sought
geographical separation and the outward
expansion of the city gained pace. Separation from

poorer neighbourhoods was however not
sufficient. The Victorian family sought sanctuary
from unplanned encounters with neighbours not
just of different classes but also their own. The
detached villa was therefore favoured surrounded
by a high wall and with a sweeping drive to block
views from the street. Thus the middle classes
were able to recreate their own miniature version
of the country estate yet remain within reach of
their employment in the city.

As is so often the case the lower-middle-
classes, uncertain in their newly acquired position,
were all the more concerned to adopt middle-
class values which is the comic value of the Pooters
in Grossmiths *Dairy of a Nobody*. Unable to afford
a detached villa the solution was the semidetached
villa complete with porch and boot scraper.

Burnett cites the first example of semidetached villas in 1794 and the revolutionary idea was further developed by Nash alongside the grand terraces and detached villas of Regent's Park. However by the end of the century the semi-detached house had made the benefits of sub-urbia available to a much larger part of the middle class and the foundations of twentieth century housing development were being set. As Dyos and Reeder have said: 'The middle class suburb was an ecological marvel... it offered an arena for the manipulation of social distinctions to those most conscious of their possibilities and most adept in turning them into shapes on the ground; it kept the threat of rapid social change beyond the horizon of those least able to accept its negative as well as positive advantages.'[10]

The development of flats

Throughout the great boom of urban population in the nineteenth century it is remarkable that people in England and Wales remained so attach-ed to the individual home on its own plot of land. In Scotland and on the continent the res-ponse to overcrowding had been to build upwards

Early council housing in Manchester:
In the background, Victoria Square, the first flats to be built in the city. The street in the foreground was originally called Sanitary Street after the council committee which commissioned the housing. The 'S' and 'ry' have since been dropped at the request of residents so that it is now called Anita Street

– possibly encouraged by a different legal system which allowed 'flying freeholds'. In England and Wales this rarely happened, with occasional exceptions such as the two storey Tyneside flat and the London mansion block often used as bachelor flats. In 1849 the *Builder* published an article which argued that 'the time has now arrived when the expansion and growth of this city [London] must be upwards in place of outwards – when "houses" must be reared above each other... instead of straggling miles farther and farther away from the Centre'[11]. The only deve-lopers to take up this call were the housing societies which started to emerge in London and to a lesser extent provincial cities like Leeds. The early associa-tions such as the Society for Improving the Conditions of the Labouring Classes were joined by the Peabody Trust in 1862 and the Guinness Trust in 1890. From the start these societies concentrated on building flats as demonstration projects to show that quality working-class hous-ing could generate a return for investors. By 1870 Peabody had produced more than 5 000 flats in dense six-storey blocks, something which had never before been seen in England. The flats were accessed by wrought iron balconies around in-ternal courts. These models were to influence the earliest council housing in London, Leeds and Manchester such as Victoria Square in Manchester (left). Were it not for the Tudor-Walters Report, such flats could have become the predominant housetype in the twentieth century with far-reaching effects on our towns and cities. A further constraint on the development of flats was lack of finance on a sufficiently large scale, unlike Paris where Napoleon III set up a national bank to fund Haussman's apartment blocks.

However despite the development of middle-class suburbs and flats the nineteenth century home remained the terraced house. In 1911 only 10% of houses were detached or semi-detached and only 3% were flats[12]. The vast majority of housing was therefore terraced and this had become as ubiquitous in the nineteenth century as the semidetached home would become in the twentieth.

The twentieth century home

As we have seen major improvements were being made to the standard of housing in the second half of the nineteenth century. The growth of middle-class housing and the introduction of by-laws had largely overcome the worst problems of the early industrial revolution at least for new housing. However this did little to address the legacy of substandard housing from the early nineteenth century which still dominated most industrial towns at the turn of the century. There were for example still 42 000 back-to-backs in Birmingham in 1914.

The next major development in housing was to come about at the end of the First World War when there was the prospect of a severe housing shortage as millions were 'demobbed' at a time of widespread unemployment. The major housebuilding programme launched by the Lloyd George government therefore sought both to address the housing shortage and to create jobs. However in doing this the government was also keen to rethink the sort of housing that was produced. The Homes Fit for Heroes campaign turned for inspiration to the garden city movement. The vehicle for this was a committee chaired by Sir John Tudor-Walters and including Raymond Unwin which published its report *Dwellings for the working classes* in 1918[13]. The recommendations of the committee were incorporated in their entirety in the Local Government Board's *Manual on the preparation of state-aided housing schemes* published in 1919[14] which established the model for interwar housing development. This model was largely based on the work of Parker and Unwin. The houses recommended by the committee and illustrated on advisory plans were widely adopted by local authorities. The preferred housetypes were semidetached or short terraces of up to eight units. They had wide frontages and narrow plans to maximise the amount of internal daylight. In terms of layout, Tudor-Walters recommended a mixture of housetypes for different classes of tenants. Cul-de-sacs were suggested for economy and the removal of through traffic, and houses were to be at least seventy feet apart to allow the proper penetration of sunlight.

The Tudor-Walters Report was concerned with public housing and its far-reaching impact was due to the great boom in public housing after the First World War. Indeed council housing did not exist until the Housing of the Working Classes Act of 1890 which gave local authorities the power to build housing. The 1919 Housing Act, for which the Local Government Board's manual was produced, transformed this power into a duty and the twentieth century council house was born. This heralded a great step forward in housing quality and was only made possible because the 1919 Act severed the link between the cost of housing and the rents that could be charged. The government undertook to provide the majority of the funds whilst rents were to be

The suburban ideal: This illustration and the one on the following page are taken from the handbook of the Building Employers Federation 1932

set independently in line with the wartime rent controls. Quality could therefore be improved without the costs being passed on to tenants. As a result housing built in 1920 typically cost four times more than the housing of 1914. The alarm that this caused resulted in new approvals being halted in 1921. However when council house building was resumed in 1924 by the incoming Labour government the standard had been set by Tudor-Walters, and despite lower levels of subsidy and less regulation, standards remained high.

The 30 years between 1890 and 1920 therefore saw a radical change in ideas about housing. This provides a valuable lesson for those seeking to promote an equally significant change into the twenty-first century. The Utopian ideas of Ebenezer Howard were first translated, some would say compromised, into demonstration schemes such as Letchworth and Hampstead Garden Suburb. These received widespread attention in the professional press and in policy-making circles. As a result, when a major increase in housing output was planned by councils with little or no experience in housebuilding the garden city model was enthusiastically adopted, first through an official report and then through government guidance. In this way the model for working-class housing was completely transformed over a relatively short period of time.

The Tudor-Walters Report was to have an equally significant impact on private house-building which is another twentieth century phenomenon. In the nineteenth century virtually all housing was privately rented. The only exceptions were the upper echelons of the middle classes and the working-class building clubs (which could be seen as precursors of today's self-build co-operatives). This however changed after 1918 and, of the four million or so homes built in the interwar years, around two-thirds were for owner-occupation. There are many reasons for this, the growth of the middle classes, the provision of state subsidy in the 1923 Chamberlain Act, the opening up of cheap land through the construction of suburban railways and roads and the development of building societies to provide mortgages. The building societies which, like the co-operative movement, grew up in northern towns to help the working classes improve their conditions, ended up reinforcing middle-class ideals of the desirable home. This expansion in owner-occupation took place in the suburbs where the image of the Victorian villa was combined with the practicalities of Tudor-Walters to create the ubiquitous semi which was to come to dominate private housing provision.

It is however debatable whether the demand for owner-occupation created the suburb or whether the suburb made owner-occupation possible. Suburbs grew around most British industrial cities as a consequence of commuter railway lines in the latter half of the nineteenth century and electric tram lines and buses towards the end of the century. This opened up great swathes of cheap land for development. As a result house and land prices fell in relation to average incomes to an all time low in the 1930s[15]. Home

Housing since 1945

Since the Second World War housing has been through a rollercoaster of change unprecedented in the previous 150 years. The pendulum swung first to an almost total reliance on the public sector and then to a similar reliance on the private sector. Housing became, for a period, the prime concern of architects, sociologists, academics and politicians before falling out of favour and becoming once again a largely technical and financial issue.

The situation immediately after the last war had many parallels to the aftermath of the First World War. There was, once again, a severe housing shortage due to wartime damage and a commitment, as in 1918, to improve conditions for the returning troops. In this postwar climate the Labour government swept to power and housing was seen as a central plank of the new welfare state. Indeed political parties vied over how many houses they could build. As in 1918 there was also an influential report, the Dudley report of 1944[16] which set the standard for postwar development. The Dudley Report was very much a progression and updating of Tudor-Walters. It further increased internal space standards as well as considering the layout of housing to overcome the monotony which had been seen as a problem of interwar housing. As with Tudor-Walters, the Dudley recommendations were incorporated into government manuals but were soon being undermined by economic pressures.

A further attempt to increase standards came with the Parker Morris Report[17] of 1961 which updated Dudley in line with changing social trends and was, for a time, mandatory for council housing. Since that time the trend has been to move away from prescriptive standards. The RIBA/Institute of Housing, Homes for the Future Group[18] sought to set standards in 1983 but these were purely advisory and were not taken up by government. Indeed in 1994 the Joseph Rowntree Foundation inquiry into housing standards[19] concluded that housing standards were no longer politically acceptable and published instead a consumer guide to help residents to exercise choice more effectively.

The future is bright: An artist's impression of a proposed council high-rise block in Sheffield in the 1960s. It captures some of the excitement and idealism that must have attracted the architects and councillors of the time.

ownership therefore became a real option for most of the middle classes and for the upper sections of the working classes. This growth in owner-occupation is perhaps the most influential trend in the twentieth century. Whilst professionals and academics have spent their time debating housing, their ideas have been applied almost exclusively to council housing. Meanwhile private developers and their customers have been quietly working to create a much more practical and enduring Utopia in the suburbs. Unconcerned by the scorn of professionals and designers, private housing has evolved slowly in stark contrast to the grand innovations and disasters in the public sector.

However our concern here is not so much with housing standards but with the effect that they have had on the design and layout of housing. Here the crucial issue is the interaction between the costs imposed by compliance with the standards and the finance available to build the housing. Whereas in 1918 Tudor-Walters led to a huge increase in the cost of new housing, after the Second World War this could not happen because budgets were capped. It is estimated that Parker Morris's recommendations added 8–15% to the cost of a home so that within fixed budgets commensurate savings had to be found elsewhere. In order to comply with the recommendations of both Dudley and Parker Morris within their budgets, councils opted for standardisation, system-built construction, and higher densities to reduce land costs. The drive to increase internal standards is therefore at least partly to blame for the despised high-rise development of the 1960s.

Immediately after the war the concern was not so much with urban development as with overspill. Council minutes from Liverpool after the war show that the intention was to build self-contained houses with a minimum of terraces and flats of no more than three storeys[20]. This was possible because the majority of new housing and displacement from slum clearance was to be accommodated through overspill in areas like Kirby and later the new town of Skelmersdale. The most influential element of policy in the immediate postwar period was the constellation of new towns which was launched by the 1946 New Towns Act. There were initially twelve new towns with planned populations of 50 000 to accommodate overspill from London. A second round of ten larger Mark Two new towns was launched in the

1960s for populations of up to 250 000, included Milton Keynes, Cumbernauld and Warrington/Runcorn. In many respects these new towns represented the fulfilment of Howard's garden city vision, if in practice they bore little relation to the original concept. They were important because they provided great laboratories for public housing development. They attracted the best designers and planners and provided an opportunity to put into practice many of the concepts propagated by CIAM and others between the wars. Because they had a blank canvas on which to work, the new town planners could implement the ideas of neighbourhood units, pedestrian vehicle separation and open space described in the previous chapter. Through extensive coverage in the professional press they had a far-reaching impact on new housing throughout the country.

However by 1982 only two million people or 4% of the population lived in new towns[21]. The vast majority of population growth was actually accommodated through suburban expansion and the development of overspill estates. Indeed the vast new town building programme over the last fifty years has accommodated less than half of the projected growth in households over the next two decades.

For the early years after the war the pressure had therefore been taken off urban areas.

Municipal megalomania: Hyde Park in Sheffield is one of the most monumental examples of high-rise council housing

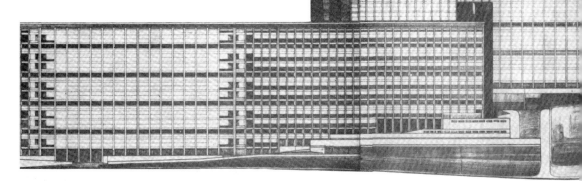

However in 1951 the incoming Conservative government enacted a number of measures which radically altered the situation. The new town programme was halted, save for the completion of those which had already been designated. Budgets were reduced, making it difficult to implement Dudley's recommendation and most importantly the regional offices which had previously been responsible for managing urban overspill were abolished. This, together with the introduction in 1955 of the first green belt, made it increasingly difficult for urban authorities to plan for overspill estates. Many had planned to accommodate growth through the expansion of smaller towns by agreement between urban and rural authorities. However two major inquiries about Manchester's plans to expand Knutsford and Birmingham's plans for Wythall were resolved in favour of the rural authorities. Urban authorities were therefore placed in an increasingly difficult situation. Populations were expanding and household sizes were falling yet the overspill option to deal with these pressures was being closed off to them. The need to accommodate families displaced by the slum clearance programme which was reactivated in 1955 potentially made

the problem worse. However it also offered a partial solution since it released land for new development.

So by the late 1950s pressures for higher standards and lower costs, household growth and restrictions on overspill created the conditions where Le Corbusier's ideas seemed to make perfect sense. This was reinforced by higher government subsidies for housing over six storeys so that by 1964, 55% of approved tenders were for the development of flats. At this time around 90 000 slum properties were being cleared each year, mostly to be replaced with high-rise and deck-access council housing. Many developments made use of continental prefabricated systems ill suited to UK site practice or weather or site conditions. This was the period when architects and planners

POST-WAR COUNCIL HOUSING IN LIVERPOOL

1945–1954. The council was committed to building self-contained houses. However in the inner city land was scarce and most new housing was three-storey walk-up blocks on clearance or bomb damage sites. These blocks 'standing forlorn in a sea of tarmac open space' remain some of the least popular in the city.

1954–1960. Liverpool councillors visited America to study high-rise housing and were impressed. This combined with government subsidy and architectural fashion unleashed 'municipal megalomania'. The housing committee observed that there was 'no reason why the twenty storey mark should not be passed... as important a step in the construction of domestic dwellings as was the breaking of the sound barrier in flight'.

1960–1973. The era of comprehensive neighbourhood policy in which whole sections of the city were razed for redevelopment not only with high-rise housing but also roads, shops, schools and other facilities. During this period Liverpool was building 2 000 houses a year, most of the worst slums in the city were removed and most of today's problem estates built.

1973–1985. The council resolved not to build above five storeys and embarked on a disastrous programme of high- density low-rise development. Even-tually it was decided not to build above two storeys. The final phase of council housing in the city which, due to the politics of the city, continued after council house building elsewhere had ceased, was traditional, low-rise and semi-detached.

Liverpool was left with a legacy of unpopular housing which is difficult to let and expensive to maintain. It had also created a hugely unbalanced housing stock, 86% of properties in the south of the city were flats and large parts of the city became mono-tenure council housing.

came to the fore and were given the opportunity to apply the ideas taught in planning and architecture schools to large areas of the city. As Martin Richardson says of the London County Council in the 1960s, 'The whole of the housing division seemed like a giant nursery school whose principal objective was the happiness of the architects'[22]. Architects praised the new megaliths for their exciting contribution to urban form whilst dismissing bland petty suburbia and even suggesting that 'aesthetically pleasing' housing may be difficult to live in. Great problems were seen as requiring great solutions and the bulldozer was king. Anything other than blocks of flats was dismissed as 'noddy housing' and not proper architecture! The model of walk-up blocks, so common in European towns was largely ignored, perhaps because it was too prosaic or because people were obsessed with technological breakthroughs at a time when Harold Wilson was talking about the 'White heat of technology'. Christopher Booker has summed up the effect of all this on our cities: 'We have seen one of the greatest fantasies of our time burgeon forth from the minds of a few visionaries to make a hell on earth for millions of people ... leaving only what remains of our wrecked, blighted, hideously disfigured cities behind'[23].

In theory high-rise development came to an end in 1967 with the explosion at Rowan Point in London and the ending of additional subsidy for properties over six storeys. However, in practice, the development of deck-access housing continued apace. Much of Hulme in Manchester including the infamous Crescents was not completed until the early 1970s. Indeed in Manchester the bulldozer had been particularly effective and the scale of the city's 'achievements' was used to criticise other local authorities.

However by the early 1970s the emphasis had changed to low-rise high-density development. This was largely done through standard housetypes so that the main concern of architects became layout. This has been characterised by Bill Hillier[24] as based upon enclosure, repetition and hierarchy to invoke traditional urban courts, squares and greens. Housing would be built in

The end of an era: The Byker estate in Newcastle designed by Ralph Erskine in the 1970s. It can be seen both as the last of the great slum clearance schemes which characterised the 1960s and 70s and also the first major example of a more community-based approach to housing development. It was designed from an architect's office based in the heart of the area and involved extensive community consultation. While not without its problems, it remains the most successful major redevelopment of the era

small groups around courts to foster community. In many respects this was the age of social engineering as housing became the concern of social scientists as much as designers. Oscar Newman's book *Defensible space: People and design in the violent city*[25] published in 1972 was an important influence, as was the idea that the design of housing estates could create close communities. There was still a commitment to pedestrian/vehicle separation and the result was to create a warren of deserted walkways and blind corners. Whilst these estates have received less attention than the earlier high-rise developments the problems, particularly of crime, that they have experienced have been equally severe.

Towards the end of the 1970s it is possible to argue that council housing departments were starting to get it right. Developments by architects like Darbourne and Dark in London and Ralph Erskine's redevelopment of Byker in Newcastle illustrated the quality of what councils could achieve. They showed that innovation was not incompatible with the creation of successful areas. The key to success was often the close involvement of residents in design, something which councils had started to recognise just in time to see their house building programmes curtailed by the incoming Conservative government in 1979.

The private house building industry since 1945 has been almost entirely untouched by the changes in fashion in public housing. In Colquhoun and Fauset's review of housing design[26] only one private developer, Span, is deemed worthy of significant mention prior to the 1980s. Span developed innovative private housing, in partnership with the GLC, in the late 1960s such as New Ash Green – only to go into liquidation when the GLC failed to take up their allocation. However they were very much the exception. For most developers there was no need to innovate. Until 1974 mortgages were cheap, building costs were stable and demand outstripped supply. Private developers could therefore sell pretty much anything they cared to build and space standards at the lower end of the market declined markedly[27]. This meant that the differential between private housing and council housing was eroded and eventually reversed so that by the 1970s council housing was generally larger and built to a higher standard than private housing. Private developers therefore sought to differentiate their product and increase its 'kerb appeal' with ornament and suburban frills. Indeed suburban owner-occupation was as much about status as housing requirements. As a participant at a RIBA client focus group on housing[28] stated: 'People are judging a potential new home not on what's inside it, but on what it says about them'. In design terms private housing followed the continuum established between the wars with semidetached ribbon development and cul-de-sacs at ten houses to the acre.

This period was also marked by an increasing geographical separation between public and private housing. While local authorities may have been forced to build within their administrative boundaries, private developers operated under no such constraints, and in any case urban land was scarce. Private housebuilding therefore took place in the very rural districts which had been so active in opposing council overspill. It is this development that accounts for much of the urban dispersal during the period. There was little or no private housing in the inner city and metropolitan areas increasingly became a monoculture of council housing – at one point 82% of households in Tower Hamlets in London were council tenants. Thus was established the pattern of unpopular high-rise council housing in urban areas and popular low-density private housing in the suburbs and smaller towns. This was partly the result of a desire to escape the city but, as social segregation became more marked, it also became one of the reasons for dispersal. It was no longer the problems of heavy industry and over-crowding which repelled the suburban emigrants, it was the council estates and poverty which had now come to dominate urban area. The history of the last fifty years suggests that this situation is the result of a very specific set of circumstances and by no means inevitable. It is not long ago that urban areas accommodated up-market housing and there is no reason to believe that they should not do so again in the future.

Housing since 1980

Throughout the 1980s and 1990s radical change in the housing world has subsided only to be replaced by uncertainty over funding and markets. Council house building has all but ceased and the redevelopment of council estates, 'right-to-buy' sales and stock transfers have eroded council stocks. There has been a massive promotion of home ownership yet the private sector is in no real state to play a leading role having been through a series of boom and bust cycles which has destroyed the certainty which prevailed until the mid-1970s. In the social sector housing associations are still coming to terms with their role as the primary providers of new social housing whilst their grant rates are being cut and competition to reduce capital costs has put pressure on standards.

The good times in the private sector came to an end with the slump of 1974 when high interest rates and inflation increased costs and reduced demand. Over the following decade minor recoveries were followed by further slumps. This led Tom Barron of Christian Salveson in 1983 to state: 'The housing industry has at long last accepted that it... must produce the sorts of housing that customers will want to buy and not the sorts of housing it wants to build'[29]. However if this lesson was ever really learned it was forgotten in the boom of the late 1980s. In 1988 the annual housing inflation rate exceeded 30%, outperforming virtually all other forms of investment. In the naïve belief that this would last forever, people rushed to put their money into housing and developers could once again sell virtually anything they wished to build. As a result the percentage of UK owner-occupation rose to 66%[30] and personal sector debt, which was largely devoted to mortgages, rose from 55% of disposable income to 110%[31]. The housing market and interest rates came to have a major influence on the national economy in a way that does not happen in other European countries where rich countries like Switzerland paradoxically have very low levels of owner-occupation.

The party ended in 1988 as basic variable mortgage rates started to rise from 9.5% to 15% and double tax relief on mortgages was abolished.

As a result house prices fell by 30% between 1989 and 1992 and the number of transactions fell from 2.1 million to 1.1 million[32]. Since then more than a quarter of a million homes have been repossessed and almost a million have experienced negative equity. In most parts of the UK house prices have now recovered and over the last few years there have been occasional predictions that rising incomes, low interest rates and affordability will lead to a return of the boom years[33] but house price increases have remained modest.

It is too early to say whether the slump at the end of the 1980s will have a lasting effect on the housing market and the nature of private housing. Certainly the belief that housing is a guaranteed investment which will always increase in value had been severely dented. Analysts such as John Wrigglesworth[34] have suggested that 'The typical buyer in the 1990s will be buying for 'nesting not investing'. It is likely that with job insecurity, flexible employment patterns and memories of the slump, people will be more cautious about what they buy and developers more cautious about what they build. It may even be that we follow a more European model where people buy later and buy for life rather than relying on trading up through the housing ladder. There is some evidence that this is happening. As Savills Residential Research have reported[35], the average first-time buyer in the mid-1990s is in their early thirties, almost ten years older than in the late 1980s. They state that the successful housebuilder of the future will find opportunities in 'unconventional product ranges' which might involve homes for letting and single person households rather than 'bulk estates for mortgage reliant families'. They conclude that 'never before has it been so important to find new markets and break new ground in housing construction'. It is clear that the certainties which have driven the

Private sector innovation: Much of the housing innovation in the 1980s took place in the private sector in areas like London's Docklands

housing market for almost 100 years are increasingly being called into question.

In terms of design, the period from 1980 onwards has seen a reversal in the attitudes of some private housebuilders to innovation in design. Before 1980 virtually all innovations in housing design took place in the social sector and private builders stuck to the tried and tested formula of the suburban detached and semi-detached house. It is true that throughout the 1980s and 90s the majority of private developers have continued to shun innovation. However, in stark contrast to the situation prior to 1980, most of the housing innovation which has taken place has been in the private sector in town centres and particularly dockland developments.

The 1980s and 90s have been an equally uncertain period for the social housing sector. Whilst council housing accounts for more than 87% of social housing in Britain, new council building has fallen to fewer than 1 000 units per year compared to 20–30 000 units being constructed by housing associations. The housing association movement has existed since the mid-nineteenth century but, as councils took the lead, housing associations were largely confined to specialist needs such as young people or the elderly. This all changed in the 1980s as the government encouraged housing associations to step into the void left by the ending of council building.

This was made possible by the 1988 Housing Act. Before this housing associations benefited from 95% grant rates but operated under rent controls and were limited in terms of what they could build. The 1988 Act transferred development risk to associations, reduced grant rates, introduced private finance and established a system of competitive bidding for funds. The wind of market forces blew through the social housing world as it had done through many other areas of public life in the 1980s. This was accompanied by a doubling of resources for new housing from £1 billion in the late 1980s to £2 billion in the early 1990s with grant rates falling to 58% in 1994–95. The response of housing associations was at best confused and at worst politically naïve.

GREATER LEYS – OXFORD

Greater Leys on the edge of Oxford is typical of the sort of social housing that caused people to question the sustainability of large social housing estates in the early 1990s. The estate is adjacent to a large council estate, Blackbird Leys which was the scene of rioting a number of years ago. It covers 34 acres and is one of the largest housing association developments in the country with 1232 social housing units having been completed between 1992 and 1998. In addition to this almost 500 private houses were built.

The fact that the scheme is built on open land five miles from Oxford is inevitable in a city where there is very little housing land within the urban area. As a result

a great deal of effort has been required from the Council and the developers to ensure that shops, facilities and services are provided.

Approximately £12 million has been invested by the Council in infrastructure including a new school, community facilities, play areas, sports facilities and extensive landscaping. However local shops and employment

uses have proved more difficult. It was also difficult in the early phases to provide bus services which are still subsidised by the council. Therefore while the development of such sites is inevitable in places like Oxford the danger is that, in the early years at least, people will be isolated without access to facilities, employment or transport.

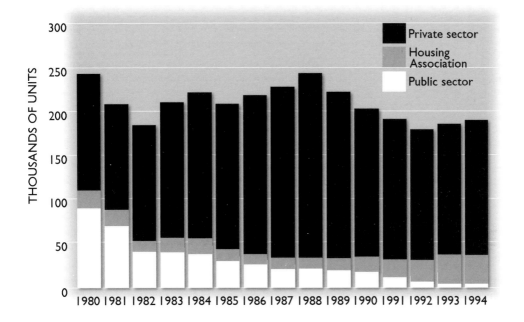

On the one hand they embraced their new-found importance and launched huge expansion programmes. At the same time they complained bitterly about falling grant rates. However even here the response was confused as pointed out by Adrian Coles, Director General of the Council for Mortgage Lenders when he said: 'It is noticeable that each successive reduction in grant rates has been accompanied by dire threats that development will no longer be possible, accompanied by increased competition between housing associations to underbid the new grant rate'[36]. It became a matter of pride for associations to be able to announce that they had developed schemes with as little as 25% grant[37] and it was therefore hardly surprising that the government saw the potential for further grant cuts.

In the mid-1990s this building boom has ended and housing association capital funds have fallen back to their late 1980 levels. However this has, if anything, made the situation worse. Housing associations have committed themselves to business plans and staffing structures based upon development-led expansion. Rather than cutting back on development they have respond-ed by cutting costs to maintain volumes which has inevitably meant cutting standards. They are forging ever closer links with private builders, as a result of which what are basically private sector starter homes are being built by housing associations for families condemned by poverty and unemployment to spend much of their time at home and with little opportunity to move on.

Less social housing is being built today than at any time in the last 100 years. The housing which is being built is therefore being prioritised for those in greatest need. New tenants of housing associations are poorer and have more children than at any time during the last hundred years due to housing allocation policies. Yet the quality of new housing is falling as illustrated by research by Valerie Karn and Linda Sheridan for the Joseph Rowntree Foundation[38]. They state that associations are becoming the 'mass providers of poor homes for poor people' and that these people are being consigned to life squashed into a starter home designed as the first rung on the housing ladder. Further concerns have been raised in research by David Page, also for the Joseph Rowntree Foundation[39]. He illustrates graphically

Housing Output:
Housing completions in the UK by sector, Source: JRF Housing Review 1996/97

that, in an attempt to meet urgent housing needs, housing associations are filling estates with a mix of tenants that is almost bound to create problems. As an example he points out that, whereas in the general population there is one child to every four adults, in new housing association estates there are sometimes more children than adults and this 'child density' is closely correlated with a range of social problems. Associations, to save money, are building larger schemes to inappropriate private sector designs often in isolated locations. As a result Page states: 'There is now evidence that the process of rapid decline of large social housing estates, which some had thought peculiar to council housing, can also apply to the stock of housing associations'. What is more, while council estates have often taken years to decline with some housing association estates decline is taking place in as little as four years.

Towards the twenty-first century

There is a sense in social housing of history repeating itself. Just as a seemingly unrelated range of factors in the early 1960s gave rise to high-rise council estates, so a similar conspiracy of circumstances means that we are in danger of building today the slums of tomorrow. As we approach the end of the century there is a sense of fatigue in the housing world. The principles which guided housing providers for many years have been overturned yet the problem of social housing is as intractable as ever.

Innovation has come to be seen as a dirty word since virtually every housing innovation in the last 50 years has failed. The response has been to resort to the private sector housing forms which are seen to have survived the test of time. These hark back to an idealised vision of family life dating from the golden age of interwar suburbia. A vision of 'leafy suburbia that apparently, for a great swath of the British middle class, is the ideal home'[40]. The prevalence of advertising images has firmly embedded the suburban ideal in the consciousness and aspirations of the providers and residents of both social and private housing. This is reinforced by the housing market which puts a premium on traditional designs and stifles innovation. Inadequate as they may be, the use of suburban housetypes by housing associations, portrays exactly the image that many of their tenants seek.

So engrained is the suburban ideal that it is difficult to imagine any other type of housing dominating the UK market. However the history of housing over the last two centuries shows that received wisdom can be overturned. It is not unreasonable to consider that quite different types of housing may be built in the future, particularly given the changing planning context described in the previous chapters. But where are the alternative models for the twenty-first century? To predict what these might be it is necessary to look at the forces which shape housing and development patterns which is what we will do in Part 2 of this book.

Part 2

THE INFLUENCES

Underlying the sedimentary strata of theory and policy described in Part 1 of this book is a bedrock of influences which has always shaped housing and urban development and is likely to do so in the future. The second part of this book describes these influences and how they are likely to shape the home of the future. These we have characterised as the 'Four Cs': Conservation, Choice, Community and Cost.

'We continue to build post World War II suburbs as if families were large and only had one bread winner, as if jobs were all downtown, as if land and energy were endless, and as if another lane on the freeway would end traffic congestion'

Peter Calthorpe - *The Next American Metropolis: Ecology, community and the American dream*, Princeton Architectural Press, 1993

CHAPTER 5
Conservation
Environmental pressures on future settlements

The growth in the environmental movement has been one of the most significant influences on government policy and public attitudes in the last two decades of the twentieth century. It has developed from a fringe concern of fringe groups into a principle which, whilst not always followed, is at least accepted by a large majority of decision makers. Ever since we ventured into space and were able to look back on the earth it has somehow seemed a much smaller and fragile place than we hitherto assumed. Pollution and resources have probably always been a concern to city dwellers. In the past however these were local concerns about smog or contaminated drinking water and it was generally assumed that the capacity of the atmosphere, rivers, land and sea to absorb pollutants was limitless. However with the advent of nuclear power and scares about man-made pollutants such as dioxins it has became clear that there was much we did not understand about our effect on the environment. We have come to recognise that natural resources are much less abundant than had previously been assumed and natural ecosystems much less resilient. Evidence has accumulated that natural systems are being thrown out of balance leading to global warming, ozone depletion, the loss of species and habitats and the poisoning of seas and lakes. While there has been a great deal of scientific debate about the nature, extent and causes of these environmental changes it is now widely accepted that

policy should be guided by the 'precautionary principle'[1]. This suggests that the consequences of environmental change are so significant that we should act now rather than wait for scientific proof by which time it is likely to be too late to repair the damage.

The environment and the shape of settlements

It may seem that the influence of the environment on housing and urban development is a relatively recent phenomenon. However, as we saw in Part 1 of this book, certain environmental issues have been a concern of housing reformers for much of

on foot and factories had to be multistorey to allow the efficient use of belt-driven machinery. When workers had no way of commuting over any distance, it was inevitable that their houses should be tightly huddled around the factories or mills where they laboured.

The dispersal of housing and industry over the last 150 years has been made possible by the harnessing of energy through technology. The development of electricity and gas supplies, the railway system and, most important of all, the internal combustion engine, have shaped the way that human settlements have developed in the twentieth century. This has largely been unconstrained by the notion that energy is a finite commodity, particularly in the area of transport. The availability of cheap fuel in the first half of the twentieth century allowed people to write off energy costs as a locational factor so that settlements were able to disperse.

The same is true of waste; indeed the ability to dispose of human wastes and other pollutants has in the past been an important constraint on the growth of human settlements. The medieval city may have been able to dump its waste over the city walls but, if cities were to grow, more sophisticated means of disposal were required. The city of the industrial revolution is infamous for its pollution, smogs and the resulting mortality rates of its population. The solution however was not to curtail harmful activities, such is not human nature. Instead technologies were developed to mitigate the environmental effects of growth such as smokeless fuel, clean electricity and gas, piped water supplies and sewage systems. More importantly for the city, zoning policies were developed to separate the people and their homes from the polluting industry.

It is not the nature of cities to accept external constraints on their growth. There have been cities in history which have disappeared as a result of environmental factors such as drought or pollution but there has never been a city which has averted such disaster by limiting its own growth. Indeed it is doubtful whether the citizens of cities or their governments have the capacity to limit growth. Jane Jacobs has argued[2] that cities

the century. Tony Garnier's *Cité Industrielle* in 1917 incorporated very careful passive solar design and was self-sufficient in terms of energy through hydroelectric power. His main concern however was the health-giving properties of daylight and fresh air rather than energy and heating. Indeed for much of the Victorian period daylight and fresh air were important guiding principles and lay behind the development of by-laws as well as the recommendations of the Tudor-Walters committee.

Compared to today's global environmental concerns these were however peripheral issues. To uncover the fundamental trends which have guided development we need to consider the impact of resource consumption. As we have seen, the pre-industrial city was far more compact than today's settlements due largely to the limited availability of resources and the technology with which to exploit them. When the main sources of energy were water and the horse, settlements had to be located on rivers or streams and their scale was determined by distances that people and goods could cover on foot and by horse. With the advent of steam power and canals, locational constraints were not so severe but settlements still had to be sufficiently dense for people to get about

are always impractical. Cities in every age have grown beyond the point where the problems of energy supply, water, food and waste can be easily solved; just as cities today are not practical in terms of car use and congestion. She suggests that this impracticality is an essential spur to technological innovation to solve these problems which in turn drives economic development. London was more impractical in the seventeenth century as witnessed by the Black Death and the Great Fire than it is today despite being almost hundredth of the size it is today.

Profligate use of energy has characterised much of the nineteenth and twentieth centuries. This was brought to an end not so much by the environmental movement but by the oil crisis of 1974, which led to escalating energy costs and a far greater concern to reduce energy use. The environmental movement was able to use this concern to change attitudes through ground-breaking books like Rachel Carson's *A Silent Spring* and *The Limits to Growth* published by the Club of Rome[3]. Since then attitudes have changed and it is no longer assumed that traditional energy sources and natural resources are infinite, nor indeed the capacity of the environment to deal with the effects of consumption. Growth remains the driving force of world economies and has been

synonymous with increased consumption. However environmental considerations can no longer take a back seat and governments in the developed world have been wrestling with the seeming contradiction of sustainable development.

Attitudes to resource consumption have been closely linked with the growth of cities in which human activities have become increasingly divorced from nature and natural ecosystems. In modern cities energy is available at the flick of a switch, water is on tap, resources from all over the world can be purchased in supermarkets and waste can be flushed away or left out for collection. The environmental consequences of our urban lifestyles are effectively hidden or packaged up and located at a distance. As a result there is little incentive for people in cities to pursue more environmentally-friendly lifestyles because the benefits of this are hidden from them. However Ulrich Beck in his book *Ecological politics in an age of risk*[4] has argued that this is changing as a result of health scares. In recent years such scares have been legion in the UK with concerns such as BSE, E.coli food poisoning, air pollution alerts and the huge growth in asthma cases, summer droughts, and concerns aired in the press about toxic and carcinogenic substances. Beck suggests that, while these risks may seem unconnected,

A sustainable settlement? New development models like the American Pedestrian Pocket are also based on the needs of travel by foot and public transport

they are bringing home to the public the fact that environmental issues can have a direct effect on them and their families. When we have to ask whether our food and water are safe to eat and drink and our air safe to breath we might increasingly question a system in which these necessities are controlled by distant authorities beyond our control and influence. This, he suggests, will increasingly influence public attitudes to the environment.

Cities may no longer belch smoke and pollution as they did in the industrial revolution. They have however become symbols of our resource-hungry society sucking in energy and raw materials and spewing out waste and pollution in linear systems which are entirely divorced from natural ecosystems. Yet the availability of energy and resources in the twenty-first century is likely to be much more limited than it has been in the past. Just as profligate energy use and a disregard for environmental consequences allowed settlements to sprawl, so resource austerity may make this sprawl seem immoral and may cause a return to more compact settlement forms. Thus transformed the city may come to be seen as a tool to address many environmental concerns. This was the conclusion of the *European Green Paper on the Urban Environment*[5], which saw a new type of city as the answer to many environmental concerns – the compact, walkable city. In advocating the compact city the European Union referred back to pre-industrial cities such as Siena as a model. The same has happened in the UK and US where models such as the Urban Village[6] and Pedestrian Pocket[7] have been put forward as sustainable settlement forms to promote walking and public transport. Thus the influence of the environment on human settlements could come full circle and the sprawl of the twentieth century may come to be seen as a temporary aberration.

The impact of environmental concerns

The growing awareness of environmental issues has resulted in international agreements, most notably the 1992 Rio Summit which committed national governments to strategies for sustainable development. The best definition of sustainable development is still that put forward by the Bruntland Commission[8] – 'Development that meets the needs of the present without compromising the ability of future generations to meet their own needs'. In tune with the spirit of the 1980s the UK government summed up the same sentiments using the language of the market: 'Sustainable development means living on the earth's income rather than eroding its capital. It means keeping the consumption of renewable natural resources within the limits of their replenishment. It means handing down to successive generations not only man-made wealth… but also natural wealth, such as clean and adequate water supplies, good arable land, a wealth'[9].

Yet defining sustainability is one thing, achieving it is quite another. The fact that agreement was reached at Rio may have been remarkable but many of the targets set have not been met. Indeed many governments – most notably the US – have failed to put in place policies which make meeting the targets even a remote possibility because of their reluctance to sacrifice the nirvana of growth. Policies instead have been driven by crisis management with individual initiatives introduced in response to environmental scares, such as the banning of CFCs in response to the discovery of the hole in the ozone layer. Whilst individual initiatives can be important, what is needed is a more comprehensive approach to ensure that human activities are more sustainable. It is true that this may mean accepting lower levels of growth, but this is a small price to pay compared to the impact on growth of environmental collapse if we do nothing.

The development of a more comprehensive approach lies at the heart of the United Nation's and European Union's[10] current thinking on environmental policy. They are developing a more system-orientated approach which looks at the whole cycle of production, consumption and disposal to get a clearer picture of environmental impacts. Another important concept is BPEO (Best Practical Environmental Option) which suggests that all decisions should be taken to minimise their environmental impact within the constraints at the time of the decision. The Environment Agency in the UK is starting to adopt these approaches and it is likely that they will lead eventually to a situation where environmental considerations lie at the heart of government decision-making. This would have far-reaching effects on urban planning, housebuilding and transport policy.

The impact of environmental concerns is not however confined to public sector decision makers. Far more important in terms of its global environmental impact is the private sector. On the surface the environmental movement would appear to have deeply affected the private sector. The green consumer has become a force to reckon with and most companies are now concerned to emphasise their green credentials. It is however far from clear whether this represents a cultural change in the attitudes of the private sector or is little more than clever marketing and public relations. In some cases it can be both, as with the introduction of a set of ethical and environmental principles by the Co-operative Bank in the UK. There is little doubt that this was a sincere attempt by the bank to put environmental and ethical considerations at the heart of its corporate decision-making. Yet it was also a very powerful marketing tool and helped the bank to firmly establish itself as one of the big players in the UK market.

Even if the private sector's new-found environmental awareness is only public relations it can still be a powerful force. A good example is the Brent Spar oil rig incident in 1995 where public pressure forced a multinational oil company to abandon its plans to sink the rig at sea despite good scientific advice which suggested that this would be no more damaging than other options. In the face of such public opinion manufacturers are concerned to review their policies and to trumpet the 'greenness' of their products. Goods labelled as environmentally-friendly sell from supermarket shelves, ethical bank accounts attract new customers and environmental pressure groups attract larger memberships than political parties. These private sector concerns spill over into the development industry as companies ensure that their buildings comply with their environmental policies. They are however yet to have any real impact on the housing market. The green consumer may be happy enough to criticise a large company for its environmental performance but is less willing to apply these same principles when spending their own money on a house.

While the environmental movement may have achieved many successes in changing public and corporate attitudes as well as the emphasis of government policy, progress has been painfully slow. Targets are set on the basis of what can be agreed rather than what is needed and the unsustainable forces of private consumption continue largely unchecked. Looking ahead to the twenty-first century there would appear to be only three possible scenarios. The first is that we continue as we are at present in the hope that technological developments will avert the prospect of environmental collapse. The second is that the world somehow turns out to be a much more robust place than many scientists currently believe. The third is that policies to address environmental issues become much more effective than they are at present. The only responsible option open to us is to plan on the basis of this third scenario. In this case it will no longer be sufficient to pay lip service to environmental concerns in the twenty-first century, some much more fundamental changes will be necessary and this is likely to have a fundamental affect on housing and urban areas.

In order to assess the extent of this impact it is important to review the range of environmental issues which are likely to be important in the next century. These are summarised in the table on page 78.

Global warming

The overriding environmental issue today is global warming caused by the greenhouse effect. The Inter-Government Panel on Climate Change[11] has estimated that global temperatures will rise by $0.2 - 0.5°C$ per decade in the next century leading to extreme weather conditions, crop failure and coastal flooding. The British situation was documented by the UK Climate Change Impacts Review Group in its report published in July

Summary of environmental issues and their impact on urban development

Issue	Impact	Policy context	Implications
Carbon dioxide	Global warming leading to temperature rises of up to 0.5°C per decade and a rise in sea levels of up to 6 cm per decade	Rio targets to reduce emissions to 1990 levels by 2000. Kyoto targets agreed in 1997 to reduce global emissions by a further 6% by 2008 and European emissions by 8%. The UK government has set a target for a 20% reduction on 1990 levels by 2010	30% of CO_2 emissions relate to housing and 23% to transport although the latter is growing rapidly. Need to increase energy efficiency and reduce car use
Ozone depletion	Destruction of the ozone layer by up to 8% in northern and mid latitudes threatens an increase of 25 000 skin cancers and a 15% drop in global food production	Montreal Protocol 1989/90/92 and the UK Environmental Protection Act 1990 seeks to phase out CFCs and to reduce HCFCs	The main impact on the building industry will be the phasing out of insulation materials which incorporate CFCs and HCFCs
Rain forest	The destruction of rain forests is increasing global warming, reducing natural diversity and a possible source of new drugs	None	The avoidance of tropical hardwoods in buildings such as window frames and plywood
Car use	Has risen from 219 billion km/year in 1981 to 330 billion km/year in 1990. Similar increases predicted into the future unless action is taken	Government committment to reducing car use in Sustainable Development - the UK Strategy (currently being revised) PPG 13, reduction in road building, Integrated transport policy being prepared	60% of housing on brown field sites, increased densities, road pricing, limits on out-of-town development, improvements in public transport, restrictive parking policies
Natural resources	The environmental impact of materials in terms of extraction, manufacture, transport, use and disposal	Government policy to ensure sustainable supply through minerals PPGs, alternative sources, more efficient use and recycling	The use of locally sourced materials, timber from managed sources, bricks fired with landfill gas, recycled materials such as PFA
Recycling	The UK produces 20 million tonnes of domestic waste per year only 5% of which is recycled. This is wasteful of resources and energy as well as using up landfill sites and producing methane which contributes to global warming	Government target to recycle 25% of household waste by 2000. Landfill tax introduced in 1994 and increased in the 1998 budget.	Domestic and trade waste recycling, segregated collection, local recycling points, segregation of waste within the home
Water	Water use is increasing leading to droughts and potentially limiting development in the SE. Purification and disposal uses large amounts of energy	Government regulation of the water companies, targets for the reduction of leakage, domestic water metering.	In an energy-efficient home water bills can be more than all other utility bills. Water capacity may limit development. Greater demand for water saving features.
Ecology	The loss of ecosystems, diversity, and the extinction of species	Government biodiversity Action Plan seeks to protect specific areas and species and increase overall diversity	Protection of habitats may limit green field development. Site ecological surveys, permaculture, planting, gardens, parks, landscape
Acid rain	Acid rain is caused by sulphur dioxide, smoke, and oxides of nitrogen. 20% of UK trees are affected plus northern lakes	Government target of 60% reduction in sulphur dioxide emissions by 2003 and 30% reduction in nitrous oxide by 1996 achieved by switch from coal-fired power stations	The main cause of acid rain is now car emissions which will be a further justification for measures to reduce car use

1996[12]. This predicted that by 2050 UK average temperatures will rise from 9°C to 10.6°C, sea levels will rise by 35 centimetres and rainfall by 10%. Climate systems will move northwards by about 200 kilometres so that southern England will acquire the climate of the Loire region in France. This suggests that the south will become drier and subject to droughts whilst the north will become wetter and prone to flooding. The impacts are however very difficult to predict because of the complexity of global climate. It is possible that melting polar ice could cause the Gulf Stream to change its course which would leave the UK icebound like other countries on the same latitude.

The problem with such predictions is that they sound like scare stories. Compelling as the evidence may be many people, including decision makers, find it difficult to imagine the loss of large areas of coastal land to rising sea levels or the collapse of agricultural production. These are however not theoretical predictions. Global average temperature rises have already been measured and many scientists believe that the exceptional storms and heat waves across the world in recent years are the results of this.

Global warming results from the collection of greenhouse gases in the troposphere which then act like a greenhouse to trap infrared radiation. About 50% of the greenhouse effect is caused by carbon dioxide (CO_2). Other gases such as CFCs and methane are more damaging but are produced in much smaller quantities. Fossil fuels account for 80% of CO_2 emissions, 30% of this relates to housing, half of which comes from space heating. Transport is responsible for 23% of emissions and is of particular concern because, whilst other sources of CO_2 are being reduced, transport is projected to rise to 26.7% of emissions by 2005[13].

In 1992 the Rio Summit set global targets to reduce CO_2 emissions to 1990 levels by the year 2000[14]. In the UK we produced 158 million tones of CO_2 (MtC) in 1990 and in order to get back to this level by the year 2000 annual emissions have to be reduced by 24 MtC. The UK and Germany are the only Rio signatories which look likely to meet these targets although in the UK this is largely the result not of energy saving but the switch from coal to gas fired power stations.

In Kyoto in 1997 governments signed up to binding targets for a 5.2% global reduction in CO_2 emissions on 1990 levels over the next 15 years although, within this, different targets were agreed for different countries, Europe's being 8%. While an agreement was eventually reached, the meeting uncovered a range of international tensions. The UK for example has already committed itself to a 20% reduction in emissions by 2010[15] whereas in the US a coalition of interests has been lobbying hard for their government not to sign up to any reductions fearing loss of jobs and economic activity. On the other hand developing nations argue, with some justification, that pegging their emissions to 1990 levels will prevent them from catching up with the established economies of the west which are pegged at much higher CO_2 levels.

It could be argued that these international agreements are determined by what it was possible to agree rather than what was necessary. As an illustration of this the UK government's scientific panel on global warming estimated in its July 1996 report[16] that even if greenhouse gas emissions

Carbon dioxide emissions by sector: Source UK Government

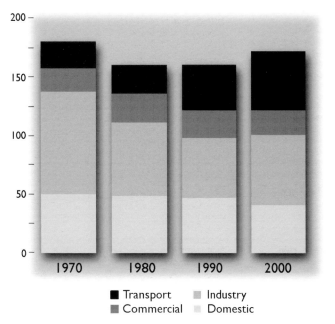

■ Transport   Industry
■ Commercial   Domestic

were 'chopped off at the knees' it would be 50 years before improvement in global warming would be possible to measure. It is therefore likely that by 2050 we will be looking at reductions of up to 60% on 1990 CO_2 emission levels in western nations in order to stabilise emissions at a sustainable level[17]. This will bring into stark focus issues of equality between nations. Is it right for the US to peg its emissions to a per capita level ten times greater than a developing nation? There are many who argue that a common per capita emissions target should be set for all nations which would mean that the burden will increasingly be placed on the developed world.

CO_2 production is a function of energy use from fossil fuels. Measures to reduce CO_2 emissions are likely to be a more important constraint on energy use than scarcity of supply. For years the hope was that nuclear power would overcome problems of scarcity. This however has its own environmental and financial problems not least with decommissioning. Recent announcements suggest that there will be no more nuclear power plants developed in the UK and it would be unrealistic to rely on this sector. A better option is renewable energy such as hydroelectric power, wind, wave and tidal power which do not pollute or produce CO_2. These may also carry environmental costs, such as the flooding of valleys or tidal estuaries or the erection of wind turbines on

attractive hillsides. However while these problems are of local concern, they are as nothing compared to the global impact of fossil fuel use. The fossil fuel levy in the UK, while designed to support the nuclear industry, has led to an increase in wind generation and there are proposals for tidal barrages on the Bristol and Mersey estuaries. It is however unlikely that renewable energy will replace fossil fuels in the foreseeable future as the market remains dominated by short-term financial considerations. The decline of the coal industry and the deregulation of the electricity market has, for example, meant that the main area of investment has been in gas fired power stations yet gas supplies will not last for more than a few decades.

One of the problems with the current approach to power generation is that it is based on large power stations which are inefficient. Even the most modern plant only converts about 30% of available energy into electricity. Much is lost as surplus heat, or because the plant must be sized to peak demand. Losses are also incurred through the distribution of power over long distances. The solution to sustainable power generation may therefore not lie in large capital investments. A more realistic option may be more local power generation, such as the plans by the Japanese government to have a million roofs generating solar power or neighbourhood combined heat and power plants. Such solutions would be more responsive to demand, avoid distribution losses as well as making it possible to use surplus heat. The experience of continental Europe suggests that we may be on the threshold of major change in the power generation industry. Market intervention by the German government, for example, to reduce the cost of photovoltaic technology is transforming the economics of power generation. Carbon taxes are also being considered by many governments[18] which will increase the costs of fossil fuel generation. It is therefore possible that housing and urban areas in the future will need to be designed for a much less energy-intensive way of life and also to accommodate a range of local power generation technologies.

Other global environmental issues

The other great global environmental concern is the loss of the ozone layer, although this is of less relevance to physical development. Ozone in the upper atmosphere protects the earth from ultraviolet rays that can cause skin cancers and crop failure. The British Antarctic Survey first identified an ozone 'hole' over the Antarctic in the 1970s but this did not affect populated areas. However in recent years ozone depletion has been documented globally amounting to 8% per decade in northern latitudes. This has been associated with an increase in skin cancers and unusual and persistent weather patterns in the winters of 1992 and 1993. A number of substances are responsible for ozone depletion, the most damaging of which are chlorofluorocarbons (CFCs). These substances are controlled by the 1989 Montreal Protocol, which has been twice updated and sought to phase out these chemicals by 1996. In the short term they are being replaced with less damaging hydro-chlorofluorocarbons (HCFCs) although these too will be phased out by 2030. This will affect household goods such as fridges as well as insulation materials. There is also widespread concern about the loss of the rain forests which reduces the planet's ability to absorb CO_2 as well as harming biodiversity and removing a rich source of new drugs.

This will affect the building industry which will need to find new forms of insulation and phase out of the use of hardwoods from unsustainable sources in building components such as window frames and plywood. It is however unlikely to affect the way that settlements are planned.

Pollution

Local environmental issues are likely to affect the planning of settlements to a far greater extent. One of the most important is air pollution. British cities have suffered from air pollution for well over a century. As late as the winter of 1953 urban smogs caused 4 000 deaths in London, largely as a result of the burning of coal in domestic fires and emissions from industry. The 1953 smogs gave rise to the Clean Air Acts of 1956 and 1968 and the introduction of smokeless fuels meant that smogs became largely a thing of the past. However air pollution remains a problem and domestic heating has been replaced by transport as the main source of the problem. Today's pollutants are oxides of nitrogen (NO_x), carbon monoxide (CO), particulates and volatile organic chemicals (VOC). NO_x and VOCs can react with sunlight to create ozone, something which may be of benefit in the upper atmosphere but is damaging to health and plants at ground level. Background ozone levels have doubled in Britain over the last century and we now regularly break

World Health Organisation guidelines particularly in hot summers.

NO_x is also an increasingly important cause of acid rain. This was previously caused largely by sulphur dioxide (SO_2) from manufacturing industry and power generation. While SO_2 emissions have been reduced (by 45% since 1970) NO_x from road transport has risen steadily and is now a significant cause of acid rain. Twenty per-cent of UK trees are estimated to be affected by acid rain as well as a number of lakes in Scotland, although there is some evidence of recovery in northern forests. The trend with chemical emissions has therefore been for industry to put its house in order as a result of regulations but for these gains to be partly cancelled out by the growth in pollution from cars. Here progress has also been made with more efficient engines, catalytic converters and lead-free petrol. Yet while individual cars may be less polluting their numbers and use are growing so that overall pollution continues to increase.

Water and sewage

Another important local issue is water use. In a wet island like Britain it has in the past been difficult to persuade people that water is a scarce resource. However the severe droughts since 1988, particularly 1995, which may be an early

sign of global warming, have exploded this perception. In hot summers reservoirs have run dry and river extraction has caused levels to become dangerously low, endangering wildlife. In the south-east in particular the margin between available rainfall and demand is perilously small and is being eroded by new development. Indeed water companies in the UK have demanded rights of consultation on major planning applications and have predicted that they will be unable to meet the anticipated demand from the projected increase 4.4 million households in the next twenty years.

Water saving is also important because of the vast amounts of energy used in purification and sewage treatment. The quality of water in the UK is very high but having expended so much energy in purification, up to 25% of the water leaks away in the distribution system and once it gets to the home a further third is flushed down the toilet. It then creates problems with disposal and in many coastal areas sewage is still pumped into the sea, something which is being phased out by European directives. Like power generation the response to these problems has been seen in terms of capital investment and new technology, such as the London ring main. Plans are also being considered to pump water between catchment areas, to develop desalination plants for sea water and to incinerate sewage sludge. All of these will be tremendously expensive both in terms of finance and energy use and yet will do little more than prop up a linear system of resource consumption. A more economic and sustainable option would be to turn this linear system into a circular system by which water is recycled and reused.

Water saving may therefore play an increasing role in future development. The first steps have included the introduction of water metering to give users a financial incentive to save water. Requirements have also been placed on water companies to reduce distribution losses. To go further than this, homes and urban areas in the future will need to be designed to make much more efficient use of water. This might include water collection from roofs, the restoration of grey water (water from sinks and baths) to flush toilets, and composting toilets. At present there are only a few environmental demonstration projects which include such systems. Schemes like Hockerton in Newark and Sherwood include reed beds to recycle water and in Berlin there is even an urban block which purifies waste water through a series of reed tanks down the side of the building. While these may not become a common feature of urban areas, technologies are developing for the local treatment of household sewage. One example is the bioworks developed as part of a regeneration project in Kolding in Denmark (see page 163).

Domestic waste

Domestic waste is a further concern. The UK produces 20 million tonnes of domestic waste a year, only 5% of which is recycled. This represents an enormous waste of energy and natural resources and blights huge areas of land with tipping. Landfill sites also produce methane which contributes to global warming. While the UK lags behind on many environmental issues, nowhere is this more true than in domestic waste recycling. In cities like New York, where landfill sites are scarce, recycling has become compulsory, and in Holland segregated waste collection bins are available on every street. Vienna recycles 43% of its waste compared to only 4% in London[19].

Yet in the UK recycling is little more than a middle-class fad. Local authorities have made progress in the provision of public recycling points but recent research has suggested that the environmental impact of people driving to these recycling points outweighs the environmental benefits of the materials recycled. Beyond this recycling has been left to the voluntary sector and (where it is profitable) the private sector. It is extraordinary that in the UK we have just been through a major reform of waste collection through compulsory competitive tendering (CCT) yet in virtually no cases did the tender documents make provision for segregated waste collection which is a prerequisite for recycling. What happened was that we switched from dustbins to *wheelie bins* which required equally significant

investment in new bins and refuse vehicles. However because the wheelie bins were larger and easier to collect they actually increased the volume of unsegregated waste.

The response to increasing waste has again been to look for technological solutions. One of the most popular has been waste incineration which is currently the subject of a number of major Private Finance Initiatives. This can have benefits if incineration is used to produce domestic heat, as in Sheffield, or even for power generation. It can however create environmental problems due to the emission of dioxins and is also fiercely resisted by local people. It is, in any case, a very inefficient means of unlocking the energy in waste.

It is therefore likely that the segregated collection and recycling of waste will become much more common in urban areas. At present only a few areas like Milton Keynes have segregated collection, although it is being considered in detail in London. Indeed an indication of what segregated collection might mean for urban areas can be seen from a detailed study recently completed for the London Planning Advisory Committee[20] which was piloted in a number of areas. The key breakthrough in making the scheme viable was for residents to put out all recyclable material in one container. This is then collected by an operative using an electric hand cart which

runs on pavements. The cart carries a number of sacks for different types of material which are sorted on the spot by the operative. When full the sacks are then left at a pick-up point to be collected by an electric refuse vehicle called the 'Mother ship'. This system has brought the cost of segregated collection down below that of normal refuse collection. It is ideally suited to high-density housing areas, including flats, and the take-up rates by residents on the pilot projects have been very high. It will be adopted in London in the near future and interest is being shown by other authorities so that it is likely to be widely adopted in urban areas.

The impact on development

It is clear that environmental concerns go far wider than domestic energy consumption. There is a bewildering range of issues for the would-be environmentally-conscious developer to consider and on many of these issues the advice from experts is confused and sometimes contradictory. One very specific example illustrates the point. In the Homes for Change scheme in Manchester (see Chapter 13) there was a long debate about the roofing material for the building because members of the co-operative wanted something other than a traditional roof. The roof of the building was curved and it was eventually decided to use aluminium, which received wisdom suggests is environmentally harmful because of the vast quantities of energy used in its smelting. However it allowed a lightweight roof so saving on construction, was very recyclable and, if it was sourced from hydroelectric powered smelters in Canada, produced no CO_2. Just as the group was feeling good about this decision it was pointed out that the energy used in transporting the aluminium from Canada probably cancelled out any benefits and a locally sourced material would have been better! Such confusion illustrates one of the reasons why progress has been slow. It is likely that in the future new information systems and concepts such as the Best Practical Environmental Option[21] will make these decisions easier and will become an increasingly important part of development decision-making.

This assumes that the developers of housing and the planners of cities are committed to more sustainable forms of development. Yet they are unlikely to be converted into environmental pioneers by conscience or consumer pressure. More important will be increasing legislation stemming from international agreements and fiscal measures such as carbon taxes which will give them no option but to become greener. But there is as yet little evidence that this is happening. Whilst the green consumer may have caused toilet roll manufacturers to rethink their product they have had little impact on house builders. As a recent survey of house buyers concluded[22]: 'Energy efficiency is said to be important but only when prompted. It is perhaps an aspirational necessity rather than something which will actually influence the decision to purchase'. Why is it that people are concerned about the fuel consumption of their car but not their heating system? Why do they care that their washing up liquid is green but not their house? A few developers, such as Admiral Homes through their Green Ribbon scheme, have developed and successfully marketed green housing. They are however very much the exception and to most developers and buyers the quality of the fitted kitchen is of far greater importance. The situation is not much better with social housing. True there have been a number of high profile low-energy housing schemes by developers such as North Sheffield Housing Association and Gwalia in Swansea. However these exceptions disguise the fact that the majority of new social housing does little more than meet Building Regulations and energy efficiency is seen as an expensive luxury despite the benefits to tenants in terms of comfort and running costs.

What is more, efforts to improve the environmental performance of housing have gone down something of a blind alley. Most effort has gone into the thermal efficiency of a small number of new houses and has largely ignored the existing stock as well as other forms of domestic energy use such as appliances and transport. In new super-insulated housing, heating is now a minor energy user. Yet effort continues to be put into further improvements whilst the houses are often located

AUTONOMOUS HOUSING

There have been a number of autonomous houses built in the UK such as the house illustrated to the right which was designed and lived in by the architects Robert and Brenda Vale. They also designed a scheme that has been hailed as the UK's first genuinely self-sufficient settlement, a group of five autonomous houses in Nottinghamshire. The houses promoted by Nick Martin of the British Earth Sheltering Association produce their own power and water and recycle their waste. The development is partly underground with south-facing sunstores. The plans include 3 000 trees to be planted for shelter, wildlife, and coppicing along with ponds for water supply, sewage treatment and fish farming. A wind turbine will provide power and residents will farm the surrounding 25 acres for food.

The scheme is on green belt land and despite 'breaking all of the planning rules' has been welcomed by the local Newark and Sherwood Council which is planning to build a hundred autonomous council houses within the next five years.

in remote areas and require gas-guzzling cars to get to vital facilities. What is more this esoteric research into energy-autonomous housing is leaving behind the vast majority of new houses which are still being built without tried and tested, cost-effective energy saving measures.

It is therefore unlikely that public pressure and housing developers will bring about change on their own. Action from government is required and is already forthcoming. Most high profile are the occasional government energy-saving campaigns. However more significant is the increase in insulation standards introduced through Part L of the 1995 Building Regulations. This is now equivalent to the standards achieved in some of the early energy-saving schemes in the 1970s. These thermal efficiency standards will be further increased next year as part of the overall strategy to reduce CO_2 emissions. The political minefield of VAT on fuel is also part of the strategy. Despite the controversy that this has promoted it does highlight the fact that taxation will increasingly be used to reduce demand, as in the 'carbon taxes' being considered in California and proposed by the Green Party in Britain.

The stranglehold of the car

The environmental villain of the twenty-first century will be the car not the home. The effect of environmental concerns on housing design will be as nothing compared to attempts to reduce

car use. As well as being the fastest-growing source of CO_2 emissions, cars are responsible for low-level ozone pollution, acid rain, the use of resources through road building, and carcinogenic particulates. Roads cover 1.5% of the UK land area and passenger kilometres travelled by car have doubled since 1981[23]. Congestion costs industry £15 billion pounds a year[24]. For years governments have attempted to respond to the congestion caused by this increase by building more roads. More than 9 000 kilometres of new roads were built between 1985 and 1990 in England and Wales. However even government is beginning to recognise[25] that new roads are as likely to increase car use as to reduce congestion and so can make the problem worse. This has been picked up by the Labour government which has launched a major consultation on its proposals for an integrated transport policy. It is therefore likely that the battles over Twyford Down and Newbury in the mid-1990s will mark the end of major road building in the UK and the emphasis will change to demand reduction.

The attachment of people to their cars will however be hard to break. People sit for hours in traffic jams and car speeds in many towns can be easily outstripped by a sprightly pedestrian so that mobility is not the only consideration. Investment in public transport is important but bus travel now accounts for only 6% of distance travelled[26]. This is partly due to the quality of public transport but also to social attitudes since buses have increasingly been abandoned by the middle classes and are unable to serve dispersed settlement patterns efficiently. The development of trams in cities like Manchester, Sheffield and Birmingham may start to change the image of public transport but can only serve a small part of these conurbations. It is therefore likely that further measures will be used such as road pricing and taxation on fuel. Jorge Wilheim, who was responsible for organising the Habitat II conference in Istanbul, postulates in his book *Fax messages from a near future* [27] a city where the private car has been abolished following the 'Big Jam' and transport needs are served by public cars which can be picked up and returned at service stations around the city. Such systems are already a reality in some European cities and are being actively considered in UK cities such as Edinburgh.

Cities such as Athens, Florence and most recently Paris have already taken much more radical action to exclude traffic due to severe en-

vironmental problems. Florence has banned cars from the city centre altogether while Athens bans cars with odd and even number plates on alternate days. The same was tried for one day in 1997 in Paris combined with free public transport following the incidence of very high pollution levels (even higher levels have since been measured in London without action being taken). Other cities in Denmark and the Netherlands have made great progress in promoting cycling and walking, to a far greater extent than even the most advanced British cities like Oxford and York. In Britain the erection of road blocks around the City of London as a result of terrorist bombing in the early 1990s is an interesting case study. Computer traffic models of the city illustrated that this was not possible without creating grid-lock. Yet it was done, and resulted in a large reduction in traffic without causing inconvenience whilst making the streets of the City much more pleasant.

It is likely that in the coming century the practicality and social acceptability of driving into town will be greatly reduced. Cities must both

CONTROLLING THE CAR – EDINBURGH

Many cities have laid claim to environmental credentials over recent years. However the city of Edinburgh is now showing the way with radical measures to reduce car use. This is a good example of the sort of policies which are likely to become more common in cities in the future. The aims of Edinburgh's policy are to reduce car dependency, congestion and pollution.

Traffic has been rerouted to deter motorists from driving into the centre along with simple measures such as increasing the delay at traffic lights. A road-pricing scheme encompassing the whole city could be in place by the year 2000. This will create a cordon around the outskirts of the city where motorists will have to pay £2. The dual aim is to reduce traffic and to raise revenue for public transport improvements. Because the city is relatively compact, has few entry points and little through traffic it is considered ideal for this scheme.

A car-sharing scheme is also being established with a taxi-style booking system to hire communally owned cars parked in reserved spaces. A club card will be used for fuel and a contract agreed for maintenance and insurance.

This will give people easy access to a car without having to own one and it is also hoped that it will make people think more carefully about their car use. There are now 300 similar schemes in Europe, one of the largest being Berlin which has 3 000 members of car sharing clubs. See also the case study of car-free housing in Edinburgh in Chapter 10.

respond to this and to the threat that people will abandon town altogether in favour of out-of-town facilities so increasing car use. The other plank of government policy through Planning Policy Guidance Notes 6 and 13 is therefore also important since it seeks to limit out-of-town development in favour of urban infill and town centres.

It is clear that the first of the 4Cs, conservation, will have a far-reaching effect on future housing and development patterns. This will result partly from public pressure but much more significant will be regulation and financial necessity as governments and markets come to terms with finite resources and the potentially catastrophic effects of climate change.

FREIBURG – GERMANY

Freiburg has won the accolade of 'Environmental capital' in Germany through its work to reduce car dependency by offering cheap alternatives.

Its strategy includes an employment location and density policy to maintain the traditional urban structure of the city. A street-car network has been developed with rights of way over cars linked to a 'Regio-Ecoticket', a cheap one-fare pass valid on 2 400 km of regional rail, street car and bus routes.

High parking charges and resident-only parking have been introduced along with a park-and-ride system. Speed limits throughout the city have been limited to 30 km/hr and roads have been narrowed to reduce car flow. The city has also created 400 km of cycle routes and parking for 700 cycles.

Over the last five years public transport use has increased by 30%. Between 1976 and 1989 car ownership in the city rose by 46% but car use did not increase.

CHAPTER 6
Choice
Changing household characteristics and the 21st century home

Choice was the mantra of the 1980s. It was the justification for a raft of legislative change, an important part of which related to housing. It would however be a mistake to assume that policies to increase housing choice did anything of the sort. The only real choice on offer was to move from renting, and in particular the council sector, into owner-occupation. The choices that we are interested in here relate not to tenure but to design and location. In many respects the last few decades have seen a diminution of choice in these areas. As housing provision has become dominated by private builders so housing design and location has been driven by profits from land development rather than by meeting the needs of people. This means that the housing stock is increasingly out of step with society's changing needs.

The driving factor in much housing provision is market forces which dictate the location of housing (do not build in the inner city), its form (avoid flats where possible), its design (detached best, semidetached good, terraced bad), its layout (cul-de-sacs with large gardens preferred), detailing ('Tudorbethan' trimmings a bonus) and technical specification (you should have central heating whether you need it or not). In other parts of the world such as Scandinavia, North America and Japan a sophisticated house building industry allows consumers to choose from a catalogue of factory-made high specification houses. By contrast in Britain houses are built in the same chaotic manner as they have for most of

this century. This is possible because market places a premium on the sort of traditional suburbia which has come to so dominate the UK in twentieth century. In the last two years 53% of new housing was either detached or semidetached and only 13% was flats[1].

The preference for traditional suburbia is shared by many of those who buy new houses. A survey for the Housebuilder's Federation[2] of 818 households who had recently bought new houses found that 76% rejected the idea of living in urban areas, citing as their reasons hostile environments, traffic, noise, dirt and the poor quality of schools. They were concerned about the 'density' of urban areas, particularly space standards, small gardens and lack of parking, and summed up the attraction of their new home with phrases like: 'it's a nice cul-de-sac, not close to shops or pubs… you're just away from every-thing'. Indeed these attitudes were most pro-nounced amongst lower socioeconomic groups and those who had experience of living in urban areas.

The desire to escape into 'your own little world' which has driven suburban growth for much of this century would appear to be as strong as ever. This certainly is the view of the Housebuilder's Federation, who have suggested that the survey is representative of the aspirations of the majority of households. It confirms the view of many in the housebuilding industry that the predominant household in the UK is made up of two parents with children, is able-bodied, mobile

TOWN CENTRE HOUSING: Is the popularity of city centre housing catering to a niche market or indicative of a more fundamental change in the housing market?

MERCHANT'S CITY: GLASGOW

In Glasgow City Centre over 1 200 housing units were created during the 1980s. Of these 41% involved the conversion of existing buildings, many in Merchant's City. These were made possible by grants which averaged £5 100 per dwelling. The early pilot schemes required grants amounting to 39% of the development costs, plus the value of the buildings gifted by the Council. However subsequent schemes have required much lower grants and one scheme has now taken place without grant. One of the largest schemes, Ingram Square, involved the renewal of a complete block, including three warehouses, a department store, and new build to create 239 dwellings. This was developed by a partnership with the city and the Scottish Development Agency each taking a 25% share.

WHITWORTH STREET: MANCHESTER

Over the last ten years over 2 600 flats have been developed along the Whitworth Street corridor in Manchester. Twenty buildings have been converted representing investment of over £120 million. The area is characterised by huge Victorian commercial buildings, rising to 10 storeys. Two of the developments have been undertaken by housing associations for rent, the conversion of India House by Northern Counties Housing Association into 100 flats and a 6-storey new-build scheme by Tung Sing, an association catering for the large local Chinese community. The first residential conversion was Granby House in 1986. This 6-storey, 70 000 sq ft building was converted by Northern Counties to 70 flats for sale at a total cost of £1.7 million with subsidy of £785 000 although the caution of lenders meant that Northern Counties had to invest over £400 000 of their own resources. The flats sold quickly at average prices of £16 000 and on the resale market the value of the flats doubled within a year. This was a very practical demonstration of the market potential in the city which persuaded other developers, and lenders, to follow the lead.

and in regular employment. This may be the view of many of the middle-class housing professionals, estate agents, developers and architects who shape the housing that is built, but it no longer reflects the demographic make-up of the country. The Housebuilder's Federation survey was of families who had recently bought a brand new home on a suburban housing estate. Even if these people were typical of housebuyers (which they are not since nine out of ten housebuyers buy 'second-hand' houses) a it is hardly surprising that they should express a preference for the sort of housing that they had recently bought. However, more fundamentally, while this group may have been a majority in the interwar years they are increasingly becoming a minority of households.

Another survey by Brian Robson[3] of people who had recently moved into city centre apartments in Manchester tells a very different story. Of the 170 households surveyed 40% were single people and only five had children. The survey was equally unrepresentative since it was of a group who had recently decided to move into a city centre apartment, but it does illustrate that the Housebuilders' Federation survey does not give the whole picture. Nearly two-thirds of the households had all of their adults in full time employment, mostly in professional occupations, and two-thirds of the owner-occupiers were first-time buyers. When the first warehouse in Manchester was converted to housing in the early 1980s the flats were sold for £16 000, so uncertain were the valuers about the market for this type of housing. When the flats started to change hands for more than £30 000 within a few months it was clear that a market existed and a flood of residential warehouse conversions followed. As the survey confirms, the buyers were young professionals without children and 'empty nesters' whose children had left home and who worked in the city centre. At the time they were regarded as a niche market but this may no longer be the case.

Just as the nineteenth century home changed in response to the growth of the nuclear family so the twenty-first century is likely to reflect its decline.

Changing household composition

It seems reasonable to assume that the design and location of housing should match the characteristics of the households for which it is built, although this sometimes seems a radical concept in the housing world. As household characteristics change housing should therefore also evolve. The trend which has dominated the last two centuries is declining household size and increasing household numbers. As a result the need for new housing has consistently outstripped population growth. In crude terms this can be seen from overcrowding figures which saw a fall from an average of 5–11 persons per dwelling in 1861 to 2.97 in 1966[4]. The same trend can be seen with average household size which fell from 4.6 persons in 1901 to 3.1 in 1961 and to just 2.4 in 1993. So, whilst the UK population rose by just over 20% between 1921 and 1961 from 38 to 46 million, household numbers leapt by more than 70% from 8.7 to 14.9 million, an increase of 1.75% per year. In the process the proportion of two-person households in the UK rose from 21.5% of households in 1911 to 55% in 1983.

Figures from the 1991 census[5] show this trend is still at work. The nuclear family made up of a mother and father with children now makes up just 19.8% of households, rising to 25.1% if families with more than two adults, such as an elderly relative are included. Indeed even when you include single-parent families the total number of households with children is only 30%. Compare this to the 40% of households who have no children and 30% who are pensioners and one may question why most of the housing

that we build is designed for families. The reason is probably that most of society's decision makers – developers, investors and politicians – tend to be married with children and fall into the trap of assuming that everyone lives this way (or in the case of politicians, should live this way). They are however no longer representative of the people whose lives they influence.

Indeed the most important household type is below pensionable age and childless. Of the 40% of households which fall into this category 15.6% are childless couples, 13.2% are all-adult households and 11.7% are single people. Yet most of the housing industry regards this group as a niche market, assuming that most people will buy a house when they have a family and settle down. The reality is that more people are delaying having a family and enjoying a more affluent lifestyle in their twenties (particularly if they have not taken on a mortgage). Their housing requirements at this childless stage of life are very different from those of families. While some will undoubtedly be drawn to suburbia, a proportion – maybe a significant proportion – will value activity and vitality over peace and privacy and proximity to facilities over space and gardens. This is the market which the warehouse conversions in Manchester and other cities have tapped and the demographic figures suggest that it is a far larger market than planners and developers have thus far appreciated.

The other great area of household growth is pensioners who now make up 30% of all households and are increasingly recognised as an important consumer and political group. Just over 13% of the population were aged over 65 in 1971;

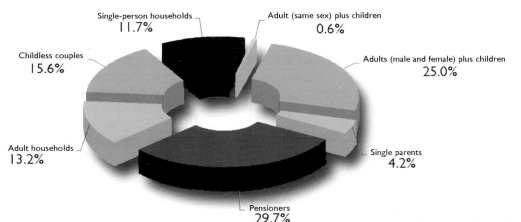

Single-person households
11.7%

Adult (same sex) plus children
0.6%

Childless couples
15.6%

Adults (male and female) plus children
25.0%

Adult households
13.2%

Single parents
4.2%

Pensioners
29.7%

McCARTHY AND STONE

The growth of McCarthy and Stone is a good example of the development of new housing forms for emerging demographic groups. The company specialise in the development of blocks of flats near the centre of small towns for people aged over 60. Since 1977 they have built over 17 000 units on 70 sites.

A typical development is Deans Mill Court 800 yards from the centre of Canterbury. This consists of 43 one and two-bed units with fitted kitchens and bathrooms incorporating mobility features. All flats have telephone entry and 24 hour 'Careline' support from a resident manager. A service charge is made to cover all maintenance and gardening.

The brochure stresses the fact that the scheme is within easy walking distance of shops and facilities such as doctors, dentists and a post office. This means that most schemes are in urban locations which tend to be favoured by elderly households. Whilst privacy and independence are stressed, the schemes create a strong sense of community. A range of communal facilities are provided such as a residents' lounge, a guest suite for visitors and a laundry room. These are however not sheltered housing schemes and the flats in Canterbury sell for prices starting from £60 000.

this had risen to 15% by 1993. The number of people aged over 85 has increased from 0.5 million in 1981 to 0.9 million in 1991. Whilst it is true that there has been a significant growth in the development of sheltered accommodation it would be a mistake to suggest that most pensioners either need or want to live apart from the rest of society. Most are healthy, active and independent and can expect to live for as many years in this state as they did as a family. This again has implications for the type of housing that we build. Whilst many pensioners may aspire to live in a modern bungalow a short walk from the shops, most end up living in their old two-storey family home only accessible by car. Over the years this is likely to become less well-suited to their needs, with the large garden, so good for children, becoming a chore to look after and the peace and quiet, once so welcome, becoming the backdrop to fear and loneliness. It is interesting to look at the trends in the US where retirement villages are one of the fastest growing forms of development. As Andres Duany has pointed out[6], so car-dependent has American society become, that it would be possible to starve in a suburban housing estate without a car. This means that it is impossible for people to continue living there when they are no longer able to drive, so that old people are forced to sell their homes and to spend their life savings to move to a retirement community. Similar trends exist in

the UK although not to the same extent. Developers like McCarthy and Stone, who have a very profitable business specialising in housing for the elderly, are increasingly building urban apartment blocks in smaller towns rather than separate retirement communities. Their brochures emphasise not seclusion and privacy but community and access to facilities.

There are other demographic factors which should influence housing. One is disability, since one in four households will have one of their members disabled in their lifetime[7]. Disability is not a need that can be met with a couple of specially adapted units in the corner of an estate, it relates to all new housing. Since one cannot predict which households will be affected, all housing should be designed with the needs of the disabled in mind. This means that if a household member becomes disabled the home should be sufficiently flexible to prevent the family having to move or to undertake expensive conversions. The Joseph Rowntree Foundation's Lifetime Homes standards[8] provides practical guidance including level entry to houses and sufficient internal circulation space for wheelchair access. The units do not look any different from normal homes and are lived in by households who are not disabled. It is possible that these standards will be incorporated into the Building Regulations in the future.

It is also important to consider ethnic minority households which form a significant proportion of urban populations. Eighty per-cent of Afro-Caribbean and Bangladeshi and 68% of Indian households are urban dwellers and their household characteristics can differ markedly from the national average. For example 42% of Afro-Caribbean and 67% of Asian households have children compared to a national average of 30%. The Afro-Caribbean population also has a greater proportion of single people and single parents but significantly less pensioners. The Housing Corporation sought to promote ethnic minority housing associations in the early 1990s, both as a means of empowerment and to ensure that housing better reflected the needs of ethnic groups. A good example is Manningham Housing Association in Bradford which has specialised in producing very large units for extended Asian families.

The mechanisms of demographic change

The reasons behind household change are varied and complex and have become mixed up with political dogma about traditional family values. The evolution of the large nineteenth century household to the small twentieth century family was driven by two parallel trends. For the middle classes the reduction in household size was not so much a matter of falling birth rates but a reduction in servants and other household members. In the mid-1800s even the lowliest middle-class household – say a bank clerk with an income of £200 per year – would employ a servant, whilst a family with £1 000 per year would have three female servants, a coachman and a footman. Given an average household size of three children plus mother and father this would mean an establishment of ten people[9]. A survey of households in York in 1851 showed that middle-class households were on average one person larger than working-

THE WIGAN FOYER

Changing demographic trends are causing new forms of urban housing to emerge in the UK. A good example of this are foyers which are being developed in many British towns and cities.

The concept of foyers has been imported from France where they have existed for many years. French foyers can best be described as a combination of a youth hostel and a student hall of residence and are targeted at young people. They include a café and are a focus for local social services. In the UK the concept has been developed to include a much greater emphasis on training and employment.

One of the best UK foyers is to be found in Wigan, a town which still has a substantial stock of council housing almost all of which are family units. The council has therefore been concerned to target new housing at groups not served by the existing stock, particularly the elderly and the young. The foyer was developed to meet the needs of young people. It provides short-stay accommodation for 42 young people aged between 16 and 25 along with a communal lounge

and a range of resources and facilities to assist them in finding work. The foyer opened in September 1996 as part of a major mixed-use refurbishment of the Coops Building on the edge of the town centre by Grosvenor Housing Association. The building has been developed as a package but is split into three sections: The foyer occupies the left wing, the central section has been converted to 15 000 sq.ft. of managed workspace and the right wing to 11 flats for social letting and 18 for market rent both for single people.

The scheme cost £4.2 million and was financed through a complex cocktail of funding. The foyer also requires ongoing revenue support from a variety of sources. The complexity of the funding package is indicative of the difficulty of developing schemes of this kind. There is very little crossover between public funding for workspace and housing so that schemes which blur the boundaries

between the two are very difficult to fund. This suggests that funding mechanisms need to change in recognition of the need for new kinds of housing development.

class households and the average middle-class household contained 1.15 servants, 0.42 lodgers, 0.41 relatives and 0.21 resident visitors. The reduction in the size of middle-class households stems from the gradual loss of these servants and dependants. This was particularly true after the First World War when the returning troops turned their back on domestic service. This is how the ten-person establishment of the 1850s evolved from its rambling gothic villa to the interwar four bedroom detached house with its domestic labour saving appliances.

At the same time the working-class household was also shrinking. In the 1870s 61% of households had more than five live births and 18% had more than ten. However infant mortality was high; in Nottingham, for example, less than 20% of families had more than four surviving children. Initially medical advances would have increased household size by improving infant mortality. However as time went on families had less need to insure against infant deaths with large families so the number of children fell. These trends were reinforced by an increasing understanding of contraception. As housing conditions gradually improved throughout the last century overcrowding was also reduced. Houses which once accommodated a number of families became home to just one. As access to housing became easier extended families found it less necessary to live under the same roof. Unlike middle-class housing, the trend with the working classes was for house size to grow whilst household size decreased.

Household characteristics therefore changed dramatically at the end of the last century as did the housing built to meet their needs. For different reasons both middle-class and working-class households shrunk, heralding the emergence of the nuclear family. As the middle-class home got smaller and the working-class home improved, both evolved into the semidetached home which has come to so dominate the twentieth century.

The change from the twentieth to the twenty-first century household is likely to be just as dramatic. As we have seen, the nuclear family which dominated provision in the 1920s has become a minority household type in all but the minds of traditional politicians and the housing industry. This does not however herald the disintegration of family life and all that the traditionalists hold dear. Instead it means that people are spending less of their life in child-rearing. The Victorian family may have had their first child in their twenties and continued childbearing into their late thirties. This would put them into their dotage before all of their children left home, with perhaps a few years of retirement before their allotted three score years and ten. The modern family by contrast is having a modest brood of children in their thirties and can confidently expect their offspring to have flown the nest, or at least to be living independent lives, by their early fifties. With modern life expectancies they can expect more than thirty years of life ahead of them and for the first part of this they will be at the height of their earning potential, if, that is, they have kept their job.

Two significant demographic groups have therefore emerged which are yet to be reflected in the housing stock. In the past people would have stayed at home until marriage and then fairly quickly started their own family. Today they are living single, or certainly childless lives in their twenties before settling down and having children in their thirties. These 'swinging singles' or 'urban venturers' in the parlance of the marketing industry are an important and growing market with high levels of disposable income which the housing industry has only just started to recognise. The other group are the parents of these 'swinging singles', what the marketing industry call, 'empty nesters'. This latter group is also being swelled by the growing divorce rate (every divorce creates two households where once there was one) and increasing life expectancy. Add to this the growing number of single parents and the trend of declining household size and rapidly increasing household numbers becomes even stronger.

Future trends

Government projections[10] based on these trends predict a 4.4 million increase in households between 1991 and 2016, an increase of 23%

from 19.2 million to 23.6 million. Some have resorted to questioning the figures but in the historical context they are no more dramatic than past household growth. Indeed rumour is that the next set of forecasts due in autumn 1998 will substantially increase the projections, perhaps, as high as 6 million.

The figures have scared the life out of planning authorities up and (mainly) down the country who fear the march of suburbia across precious green belts. But family housing is not what is wanted. Unfortunately the household projections do not break down household growth by the size or age of the household. Instead they project figures for married couples, cohabiting couples, lone parents, multi-person and single person households. The married couples' category includes people with and without children as well as the elderly. This is why 55% of households are married but less than 20% are couples with children. Despite the scale of household growth these married couples are actually predicted to decline by 2016 from 10.5 million to 9.9 million households. Small increases are projected in other categories; however the increase which over-shadows all of the others is single-person house-holds. These are predicted to rise from 3.5 million to 5.1 million. Single-person households therefore make up more than 80% of the 4.4 million net increase in household numbers.

The numbers of elderly people are also projected to rise from 10.5 million in 1992 to 16 million by 2032 when they will make up just over 23% of the population[11] with the number of people over 85 rising to 1.3 million. As people live longer, and three-generation households decline, the number of single elderly, particularly elderly women, will increase rapidly. The reducing level of state care for the elderly and the dispersal of children in search of work will mean that these people stay in their homes for longer, reducing the stock of housing released back onto the market and placing new demands on the home. Fears for personal security mean that the traditional practice of taking a lodger has largely disappeared, al-though economic necessity coupled with better housing management may lead to a revival.

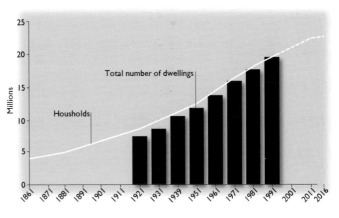

The average household of the twenty-first century will therefore be significantly smaller than its twentieth century grandparents. But will the twenty-first century home be smaller? After all working-class housing last century grew whilst household sizes fell. Alan Holman[12] argues that there is no evidence to suggest that smaller households will opt for flats rather than houses. He points out that elderly widows and widowers tend to remain in their family home. He also suggests that since most single and divorced people are under 60 and 77% of these live in houses (three-fifths of which have more than three bed-rooms) then that is the natural state of things. He rightly suggests that single people are no less affluent than married couples and will therefore exercise their free choice to live in what they can afford, namely a house. But this argument is open to question. While Holman points out that basing house building on housing projection is a self-fulfilling prophecy he fails to recognise that people may not be opting for flats because there are few

Household growth is nothing new: Historic and projected growth in household numbers compared to the total stock of dwell-ings. This shows that projected household growth rates are no different from past rates and that housebuilding has actually outstripped household growth Source: DETR

The nature of household growth: Projected household growth by household type. Source: DETR

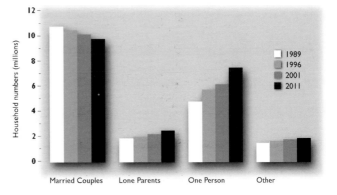

suitable flats available. Implicit in his argument is the idea that flat dwellers are second-class citizens and it is therefore logical that people will opt for a house if they can afford it. This would not however be the case on the continent where flats (or apartments; a word which has altogether different connotations) are perfectly respectable and sought after. The Swiss, for example, expect to live in an apartment, looked after by a landlord whilst they get on with the important matters of life like running a business.

This brings us back to the issue of choice. Many single people and childless couples would probably welcome the benefits of living at higher densities in urban areas near to a range of facilities within an easy walk. Indeed where such housing has been provided, as in Britain's historic towns, it has proved very successful. But at present they are hardly given the choice. We are not suggesting that all childless households would make this choice but it is reasonable to assume that a proportion would, maybe a significant proportion. In doing this they would not be sacrificing their living standards to live in a flat as Holman suggests but living in lively urban areas more suited to their needs.

Second class citizens? A number of developers are tapping the market for urban housing for childless households. Urban Splash are developing apartments in areas which would previously not have been considered for housing in Liverpool and Manchester. Their conversion of the former Affleck and Brown Department Store on Oldham Street in Manchester to 80 loft apartments was completed in 1998 and has achieved some of the highest prices ever in the city centre

Re-instated four storey atriums providing natural light to internal elevations

Duplex and triplex Lofts on Oldham/Church Street

New ground floor retail frontages and 1st floor loft balconies

Existing Victorian elevations fully renovated

Changing social and economic trends

As important as demographic change is the influence that social and employment trends will have on future housing. These include the increasing number of women in the workforce, job insecurity, increased leisure time and changes in employment patterns. Just as suburbia developed in response to the nuclear family so it also responded to a particular way of life and set of economic circumstances. As we have seen in previous chapters, suburbia developed with the expansion of the middle classes and the desire to separate the home and work environments. It was based on stable employment to pay the mortgage and an assumption that the family would be a self-sufficient unit with the wife managing the home and the husband bringing in the money.

These assumptions are increasingly open to question. Women are making up an increasing proportion of the workforce, partly because they are having children later in life. Economic activity rates for women aged 25–34 rose by 25% between 1971 and 1993 while activity rates for men declined for all ages but particularly over 55[13]. As a result the proportion of women as a percentage of the workforce rose from 37% in 1971 to 44% in 1993. Indeed because female unemployment rates are lower, women already account for half of all employees. A recent report by the Henley Centre for Economic Forecasting[14] has highlighted some of the potential effects of this groeth in female employment. They suggest that women will be less willing to tolerate a long commute to work or other facilities, particularly if they have to juggle working life with the needs of children. They may therefore be attracted to urban areas but are likely to be very choosy and are only likely to be attracted to urban areas capable of providing a high quality of life.

The nature of employment is also changing. Twenty-five years ago half of all men in the workforce and 30% of women worked in manufacturing or construction. Today this has fallen to just one in three men and 13% of women. At the same time employment in financial and business services has doubled from 13% to 26% of the workforce. This has not however been reflected in better working conditions. For years we have been told to expect greater amounts of leisure time whereas in practice UK males now work an average of 43.3 hours a week, longer than any of their counterparts in Europe. At the same time unemployment remains persistently high. Those with the money to enjoy leisure time are therefore getting less of it while those with time on their hands do not have the resources to enjoy it. This reflects Will Hutton's analysis the 40:30:30 society[15]. The 40% of the population who are in secure employment are working longer hours and being well rewarded for it while 30% are struggling, poorly paid and insecure and 30% are excluded due to unemployment or incapacity.

It is clear that this situation is very different to the economic circumstances that created the suburb. The availability of cheap mortgages fuelled suburban growth whereas insecurity is now undermining the ability of people to make long-term mortgage commitments. Travel to work is also changing. It is argued that the dispersal of employment will reinforce suburban growth[16] but the situation today is very different from fifty years ago when the man as bread winner could commute to a stable job. If two or more household members are working they will either have to live near to public transport or each run a car. If we already work the longest hours in Europe we may increasingly question spending the most valuable hours of the day travelling to and from work by car. It is therefore possible that changing employ-

LIVE/WORK HOUSING

While people still argue over the viability and desirability of mixed-use development a few intrepid developers are taking the concept one step further by mixing uses within units. Live/work units, sometimes called atelier units, are places designed both for living and working behind the same front door.

This is similar to the traditional corner shop although new live/work units owe more to the original New York loft which was a place where people, often artists, both lived and worked. While most UK loft developments have not been designed for working, there is a growth, in London in particular, of live/work loft conversions. Indeed so common have these become in Hackney that the council has adopted supplementary planning guidance on the issue. Live/work units are generally to be found in converted warehousing which is fitted out to shell standard and are available both to rent or buy. The impetus behind their development is not so much a demand to work from home but local planning policy which prevents residential development in designated employment areas. The cheap buildings in these areas are attractive to housing developers yet they can only get planning permission for live/work units. This means everyone is happy, the developers get a residential development and the council is happy that it has attracted employment into the area.

There are however a handful of live/work schemes outside the private sector where the roots of new development form may just be starting to emerge. Here the aim is to combine housing with economic regeneration. Schemes are being planned in Liverpool, Birmingham, Bolton and London.

A good example is the Westferry scheme (below) by the Peabody Trust on the St. Vincent site near Canary Wharf. This is part of a wider development by Peabody and is aimed at promoting local economic development, particularly in the cultural industries. The courtyard scheme will include nine business units on the ground floor below twenty seven live/work units on the three upper floors. The live/work units have a floor area of 800 square feet. They have heating, a shower and a basic kitchen but will otherwise be fitted out by incoming tenants and will be let on standard business leases. It is anticipated that 60% of the floor area will be used for business with 40% used for living.

A common thread to these schemes is that they are targeted at artists. Indeed artists and other individuals working in creative industries are probably the main market for this type of development. They are often young and unable to afford separate premises to live and work. They also work irregular hours and some activities, such as the firing of pottery, require constant attention. As a result many artists work from home and find the bespoke live/work unit more appropriate than the restrictions of the spare bedroom or the kitchen table. They are a good example of innovation in urban development as demographic and economic change creates demand for new types of unit. A comparison with the range of cars now available may suggest that there are other niches to fill.

97

ment patterns will reinforce the benefits of urban living and the attractions of alternative tenures such as private renting.

While it is possible that changing social and employment trends will reduce the attractions of the suburb, it is far less clear what sort of housing they will lead to. Great play is often made of electronic communication and the scope for teleworking from home. The Labour Force Survey shows that there are 3.3 million self-employed people in the UK[17]. Most of these do not however work from home. There are currently only 650 000 people in the UK who work from home – about 2.5% of the workforce – although this rises to 5% in associate professional and technical occupations. Eleven per-cent of employers employ homeworkers, half of whom use new technology[18]. The impact of these trends on housing and cities may however have been overestimated. For desk-based homeworkers the main need is for a telephone line and a space to work away from household distractions. For most people a spare bedroom meets these needs and it is unlikely that it will lead to the emergence of new housing forms. There are however activities which are too noisy or dirty for the spare bedroom or kitchen table. Homeworking also becomes more difficult if a self-employed business grows and needs to employ other people. There is some evidence that the growth of self-employment in areas like the arts is leading to new forms of housing such as live/work units.

Another important trend is the decline of large employers and the growth of small businesses and self-employment. Organisations like the BBC which once carried large workforces now contract out much of their work often to former employees. These self-employed workers and small businesses rely on networks of contacts to get business and to stay in touch with developments. They therefore tend to gravitate to cities where there is a market for their work and a critical mass of similar businesses.

Another potential influence of information technology and flexible working is on the very shape or even existence of cities. When the impact of the Internet became clear there were some who argued that there would no longer be a need for cities. With homeworking, computer shopping and banking, and the availability of information over the World Wide Web people would be freed to live where they wished and their remaining ties with the city could be broken.

While isolated televillages have been developed in the US, the predominant trend has been for telecommunications to actually reinforce the city. Graham and Marvin[19] have pointed out that the top fifteen metropolitan core regions in the US account for just 4.3% of the national population but 20% of Internet use. They argue that more, not less, face-to-face contact is required to interpret and harness the huge amount of information on global networks and to respond to increasingly volatile international markets. More than anything else, the commodity that cities deal in is information. Therefore cities are not only being strengthened by the Internet, they are actually driving its growth. It is also in cities that the infrastructure is being put in place, such as fibre optic and broad band home media networks, which will reinforce the urban dominance of information technology. It is therefore unlikely that teleworking will lead to an urban exodus. Working alone at home increases the need for human contact, even if this is just a walk down to the shops. Indeed teleworking may allow people to benefit from city life while avoiding the frustration of commuting through congested streets.

In this chapter we have reviewed the demographic and social trends which will shape future housing and settlements. These are no less potent than the trends which transformed the city a hundred years ago. It is too early to judge the impact they will have on housing and cities. It is however clear that the choices that people make in the future will not necessarily lead to continued suburbanisation which many commentators assume to be the natural state of things. The question is whether other choices will be available.

HALL · MARKET

The information city: London is booming as global markets and information technology increase the need for the face-to-face contact that only large cities can offer

CHAPTER 7
Community
Social sustainability in the suburb and city

In the last chapter we looked at how people live together as households. In this chapter we cast the net wider to look at how households live together as communities. The word 'community' like 'choice' is a word which has been devalued by overuse. Because community is generally seen as a good thing the word has become a euphemism to disguise unpopular policies, from care in the community to the community charge. In other contexts the word has become little more than a collective noun for human beings as in the black community or the gay community.

Yet when we talk about community in a geographical sense we still have a fairly clear idea of what we mean. Be it the rough-edged urban communities of Coronation Street or East-enders or the rural fraternity of the Archers in Ambridge, community implies a sense of be-longing and pride, a common bond and shared identity, the willingness to help neighbours and support them in times of need, and perhaps also a suspicion of outsiders. Indeed the community is probably the most basic form of human organisation dating back to the earliest hunting groups.

Community is motherhood and apple pie. No one would suggest that it is a bad thing. This is not, of course, to say that everyone wants to live in a community. To paraphrase Oscar Wild; 'a community may be a fine institution but who wants to live in an institution?' Indeed, as we have seen, urban trends over the last hundred or so years have been driven not by the desire of people to live in communities but by a desire for separation. People, while paying lip service to the idea of community, have sought, through the location and design of their home, to reduce contact with others. The basic building block of society has become not the local community but the nuclear family. It therefore seems that there is an increasing divide between our idealised notions of community and how we actually choose to live our lives. It is this tension which has shaped our housing and the way that our towns and cities are organised.

However when we look to the future it may well be that our reliance on the family rather than the community will become less tenable. As we have seen in the last chapter the family is much less common than it once was and will become even less so in the future. As family members disperse in search of education, employment or a partner they may find more need of community as an antidote to loneliness. The single person and elderly households of the twenty-first century may well place more value on community life than did the self-contained nuclear family of the twentieth century. The self-employed home worker, the unemployed and retired – deprived of their workplace community – may look to their home environment for support and social contact. In short we believe the concept of community will be a potent influence on the twenty-first century home. It is therefore important that we understand the nature of communities.

The value of community

The existence of a strong community is often the difference between successful and declining urban areas. It is however less clear whether the existence of a community creates a successful area or whether a community is only able to develop once the area has become successful. Certainly most of the urban areas with severe problems lack any sense of community. Yet estates with a fierce community spirit and pride are not immune to problems whilst other areas without any obvious sense of community do perfectly well.

By all accounts the back-to-backs and courts of the Victorian city fostered strong communities but they are hardly a model for the future. Indeed there is an element in the character of communities which thrives on adversity. This might be a feeling of being 'in this together' or uniting against a common enemy. It is certainly common for tenants' associations to thrive when an area is being ignored only to wither when their demands are accepted and improvements to the area start taking place.

It does however seem that the existence of a sense of community can help an area to avoid problems and can lessen their impact when they do occur. The reason for this is that a community gives people a reason to care for their area through a sense of pride and belonging. This is one of the reasons why the middle classes have less need of community. In owner-occupied areas people have a keen sense of the value of their property and a strong financial incentive to discourage antisocial behaviour which might affect this value. With social rented housing this has never existed and needs to be replaced with other reasons to care. In the past this may have been a sense of affinity or respect for the council landlord and today it can be provided through structures like co-operatives or estate management boards. However the most effective means of engendering pride is the existence of a community.

This works in a number of ways. Communities share a common sense of identity and pride. They also involve peer pressure to control antisocial behaviour and an understanding that community members will support each other. In a strong community people will be more inclined to keep their property in a reasonable state, to pick up litter or at least not to drop it in the first place. They are more likely to make the area their long-term home so creating a stable population. They will support their neighbours in small ways such as holding a spare set of keys or feeding the cat. These may be small things but they are the mortar which binds together urban areas and can make the difference between success and failure.

These elements of community are fundamental to many aspects of urban life not least to the control of crime and social order. In the past a community member challenging antisocial behaviour could do so in the knowledge that they would be backed up by other members of the community. In today's more violent urban environment this may be a little over-idealistic, but perpetrators of antisocial behaviour are likely to feel more vulnerable to challenge in a strong community which is a deterrent in itself. Indeed this is the basis for much of the thinking about 'secure by design' approaches to address crime. Whilst a great deal of attention has been given to surveillance cameras and security guards, the majority of secure by design work depends on surveillance by residents. There is much talk of windows being eyes onto the streets. This however is of no value if the people behind those windows feel no connection with their neighbours and have no incentive to intervene.

To social landlords communities can also bring very real financial benefits. They make areas easier to manage and mean that problems which would once have been reported to the landlord are dealt with locally. It is significant that David Page's 1993 report for the Joseph Rowntree Foundation was called *Building for Communities*[1]. In this he paints a disturbing picture of the problems arising on new housing association estates where communities have not taken root. The reason, Page argues, is that we are building houses, not communities, and are failing to recognise the problems that arise when communities do not develop. Following on from this report the Housing Corporation has adopted the development of 'sustainable communities' as one of its key objectives. Indeed URBED have recently completed a major piece of research for the Housing Corporation[2] in which we explored the components of sustainability in new social housing.

Communities are good for you

Recognising the value of community is one thing, understanding how communities work is quite another. Yet without this understanding attempts to create communities can go hopelessly wrong. This is where the paternalism of public authorities has devalued the concept of community and where academic and professional debate has been dominated by some very muddled thinking.

Why is it that no one ever agonises about the need to build middle-class communities? Is it that middle-class communities are so strong that they do not need professional help or that middle-class areas do not need strong communities to ensure their success? The debate about community over the last fifty or so years has been almost entirely focused on social housing. The reason is that communities have come to be seen as 'good for you' rather than just good. There is just a short step from this to the philosophy that 'our idea of community is good for you'.

Many of the professionals and academics who debate the value of community live in sub-urban areas. In the suburbs what people tend to mean by community is the rich network of voluntary groups such as churches and amateur dramatic societies which thrive in such areas. People may only be on nodding terms with their neighbours but they play an active part in networks of people who share similar interests and values often over quite a wide geographical area. At the same time behaviour is controlled by a milieu of social pressures which ensures that lawns are trimmed and disturbance is minimised.

This is not however the sort of community which has exercised academics and professionals concerned with the inner city and social housing development. Their idea of community has not

SUBURBAN OR URBAN COMMUNITIES?

The debate about what sort of communities we should be creating in urban areas permeates discussions between professionals and local residents as illustrated by the examples of Hallwood Park in Runcorn and, on the following page, the Divis Flats in Belfast and St. Wilfred's in Hulme.

HALLWOOD PARK: RUNCORN

The Southgate Estate in Runcorn will be familiar to anyone who studied housing and planning in the 1970s and 80s. Designed by James Stirling, it attracted tremendous attention with its external servicing, multicoloured cladding and round windows. The scheme, which included 1100 deck-access flats and 255 three-storey town houses, was a development of the system-built schemes of earlier decades. Yet even as students were being shown around, it was clear that it was not working and residents were campaigning for demolition.

The task of redevelopment fell to Merseyside Improved Homes who have developed a scheme of 226 three-and four-bedroom homes plus 16 one-bedroom units and renamed the area Hallwood Park. This is the first part of a two-phase development which has been planned to maintain the community by allowing people to stay on the estate. The new development was subject to extensive consultation. Having lived in an architect's vision the community wanted something much more traditional and low density. The resulting scheme is characterised by traditional semidetached homes (14 different styles) on cul-de-sacs with front and back gardens.

It is too early to say whether the new Hallwood Park will fare better than the old Southgate. The developer is proud that they were able to give the community exactly what they wanted, which was to feel like owner-occupiers which Hallwood Park achieves very effectively.

been the social networks and interest groups that characterise suburban areas. Rather it seems to be some vague notion of conversations over the garden fence, corner shops and being able to leave your front door open while children play on the street. This lies at the heart of the confusion over what we mean by community. We have been seeking to promote a vague and idealised notion of urban community yet we have judged such communities by suburban standards so that we have failed to recognise and value them even where they do exist.

This is perhaps best illustrated by a personal example from Manchester. I (DR) remember walking around the terraced streets of the Great Western Street area of Moss Side with a group of fellow council officers in the mid-1980s on a warm day which could have come from the memoirs of those elderly residents who moan that things were so much better in the old days. Front doors were left open, children were playing in the street, people were chatting on doorsteps, a couple of men were fixing a car propped up on bricks and one particularly blasé dog was snoozing in the middle of the street. The perfect picture of an urban community, one might think. However this was not what my fellow council officers were seeing. What they noticed was the loud music emanating from some of the open doors and the group of youths on the corner who could have been muggers or drug dealers. The children playing amongst the parked cars were in dreadful danger (not to mention the dog!) and should be tidied away into a play area. The car mechanics were an unauthorised use on the public highway. They noticed the overturned bin, the broken glass, the graffiti and could no doubt have found a syringe or two if they had looked hard enough

DIVIS FLATS: BELFAST

The 800 unit Divis Flats estate is one of the most notorious in Belfast and has been redeveloped by the Northern Ireland Housing Executive. As part of this extensive consultation and participation work took place with tenants organised by the Town and County Planning Association. While residents wanted individual homes they opted for a layout of traditional streets and for relatively high densities. This however was not accepted by the authorities and subsequent revisions to the masterplan saw densities reduced from 562 to 366 and eventually to 244 units developed in a suburban layout based on cul-de-sacs.

ST. WILFRED'S: HULME

As part of the development of Hulme in Manchester, North British Housing Association have undertaken the redevelopment of a system-built estate for 215 houses working in close partnership with a traditional local community. The initial scheme involved the creation of three cul-de-sacs with a mixture of semidetached and terraced housing at medium densities. The tenants welcomed the scheme but it was not accepted by the Council who were seeking to promote Hulme as an urban neighbourhood (see Chapter 13).

A series of intensive workshops were therefore undertaken by the Hulme Community Architecture Project to look again at the designs for the scheme. This started by going back to memories of the area that had existed prior to the original redevelopment of the 1960s. Many of the older residents remembered the old terraces and started to develop ideas based on urban rather than suburban ideas of community. As a result they threw out the initial scheme and redesigned the scheme to recreate the traditional streets that many of them remembered.

in the back alleys. In short, what they saw was not a tightknit urban community but a stressed inner city district in need of their help.

This is the way that many professionals view urban communities – through suburban eyes. Most of my fellow council officers commuted in from the leafy suburbs of south Manchester and had a very different idea of community from the people of Moss Side. This is not to say that either idea of community is right or wrong or to suggest that Moss Side's community is perfect. It does however illustrate some of the confusion that muddles the debate about community. The community in many of the older parts of Moss Side has many of the characteristics that professionals and academics have been promoting for years yet when confronted with such a community, warts and all, in a deprived inner city area they either do not recognise it or do not like what they see. Instead they start judging urban areas by suburban standards. This is when attempts to build or engineer communities can go badly wrong.

Different types of community

There are different types of community in suburban and urban areas, something which is rarely discussed except by sociologists[3]. To listen to planners and politicians one could be forgiven for thinking that community is a homogeneous concept and local differences are aberrations. This probably means that different groups have spent years talking the language of community and meaning entirely different things. It is therefore important to explore in more detail different ideas of community. The attachment of people to these very different ideas is one of the forces which shapes human settlements.

The first community ideal, which many people think of when visualising a community, is the close-knit village of Miss Marple or James Herriot. A place where everyone knows each other and everyone knows their place. It is a community with a natural focus, the church, pub and local shop which brings people together and allows news (perhaps gossip is a better word) to be shared. The community has clearly defined boundaries, both in terms of the people who lay claim to membership and the geographical area covered. As such the community is suspicious of strangers and reluctant to embrace newcomers, as many an émigré from the city has found to their cost. The village community is mixed and includes everyone from the squire to the labourer. This is not, of course, on an equal basis, but as part of a strict hierarchy. The village community is guided by

The ideal urban community? The Moravian Settlement in Ashton. Is this perhaps what we have in mind as the ideal urban community without any rough edges?

105

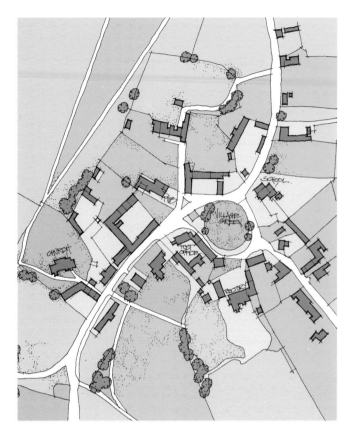

The English village: Home to an idealised vision of the village community

unwritten rules which are as rarely stated as they are transgressed. It is an ordered, civil society where people feel at ease and where a certain image of English life has continued undisturbed for centuries. Whether or not such village communities exist is not the point, the ideal exists in people's imagination and shapes their ideas about the ideal community in which they would like to live.

The other community ideal is almost the complete opposite of this. This is the urban street as described by Jane Jacobs. If the village community is a rock pool the urban community is the shoreline washed by the ebb and flow of the tide. In the *Death and Life of Great American Cities*[4], Jane Jacobs recounts an incident on her own street which serves to illustrate the qualities of an urban community. She describes how she noticed from her window a small girl being dragged against her will along the opposite sidewalk by a suspicious looking man. Before Jacobs could decide whether to intervene she noticed '…from the butcher's shop had emerged the woman who, with her hus-

band, runs the shop; she was standing within earshot of the man, her arms folded with a look of determination on her face. Joe Cornacchia, who with his son-in-law keeps the delicatessen, emerged at about the same time and stood solidly on the other side. Several heads poked out of the tenement windows, one was withdrawn quickly and its owner reappeared a moment later in the doorway behind the man. Two men from the bar next to the butcher came to the doorway and waited, …the locksmith, fruitman and laundry proprietor had all come out of their shops and the scene was also being surveyed from a number of windows besides ours. The man did not know it but he was surrounded.'

This is very different to the village community, although successful urban communities like Greenwich in New York often come to be known as villages. Yet there were probably more people living on Jane Jacobs' short street than in the whole of our ideal village. They did not know each other although most of them did, like Jacobs, know Joe Cornacchia and the other shopkeepers. They also quite clearly felt a responsibility for the street but this did not translate into a hostility towards strangers. Indeed the little girl in the story effectively became a co-opted member of the community with full rights of support and protection for the duration of her short walk down the street with, what turned out to be, her father. The urban community therefore embraces the stranger as someone who enriches it rather than as a threat. Indeed a stranger need only visit the street on an occasional basis to feel part of the community.

Jacobs described how her street changed during the day with the commuters leaving for work in the morning followed by the arrival of the local office workers and the children going to school. Later in the morning mothers with young children and 'bums' tended to dominate followed by the frenetic activity of lunchtime and so on throughout the day. This cycle of activities continues day after day as part of wider weekly and annual cycles so that the constantly changing street scene is accommodated within a regular and unchanging structure.

Jane Jacobs was writing in 1961 and she has been accused[5] of sentimentalising urban life. Some question whether such urban communities exist any more or even whether they ever really existed in the past. This again is not the issue. Like the village ideal, the urban community is an idea which inspires many city dwellers. It seems likely that most people's vision of community is at least partly based on one of these two models. While the same may not be true in continental Europe, in the UK it is the village community which has held sway. Most surveys of house-buyers show that what they aspire to is the rural ideal even if very few actually achieve it. What they do achieve is the suburban community which is, in many respects, a hybrid form of community which is a development of the village in an urban context.

We have already discussed the communities based on networks of interest that thrive in suburban areas. There is however a more local dimension to the suburban community which is more rarely achieved. A good description of such a community is Allen Jacobs' evocation of the street where he once lived in his book *Great Streets*[6]. In this he describes Roslyn Place in Pittsburgh, a short tree-lined cul-de-sac of eighteen detached and semidetached houses: 'in a small space there are eighteen doors that people walk into and out of so people pass each other and each knows where the other lives… Recognition, discussion, communication, community are encouraged by the nature of the street. On a Saturday morning in Spring, Izzy Cohen, chemist, is screaming at the retired butcher who parked last night where Izzy usually parks… later more intimate discussions of what went on and why will take place in small knots of two or three neighbours. Surely Izzy will want to explain to each group what happened. The butcher doesn't speak. He is a quiet man.

The village in the city: Successful urban communities like Moseley in Birmingham often come to be known as villages. Indeed many, like Moseley, were originally villages which have been absorbed into an expanding city

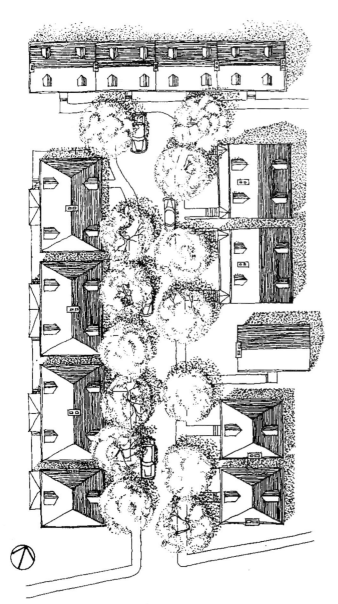

The suburban community: Roslyn Place in Pittsburgh, the street described by Allen Jacobs

is much more like the village. Everyone knows each other and strangers are not welcomed. There is no sense in the description of the wider urban area, which one feels is probably part of the attraction. However unlike the village this suburban community is not mixed. Its strength is social homogeneity rather than variety. It works, not because it can accommodate different lifestyles but because its residents share similar values.

However not all suburban environments are as supportive as Roslyn Place. Few manage so skilfully to balance the desire for privacy with the need for contact. Indeed as Allen Jacobs points out, a host of regulations would prevent Roslyn Place from being built today. Much suburban development takes place on a far greater scale. David Popenoe in his book the *Suburban Environment*[7] looks at Levittown, a private suburban estate of 17 300 single-family homes on 5 750 acres of land near Philadelphia. Levittown is divided into neighbourhoods which contain not eighteen but 430 homes, each on its own plot. As Popenoe summarises: 'In the early years of Levittown the teenager, the elderly person, the widow or divorced female… the working class women living in tight financial straits and cutoff from relatives were unfamiliar figures. Today they have become common and the environment is not as congruent with them as it was with their predecessors. For adults in anything but a fully functioning, economically secure family system, Levittown may be an invitation to trouble'. This, again is an extreme example, but it illustrates that the development of mass suburbia has done little to foster the sort of communities described in this chapter. Such environments have been created for the nuclear family and are increasingly inappropriate for the demographic groups who are likely to dominate the twenty-first century.

Here are three very different views of community – the village, the urban street and the suburban hybrid. Each may be rarer than we would like to think but undoubtedly provide valuable models. Each can deliver the benefits that flow from a strong community but will only thrive in a particular context. Indeed none of the models transplant well from one situation to

Solitude, if you want it, is also possible… people will sweep a walk, others will garden, people will come and go. Maybe a date will be made for coffee later or for a dessert after dinner'. This is also an idealised vision and is not typical of most suburban areas. As Allen Jacobs points out the street has no off-street parking so that houses are closer together with uninterrupted sidewalks and the parking of cars provides an endless topic of discussion for Izzy and his neighbours. Whilst the description of street life has overtones of Jane Jacobs, the community that Allen Jacobs describes

another. The rural village may be a model that many people aspire to but translated, as it was, into the tight courtyard council house developments of the 1970s it was always destined to fail.

It is however the suburban model of community which has been most consistently misapplied. It is this type of community, at least as described by Allen Jacobs, that many professionals have been striving to achieve for decades. For ourselves we may strive for the village or urban communities but when planning communities for others it has generally been the tightknit, homogeneous community that we have had in mind. It is however far from clear whether such communities can be created, particularly on a large

scale. It is also questionable whether such communities will thrive if the only thing that people have in common is the fact that they are disadvantaged, which is often the case on new housing association estates.

However if, as we have suggested, environmental and demographic trends are pointing towards a more urban society in the future, the question is whether the suburban community can be transplanted to urban areas. This has been done by people like the Old Eldonians Housing Cooperative in Liverpool. However generally this type of suburban community is not tolerant of the strangers which are inevitable in cities. This can make them vulnerable to crime and antisocial

BENTILEE: STOKE-ON-TRENT

The Bentilee Estate on the outskirts of Stoke-on-Trent is an interesting example of the application of a community ideal. Bentilee is a council estate of some 5 000 properties which was developed in the garden city style in the 1950s. Over the years the estate has acquired a poor reputation and has struggled to achieve a community identity because of its scale and isolated location. In 1996 the opportunity arose to improve the estate through the government's Single Regeneration Budget. The concept behind the scheme was the transformation of the estate into a series of villages and the programme was called the Villages Initiative.

URBED recently carried out a study to explore the transformation of the estate into a series of eight village centres. By studying the history of the area and building upon local nodes such as shopping parades, pubs and schools, a series of village centres were identified. These were reinforced by creating community halls, and introdu-cing new housing development to create a sense of

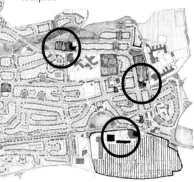

Illustration by Levitt Bernstein Associates. The circles indicate proposed village centres with the larger centre being the existing shopping centre. The hatched areas indicate sites for new housing development

enclosure and increased density. It had originally been suggested that the key to creating village identities was the selective demolition of properties to create open space between each village. However the study concluded that this would not work and was in any case based on a model of a village community which was not appropriate for the area. Rather than a rural village a concept was developed based on the villages which exist in urban areas. These are defined by their centre rather than their edge and tend to merge into the surrounding urban

areas. The idea in Bentilee was therefore to create a series of village centres and to allow the population to gravitate towards whichever village centre they preferred.

In Bentilee these ideas were subject to extensive consultation with local people. It was clear from this that not everyone viewed the idea of a village community as a positive thing. Indeed young people saw it as somewhere where people stuck their noses into your business and stifled individuality. However the word village still held a strong appeal, particularly to the older members of the community, and the proposals received widespread support.

behaviour which in turn creates pressure for overt security measures. Indeed a third of all new housing development in the US is taking place in 'gated developments'[8] separated from the rest of the world by fences, gates and security guards. Is this what we must resort to if we are to preserve the suburban community in the city?

In the twenty-first century people's ideas about the ideal community, both for themselves and others, will continue to shape the city. However we must recognise that different types of community only thrive in the right context. The village and suburban communities are attractive ideals to which many people aspire. These aspirations will continue to drive suburbanisation as people seek to achieve their ideal of community. These ideals should not however drive urban planning. The village or suburban community transplanted to the city simply will not work. If we are to make cities more popular we need to develop new models of urban communities to complement the suburban communities which will continue to serve large sections of society. Jane Jacobs' description of urban community life may already have been dying out in the early 1960s when she was writing. However it is still a vision which is attractive to a large section of society. These people are not the majority but demographic change suggests that they are growing. If urban areas are to be revitalised it will be by tapping these very urban ideas of community rather than importing inappropriate models from the suburbs.

It is likely that the notion of community will be an increasingly important influence on the twenty-first century home. This will however require a rethink of our preconceptions about the 'good community' and the development of concepts of community more suited to non-family households and urban living.

CHAPTER 8
Cost
The economies of urban development

The final 'C' stands for cost, a factor which has always influenced housing design more as a constraint on innovation than as a respectable goal like green design, consumer choice or community. Great improvements tend to be made in housing design when cost constraints are less strong, as in the 1920s. However when concerns focus on value for money – as has happened in the recent past – fears are raised that standards are falling and innovation is being stifled. It may be simplistic to suggest that spending more money will always produce a better product but we must raise our sights above the penny-pinching battles which have characterised late twentieth century housing. In doing this it would be reckless to ignore the issue of cost.

Innovation and cost

The transformation in housing design which took place at the beginning of the century shows the impact that innovation can have on cost. While Ebenezer Howard devoted large parts of his writings to the economic structures of the garden city, his object was not to show that it could be built as cheaply as the terraced housing which made up the majority of development at that time. When the garden city ideas were first put into practice on a large scale in the council housing of the 1920s the costs increased four-fold over what had been produced before the First World War. The result so alarmed the Conservative government of the time that council house building was

stopped. When it resumed in the mid 1920s efforts were made to reduce costs. However, having seen the future and liking it, councils, their architects and their tenants were not going to go back to prewar standards. Thus a great leap forward in housing standards and a great burst of innovation was accompanied by a huge increase in costs. The new standards also had a profound influence on private production and, whilst private developers undoubtedly built cheaper than councils, they had to match the new public sector standards and therefore also saw a substantial increase in their costs.

Finance is unlikely to be so readily available in the future despite pressures from those who argue for higher standards. Indeed the Latham Report[1] has argued that construction costs should be reduced by 30%. While this is largely based on reform of the construction industry it holds out little prospect of resources being made available to increase standards. Yet there are dangers in pushing through higher standards without increasing costs. The Parker Morris standards which were mandatory for a time in the 1960s are estimated to have increased construction costs by up to fifteen per-cent, yet without an increase in overall budgets the result was that savings were made elsewhere through high-rise and system-built construction and lower labour costs. In real terms, the amount spent on new housing today is less than was spent in the 1960s and one could despair at the potential for improvement and innovation in such a climate. What choice have we but to continue building the cramped brick boxes that are the 1990s equivalent of the system-built flat?

Continental approaches to cost

The prospects of improvement seem even more remote when we look to the continent, as we so often do, for inspiration. In the 1980s German construction costs (excluding land and external works) were £1 200–£1 500 per square metre, whereas the equivalent figure in the UK was just £450–£600 per square metre[2]. What is more the average floor area of German housing is some 50% greater than the UK average. The result is that the Germans spend up to four times more on the construction of their housing than we do in the UK and the Germans are by no means unique. If anything the Swiss spend more on their housing

Continental approaches: Social housing by Herman Hertzberger at Lindenstrasse in Berlin, designed with high levels of resident involvement

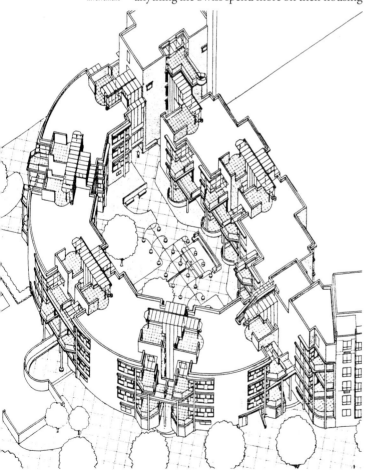

although it is significant that most of this, even at the top of the market, is for rent rather than sale.

Since the 1980s the gap between UK and continental construction costs has widened as a result of a steady downward pressure on UK housing costs. It is true that part of the greater costs in Europe can be accounted for by higher labour and materials costs as well as exchange rates. This does not however explain the whole difference, which is the result of a radical difference in UK and continental views of housing as a long-term investment.

The German people view home ownership very differently from the British. The UK approach has been to struggle onto the first rung of the housing ladder at the earliest opportunity and to rely on rising values to trade up to the house of your dreams later in life. People will therefore put up with a cramped, substandard house in their twenties in the hope that it is only a staging post to something better. In Germany, by contrast, a house is an investment made much later in life with the intention that you will live there for a long time and pass it on to your children. People therefore make do with rented accommodation in their twenties or even live with their parents until they have accumulated sufficient capital to invest in a substantial home.

These attitudes also influence German social housing developers who see private housing as a benchmark, as happened in Britain in the 1920s. In Germany social housing is built to last with a view to maintainability, running costs and long-term value. In the UK, by contrast, the attitude is that if the private sector can produce a perfectly saleable starter home for £40 000, why should social providers spend more? As Valerie Karn describes in her report for the Joseph Rowntree Housing Standards Committee[3] this means that housing designed by private developers as the first rung on the housing ladder is being filled to capacity by housing associations with families who have no realistic capacity of moving on as their needs change. In a depressed housing market the same fate can befall owner-occupiers as negative equity denies them the ability to 'ladder up' to something more suited to their needs.

Market constraints

Some commentators[4] have argued that the UK housing market is becoming more like the continent as people buy for 'nesting not investing'. However there is little sign that this is influencing the housing that is built. The reason for this is the workings of the housing market. Defenders of the volume-housebuilding industry argue that the market is only providing what the customer demands. Housing is produced at a cost which allows it to be sold at a profit and the market regulates the balance between the quality of the product and the price. However the housing market is imperfect and does not always make it possible for needs to be met. If this is not heresy, we would also argue that the buyer does not always know best because of the narrow way in which UK housing is valued.

As the joke goes in estate agent circles, the three most important factors in property value are location, location and location. Not the quality of construction, the energy-efficiency or the floor area, not even the attractiveness of the design – all come a poor second to location. This is clearly very significant if we are to attract people back into urban areas because the locations to which estate agents attach the highest values, parts of London excepted, are not urban. It could be argued that this simply reflects where people want to live. However the workings of the market can work to inhibit these preferences. If housing in urban areas costs as much to build as housing in the suburbs, yet can only be sold for half of the price it would, at present, be economically foolhardy to develop or buy unless the price is substantially discounted by subsidy (as indeed is the case with much private urban housing). If more people choose to buy housing in urban areas, the value of urban housing will increase. However at present if they choose urban housing they risk buying a low-value product and one which is likely to give poorer returns on their investment than the suburban alternative.

The flip side of this coin is that the greatest value is attached to housing in locations where green belt policy means that development sites are scarce. This has the effect of artificially increasing land prices so that while we may not spend as much on housing construction as the Germans we make up the difference in the price that we pay for land. As Colin Ward described in a recent column in 1945 land prices accounted for 5% of the cost of housing. By the 1960s this had risen to 40% and in parts of the south-east today it is as high as 65%[5]. This means that the UK housebuilding industry tends to make its profits not from building housing but from trading in land and they have a strong vested interest in keeping things this way. The success of private housebuilders depends on their ability to buy land at the right price. This they do through 'land banks' which are built up when prices are low and then developed when the market rises. Given the importance of land to developers it is not surprising that they are reluctant to trade in the damaged product that they consider most urban brownfield land to be.

There are other inconsistencies in the market. While surveys[6] may show that people consider energy efficiency as an important consideration when buying a house, the reality is that it plays far less of a role than the quality of the kitchen or 'kerb appeal'. This may be because buyers and tenants are not being given enough information about savings on running costs. However even where they are given this information, for example through a National Home Energy Rating, it does not play a major part in their decision. The real reason is that energy efficiency is not reflected in the value of the house unlike the fitted kitchen. This means that they are faced with paying more for a better insulated home which is worth no more than a poorly insulated home. Indeed houses built in Milton Keynes, which were so energy efficient that they did not need central heating could not be sold[7]. The estate agent could not tick the central heating box on the valuation form so that the houses were valued as 'unimproved'. It is true that energy efficient homes cost less to run but buyers rarely make the link between purchase costs and running costs. This is partly because, unlike fridges, washing machines or cars few houses are sold with details of their energy consumption.

The same is true of floor areas, which may explain why German and indeed American housing is 50% larger than in the UK. In Germany and America housing is valued by floor area and everyone can tell you the square metreage of their home. In the UK by contrast housing is valued by the spurious measure of the number of bedrooms. So for example a seventy square metre house will have a greater value if it has three bedrooms than it would with two. No matter that the storage cupboard masquerading as the third bedroom can accommodate nothing other than a single bed, it gets a tick on the valuer's chart and puts the proud homeowners a notch above their two-bedroom neighbours. Another example from that great laboratory of housing design, Milton Keynes, serves to make the point. Here a private builder developed a number of 200 square metre two-bedroom houses intended for affluent couples whose children had left home. Again these units caused headaches for the valuers since as two-bedroom units they should have been starter homes yet clearly they could not be valued as such.

It would be easy to blame the house-buyer for these market inconsistencies, but that would be to miss the point. In the UK housing is viewed both as shelter and as an investment. With an investment it is safety, not innovation, that counts. For something to be a good investment, you must be sure that other people will accept its value. The further that you move away from the market norm the more you run the risk that this will not be the case. An example of this is the rule of thumb that an architect-designed home is worth ten per-cent less than an equivalent house of standard design. People buying a home therefore face a dilemma if their idea of the ideal home is different to that of the market. Do they maximise the return on their investment or go for the home that they want? The same is true of private builders who need to be sure that what they built will sell quickly and for a good price. It is, of course, possible for market norms to change. The people who bought the early city centre apartments in cities like Manchester were buying a product which the market regarded as low value but the market has changed and they have been handsomely rewarded.

However the safest investment in UK housing remains the suburban semi; it may not suit your needs or even your aspirations but at least you know that when you come to sell it will have increased its value. The UK housing market is therefore inherently conservative in both what and where it builds. We pay too much for building plots while the valuation formula leads us to cut costs on construction. By providing features such as the maximum number of bedrooms, the fitted kitchen and the mock Tudorbethan exterior the development industry is still able to achieve a good price for producing a product which is by any international comparison substandard. This will remain the case while the housebuilding industry is insulated from international competition by the localised nature of the housing market. However, like the car industry in the 1960s, if international housebuilders do manage to establish a UK base – as a number of Japanese and Scandinavia firms are trying to do – the UK industry may find itself very vulnerable to competition.

Cost constraints in social housing

The situation in the social housing sector has many parallels as social housing providers produce housing which is almost indistinguishable from low-cost homes for sale. This is partly because, as one participant at an RIBA Focus Group said of social housing tenants: 'They want Brooksides… ask your average council tenant what they want and you will discover that they want to live in a house that makes them look like an owner occupier'[8]. However, despite the community architecture movement, it is not often that social housing tenants are asked what they want other than the right to refuse a limited number of offers. The real reason why housing associations are lowering their sights to those of the starter home is once again cost. With social housing costs are set not by the market but by a government appointed body, the Housing Corporation. This operates a system of cost yardsticks called Total Cost Indicators which vary by housetype and region and are adjusted annually in line with scheme out-turn costs. In the 1980s these yardsticks lagged behind spiralling tender prices and were very difficult for developers to meet. In the more competitive tender climate of the 1990s the yardsticks have been relatively easy to achieve.

However a downward pressure on costs continues to be applied not through cost yardsticks but by the desire to reduce grant requirements in a competitive bidding market. The most successful and efficient housing associations have come to be seen as those who can develop with the least public subsidy or rather those who can provide the most housing with the subsidy available.

In many respects the desire to produce the maximum number of units with the grant available is understandable given the acute shortage of social housing. With huge housing pressures and limited resources, it must be right, so the argument goes, to build three houses with the money which once built two as one London housing association recently boasted[9]. Yet it is this shortage of social housing that removes any choice from social housing tenants. If you are offered a new house after being stuck in a bed and breakfast hostel you are not going to quibble about details like the quality of your home. However as the years pass and your family grows, you will notice the lack of space, the heating bills, the dearth of local facilities and the bus which never comes. By that time, unless you are lucky enough to afford to buy somewhere, you will be stuck.

Housing associations hotly contest this. They point to the flagship projects in their annual report where tenants were involved in design and quality was a priority. Yet for every flagship estate there are maybe four or five estates built in peripheral locations in consortium deals with private developers using their standard housetypes[10]. Indeed on a site visit organised as part of the Joseph Rowntree Foundation's Housing Standards Committee the director of a medium-sized housing association was shocked to discover the poor quality of housing being built on some of their less high profile new estates. Here cost, or what it is euphemistically called 'value for money', is the name of the game. The problems which this is storing up for the future are increasingly being recognised but there is as yet no indication of the money available for new social housing being increased.

The Housing Corporation have however published URBED's sustainability checklist[11] with the aim of avoiding the problems that have affected some recent social housing developments. This will be used to assess all new social housing and discourage large developments in peripheral locations. It may therefore be that to ameliorate the potential problems of new social housing at a time when costs are not going to rise, more emphasis will be placed on building within existing communities and urban areas.

The future influence of cost

In both the private and social housing fields there are therefore powerful forces at play which reinforce both suburban designs and suburban locations as well as exerting a corrosive effect on quality and stifling innovation. While there are signs that things may be changing these forces must currently be seen as a major constraint on the promotion of more urban housing. But what of the future?

We could argue that the pressures for change described in the last three chapters will cause us to reassess what we spend on housing in the future and invest much more. In doing this we would be in good company but would probably not be being realistic. The trends in consumer spending and public finance suggest that the investment available for future housing will not be much more than that which is spent today. Indeed increasing household numbers may mean that we will need to produce more housing than we are currently doing within current budgets. As with Parker Morris, any increase in standards will therefore have to be paid for with savings elsewhere.

This however may not be as unrealistic as it seems. As we have suggested, a large part of the costs of new housing in the UK lie not in construction but in land costs. This is confirmed by government research on housing costs[12] which has shown that as little as 30% of the costs of a typical new house are in construction. This is eclipsed by land costs at 35%, whilst developers' overheads are 19.7% and infrastructure is 12.8%. This suggests that cutting corners on construction is a false economy since it has only a minor impact on overall costs. The reverse, of course, is also true

and better specifications need not hugely increase total costs. This is where the real influence of cost on the twenty-first century home lies, not on what it will or will not allow us to build, but rather on where and how we build housing.

Where we build

The peculiarities of the UK land market are a significant influence on the location and cost of new homes. The curve of land prices in UK cities follows a very different track to continental cities. On the continent high values in central areas fall off in a gradual but relatively flat curve to the periphery. In the UK, by contrast, high values in the centre fall rapidly in the inner city before rising into the suburbs to a peak on the periphery. This is became the aspiration in the UK has been to live as far away as possible from the centre of the city. However the tendency to dispersal has been partly checked by green belt policy so that land is scarcest on the desirable periphery which relates not just to housing but to commercial and retail development.

Whilst accepting that the continental model may be changing with the advent of affluent suburbs and out-of-town development, the tradition has been very different. Here the centre is most desirable and hence is where the land values are highest. The difference is that the highest continental land values created by scarcity in central areas have naturally led to higher densities and urban development. If land is expensive it makes sense to build more intensively on small plots leading to higher buildings, a mix of uses and a greater use of apartments. Such forms are, of course, historically more acceptable on the continent. In the UK, by contrast and rather perversely, higher land values have combined with suburban aspirations for low densities, which is why land costs on new housing are so high.

In addition to this, peripheral locations may be poorly served by infrastructure. On green field sites developers have to put in the roads, sewers, street lighting, cabling etc. They may have to pay to increase the capacity of the local sewage works or water pumping station and may even, through planning gain, be asked to build or extend a primary school. To make such investment worthwhile there is a tendency to look for economies of scale by building ever larger estates.

This suggests that there may be real cost savings (as well as environmental benefits) to be made by building within existing settlements. Here the land is cheaper, roads and other infrastructure already exist, there is spare capacity in schools, as well as in services like water and sewage. This was an argument that we sought to test through our *21st Century Homes* research through a series of demonstration projects, although the results were inconclusive[13]. Certainly the land costs for the urban demonstration pro-jects that we developed were low and some infra-structural savings were possible. However poor ground conditions caused by back-filled base-ments cancelled out some of these savings and in other areas contamination may also be a problem. Much of the urban infrastructure is also in need of renewal, particularly on redeveloped council estates. Indeed on larger brownfield sites the need to provide infrastructure may be almost as great as on green fields. It is possible that smaller scale infill development would overcome the problems of infrastructural costs, although here developers would not be able to achieve economies of scale and lack of space may increase site costs.

However the real constraint on urban, as opposed to peripheral, development is that even if the costs are lower savings cannot be put into improved housing because the value of the housing is also lower. Yet when land needs to be found for 4.4 million homes, urban infill is likely to be a more cost-effective, sustainable and politically acceptable solution than abandoning green belt policy. It is therefore important to stimulate urban housing markets by subsidising costs such as land contamination. Over time this would increase urban housing values so making it more financially attractive to developers. While subsidy may be politically unattractive it should be recognised that peripheral development is already subsidised by road building and other public services and it is in our best interests to make better use of what we already have in existing towns and cities.

How we build

The other area in which cost will exert its influence is in the way that housing is built. There has been a common misconception in the past that housing is architecture so that has to be procured in the same way as one would a concert hall or an office building. Architects have been appointed along with engineers, quantity surveyors and service engineers and they have worked their creative magic to produce a design which meets the clients' needs, fits the location and, hopefully, enhances our quality of life. There is no doubt that this system can produce fine housing developments (although it can also produce disasters). However it cannot be a cost-effective way of building what is our most common form of building in the UK. Indeed it is a bit like a car manufacturer commissioning a team to design each run of fifty cars coming off the production line.

Because architecture is a creative profession it somehow does not feel right for architects to reproduce the same designs for each new scheme they undertake. The tendency is therefore for the wheel to be reinvented on every site with all the attendant fee expenditure that this entails. Indeed even when housing is not built this way the fee scales assume that it is and the job is priced accordingly. The system by which fees are linked to construction costs also means that consultants' fees rise the more the scheme costs. Increases in specification are therefore reflected in higher fees regardless of whether they incur extra consultants' time. This is partly addressed by systems such as Design and Build construction where the contractor takes responsibility for either all or part of the design. However it is only a partial solution because, whilst insulating the developer from the risk of rising costs, it puts design decisions in the hands of the contractor who does not have a long-term interest in the quality or value of the housing.

Of course not all housing is built by this traditional route. Whilst it may be the way that many of the schemes that we read about in the architectural press were developed it is not how the majority of our housing is procured. Pressures on cost in the public sector meant that most council housing was produced using standard housetypes, a system which dates back to the standard designs in the *Local Government Manual* of 1920. In Manchester low-rise housing estates can be dated by the design of their houses from the earliest 'H1' to the 'H6' which were the last council houses built in the city. When councils were not using standard housetypes they were using building systems, often imported from the continent for the high-rise and particularly the deck-access property of the 1960s and 70s. Then as now, the architect-designed estate was something of a novelty and was confined to flagship developments like the Crescents in Manchester, Hyde Park in Sheffield or the last great council estate, Byker in Newcastle.

The same is true of private production where the architect-designed estate is a rarity. Here the standard housetype has dominated, albeit with names which are more appealing than the strict numbering system used in places like Manchester. The private sector has also been more skilful in disguising standard types with exterior decoration which can introduce endless variation into an estate of houses which are basically the same.

Historically there have therefore been two solutions to the problem of maintaining standards

whilst reducing costs, standard pattern books and the use of prefabricated systems. Both are still relevant and have an important role to play in the building of the twenty-first century home. Standardisation can reduce design time and therefore fees, whilst increasing cost predictability and allowing the mass-production of components. Likewise prefabrication reduces design fees, allows mass-production under orderly factory conditions and can cut construction times with associated savings in interest charges and site costs. However standard types and prefabrication encounter resistance. Pattern books are seen as leading to monotonous repetition and to a stifling of innovation. Prefabrication by contrast is seen as unreliable and is tainted both by the memory of system-building and the timber frame scandals of the early 1980s.

These objections relate not to the principles involved but to the application of the techniques in the past. There has been a great deal of resistance in the social housing world to the use of pattern books. In Wales, for example, Tai Cymru (the Welsh equivalent of the English Housing Corporation) has introduced a mandatory pattern book of sixteen designs which are to be used for

Model plans:
A series of standard housetypes designed for Noel Park in London in 1833. In the nineteenth century pattern books were common, perhaps the most influencial being Banister Fletcher's *Model Houses for the Industrial Classes*, 1871

The Artizans Labourers' & General Dwellings Estate
at HORNSEY

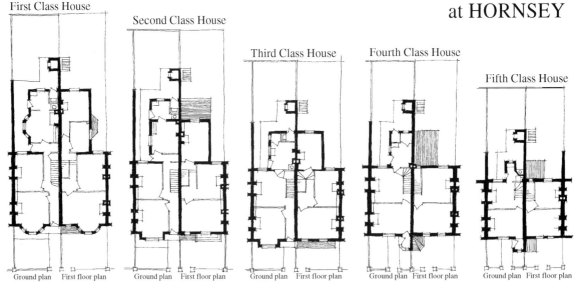

First Class House   Second Class House   Third Class House   Fourth Class House   Fifth Class House

Ground plan   First floor plan   Ground plan   First floor plan   Ground plan   First floor plan   Ground plan   First floor plan   Ground plan   First floor plan

all new housing which they fund[14]. This has led to considerable resistance from associations wishing to innovate or fearing that they will be unable to respond to local circumstances or to tenant concerns. They also fear that they will be unable to build on tight sites in urban locations where the standard types do not fit. Yet Tai Cymru argue that the standard types meet their standards, have proved popular, and can be built within budget. The problem is that the pallet offered by sixteen standard types is very limited. Compare this to Bellway Homes, a developer which has prospered through the housing slump of the early 1990s. They have over a hundred standard types which vary from region to region and for different locations. Bellway's range includes three storey town houses and flats which can be used to close the corners of urban sites and has sufficient breadth to be able to respond to a wide range of needs, markets and locations. Their pattern book is also dynamic – where a site throws up interesting new designs they can be added to the range and used elsewhere while designs which develop problems or which do not sell can be dropped. The problem with the pattern book is therefore not so much with the principle but with the tired, limited range of designs that so many pattern books contain. If it is treated as a positive tool standard housetypes could have an important role to play in reducing costs and allowing the dissemination of good practice without the need to constantly reinvent the wheel. This, after all, is how most houses used to be built. In Georgian and Victorian times only the very grandest houses would have been designed by an architect. Most were developed speculatively by small developers who would get the floor plans and elevations from pattern books which they would buy. This was particularly true in urban areas where terraces allowed for the repetition of elements and continuous elevations.

Potential cost savings also lie in the even more unpopular standardisation of construction. This goes to the heart of our construction industry which continues to build in much the same way that it has done for the last 200 years. Houses are still built laboriously brick upon brick by skilled labourers often standing in six inches of mud or

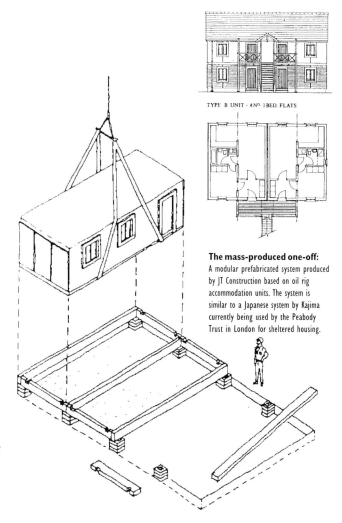

TYPE B UNIT - 4 Nº 1 BED. FLATS

The mass-produced one-off:
A modular prefabricated system produced by JT Construction based on oil rig accommodation units. The system is similar to a Japanese system by Kajima currently being used by the Peabody Trust in London for sheltered housing.

freezing in a biting wind. This cannot be the best or most cost-effective way of building what is a very sophisticated and valuable product. This was pointed out by Michael Ball in his report *Housing and Construction: A troubled relationship* for the Joseph Rowntree Foundation[15].

Jane Jacobs in the *Economy of Cities*[16] identified three stages of development for manufacturing industry: craft production, mass production and differentiated production. She pointed out in the 1960s that the construction industry was only just emerging from craft production more than a hundred years after most industries. Yet its attempts at mass production were, on the whole, disastrous and it has since reverted back to craft techniques. The future is

119

however with differentiated production where a product can be produced with endless variations whilst still retaining economies of construction. This must be the future for the housing industry which is so ill-suited to mass production.

An example of what this might mean can be seen in Japan[17] where the greatest advances in prefabrication have been made. The Japanese housebuilding industry constructs eight times as many new homes a year we do in Britain, for a population only twice as large, and the largest developer, Seki Sui Heim, produces 70 000 units a year, more than 10 times the largest UK housebuilder. They do this using computer-aided design and computerised manufacture to customise each unit to the resident's requirements. Purchasers can choose a house style from a catalogue or exhibition and then adapt it to suit their own requirements. Japanese companies began research into increased industrialisation of housing production in the 1950s in response to oil price rises, the threat of earthquakes, skills shortages and the need to replace low-quality housing. Heavy investment has been made in marketing and production facilities made possible by the involvement of large companies such as Toyota. A house frame can be erected in as little as 3 hours and from order to completion, design and construction times have been reduced to just 50 days. Companies are able to achieve economies of scale through mass-production of some elements while tailoring the product to the varied needs of their customers. The trend has been to move away from timber frame in favour of steel frame construction. This is more reliable in terms of quality. The systems also include pre-made modules such as bathrooms, kitchens and exercise rooms which can be added on to the house or used for extensions at a later date. Such prefabricated systems are by no means confined to the Japanese. They are widely used in

THE MILLENNIUM VILLAGE: GREENWICH

One of the most significant prefabricated housing schemes in the UK is likely to be the Millennium Village in Greenwich. The winning design by Ralph Erskine proposes the use of a new prefabricated system based on a steel frame. This is then to be clad with factory-made timber panels to which glazing and external finishes can be attached. The system uses timber intermediate floors up to eight storeys with concrete floors for higher buildings. Bathrooms and kitchens are to be factory-made timber pods fully fitted and ready for attaching to services.

The system is being designed specially for the project and is targeted to reduce construction times by 5% in year one, rising to 25% over the three years as well as reducing total costs by 15% in the first year and up to 30% over the life of the project. It is also projected to eliminate defects by year three and to reduce accidents from eight per thousand

employees to two. The project literature suggests that 'by designing a new panel-based, cost-effective system for housing, the project will achieve a global lead for the UK which can be exploited beyond the year 2000'. The Millennium Village is likely to be the most important opportunity to demonstrate and sell the benefits of prefabrication in the near future.

Scandinavia, Canada, the US and Europe.

Prefabrication need not need to be based on steel or timber. In much of continental Europe concrete systems have been used. In Holland, for example systems are used based on a prefabricated concrete structural shell. External cavity walls are also factory-made to include insulation, doors and windows and factory-made timber roofs arrive on site ready for craning into place and tiling. These European concrete systems have developed hugely since they were last used in the UK in the system-built housing of the 1960s. They are now used to create housing which is as individual and flexible as anything produced in the UK.

Is this the future for the British twenty-first century home? Much of the work on prefabricated housing has been based on individual homes but prefabricated systems are now widely used for flats and high-density developments in urban areas in Japan. However it may well be that the British, brought up on the three little pigs, are committed to the brick -built house which will not blow down however hard the wolf huffs and puffs. In our *21st Century Homes* research we concluded that the prefabrication industry in the UK was a graveyard of good intentions and questioned whether it really had any future in the face of market and industry resistance. However our more recent research also for the Joseph Rowntree Foundation[18] has shown that the situation is changing, not least due to the potential competition to UK housebuilders from foreign competition. An important role may be played by the Millennium Village in Greenwich which is being developed with a prefabricated system and will illustrate the advantages of alternative forms of construction on urban sites.

While the total amount of money available for new housing in the future will not be very different to the budgets available to us today, this does not mean that we must resign ourselves to building the mean houses which characterise so much of our current production. We should instead look to the economics of the land and housing market to reduce plot costs and ensure that quality is recognised in higher values. We should also look to the way that housing is procured to ensure that we are getting the full benefits of efficient volume production without the disbenefits of standardisation and monotony. People want their home to be unique as witnessed by the huge sums that people who have bought their council homes will lavish on stone cladding and external decoration. The challenge of the housing industry in the next century will be to produce what has been called the 'Mass-produced one off'[19] which can economically meet these diverse needs. However the influence of cost on the location of housing is less clear-cut. While environmental pressures and demographic change may be pointing to a return to urban living there remain economic forces preventing this from happening. It is possible that in the future urban sites will become more attractive financially, particularly if urban housing values rise. However in the immediate future incentives are required for many urban housing developments if urban repopulation is to gather momentum. It should however be remembered that the taxpayer has been subsidising peripheral development for years through commuter rail lines, roads and more recently motorways. Massive public investment has opened up land for development and created profits for developers. In this context money spent on urban housing is a good investment because it makes use of existing infrastructure and over time will create a market allowing subsidy to be reduced.

THE SUSTAINABLE URBA

The twenty-first century home is likely to evolve over coming years until it bears little resemblance to the suburban product that we are so used to today. The influences described in Part 2 of this book could lead to a reversal of the centrifugal forces of dispersal. However while pressure for change may be building, the mechanisms to release this pressure do not yet exist, nor is there any clear agreement about what we should be changing to. The principles of suburban development have become institutionalised. They are inherent in the land-use planning system, in detailed planning controls and in our highway standards. They underlie the

'The multifunctional, creative city, which is also the liveable city, is the one that pollutes least'

European Green Paper on the Urban Environment

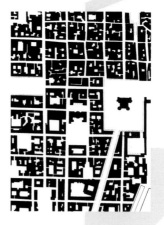

EIGHBOURHOOD

workings of the land market, are reflected in public aspirations and have penetrated the very heart of professional philosophy. These are powerful forces which will inhibit change which might otherwise take place. Furthermore the urban areas to which people might return have been disfigured by years of misguided planning and urban decline. People may initially have fled from the overcrowded industrial city but they now fear to return to cities which they see as ugly, alienating environments, strangled by roads and beset by crime. Today's anti-urban sentiments are a result of what we have done to our cities rather than a rejection of the principle of urban living.

We therefore combine prediction with advocacy. The influences that we have described will only result in people and investors returning to urban areas if urban areas are reformed and are able to provide attractive places to live and work. We will not do this by turning urban areas into counterfeit suburbs or by recycling the outdated Utopias of the twentieth century. What is needed are new models for urban development which can create the successful, humane urban areas required by the twenty-first century to attract people back to towns and cities. Part 3 of this book is devoted to one such model, The Sustainable Urban Neighbourhood.

CHAPTER 9
Urban repopulation

The most fundamental feature of the Sustainable Urban Neighbourhood is its location – the fact that it is located within existing towns and cities. Unlike past urban visions we do not set out a Utopian vision for new settlements free from the complexity and muddle of existing urban areas. Ours is a reforming vision and we propose the Sustainable Urban Neighbourhood as a building block to regenerate urban areas ravaged by decline and post-war planning. However developing a vision for the reform of urban areas is of little value if people do not want to live there, if developers refuse to build there and if businesses are not prepared to locate there. We cannot assume that activity can be attracted back to the urban areas that it has been abandoning for much of this century simply through planning policy or limits on green field development. The location of development may therefore be the most radical element of our vision. This chapter is therefore devoted to the issue of urban repopulation.

Government policy to stem dispersal

Concern to control the dispersal of British cities has been a feature of British planning policy for the last 50 years. The main tool used to do this has been the green belt which has been wrapped around our towns and cities and fiercely guarded from development. In many respects this policy has been very successful in preventing the scale of urban sprawl seen in many US cities. It has not however persuaded people or developers to remain

within cities but has rather led to what has been called 'counter urbanisation'[1]. People with the means to do so have leapfrogged the green belt to live in smaller towns and remote rural areas. Bibby and Shepherd[2] have shown that between 1981 and 1991 for every hectare of land developed on the fringe of urban areas four were developed in villages, hamlets and more remote rural areas. Green belt policy has therefore distorted rather than reversed the trend of urban dispersal and in doing so has inflated land values without benefiting cities. Indeed, it could be argued, that the green belt was designed, not to prevent urban areas from depopulating, but to protect the countryside from a process of urban depopulation which was seen as inevitable and even desirable.

In recent years this view has changed. The initial impetus was to reduce car use as set out in the 1990 *European Green Paper on the Urban Environment*[3] and echoed in *Sustainable Development: The UK Strategy*[4]. However in recent years the debate has shifted largely as a result of the household projections. The prospect of accommodating 4.4 million additional households by 2016 has raised the spectre of the housebuilder running rampant across England's green and pleasant land and has led a coalition of urban and rural interests to lobby for more urban development. To this has been added another, less high profile argument – the regeneration of urban areas. This was put forward by the UK Round Table on Sustainable Development in 1997[5] and, while it may not have been the main focus for the debate, it is, in our view, of key importance. If it is true that urban areas have declined as a result of population loss, urban repopulation must be a prerequisite of their revival.

Each of these arguments has been the subject of considerable controversy. It has been suggested that urban development has little impact on car use, that the loss of green field land is not significant, and that, far from regenerating urban areas, increasing the amount of urban development will lead to 'town cramming' and a decline in the quality of life in towns and cities. We review these arguments later in this chapter. However one of the reasons why these concerns have been so forcibly voiced is the fact that the idea of the compact city has been largely accepted by government.

The government's enthusiasm for urban development took root under the stewardship of John Selwyn-Gummer as Secretary of State for the Environment in the early 1990s. Swayed, no doubt, by the views of voters in the shire counties, the government sought to tighten controls over out-of-town development while promoting higher densities, mixed-use development and encouraging more people and activities back into existing towns and cities. This policy shift was based, in part, on work by David Lock[6] into the most sustainable form of development. He identified five 'classic' ways in which housing growth could be accommodated; urban infill, peripheral expansion, the expansion of selected villages, the expansion of all villages, and new settlements. Each of these was evaluated against a series of economic, social and environmental criteria. The result was not entirely clear-cut. Urban infill and new settlements achieved the highest scores but scored poorly on certain criteria. However he did suggest three levels of sustainability for settlements:

750 – 1 000 houses: Somewhere which would support a primary school but not jobs, public transport or other amenities. Such settlements, he argued, would be heavily car-dependent.

3 000 – 5 000 houses: A place that would support a secondary school and some jobs

---

DICKENS HEATH – SOLIHULL

Since the war, new town planning has been something done by the public sector. However in the early 1990s private developers spurred on by a shortage of sites, have got in on the act. Many private new settlement proposals are hard to distinguish from run of the mill suburban sprawl, and most never manage to chart a course through the planning system. However one which did and is worthy of the title new settlement, is Dickens Heath.

Dickens Heath is a new village being built on 126 acres of green fields near Solihull. The plans include for schools, shops and commercial and recreational facilities along with 850 new homes for sale. It is being built by a consortium including Solihull Council, Laing Homes, and Bryant Homes.

The scheme has been designed by the Barton Willmore Partnership to create a clear identity for the new village with a safe and healthy environment for both residents and pedestrians. The village is planned with a low density rural fringe (six houses per acre) which gradually develops into a higher density urban village centre (eighteen houses per acre). This seeks to emulate a traditional village and allows the development of a mix of housing types in different parts of the settlement.

The aim is to create a diverse and sustainable community. A mix of land uses is also planned along with open spaces and a traditional village square to provide a focal point for the community. Sites will also be allocated for commercial and retail uses and a community hall/library, primary school and medical centre.

The village has been designed so that walking distances are minimised to reduce reliance on the car. There will be three main roads through the village however traffic is excluded from parts of the centre and dispersed along a series of residential roads with 20mph speed limits. Footpaths and cycleways will run parallel to the roads and in two circular loops around the village.

While it is not as large as proposals like Cambourne, Dickens Heath is one of the largest of the private sector new villages that are being built. Yet it barely meets the first rung on the sustainability ladder suggested by David Lock.

and amenities but would not be large enough to serve its population or to be considered self-sufficient.

10 000 houses: A settlement with a population of 25–30 000 people was considered the threshold for sustainability. It would be able to achieve a critical mass of jobs, services and amenities to serve its population and would support a good public transport service so reducing both the need to travel and the reliance on the car.

Two possible conclusions could be drawn from this work. We should either be building very large new settlements or should be building within existing urban areas. Without a state-sponsored new town programme the only new settlements being planned were those promoted by the private sector. The largest of these came nowhere near the threshold for sustainability and the inevitable conclusion was that the majority of development should take place within existing settlements.

This work formed the basis for *Planning Policy Guidance Note 13*[7] published in 1994. PPG 13 was described by David Lock as having 'such far-reaching effects that it would soon come to be regarded as a major landmark in the evolution of planning and the true start of the journey towards sustainability'. Amongst other things it sought to prevent out-of-town retail, leisure and commercial development and stated that, where possible, all new housing should be built within existing towns and cities. If this was not possible new development must be served by public transport and new settlements would only be considered if they were likely to reach a population of 10 000 within twenty years. In urban areas it stated that local plans should seek to 'concentrate higher density residential development near public transport centres... and close to local facilities'. In a section entitled Planning at the Neighbourhood Scale, it also promoted the idea of mixed-use development suggesting that '...planning for a variety of uses – shops and rest-aurants – on the ground floor of developments will help keep streets lively. Attention to preserving or enhancing continuous pavement level street-

scapes and the avoidance of blank frontages... can be a major contribution to retaining pedestrian activity, retaining the commercial life of the area and to crime prevention'. The government thus set down in official guidance in 1994 the outline of what we have called the Sustainable Urban Neighbourhood. PPG 13 has indeed been a very influential document and has led to the revision of other Planning Policy Guidance Notes, notably PPG 1 on local plans and PPG 6 on retail development. It has also led to a significant reduction in planning consents for out-of-town retail and commercial development.

The focus of government policy then moved to housing, particularly following the 1995 household projections[8] which increased the number of new households projected by 2016 to 4.4 million. This added impetus to government policy since it meant that a policy of locating more housing within existing urban areas would not only reduce transport but also the number of green fields lost to development. The 1995 Housing White Paper[9] therefore set a policy target that half of all new homes should be built in urban areas. This initially went unnoticed by many in the planning world who were still arguing that the household projections were too high. However the issue came to a head the following year when the government suggested in the Green Paper *Household growth: Where shall we live?*[10] that the target should be increased to 60%. This was based on land-use change data[11] that showed that 49% of all new housing in 1993 had been built on previously developed urban land, in other words that the 50% target was virtually being met. While this higher target was never more than a suggestion, it did illustrate the radical shift that had taken place in policy towards the control of sprawl and the promotion of urban development.

In May 1997 there was a change of government and a Labour party was swept to power which had been ambivalent about this shift in policy. In opposition shadow ministers like Nick Raynsford had poured scorn upon the 60% target for homes built in urban areas as an 'aspirational target' which was unlikely ever to be achieved and had voiced fears about the dangers of town cramming[12]. This reflected the traditional urban constituency of Labour and suggested that the party had taken to heart many of the concerns about the compact city and town cramming. The new government initially showed little enthusiasm for taking up the issue and were happy to restate the 50% target of the 1995 White Paper. However their hand was forced by the outcry over plans to extend Stevenage into the green belt which the government approved in the autumn of 1997. This outrage was fuelled by unguarded comments by the Planning Minister Richard Caboune who seemed to suggest that the green belt was 'up for grabs'[13] and culminated in the Countryside March when thousands took to the streets of London in March 1998 in support of rural areas.

In response to this the government overcame its initial doubts about the 60% target and adopted it as policy in a statement made by the Secretary of State for the Environment, Transport and the Regions, John Prescott, to the House of Commons on 23rd February 1998[14]. In this he also abandoned the traditional 'predict and provide' approach to accommodating household growth by which household growth figures were imposed on local authorities. In its place he introduced a system by which local authorities would be able to provide for less homes than projected for their area provided that they monitored house prices, homelessness and other indicators to ensure that demand was being met. He also established a task force under the chairmanship of Lord Rogers to identify ways of increasing the proportion of housing built on brown field land and hinted that the 60% target could be increased if it was seen to be working. This statement completes the work started by the previous government and opens up the prospect of a broader shift in household growth not only from green field to brown field sites but from the rural counties to metropolitan districts.

The compact city therefore appears to be firmly entrenched in Government policy yet the heat of the debate shows little sign of cooling. Indeed a change in policy has come about, not so much because policy makers have been convinced

of the merits of the compact city, but rather because of the reaction against green field development. The critics of the compact city are not convinced and continue to mount a vigorous rearguard action against government policy while environmental groups, countryside campaigners and urban planners argue that we could go further still. URBED have recently completed some work for Friends of the Earth[15] to explore the feasibility of increasing the target for housing built in urban areas from 60% to 75%. Our report, *Tomorrow: A peaceful path to urban reform* brings together all of the evidence in considerable detail. This work suggested that a higher target is both desirable and feasible but will require fundamental changes in the way that towns and cities are planned. Some of the key arguments are reviewed below.

Sustainability and the compact city

The original impetus behind the promotion of development within urban areas was sustainability. As the *European Green Paper on the Urban Environment*[16] states 'the city offers density and variety (and) the efficient time and energy combination of social and economic functions'. The idea that the city may provide our environmental salvation may initially seem strange since so many of our environmental problems are concentrated in cities. However, as we saw in Chapter 5, many of the environmental issues which will shape future housing: pollution, CO_2 emissions, damage to the ozone layer, acid rain and energy consumption, relate to the private car. What is more, while the domestic and industrial sectors are gradually reducing energy use and pollution these gains are being overtaken by the growth of transport. Governments across the English-speaking world have therefore seen the location of new development as an important means of reducing the demand for car use.

While a great deal of effort has gone into energy efficiency, there is little point building super-insulated buildings in locations which are reliant on the car. It follows that, to maximise environmental sustainability, housing should be built near to existing facilities to reduce travel distances and encourage walking, cycling and the use of public transport. This in turn implies that housing should be built within existing towns and cities.

This was backed up by a very influential piece of research by Newman and Kenworthy in the late 1980s[17]. This showed a clear correlation between per-capita petroleum consumption and population density. They found that US cities have twice the petroleum consumption of Australian cities and four times that of European cities and that there was a direct relationship between this and the compactness of urban form. This research has been used to justify urban containment policies in the United States, Australia and Europe. It has also been used to justify the British government changes described above.

Newman and Kenworthy's findings have not gone unchallenged[18]. It has been suggested that as jobs and services decentralise commuting distances from suburban housing will reduce and also that the findings take insufficient account of income levels and fuel prices. However the main objections relate to the acceptability of urban containment. This is a consistent thread running through the debate about the compact city. Critics of containment have started from the assumption that living in towns and cities is unacceptable to the majority of the population and have therefore reacted against research which has concluded that this is where they should be forced to live. They argue that holding back the tide of urban expansion will require unacceptable levels of state control on people's freedom to choose where they live and work. This is really an ideological debate about free market-led decentralisation verses the heavy hand of state control and has little to do with the environmental impacts of different settlement patterns. It is indeed remarkable that western governments, committed to the free market, remain such enthusiastic advocates of compact settlements.

In the UK research by ECOTEC[19] for the Department of the Environment in 1993 reinforced Newman and Kenworthy's findings. They demonstrated that people in the UK living at the lowest densities travelled twice the distance

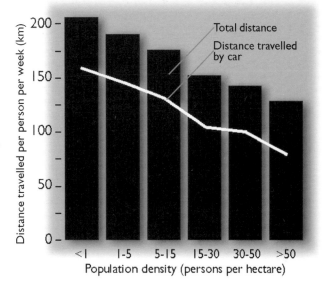

by car per week as the people living at the highest densities. ECOTEC's findings have influenced government thinking. However their figures have been used by Michael Breheny[20] to question the value of urban containment to reduce the energy consumption of car use. He has calculated that, if all of the UK population were to live at the population densities of metropolitan areas, it would save about 34% of energy used in transport. This, as he points out, is impossible and the level of savings achievable even through the most draconian use of planning powers is more likely to be 10–15%. However a better estimate of savings, he argues, can be calculated by looking at the rates of decentralisation over the last 30 years. If this had not taken place the transport energy savings would have amounted to just 2.5%. This he suggests is the most that future urban containment policies are likely to achieve and does not justify the draconian policies that would be required to bring it about. These findings are persuasive and call into question one of the impetuses behind government policy.

However it does not follow that we should abandon all attempts to control car use by promoting urban repopulation. Peter Headicar[21] has demonstrated that not only are travel distances greater in small settlements, they are also growing much more rapidly than in larger cities so that

Density and travel: There is a strong correlation between population density and both total travel distances and the distances travelled by car. Source ECOTEC 1993

the future effect may be greater than Breheny predicts. Energy consumption is also not the only reason for reducing car use. We should also consider traffic congestion, road accidents, CO_2 emissions, acid rain, and pollution. It may be that traffic reduction measures have a far greater impact in these areas than on energy use. Yet even if the benefits in all of these areas are not as great as we might have hoped, is this any reason not to take what benefits we can from the location of development? There are, after all, many areas where energy saving measures only result in a minor impact on total energy use. Domestic energy-efficiency is a case in point since improvements to the efficiency of new housing have only a very minor impact on total domestic energy use because new housing is such a tiny proportion of the total housing stock. It is not however suggested that we should abandon attempts to make new housing more energy efficient. The difference is that is that, unlike energy efficient housing, urban containment is seen as something which has disbenefits to set against the benefits. If the achievement of reductions in transport energy use implies the forced repatriation of unwilling suburbanites to the city then there many be a great deal of pain to set against very little gain.

It is not however our contention that heavy-handed planning policies should be used to achieve the repopulation of urban areas. We have argued instead that a range of demographic, environmental, social and economic factors are already increasing the attractiveness of cities as places to live and work. One of the most important of these factors is transport. It is widely accepted that projected levels of car use are entirely unsustainable. It is therefore inevitable that the mobility offered by the private car will be limited in the future if not by measures such as fuel taxes, road pricing, or parking restrictions then by rising levels of congestion. As Andreas Duaney[22] has pointed out, the unions in the US fought long and hard to reduce the working week yet these gains have been cancelled out as the average American employee now spends more than two hours a day locked in a metal box travelling to and from work. A recent survey by the Henley Centre[23] in the

UK suggested that this logic will become a powerful force attracting professional people, particularly women, back to larger cities which are able to offer a high quality of life. This is particularly true where the need to juggle children and work makes it impossible to contemplate the sort of commuting times that men have been accepting for years.

We might therefore conclude that, in identifying a correlation between the density of development and car travel, we have been confusing cause and effect. It may be that the density of the cities studied by Newman and Kenworthy was the result rather than the cause of low per-capita fuel consumption. As personal mobility is constrained by congestion or restrictions on car use, the attractiveness of low-density locations will be reduced. Conversely locations with employment and facilities within easy reach on foot or by public transport will become more attractive. This can already be seen in many of our major cities, particularly London. It is well summed up by hoardings advertising urban housing developments which suggest to passing motorists stuck in traffic that if they bought one of the apartments they could be home by now.

While compact settlement policies may not therefore be the most effective means to reduce car use, measures to reduce car use will make compact settlements more attractive. This does not require the stick of draconian planning restrictions but rather the carrot of attractive urban areas capable of attracting people back to the city.

The loss of countryside

The urban compaction debate has thrown up some interesting alliances. The Council for the Protection of Rural England (CPRE), for example, has been one of the strongest advocates of urban development[24] as a means of protecting the countryside from urban sprawl. The government and CPRE differ on the amount of countryside that is being lost to development. The government puts the figure at around 5 000 hectares a year whereas the CPRE suggests that the figure is more like 11 000 hectares a year. Either way the loss of countryside represents a

Land area required to accommodate 4.4 million households at suburban densities of 30 houses to the hectare

Land area required to accommodate 4.4 million households at urban densities of 62 houses to the hectare

Land estimated to change from rural to urban use as a result of the household projections assuming current rates of urban infill (Bibby and Shepherd)

The urbanisation of England:
The scale of land required to accommodate household growth compared to the existing urban areas of England

relatively small proportion of the total countryside area. The total land area of England, is just over 13 million hectares, of which just under 1.4 million hectares or 10.6% is urbanised. Figures from Bibby and Shepherd[25] suggest that the projected 4.4 million increase in households will lead to the loss of a further 169 400 hectares of rural land between 1991 and 2016 which would increase the urbanised area from 10.6% to 12%. This may not exactly represent the wholesale destruction of the English countryside but it does mean the loss of a land area the equivalent of the county of Surrey. It is also the case that the regional distribution of household growth means that the impact of development on the countryside will be very uneven. In southern counties the percentage loss of rural land is up to six times the national average, much of which will be valued by local people. In these areas projected growth implies a significant change in the character of rural areas and there is a compelling case for maximising the amount of development which take place within existing settlements.

The loss of rural land is of particular concern where it involves areas of natural beauty and ecological importance. However most green belt land falls into neither of these categories. In the past the concern about the loss of rural land has centred on the loss of agricultural capacity. However with the increasing use of intensive farming techniques, less land is required to meet our food requirements and European subsidies are being used to set aside land out of agricultural use. The loss of farming land may not therefore currently seem to be a compelling argument for strict urban containment policies. However land taken out of intensive agriculture should probably be exploited for its potential ecological rather than its development value. It is also possible that, in the future, we will want to move to less intensive organic farming requiring more land. We may also seek to reduce the transport of food around the world by increasing domestic production. It would therefore be prudent to protect land which may be required for future agricultural use.

Not all land in rural areas is green and pleasant; 48% of derelict land is to be found in rural areas, representing some 19 000 hectares of mine workings, military dereliction and redundant institutions or industrial sites. This creates some confusion since government land use data categorises urban land by its previous use rather

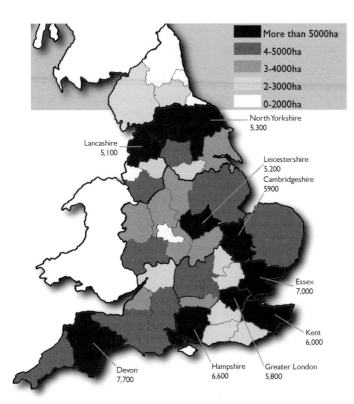

More than 5000ha
4-5000ha
3-4000ha
2-3000ha
0-2000ha

North Yorkshire
5,300

Lancashire
5,100

Leicestershire
5,200

Cambridgeshire
5900

Essex
7,000

Kent
6,000

Devon
7,700

Hampshire
6,600

Greater London
5,800

Countryside under threat: Hectares of countryside projected to be lost as a result of the household projections 1991-2016. Source: Bibby and Shepherd

may however be the most compelling reason for urban repopulation. We suggested in Part 1 of this book that the depopulation of urban areas and inner city decline are two sides of the same coin. Those with the power to do so have abandoned cities to the poor, the powerless and the vulnerable. It is therefore hardly surprising that urban areas have experienced high levels of unemployment, crime and other social problems. It is also not surprising that the billions of pounds of government money that have been spent to address inner city problems have had little or no effect on these levels of deprivation. The problem has been that the people assisted by these initiatives have often used their new-found economic power to join the urban exodus. The problems of urban areas are therefore a combination of population loss and the fact that they have become a sink for poverty.

The only way to address the root cause of these problems is to stem and then reverse the loss of population. Urban environments need to be created which can persuade people to remain in the area as they improve their quality of life as well as attracting people back to live there. Of course this needs to be handled with care to avoid problems of gentrification and rising values squeezing out local people or displacing deprivation to other areas. However without urban repopulation there is little prospect of revival in the inner cities.

The people: where will they go?
We have argued in this book that efforts should be made to encourage more people to live in existing towns and cities. In doing this we are entirely in line with government policy. Yet the debate about urban containment rages on and there are many who would argue that the government has got it wrong. It has been suggested by experts like Sir Peter Hall and Michael Breheny that the government has jumped on a bandwagon which is poorly grounded in research and which is both impractical and unlikely to produce the benefits which are claimed. It is important to disentangle the strands of this debate.

At the end of the last century Ebenezer Howard posed the question; 'The people – Where

than its location. A derelict hospital in the heart of the countryside developed for housing would therefore be categorised as an urban brown field development. This may not matter if our concern is to protect valuable countryside but it is hardly the most sustainable location for development. This raises some difficult issues about the location of green field development – which will amount to more than 1.7 million homes even if we do build 60% of new homes in urban areas. The main cause of public outcry has been the development of green belt land on the edge of towns like Stevenage. Yet if we accept the need to build some green field housing such locations may make far more sense than less attractive land which is remote from existing settlements.

The need to regenerate our cities
The final reason put forward for the development of more housing in urban areas is the need to regenerate urban areas. This was suggested by the UK Round Table on Sustainable Development[26] but has otherwise received less attention than the reduction in car use and the loss of countryside. It

will they go?' This has been a central question for urban professionals ever since but has been brought into sharp focus by the household projections. The projections have caused particular concern in the shire counties where population growth has been concentrated in recent years. The fear is that the projections will drive a coach and horses through carefully made policies and housing land allocations leading to great tracts of countryside being overrun by development. In the other corner are the private housebuilders[27] who have argued that household projections mean that more green field land should be made available for suburban expansion. They argue that County Councils are ignoring household projections and failing to make land available in the locations where growth is predicted and more importantly where people want to live. It is in this context that the Government finds it so attractive to promote urban infill and its critics find it so easy to question its motives.

This tension between planning authorities and private developers is as old as the planning system. However the debate about urban containment in the last few years has ranged well beyond these traditional rivalries. An important contribution has been made by the Town and Country Planning Association which has organised a series of major studies and enquiries starting with *The People – Where will they go?'* in 1996[28] and more recently the programme *Urban housing capacity and the sustainable city*[29]. While this work has aired a broad range of views the thrust of the TCPA's work has been to question the logic and feasibility of urban infill. As Sir Peter Hall and Michael Breheny stated in an article in *Town and Country Planning*[30]; 'The fashionable logic suggests that, by packing more people into existing urban areas we can both reduce the need to travel – thus reducing fuel consumption and emissions – and minimise loss of open countryside to development'. They go on to state that; 'This raises the critical question of whether sustainability really entails urban compaction or whether – as the TCPA has argued – it is possible to plan new developments, including new communities in ways that are perfectly sustainable'.

This reflects the TCPA's traditional advocacy of the garden city as an alternative to urban areas. Their arguments against urban containment are that the benefits of protecting the countryside and reducing car use do not outweigh the problems which include the lack of scope for urban infill, the problems of town cramming and the lack of demand for urban living. These are important issues and must be addressed if we are to promote the repopulation of urban areas.

The limitations of urban land capacity

The most fundamental argument against the accommodation of household growth within urban areas is that the capacity is simply not available. There is no point arguing that a greater proportion of household growth should be accommodated in urban areas if this is either not possible or would lead to unacceptable conditions in those areas.

The most fundamental level on which this argument has taken place has been the absolute loss of population from cities. People have pointed to the historic loss of urban populations as evidence of huge amounts of urban capacity. However others welcome this population loss and fear that urban repopulation will undo many years of good work to overcome the problems of overcrowding in cities. The picture however, as detailed on the table overleaf, is somewhat more complex. If we look at the metropolitan counties, the population loss this century has been relatively small. Indeed between 1911 and 1961 Greater London and each of the six metropolitan counties continued to gain population, albeit at a slower rate than they had done at the end of the nineteenth century. Their populations peaked at 19.7 million in 1961 and since then they have lost 7.7% of their population or about 1.5 million people. If we apply the average household size over the period this accounts for only 625 000 households.

The picture at the county level disguises more local depopulation. If we look for example at the principal cities within each of the metropolitan counties the picture is very different. These cities have lost population throughout the century and the rate of loss has sharply increased since 1961. Inner London has lost a quarter of its population since 1961 (1 million people) and Liverpool and Manchester have lost more than a third (more than half a million people between them). Other cities such as Birmingham, Sheffield and Newcastle grew rapidly in the early part of the century but even they have lost significant amounts of population since 1961 with only Leeds maintaining a modest growth rate. At face value these figures do not provide evidence for huge amounts of urban capacity. However they disguise what Tony Champion[31] has called the cascade effect of population loss from urban areas. Population has been lost down the urban hierarchy from inner urban areas to suburban districts, from these to peripheral areas and from these to more rural districts, in each case partly balanced by migration up the urban hierarchy. Much of this population change has taken place within

districts so that, for example, in Leeds it is not that the city has stemmed dispersal, but that its large geographical area has allowed dispersal to take place within the city boundaries. This is even more true of the metropolitan counties so that absolute levels of population loss fail to illuminate the potential capacity of inner urban areas.

The problem with an analysis of population loss is that it tells us little about physical housing capacity. While cities may have lost population the land occupied by these people has not remained fallow. It has been redeveloped for housing at lower densities, used, often very wastefully, for road building, or turned over to commercial use. Our urban areas have therefore become crystalised into a low-density pattern of development which is now very difficult to change. A great deal of effort has therefore been put into ways of better measuring urban housing capacity as reviewed in our work for Friends of

The lost urban populations:
This table illustrates how central urban areas have lost population to a far greater extent than the metro-politan counties
Source: Office for National Statistics

| | Population (thousands) | | | | | | | | | % change |
	1911	1931	1951	1961	1971	1981	1991	1994	1911-61	since 1961
Greater London	7,161	8,110	8,197	7,977	7,529	6,806	6,890	6,967	11%	-13%
Inner London	4,998	4,893	3,679	3,481	3,060	2,550	2,627	2,662	-30%	-24%
Outer London	2,162	3,217	4,518	4,496	4,470	4,255	4,263	4,305	108%	-4%
West Midlands	1,780	2,143	2,547	2,724	2,811	2,673	2,629	2,628	53%	-4%
Birmingham	526	1,003	1,113	1,179	1,107	1,021	1,007	1,008	124%	-15%
Greater Manchester	2,638	2,727	2,716	2,710	2,750	2,619	2,570	2,578	3%	-5%
Manchester City	714	766	703	657	554	463	439	431	-8%	-34%
West Yorkshire	1,852	1,939	1,985	2,002	2,090	2,067	2,085	2,104	8%	5%
Leeds	446	483	505	710	749	718	717	724	59%	2%
South Yorkshire	963	1,173	1,253	1,298	1,331	1,317	1,302	1,305	35%	1%
Sheffield	455	512	513	581	579	548	529	530	28%	-9%
Merseyside	1,378	1,587	1,663	1,711	1,662	1,522	1,450	1,434	24%	-16%
Liverpool	746	856	789	741	610	517	481	474	-1%	-36%
Tyne and Wear	1,105	1,201	1,201	1,241	1,218	1,155	1,130	1,134	12%	-9%
Newcastle	112	267	286	292	336	312	384	278	161%	-5%
Non-Metropolitan Cities										
Kingston-upon-Hull	278	314	299	302	288	274	267	269	9%	-11%
Leicester	227	239	285	286	285	283	285	293	26%	2%
Nottingham	260	269	308	311	302	278	281	282	20%	-9%
Bristol	357	397	443	436	433	401	397	399	22%	-8%
Plymouth	207	215	225	240	249	253	254	254	16%	6%
Stoke-onTrent	235	277	275	276	265	252	253	254	17%	-8%

the Earth[32]. From this it is clear that there are a number of potential sources of urban housing capacity which are reviewed below.

Brown field land

Much of the discussion about urban housing capacity has focused on brown field land, by which is meant land which has previously been developed. As we have already described, land-use data show that almost half of new housing is already built on urban, previously-developed land suggesting a ready supply of brown field sites. However these figures need to be treated with care for three reasons. The first is that they mask huge regional variations from 83% in London to just above 30% in the East Midlands and the South West. The second is the fact that urban land is defined by its previous use rather than its location. A significant proportion of 'urban' brown field land may in fact be in the countryside. The third reason has been highlighted by Michael Breheny[33] who has pointed out that the percentage rise in the amount of brown field land developed for housing took place in the context of falling housing output. The area of urban land developed for housing has therefore fallen. The percentage only increased because other categories declined more rapidly. He concludes that the best brown field sites are being used up and that, with the exception of the North West, brown field

COIN STREET COMMUNITY BUILDERS

Coin Street is an important example of both community-sponsored regeneration and urban brown field development. Coin Street Community Builders were formed in 1984 when they bought 13 acres of land on London's South Bank.

Since that time they have created a mixed-use urban neighbourhood in the heart of London. This grew out of a campaign to stop the area becoming a mono-functional office area and a belief that it should be a mixed residential area affordable to London people. The scheme includes a small park – Bernie Spain Gardens, a riverside walkway, the Gabriel's Wharf craft market, a range of housing developments and the mixed-use refurbishment of the Oxo Tower Wharf. An annual festival is also organised to animate the area.

The Broadwall scheme (below) was designed by Lifschutz Davidson Architects. It includes 27 units managed by Palm Housing Co-op in a four-storey block and a nine-storey tower. The flats face west but large areas of double glazed Low E glass maximise passive solar gain. The flats also incorporate gas stoves vented through stainless steel stacks up the face of the building.

The adjoining Oxo building has been refurbished at a cost of £20 million for a mixture of shops, cafés, design workshops and flats along with a rooftop restaurant and performance area. It includes 36 designer/maker workshops and 78 flats managed by the Redwood Housing Co-operative. Christine Czechowski of Coin Street Community Builders warns that the flats will not suit everyone but will be a 'hub of activity in what is very much an urban setting'.

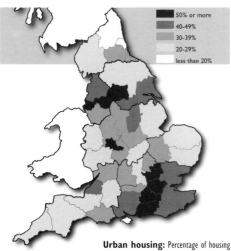

Urban housing: Percentage of housing provided through urban infill since 1991 by county. Source: Bibby and Shepherd

Legend:
- 50% or more
- 40-49%
- 30-39%
- 20-29%
- less than 20%

135

land is likely to be exhausted by 2006 so that the amount of housing that can be built on recycled sites will drop to 30–40%.

This idea that there is a finite stock of brown field land which is rapidly being used up is not however borne out by derelict and vacant land data. The 1993 *Survey of Derelict Land in England*[34] identified just under 40 000 hectares of derelict land. This had fallen by 900 hectares since 1988 despite the fact that 9 500 hectares had been reclaimed. While almost half of this land was in rural areas the greatest increases were in general industrial dereliction, much of which was in urban areas. What is more, much of the land that has been reclaimed has no end use or has been turned into low grade open space and may also be available for development. This suggests that, far from being used up, the rate at which urban brown field land is being created is only marginally less that the rate at which it is being reclaimed or developed. It may be true that the rate of industrial restructuring and its associated dereliction is slowing – there are few mines left to close for example. However urban areas are constantly evolving and vacant land is a natural result of this process. Vacant land today is as likely to be the result of institutional closures due to policies like 'Care in the Community' as industrial closure. Future sources of vacant land are difficult to predict – maybe supermarkets will close due to home shopping or car parks will become surplus to requirements due to policies to reduce car use. However it is reasonable to assume that vacant land will continue to characterise urban areas and will continue to provide a source of urban housing capacity.

Derelict land refers to land 'so damaged by industrial or other development that it is incapable of beneficial use without treatment'. It therefore does not include all vacant urban land as illustrated by the *National survey of vacant land in the urban areas of England*[35] which was undertaken in 1990. This used Ordnance Survey mapping data to survey all of the urban areas of England with a population of more than 10 000 people and estimated the national stock of vacant land to be around 60 000 hectares 'an area the size of a small county the size of Cleveland'. However more than half of this is land which has never previously been developed.

There are considerable discrepancies between the derelict land data and the vacant land survey which the report on the latter deals

Top table: Changes in derelict land by type of dereliction

Bottom table: Urban/rural split of derelict land

Plan: Area of derelict land within urban areas (percentage indicates the proportion of derelict land within the region in urban areas)
Source: Survey of Derelict Land in England 1993 - DOE

	1974 ha	1982 ha	1988 ha	1993 ha	Change 1974-93
Spoil heaps	13,100	13,300	11,900	9,191	-30%
Excavations & pits	8,700	8,600	6,000	5,807	-33%
Military dereliction	3,800	3,000	2,600	3,275	-14%
Railway land	9,100	8,200	6,400	5,615	-38%
Other*	8,600	12,500	13,600	15,713	+83%
TOTAL	43,300	45,600	40,500	39,600	-9%

* Includes mining subsidence, general industrial dereliction, and other forms of dereliction.

	Inner city Ha	%	Other urban Ha	%	Rural Ha	%	Total Ha	%
Derelict land	5,243	13%	15,236	38%	19,121	48%	39,600	100%
Area justifying reclamation	5,060	15%	14,699	43%	14,807	43%	34,566	100%

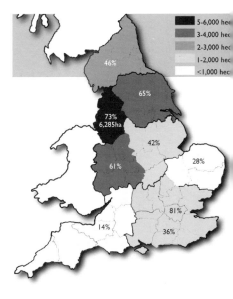

Legend: 5-6,000 hec / 3-4,000 hec / 2-3,000 hec / 1-2,000 hec / <1,000 hec

46% · 65% · 73% 6,285ha · 42% · 28% · 61% · 81% · 14% · 36%

Source	Area (ha)	Capacity at net densities of..	
		30units/ha	62units/ha
Derelict urban land justifying reclamation	19,759	415,000*1	879,000
Half of all reclaimed derelict land since 1988 in 'soft uses'	1,236	26,000	55,000
Urban land reclaimed since 1988 with no end use	772	16,000	34,000
Vacant urban land which has previously been developed	9,226*2	194,000	411,000
Vacant urban land not previously developed	13,965*3	293,000	621,000
SUB TOTAL	44,958	944,000	2,000,000
Urban land likely to become derelict 1993-2016	19,800*4	416,000	881,000
Urban land likely to fall vacant 1993-2016	9,245*5	277,000	573,000
SUB TOTAL	29,045	693,000	1,454,000
TOTAL	74,000	1,637,000	3,454,000

*1 All capacity figures assume that half of the land will be large sites and therefore subject to gross densities of 12 and 27 units/hectare rather than net densities. All figures are rounded to the nearest thousand and may not sum to the independently rounded totals

*2 Based on the figure from the 1990 survey of vacant land discounted to take account of reclaimed derelict land

*3 We have assumed that half of the vacant previously undeveloped land could be brought forward for development.

*4 Based on the annual rate of land becoming derelict in urban areas and justifying reclamation between 1982 and 1993

*5 Based on the same rate of increase as that for derelict land

Recycled land capacity: Estimate of potential recycled land available for housing within urban areas. Source URBED

with in some detail. In our work for Friends of the Earth we sought to bring together these data sets and to make assumptions about future rates of vacancy and dereliction. The findings are summarised in the table above which estimates that there are currently just under 45 000 hectares of vacant urban land available for development and that this could grow by a further 30 000 hectares by 2016. Let us for a moment assume that all of this land were developable for housing. At garden city densities of 30 houses to the hectare it would provide 1.6 million homes and at more urban densities of say 62 units to the hectare it would produce 3.4 million homes.

Even the most optimistic scenario would only accommodate three quarters of housing growth on brownfield land. This assumes that all of this land would be viable for housing in terms of access and ground conditions, that developers could be persuade to build on it and that it would not be taken up by the commercial development market all of which are pretty unlikely. It also assumes that by 2016 we would have eliminated vacant and derelict land from our cities which would be truly remarkable. The figures for brown field land alone therefore would give cause for concern about the extent of urban housing capacity if they were the only source that we could exploit. This however is not the case.

THE ROYAL FREE HOSPITAL - ISLINGTON

The brown field sites of the future are as likely to result from institutional as industrial closures. The Royal Free Hospital in North London is an excellent example of how such sites, which often include historic buildings, can be developed for housing. The hospital was designed by Charles Fowler in 1848 and closed in 1975.

The site covers 4 acres and has been developed by Circle 33 Housing Trust and New Islington and Hackney Housing Association to create 200 homes for families, single people and couples as well as disabled people's accommodation and health-care facilities. It was designed by Pollard Thomas and Edwards Architects and Levitt Bernstein Associates at a cost of £10 million. The site was acquired by the two housing associations from the local health authority in 1986. As part of the scheme some of the gateway buildings were dismantled and rebuilt to allow vehicles to access the site. The new build housing is then concentrated to the rear of the site to create an internal courtyard and a series of narrow mews streets. Despite the size of the courtyard the scheme therefore achieved an overall density of 124 units to the hectare.

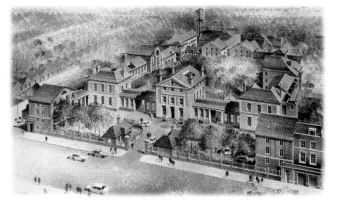

Other sources of urban housing capacity

Urban housing capacity is an elastic concept. It is not possible to measure because it is so dependent upon demand. This is why London which is already the most intensively developed part of Britain is able to accommodate more than 80% of its household growth within its urban area. People want to live and work there, developers have a market for housing and therefore have an incentive to seek out capacity beyond that which any capacity study could ever identify. Extra housing capacity is likely to come from the following sources:

The redevelopment of council estates: David Hall writing in Town and Country Planning in 1997[36] suggested that 'it should not be forgotten that there are still many thousands of high-rise flats… which within the timescale of the household growth projections will very likely have to be pulled down. High density housing is the least preferred by people when they have the choice. Thus there will be an "overspill" population from these flats'. However, outside London, many of these estates were actually built at very low densities. Hulme in Manchester, for example was built at around 15 houses to the acre which is what Ebenezer Howard suggested for the garden city (see illustrations on pages 45 and 46). The problem was that they had the worst of both worlds, looking and feeling overcrowded but accommodating insufficient people to animate public areas, support local services and make them feel safe. It is therefore possible that the redevelopment of these estates at higher densities could provide a source of extra housing capacity. Very conservative estimates suggest that the capacity from this source could be around 22 000 extra homes.

The development of car parks: At present in many town and city centres surface-level parking is the premium land use producing a healthy income with minimum investment. Many towns are therefore surrounded by a wasteland of poor quality parking, much of which is underused. With increasing restrictions likely on car use it is possible that the financial equation might change

CIRENCESTER - URBAN INFILL

Proposals have been developed by URBED for the historic town of Cirencester. These relate to the centre of an urban block, currently occupied by a supermarket with associated car parking (see inset figure ground plan). The scheme retains the supermarket while creating additional retail space with housing on the upper floors. This is achieved by building on the car parks and replacing this with a four level car park on the western part of the site. This car parking is then wrapped around with mono-aspect offices and housing so that it is not visible from the street.

The scheme creates a hundred residential units plus a substantial increase in town centre shopping provision. This is helps the council accommodate household growth without and provide affordable housing without resorting to green field development.

Redundant hospital

Car park

Supermarket

Historic core of the town (see illustration page 196)

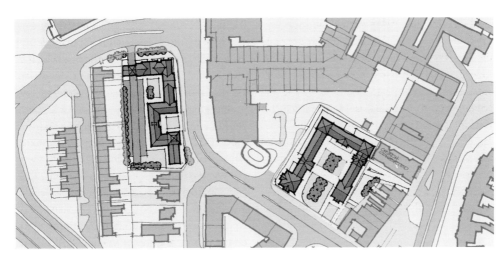

and some of this land will be released for development. Indeed local authorities might encourage this process to reduce parking capacity as part of a wider traffic reduction strategy. We have estimated that up to 200 000 homes could be accommodated in this way.

The conversion of empty commercial space: Capacity need not only exist on cleared sites. There is a huge amount of capacity in commercial property, both historic mills and more recent office space which has not been taken up by the market. James Barlow[37] estimated in 1992 that 20% of office space in London and 15% in the provincial cities was vacant. Herring Baker Research[38] estimated that there was 500 000m² of this space in London alone which represented a 'permafrost' layer which would never be let. In recent years a large number of residential conversions have taken place. This was initially concentrated in the more attractive historic buildings (see case study on page 90) but in London now also includes a significant number of more modern office conversions. On this basis LPAC have estimated capacity from this source of 54 000 homes and the capacity nationally may be more than 100 000.

Intensification of existing housing areas: The idea of accommodating more homes in existing residential areas has received a considerable amount of attention. It was the subject of a major study in

Hertfordshire[39] which suggested that intensification could produce capacity for 7 522 to 16 500 new homes in the county. The main opportunities are backlands development of areas like garage courts, back garden development, building on small areas of open space and redevelopment at higher densities. Each of these is likely to be contentious and is only likely to be attractive in parts of the country where other sources of capacity are scarce. We have however estimated that the national capacity from this source is around 280 000 extra homes.

Urban intensification: An example of one of the design exercises undertaken by Urban Initiatives in Hertfordshire to assess housing capacity of existing residential areas through intensification.

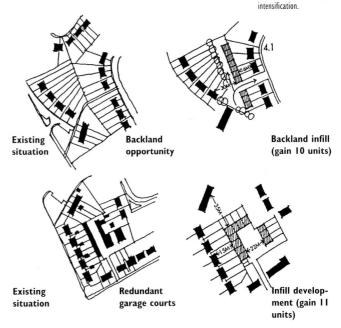

Existing situation   Backland opportunity   Backland infill (gain 10 units)

Existing situation   Redundant garage courts   Infill development (gain 11 units)

Living over the shop: A scheme of six flats in converted space over town centre retail premises in Grantham.

Living over the shop: A very significant source of capacity is the empty and underused space over shops. There are currently just over 400 000 flats over shops[41] and despite the limited impact of programmes run by the Housing Corporation and the Department of the Environment (as was) data on shopping floorspace suggests that nationally capacity could be 1 – 1.5 million units.

The subdivision of larger houses: The conversion of large houses to flats or multi-occupancy has traditionally been the way that urban areas have mopped up housing capacity, particularly for single people (who make up the majority of household growth). Work by Llewelyn-Davies for LPAC and the Joseph Rowntree Foundation[42] suggests that the potential capacity from subdivision may be up to four times the capacity from brown field sites. Based upon under-occupation data from the Office for National Statistics[43] we have estimated that if every under-occupied home were to be subdivided the capacity nationally could be as high as 6 million units. This, of course, will never happen because most home owners will not want to subdivide and the planning authorities in any case would not allow it.

The better use of empty homes: We should also consider the three-quarters of a million homes that were empty in England in 1997[40]. The majority of these are in the private sector and a proportion will be due to the natural workings of the housing market. In the public sector many will be in hard to let areas (which include parts of London) where ironically, despite household growth, it can be difficult to let even new property. However there are 250 000 homes which have been empty for more than a year and it would be reasonable to assume that half of all empty property could be brought back into use.

The housing capacity of urban areas: Summary of potential urban housing capacity (thousands of units). Source: URBED

Net densities (units/hectare)	Unconstrained capacity		Policy target	Adjusted capacity	
	30	62		30	62
Current and reclaimed derelict land	457	968	60%	274	581
Previously developed vacant land	194	411	80%	155	329
Vacant urban land not previously developed	293	621	70%	205	435
Land likely to fall vacant 1993-2016	693	1,454	60%	416	872
Redevelopment of large council estates	22	22	100%	22	22
Redevelopment of underused car parks	100	200	80%	80	160
Conversion of industrial buildings and offices	100	100	80%	80	80
Living over the shop	1,000	1,000	40%	400	400
Subdivision of larger under-occupied property[*1]	1,900	1,900	20%	380	380
Intensification	280	280	80%	224	224
Bringing empty homes back into use	325	325	100%	325	325
TOTALS[*2]	**5,364**	**7,281**		**2,561**	**3,818**

*1 To give a realistic figure the capacity from the subdivision of existing property is based upon the 30% of properties which Llewelyn-Davies suggested could get planning permission

*2 Similar estimates of urban housing capacity have been made recently in *Tomorrow's World*, published by Friends of the Earth in 1997. Based on comparable assumptions, and adapted from the UK to England, those figures suggest capacity for approximately 3.5 million dwellings in towns and cities, but propose greater additional potential for the planned regeneration of urban areas towards the end of the household projection period.

Note that figures are rounded and so the columns may not sum exactly.

Nevertheless, as Llewelyn-Davies says 'there is significant headroom in the existing stock for the conversion of homes to flats'.

These various sources of urban housing capacity are brought together in the table on page 140 which is taken from our research for Friends of the Earth. If all the potential capacity is added together and was developed at urban densities the total capacity of urban areas would be just under 7.3 million homes. This however will never happen and we set out policy targets for each of the capacity sources to achieve a target of 75% of all new homes within urban areas. Even this however will never be achieved unless we address the workings of the property market and the planning system. It is also the case that the greatest housing capacity is in the areas with the lowest levels of household growth. In the growth areas of the south most available land has been developed as is natural in a buoyant urban economy. The greatest potential exists in northern areas which have been losing population and investment for many years. It is the development of this underused capacity which holds the greatest potential both to accommodate household growth and to stem the decline of these urban areas. However if this is to happen two concerns also raised by the TCPA need to be addressed. The first is that the development of this land will lead to town cramming and the second is that there is no demand to live or work in these areas.

The 'curse' of town cramming

One of the concerns which has permeated the debate about urban repopulation is the fear of town cramming. Collis, quoted in the *Compact City* warns that 'settlements could consume themselves from within by eating up the private and public greenspace that contributes so much to urban quality'[44]. Town cramming is seen as leading to the loss of open space, increased congestion and a lower quality of life for urban dwellers. These issues have a long pedigree. They date back to Victorian concerns about overcrowding and density which have been a major influence on modern town planning but how relevant are they to today's city? While the recent literature on urban containment is full of concerns about town cramming it is rarely defined nor is the nature or extent of the problem explored. It is almost as if it is an accepted pillar of planning philosophy which is not open to question and as such casts a shadow over the entire debate.

If town cramming has a relevance to the urban repopulation debate then it surely must be in London. Parts of London, it is true, seem overcrowded and polluted and large amounts of infill development could make this worse. London is however built to much lower densities than many other European cities. Inner Paris, for example, has three times the population density of inner London and yet is not three times more uncomfortable to live in. This is even more true of northern cities which have been haemorrhaging population for much of the last century. The populations of some of our northern cities rattle around in the shells of cities built for much larger populations.

The fear of town cramming is part of the traditional confusion between overcrowding, space standards and density. This is illustrated by a quote from Professor Alan Hooper[45] '...an unreflective response which matches smaller households to smaller dwellings at high densities in concentrated urban areas is not likely to result in a sustainable form of development'. The first part of this point is well made rising incomes make it dangerous to assume that smaller households will opt for smaller units. However to equate this to high-density urban development is to make a mistake that planners have been making for many years. There is no reason why large apartments or even houses cannot exist in urban areas at high densities as witnessed by Knightsbridge or St. John's Wood in London, Manhattan in New York or Central Paris.

A useful way of reconciling these confusions has been suggested by Brenda Vale and Ernie Scoffam[46] who have suggested a distinction between the density and the intensity of development. The former is an objective measure of the number of houses, people or rooms to the hectare while the latter is a subjective measure of how crowded a place feels. They point out that the relationship between density and intensity is far from clear. Many intense environments such as high-rise council estates, are actually built to quite low densities whereas many high-density environments, particularly in historic areas do not feel overcrowded. Alice Coleman made a similar point in *Utopia on Trial*[47] when she said that 'flats certainly cram in more litter, crime and van-dalism to the acre… but they do not, in Britain, pack in more dwellings to the acre'.

Scoffam and Vale conclude by suggesting that prescriptions about density are irrelevant since 'the same density can conceal a variety of built forms which both psychologically and physically may be either compact or loose, urban or sub-urban, intense or diffuse'. Problems arise when

The density gradient:
A comparison of densities of different types of development

Area	Units/Ha	Persons/Ha	Source
Low density detached – Hertfordshire	5	20	Urban Initiatives
Average net density Los Angeles	15	60	Newman and Kenworthy
Milton Keynes average 1990	17	68	Sherlock
Average density of new development in UK 1981-91	22	88	Bibby and Shepherd
Minimum density for a bus service	25	100	Local Government Management Board Sustainable Settlements Guide (assuming that the housing is occupied to capacity)
Private sector 1960s/70s – Hertfordshire	25	100	Urban Initiatives
Inter-war estate – Hertfordshire	30	120	Urban Initiatives
Raymond Unwin 1912	30	120	Nothing gained by overcrowding
Tudor-Walters 1919	30	120	Local Government Management Board's Manual on the preparation of state-aided housing schemes
Private sector 1980s/90s – Hertfordshire	30	120	Urban Initiatives
Hulme – Manchester 1970s	37	148	Hulme guide to development
Average net density London	42	168	Newman and Kenworthy
Ebenezer Howard - Garden city 1898	45	180	Tomorrow: A peaceful path to real reform
Minimum density for a tram service	60	240	Local Government Management Board Sustainable Settlements Guide
Abercrombie - Low density	62	247	Greater London Plan 1944
RIBA	62	247	Homes for the future group
New town high-density low-rise – Hertfordshire	64	256	Urban Initiatives
Sustainable urban density	69	275	Friends of the Earth
Hulme – Manchester planned	80	320	Hulme guide to development
Victorian/Edwardian terraces – Hertfordshire	80	320	Urban Initiatives
Abercrombie – Medium density	84	336	Greater London Plan 1944
Central accessible urban density	93	370	Friends of the Earth
Holly Street – London 1990s	94	376	Levitt Bernstein Architects
Holly Street – London 1970s	104	416	Levitt Bernstein Architects
Abercrombie - High density	124	494	Greater London Plan 1944
Sustainable Urban Neighbourhood (maximum)	124	494	URBED
Hulme – Manchester 1930s	150	600	Hulme guide to development
Average net density Islington - 1965	185	740	Milner-Holland
Singapore planned densities 1970s	250	1,000	Scoffham and Vale
Kowloon actual	1,250	5,000	Scoffham and Vale

1. The grey boxes show the source figure from which the density has been calculated
2. An average dwelling size of 4 bedspaces has been assumed throughout this table although it should be noted that this is higher that the average household size in the UK.

densities are increased without rethinking the design of housing and the layout of urban areas. If the density of suburban designs are increased, lower space standards are inevitable along with congestion and a lack of open space. However this is not inevitable. Since the 1960s architects have known that the optimum form to maximise density without creating the perception of over-crowding is the three or four storey terrace around squares and open spaces. This is the traditional way in which the Georgians built within cities and there is no reason why we should not rediscover these forms as Harley Sherlock has suggested[48] to ensure that quality space standards and urban development are both achieved.

It therefore seems that there is a great deal of potential to increase the population of urban areas, particularly in the north, without running the risk of town cramming. This is why we have used the term urban repopulation rather than urban infill because we are advocating the replacement of a proportion of the populations that these cities have lost. This does however raise the question of whether people will want to return to these areas.

Will people return to cities?

The problem with urban repopulation is that people have been voting with their feet by leaving urban areas in their droves for many years. If people do not wish to live in large cities, why should they be forced to do so? As Michael Breheny has suggested: 'Clearly there are groups of people – of particular ages, occupations and levels of income – who may choose high density urban living. Likewise there are high density urban areas – usually historically and architecturally interesting and socially exclusive – that remain popular through time. However these people and these areas are very much the exception. Many

Town cramming?
There are many historic environments like Rye which are built to very high densities yet which people regard as attractive places to live

people who do live in high density urban areas, as in inner rings, are more likely to have been trapped.. than they are to have made a conscious decision to live there'[49].

Is this traditional view still relevant? Demographic change means that the groups of 'particular age, occupation and income' may constitute a far greater proportion of UK households in the future than they have done in the past. 80% of the net increase in households in the UK will be single people or childless couples who will potentially have very different attitudes to urban living. This trend is already evident in the large numbers of people who have returned to the city to live in London's docklands or Glasgow's warehouse conversions. They are not yet sufficient in number to conclude that this represents a fundamental change in British housing aspirations but they do represent more than just an exception.

It is true also that these people have been attracted back to urban areas which are generally historically and architecturally interesting although they are not necessarily socially exclusive. If these areas are the exception we should surely be questioning urban policy which has made so much of our urban fabric dull and uninteresting. We should also be learning from these popular urban areas to ensure that the qualities which make them attractive are incorporated into new urban areas. In this way the attractions which have brought people back to exceptional urban areas might be spread more widely. It is true that many of the people living in inner city council estates have been trapped there and would leave if they could. However many of these people are living at anything but higher densities. Inner city areas have lost the density required to sustain facilities, activity and community. Far from benefiting from urban life, inner city residents can be as socially and economically isolated as they would be on a far-flung peripheral estate. This is the result not of their urban location but of the legacy of bad planning and mono-tenure single-use housing which has done such damage to our urban areas.

We have reviewed in the first two parts of this book the exodus of population from urban areas and the trends which may cause this to change. However it is also important to understand how household projections and regional housing allocations have reinforced this exodus and could be a barrier to change. Because of the way that household projections have been used in the past, it is possible that they have not just responded to migration patterns, but have actually shaped them. This is based upon the circularity argument which suggests that if population growth is predicted in a particular area, that is where new housing is built and so is where more people will live. This increase in population then causes the next round of household projections to be revised upwards and so on around a self-fulfilling circle. This argument can apply on a number of levels. It has, for example, been argued that household growth itself is dependent on housebuilding and that if houses are not built fewer households will form. At the regional level it has also been argued that the fact that we build more houses in the south than the north is one of the reasons for higher levels of population growth in the south. At both of these levels the circularity argument has weaknesses. However it becomes much more important at the local level within travel to work areas. Why for example are we catering for high levels of predicted household growth in the Wirral, Cheshire and Warwickshire when the housebuilding is fuelling migration from the adjacent conurbations? The forecasts of modest household growth in these urban areas compared to the surrounding rural counties has caused housebuilding to be concentrated in the latter which has inevitably meant that these areas have further increased in population while the urban areas have further declined. This, of course, is not the whole picture and does not explain why some very good quality new housing association property in inner urban areas still proves difficult to let. However it may be that in catering for household growth governments have not just been responding to inevitable trends but have unwittingly conspired in the depopulation of urban areas.

This also raises questions about the targets for the proportion of homes built within urban areas. If we are committed to 60% of all new homes being built within urban areas why do the housing allocations continue to require the districts with the smallest urban areas to accommodate the lion's share of growth? If these targets are to be achieved it will be important to grasp the nettle and to redirect a proportion of household growth back into the larger urban areas which have surplus capacity. This does not mean forcing the aspiring housebuyers of Warwickshire into Hansworth or those of Cheshire into Moss Side. These cities also have attractive, desirable residential areas and it is possible that if they were asked to accommodate a higher proportion of household growth the process of urban repopulation could start in earnest. The approach announced by the Labour government in February 1998 makes this possible. By moving away from the 'predict and provide' approach to one where household growth in planned, managed and monitored there is the scope to shift household growth between counties which provides an important opportunity for urban areas.

This raises the issue of economic activity. The population loss of cities has, on the face of it, been the result of economic decline. As unemployment rises some people will follow Norman Tebbit's advice to get on their bike and find work elsewhere. However there is also a circular nature to this argument since depopulation is both a result and a cause of urban economic decline. This argument is expanded by Jacobs in the *Economy of Cities*[50] where she points out that population decline is always correlated with economic stagnation and that economic development is only possible if populations first start expanding. The reason is that increasing populations expand the size of local markets, generate more people capable of starting new economic activity and widen the choice of workforce for employers. It is also true that when populations decline it tends to be the most able and motivated who leave, the very people that local economies can least do without. This can be illustrated with the example of Liverpool which has lost more than a quarter of a million people since 1961, say 100 000 households. If we assume that the average household income of these households in today's terms is a modest £10 000 per year, it means that the city is losing £1 billion a year as a result of population loss. While only a proportion of this would be recycled in the local economy this would include more than £70 million worth of Council Tax as well as spending in local shops and services, dwarfing the public subsidy which currently flows into the city. This is as poorly understood today as it was in Jane Jacobs' time but it does suggest that the repopulation of our urban areas is an important prerequisite for economic regeneration, not something which must wait until regeneration is underway.

The crime, poverty and social problems which have come to be associated with residualised urban populations, like economic decline, are also a symptom as well as a cause of urban depopulation. As able people flee the inner city, it has become a repository for those members of society least able to escape. A vicious circle is thus created since people will not be attracted back into inner areas until they can see more people like themselves living in these areas. Particularly important in this respect is education because the problem of urban schools is a microcosm of the wider urban condition. Children in inner city schools are less likely to succeed and parents cannot be expected to sacrifice their children's education for an ideal of urban living. The search for better education is therefore one of the most important aspects which causes people to leave cities. Once more urban repopulation is a requirement for breaking down the social stigma which has become attached to the inner city and making it an attractive place for a far wider cross section of society. In our work for Friends of the Earth we suggested the designation of Urban Priority Areas where tax incentives would be provided for new urban housing along with targeted initiatives to improve local schools and services. Concentrating effort in this way should help to create a critical mass to overcome the barriers to urban repopulation, and the Sustainable Urban Neighbourhood provided a model for how it might take place.

It is likely that social, demographic and environmental change will increase the attractiveness of urban living. This may in turn create a virtuous circle by which urban populations start to rise and economic and social problems become easier to address. This should give some comfort to those who argue that urban repopulation will make huge demands on the public purse. Kick-starting the process will, it is true, be expensive, but if a momentum is established the process will become self-sustaining.

In this chapter we have argued that there are good reasons for repopulating towns and cities. This will bring environmental benefits as well as injecting new life into areas which have been declining as a result of population dispersal for many years. There is the housing capacity in urban areas, particularly in the north, to accommodate this growth and the traditional concerns about town cramming and lack of demand can be overcome. Much of the debate about urban containment has been driven by absolutist positions. The 'decenterists' have reacted against a perception that containment will force people to live in dangerous overcrowded urban areas or a nostalgic and impossible vision of the Italian hill town. In contrast the 'centralists' have recoiled in horror from the prospect of green and pleasant pastures being consumed by the hated suburban semi. Neither position is very helpful and the debate is really about the relative balance between urban development, suburban expansion and new settlements. As Breheny says, 'Does the answer have to lie in one extreme or the other? Will town or country only survive under decenterist or centralist regime? Could they survive satisfactorily under a middle line, a compromise?' It is possible to argue that more housing should be built in urban areas without suggesting that all housing should be built there. However whereas we are pretty good at developing suburbs we have lost the knack of building urban areas. Attracting more people to live in towns therefore requires the development of new models for urban living, which is what we turn to in the next three chapters.

CHAPTER 10
The eco-neighbourhood

The name, the Sustainable Urban Neighbourhood has been chosen with care. Each element represents an important principle. **Sustainable** refers to the ability of the neighbourhood and wider urban systems to be sustained and to minimise their environmental impact. **Urban** refers both to the location of the area and to its physical character whilst **neighbourhood** relates to the social and economic sustainability of the area, the community ties which hold it together and its relationship to surrounding areas. In simple terms our aim is to create urban areas which will endure. In this wider sense the term sustainability can be applied to economic and social as well as environmental systems. We envisage urban areas which minimise their impact on the environment but which can also be sustained economically and socially in the future; urban areas which will not require public investment and wholesale redevelopment in the future; unlike many of the urban areas built in the twentieth century. Urban character and the importance of the neighbourhood will be described in the following chapters. Here we will focus on the concept of environmental sustainability.

What is urban sustainability?

If by urban sustainability we mean towns and cities which sustain themselves without any adverse impact on wider natural systems then the sustainable urban neighbourhood is an impossible goal. The last human settlement to be sustainable in this respect, in Europe at least, was probably the small medieval town dependent on its local hinterland. It is widely recognised that the way that we plan human settlements has an important role to play in increasing the sustainability of human activities. It is therefore incumbent on those who shape towns and cities to at least ensure that they are less unsustainable and minimise their impact on the natural environment.

It is important to be clear what we mean by environmental sustainability in the urban context. To some sustainability implies self-sufficiency. This is something which has been achieved by pioneers like Robert and Brenda Vale in small-scale developments[1]. They have developed individual homes and small groups of houses which are entirely self-sufficient; producing their own energy, recycling waste and collecting and treating water. The key to achieving this has been to reduce the resource requirements of the buildings to a point where they can be supplied from natural sources such as sun and rain and from the wastes produced by the building. The Vales would argue that all housing could be built like this and have produced a number of autonomous housing schemes; some for housing associations within very tight cost constraints[2]. This is however a long way from the development of a self-sufficient neighbourhood.

There have been attempts to build self-sufficient villages often in remote rural areas. These have been described by the Gaia Foundation as 'human scale, full featured settlements which integrate human activity harmlessly into the natural environment'[3], a worthy goal for any urban neighbourhood. There are more than a hundred such settlements in Sweden alone and the Eco-Village Foundation has members in twenty-one countries across Europe, Russia, India, Australia and the USA. These settlements – like Findhorn in Scotland which is probably the best-known British example – grow their own food, generate their own power, and recycle their waste; coming as close as it is possible to an environmentally benign human settlement. They are however small in scale, rarely exceeding a population of 500, and demand time and commitment from their members. To many people they may offer an attractive way of life but only the most extreme environmental fundamentalist would suggest that the majority of the population should or could live this way.

There are precious few examples of eco-village ideas being applied in the urban context. Perhaps the only two examples are Christania in Copenhagen and Kreuzberg in Berlin, both of which were established as squatter settlements. Christania was originally a military camp which was taken over by squatters in the 1960s and has since become accepted by public authorities. Kreuzberg was a district isolated by the Berlin Wall which fell into decline and was colonised by squatter communities in the 1970s and 80s. Before German reunification transformed Kreuzberg from a backwater into a desirable district at the heart of the new German capital, it was probably the nearest urban equivalent to the rural eco-village. Like their rural counterparts the Kreuzberg squatters were driven by environmental ideals although this was given added edge by the practical realities of squatting buildings which lacked basic services. There were, for exam-

Kreuzberg: A mixed-use social housing block in Kreuzberg, Berlin

ple, blocks in Kreuzberg which created vertical reed beds with a series of oil drums down the side of the building through which sewage would filter and be purified and others which incorporated wind turbines, solar panels and food growing. Kreuzberg was the subject of a major regeneration programme from 1987 under the auspices of STERN, which can teach us much about sustainable urban development, but even at its most ambitious it could not be described as a self-sufficient neighbourhood.

Something of the kind has been researched by the Martin Centre for Architectural and Urban Studies in Cambridge. Through their work on Project ZED[4] (Zero Emissions Urban Development) with architects and academics in the UK, France and Germany, they have developed theoretical models for self-sufficient urban blocks. Like the autonomous house and the eco-village these blocks do not rely on external services. However at present they only exist in a computer to create models of urban resource systems. The practical implications of Project ZED are being explored by architects, including Future Systems, who are working up schemes for sites in London, Toulouse and Berlin.

Sustainability and the city

The development of autonomous houses, villages and even urban blocks may be a possible if complex task. However this complexity is nothing compared to the issues raised by addressing the sustainability of a whole neighbourhood or indeed city. As Robert and Brenda Vale state[5] 'Green Architecture must encompass a sustainable form of urban development. The city is far more than a collection of buildings, rather it can be seen as a series of interacting systems – systems for living, working and playing – crystallised into built forms. It is by looking at these systems that we can find the face of the city of the future.' These systems are not easy to pin down. They are not neatly confined to individual neighbourhoods or even to whole cities but operate on a regional, national and increasingly global level. It has been estimated for example that the eco-footprint of London[6] is equivalent to the entire land area of

the UK although, of course, it is not neatly confined to these shores but stretches into every corner of the world. Cities use tropical hardwoods plundered from rain forests, import food from across the globe so that fruits and vegetables are never out of season, emit sulphur dioxide which kills forests thousands of miles away whilst their CO_2 collects in the atmosphere and their wastes pollute the world's oceans. Just as cities lie at the heart of global trading systems so they dominate global systems of resource consumption and pollution.

The traditional picture of UK cities and industrial towns with smokestack industries defiling the landscape may be fading but it has been replaced with an image of the fume-clogged, resource-hungry metropolis. Something of the scale of this can be seen from Herbert Girardet's *Metabolism of London*[7]. In this he estimated the annual resource consumption of London with a population of 7 million to include more than a billion tonnes of water, 20 million tonnes of fuel oil equivalent, 2.4 million tonnes of food, about 8 million tonnes of building materials and 1.2 million tonnes of metals. As a result of this London produces 8.2 million tonnes of inert waste, 2.4 million tonnes of household wastes, and 7.5 million tonnes of sewage sludge. It also emits into the atmosphere 60 million tonnes of CO_2, 400 000 tonnes of sulphur dioxide and 280 000 of nitrogen oxides. London is not unique in this respect, indeed it is probably much better than many American cities. But it is still hard to look at the pall of pollution that hangs over the city on summer days, the barges carrying waste to landfill sites, the diminution of water resources and the congested streets and not to conclude that there can be no less sustainable way of life.

It is tempting to conclude that cities are environmental disasters and have no place in a sustainable future. But cities are here to stay. As Girardet points out[8], there will be a baby born within the next few years which will tip the balance so that more than half of the world's population live in cities. The reform of urban areas is therefore unavoidable if we are to achieve sustainability at the global level. Yet ironically cities may be part of the solution to global sustainability as well as part of the problem. We described in the last chapter how the repopulation of cities could help reduce transport energy use as well as protecting the countryside. This is only part of the story. It is possible that living in cities may be the sensible environmental choice for a number of reasons. This is based upon an understanding that it is not cities which damage the environment but the people who live in them. It is true that in the developing world cities attract people from self-sufficient rural economies leading to a huge increase in per-capita resource consumption. This is not however the case in the developed world where people in rural areas are no less demanding in their desires for commodities and services. Because of the much lower population densities in these areas the resources required to serve these needs are far greater than they would be in the city. Rural dwellers travel twice the distance by car each year than do their urban counterparts[9], the distribution distances for goods and services are greater and the infrastructure required to provide basic services more extensive.

If London did not exist where would its seven million people live and would they consume any less resources or produce any less pollution? If these people and the thousands of companies and organisations based in the city were to be spread out at garden city densities across the south of England their environmental impact could be enormous. To the environmental balance sheet would have to be added the costs of distributing goods over much wider areas, the loss of public transport as it became less viable, the increased problems of recycling and transporting waste, the difficulty of heating freestanding buildings, the miles of road to be built, serviced and lit, the fact that postage and newspapers would have to be delivered by road, not to mention the hectares of green fields that would be developed. It may be that in a dispersed low-density polycentric settlement consumer habits would change and teleworking would reduce travel. However this is not dependent on decentralisation and would have an even greater environmental impact if it were to take place within a dense urban area.

It is arguable that the massive outward expansion of British cities means that the dispersed low-density model has already been partly realised. The European cities to which Girardet compares London so unfavourably are built to much higher densities which explains the vibrancy of their streets and the fact that they can support a vastly superior public transport system and have the density of demand to make services such as recycling and local power regeneration viable. Sustainability in its broadest sense is much more difficult to imagine in a dispersed settlement than in a compact city. The dense, walkable city may therefore be the most environmentally efficient form of settlement for the majority of the population. This was probably best summed up by Roger Levett, when he was at the Scottish Development Agency, when he said; 'with the exception of food-growing virtually everything can be done more greenly within cities'[10]. We will not secure a sustainable future for Britain by building eco-villages, we must rise to the challenge and reform our towns and cities.

At present the metabolism of urban areas is a linear system with resources coming in at one end and wastes being produced at the other. Increasing urban sustainability implies the transformation of many of these linear systems into circular systems whereby waste outputs provide the raw materials for resource inputs. It

Sustainability and the city region:
An illustration from the Manchester 2020 project

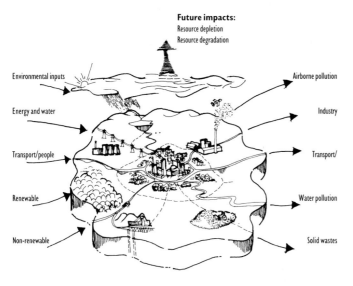

Future impacts:
Resource depletion
Resource degradation

Environmental inputs

Energy and water

Transport/people

Renewable

Non-renewable

Airborne pollution

Industry

Transport/

Water pollution

Solid wastes

may not be possible, as with autonomous housing, to completely close the system but it is possible to do this to a far greater extent than we do now. We must look at the balance between resources imported into cities and their neighbourhoods and the wastes exported in order to reduce their contribution to the unsustainability of wider systems. Something of the kind has been studied at the scale of the city region by the Manchester 2020 project[11]. This was initiated by the Town and Country Planning Association and Manchester Metropolitan University and explored the resource consumption and waste production of the Greater Manchester conurbation. The study which reported in the Summer of 1995 proposed a range of measures required to bring the impact of the conurbation within the environmental carrying capacity of the wider area. This was a mammoth task and the final report runs to several volumes. As with many environmental initiatives such a comprehensive approach to a mass of issues makes it difficult to draw out a clear message which can be used to influence action on the ground. The Manchester 2020 team have recognised this and have suggested that some of the implications of their work should be explored at a more local neighbourhood level, and indeed make reference to our work on the Sustainable Urban Neighbourhood as a possible means for doing this.

Whilst it is clear that the concept of urban sustainability is complex there are a number of fundamental principles which apply to all sustainable development be it a house or a neighbourhood.

Reduce inputs: The first is to reduce the inputs to the system in terms of the resources and energy consumed by the neighbourhood. The Vales are only able to achieve autonomy in their housing by reducing the need for heat, water and power to minimal levels which can then be supplied by the house itself. Whilst the urban neighbourhood will never reduce its resource inputs to a level which can be locally supplied the reduction of inputs must be the starting point for any sustainable policy.

Local resources: The second principle is then to make maximum use of local resources such as the sun and the rain which falls on the roofs of the neighbourhood and the food which can be grown in its gardens and allotments. These local resources also include waste produced by the neighbourhood such as restored water which can be used for toilet flushing or composted waste which can nourish gardens and allotments. By minimising the input of resources and maximising the use of local resources the neighbourhood can significantly reduce the level of resources imported into the area.

Waste minimisation: The neighbourhood must also minimise the amount of unrecycled or unrecyclable waste exported from the area, which is the third principle of sustainability. The UK government has set a target of 25% of domestic waste being recycled by the year 2000[12] and the sustainable urban neighbourhood has the potential to exceed this target by making recycling a normal part of everyday life with segregated waste collection in the home and municipal waste collection.

Making use of urban economies: However sustainability is about more than just the collection of waste for recycling, it is about the productive use of that waste to reduce the consumption of natural resources. This is the fourth principle of urban sustainability which is the role that urban areas play in economic and trading systems. The first three principles are common to all sustainable development but the fourth is where cities come into their own. Environmental efficiency is about the matching up of supply and demand. Green consumer products, waste recycling, public transport etc. are only viable if they can find a market and it is in cities that the major markets exist. Even the most committed eco-community in the heart of the countryside is going to find it difficult to smelt its waste aluminium or glass or to pulp and recycle its paper. It is going to struggle to run an efficient bus service or to manufacture low-energy light bulbs. Such activities require the sort of markets that only cities can provide. Thus urban areas as natural centres for trade have an important role to play in promoting more circular systems of resource consumption and waste production.

The eco-neighbourhood

If we are to discover the face of the city of the future we must explore the implications of these four principles on the design and planning of cities and the neighbourhoods within them. We must invent an urban equivalent of the eco-village. Concentrating, as we have tended to do, on either the design of the individual building or the broad sweep of national and international policy misses many of the most crucial issues of environmental sustainability. The latter is too remote from actions required on the ground whilst the former has become a technical challenge, producing super-green buildings increasingly divorced from the standard product of most developers, or the condition of the existing built stock. There is much that can be achieved on the scale of the individual building, but surely now the challenge is not to push back further the frontiers of ecological building, but to raise standards across the board and to address wider issues such as car use, energy production and recycling. For this we need wider canvas, and the neighbourhood is an appropriate level with which to work, large enough to address broader environmental issues but small enough to affect people's lives and to focus minds on the practicality of implementation.

New urban visions: Just as nineteenth century reformers produced Utopian visions for the city so should we. Examples include the US Pedestrian Pocket (above right) and the UK Urban Village (below)

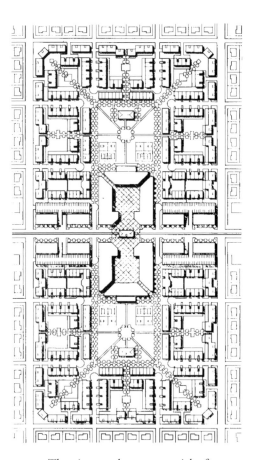

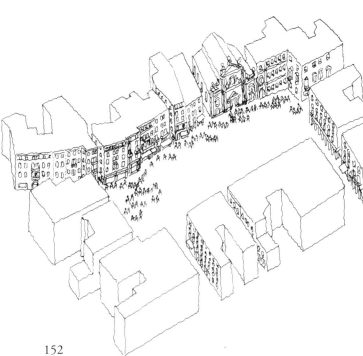

The nineteenth century social reformers produced Utopian visions for the city should not the twenty-first century environmental reformers be doing the same? While the city has tended to be seen as a source of environmental problems and as such a target for condemnation rather than reform, sustainable urban models have started to develop. Concerns about car use, in particular, have led to an emerging consensus that the answer lies in dense walkable settlements around public transport nodes. There are however two distinct schools of thought about how this should be achieved. The first adheres to the garden city tradition of relatively dense nodes of development within a general pattern of dispersal. This is the position of the UK Town and Country Planning Association, the original concept of the Urban Village[13] and the American Pedestrian Pocket movement[14]. The second school of thought favours the repopulation (or compaction according to its critics) of existing cities by increasing densities and developing brown field land. This is the current position of the Urban Villages Forum and also the policy of the UK government and European Union. Whilst a vociferous debate has raged between the two schools, both accept the need to increase development densities to make urban areas more sustainable. Both therefore require new models of urban development which respond to environmental concerns and are capable of accommodating higher densities. Both require a new vision for the eco or sustainable urban neighbourhood.

What will such environmentally sustainable urban neighbourhoods look like? One of the more extreme visions of such a reform is set out in Richard Register's book *Ecocity Berkeley* [15]. In this he describes a Utopian vision for his home town which he envisaged being transformed into a dense mixed-use urban area with cascading terraced buildings covered with plants, '...like small mountains where greenhouse roofs and glass wind screens rise above the vegetation to shine in the blue sky'. He describes a city in which buildings are laced with alleys, passages, halls, atria, galleries and bridges between buildings, so pampered will be the pedestrian. This has overtones of some of the earlier Utopian visions about which people are understandably wary. Indeed it has similarities to the 'streets in the sky' which so captured the imagination with the early deck-access developments. A more common approach has been to see the sustainable settlement of the future as being much more similar to the traditional settlement of the past. These range from the evocation of the dense Italian hill town in the *European Green Paper on the Urban Environment* to the promotion of the traditional small American town by the Pedestrian Pocket movement in the US. The Vales [16] have argued that since the city of the future will be based on the needs of the pedestrian its physical form will be similar to traditional towns which were also based on travel by foot. From these various models we can start to postulate what environmentally sustainable urban neighbourhood might look like.

Ecocity Berkeley: Is this a vision of the sustainable city of the future?

The walkable city

The reduction of car use is seen by many commentators as the most profound influence on future development forms. Just as the central location of the sustainable urban neighbourhood will reduce the need for car-borne commuting so its internal organisation should be pedestrian centred. This is the opposite of most current housing and commercial areas. The pedestrian far from being 'pampered' is subjugated to the needs of the car and forced into subways and over footbridges lest they interrupt the free flow of traffic. Even away from main roads concerns about the car still dominate. Urban areas have been designed to exclude through traffic so that even the shortest journeys can involve lengthy detours, not a problem in a car but an obstacle course for the pedestrian. At their most extreme, as in Los Angeles, such layouts make a car indispensable for virtually all journeys. In a sustainable urban neighbourhood, walking and cycling should be the most convenient mode of transport for all local trips. This has a number of implications for design.

Permeability: The first implication is that the neighbourhood should be permeable, at least to the pedestrian. Permeability as a term refers to the ease with which water passes through a substance such as rock. In the urban design context it has come to refer to the ease with which people can move through an area by a choice of routes. Permeable layouts are those where each street leads to another street which in turn leads to another street and so on. It also stresses the importance of avoiding long stretches of road without junctions. These may be attractive to highway engineers but they encourage traffic speed and reduce the choice of routes. Impermeable layouts are characterised by looping feeder roads which lead to cul-de-sacs and closes. In permeable areas all parts of the neighbourhood are accessible with particular emphasis on access to nodes of activity such as shopping centres. In impermeable areas the pedestrian is treated as a second-class citizen, large parts of the public realm are devoid of activity and the car is king.

Personal safety: Permeability like many of the principles that we are promoting has attracted criticism not least from the police who favour more 'defensible' impermeable layouts. Indeed concerns about security are probably the greatest threat to walkability in many urban areas. Fears about personal safety reduce the attraction of walking and cause developers to close routes through developments, the most extreme example being the gated communities now so common in the US. The effect of this is to make walking even less

attractive, not only because direct routes are blocked but because pavements become deserted and devoid of surveillance from surrounding buildings. This can lead to the absurd situation where pedestrians prefer to risk narrow pavements on heavy traffic routes rather than a deserted pedestrian route where they might be safe from cars but not from muggers. However in permeable urban areas where walking is not a deviant activity pavements are populated and lively and therefore much safer.

Legibility: Another important factor is the ease with which it is possible to understand the structure of a neighbourhood and to 'read' it as you walk around. Traditional urban areas are generally easy and pleasant to walk around. This relates partly to the variety of buildings and townscape. In areas with no landmarks where everything looks the same, walking is monotonous and it is easy to get lost. It also relates to the layout of the area. In traditional urban neighbourhoods main routes tend to lead to the centre and a grid of streets, whether formal or informal makes orientation straight forward. If you miss a right turn it is normally possible to take the next right and then turn right again to get onto your intended route. By contrast in modern developments a wrong turn can get you hopelessly lost in a maze of winding cul-de-sacs.

The walkable city: Traditional urban grids, whether formal or informal encourage walking (above)

The disconnected city: The plan below left shows how the layout of urban areas makes it impossible to walk and channels all traffic onto distributor roads. It is possible to reconnect the city as illustrated by the plan below right

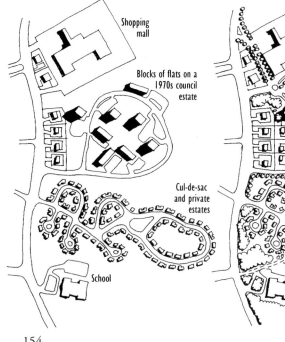

Shopping mall

Blocks of flats on a 1970s council estate

Cul-de-sac and private estates

School

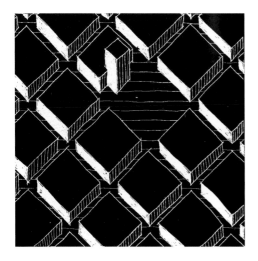

Taming the car: To many people a pedestrian-centred neighbourhood means the exclusion of the car. A number of car-free developments are currently being proposed in the UK and many city centres have successfully excluded cars. Indeed cities like Florence in Italy have excluded cars entirely from the old city bringing about huge improvements in air quality and the attractiveness of the street environment. However a pedestrian-centred neighbourhood does not mean a pedestrianised neighbourhood. The experience of the last fifty years is a warning against creating the deserted pedestrian environments which characterise many inner city estates and indeed less successful town centres. The key to the pedestrian-friendly neighbourhood is to tame rather than to exclude the car. This means reducing traffic speeds and reclaiming much more of the street area for pedestrians but it does not mean removing cars entirely from urban areas. Excluding cars and parking removes activity from streets making them feel less safe and therefore, ironically, less attractive to pedestrians. This was confirmed by research by Environmental and Transport Planning[17] which looked at the 'sociability' of streets and public spaces in nineteen towns in four European countries. They found no relationship between the extent of pedest-rianised areas and the level of social and pedestrian activity. More important was the scale and familiarity of streets and squares – streets that were too wide or too tall did not encourage walking and the most positive reactions were to historic urban areas. Streets with active frontages such as ground-floor commercial uses are also important in making streets feel safer and encouraging pedestrian activity. The urban character of an area may therefore serve an important role in promoting walking. This includes a mix of uses to create activity throughout the day and active frontages, a hierarchy of streets serving different functions and accommodating different levels of traffic and an urban form which creates a level of enclosure and intimacy without being claustrophobic. We will return to these aspects of urban character in the next chapter.

CAR-FREE HOUSING: EDINBURGH

Edinburgh is home to one of the UK's first planned car-free housing schemes to be developed by Canmore Housing Association. The scheme on disused rail land will consist of 121 flats and will provide 'energy efficient homes in a car-free environment'. People wanting to buy or rent flats will have to sign an agreement not to attempt to bring a car onto the estate in which there will be no parking facilities. It is intended to establish a car club on the edge of the site in due course. The land that would have been used for parking will be used for terraced gardens, allotments and reed beds for grey water recycling. The site being developed at densities of 50 units to the acre.

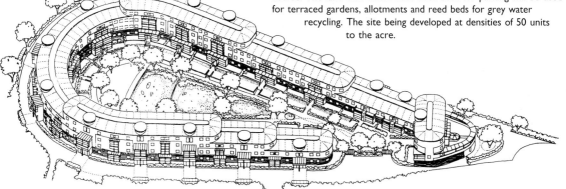

POUNDBURY IN DORSET

Poundbury is being developed by the Duchy of Cornwall as a planned extension to Dorchester. The initial phase provides 244 houses and flats (35 for renting and 209 for sale), offices, retail space and workshops. The masterplan by Leon Krier creates a mixed-use 'urban village' based on perimeter blocks and courtyards. Houses are built to the back of pavement in order to maximise urban form and street character and no two adjacent houses are to be designed by the same architect, ensuring a mix of styles. It is eventually planned that Poundbury should have a population of 6-8,000 and take up to 25 years to build so that the village and its community grows organically.

Taming the car: The plan incorporates a radical approach to the motor car developed by Alan Baxter Associates. Rather than seeking to calm or exclude traffic through engineering it seeks to civilise the car through the urban layout. The starting point was

to create pleasing urban spaces which were human in scale. Only once this was done were the pavements and roads fitted into these spaces. The highway engineering is therefore dictated by the building form rather than vice versa. Streets are shaped to avoid long vistas so reducing acceleration distances. Junctions also include tight radii and limited sight lines forcing drivers to stop rather than to glance and drive through. Parking is accommodated in wider streets and courtyards as well as being attached to individual dwellings. At the insistence of the planners the parking standards are still very high with two places per dwelling plus visitor parking.

The development is regulated by a tight building agreement by which the Duchy can render development rights forfeit if the scheme does not go ahead as intended. House buyers are also subject to restrictive covenants regulating maintenance and alterations to the homes. It is intended to eventually transfer these rights to a community controlled management company.

Creative congestion: The design and management of streets is also important in making areas pedestrian friendly. Colin Davies in his work for the Royal Fine Arts Commission[18] has explored how streets can be made more attractive by widening pavements, providing cycle lanes and calming traffic. The latter need not necessarily be through the traditional techniques of chicanes, pinch points and speed humps. Just as effective and less intrusive can be limited sight lines, tight corner radii, narrow carriageways and street trees as proposed by Alan Baxter Associates in Poundbury[19]. However one of the best forms of traffic calming is street activity, dare we say, a degree of congestion. Traffic lights, traditional cross roads, pedestrian crossings, on-street parking and turning movements all serve to reduce traffic speeds in traditional urban areas to a walking pace. It may seem perverse to suggest traffic congestion as an important characteristic of a pedestrian-friendly urban neighbourhood. However congestion is another name for vitality which is part of the

attraction of urban areas and why many urban streets lose much of their character when traffic is excluded. Provided that heavy vehicles are restricted and generous space is given over to pedestrians and cyclists, this congestion need not undermine the quality of the environment. The result is not that the car dominates but that environments are created which are more pleasant for pedestrians. Motorists are not given the impression that they have free and unhindered right of way so that they are prepared for pedestrians. In such streets it is natural to drive

slowly and the introduction of 20 mile an hour zones should make it possible for such ideas to be applied much more widely in our cities.

Indeed it is possible that the creative use of congestion could play a role in traffic reduction. We have argued through the SUN Initiative[20] that many traffic reduction measures suffer from the same weakness as road building. A new road increases highway capacity thereby making it easier to drive and encouraging more people to use their cars. The level of traffic therefore increases until the road system is once again congested when the attractiveness of driving is once more reduced and traffic growth slows. This suggests that traffic will tend to increase to a level just below the saturation point of a given road system. The weakness of many traffic reduction measures is that they reduce traffic without reducing the saturation point of the system. A park and ride scheme, for example, will be successful in taking a significant amount of traffic off a road. This will make it less congested and easier to use so encouraging other drivers to take the place of those using the bus. The only way of reducing total traffic volumes is to combine traffic reduction measures with a reduction in highway capacity to reduce the saturation point of the system – in other words to maintain levels of congestion. The urban neighbourhood could do this by reducing the number and width of carriageways so maintaining traffic calming

congestion with much lower volumes of traffic. In Copenhagen something similar has been done by giving over road space to bicycles and reducing car parking spaces by around 2% per year.

Density: A pedestrian-focused neighbourhood will also be a dense neighbourhood so that distances between facilities are kept to a minimum. Both the Urban Village and Pedestrian Pocket are based on a maximum ten-minute walking time for the majority of the population into the centre. To do this and still retain sufficient people and activity to animate streets and support local services and public transport we need to build to higher densities than has happened in the past. Again there are likely to be objections from those who believe that high-density development is synonymous with overcrowding and a reduction in internal space standards or a return to high-rise development. Rather, in the words of the late Francis Tibbalds, it means 'forgetting the spaced-out buildings of the past few decades, separated from each other by highways and leftover tracts of land and concentrating on producing intricate places related to the scale of people walking not driving'[21]. This goes hand in hand with the concept of mixed-use development since the facilities that people need should be located close at hand rather than being zoned into separate areas. This includes employment, shops, services, schools, and the other facilities needed by the community. Commercial activities should be mixed with the

Reclaiming the streets: Proposals developed by URBED for Darwen Street in Blackburn. This shows how it is possible to widen the pavements so that they can be reclaimed for public life while reducing the traffic capacity of the road.

Energy use

Whilst the development of a pedestrian-friendly environment is probably one of the most important aspects of the sustainable urban neighbourhood it is far from being the only issue which needs to be considered. Other environmental issues will play an equally important role in shaping our cities not least the reduction of energy use and the associated CO_2 emissions. Much of the recent work on energy efficiency has concentrated on the technical aspects of building construction, something that we do not propose to dwell on here. Much less attention has been given to the implications of building type and location.

The energy use of buildings needs to be considered at different stages of its life cycle. The construction of a building accounts for more than 10% of its total energy use. Energy is then used to service and heat the building, to maintain it and to refurbish or demolish it when it is no longer required. In each of these areas urban buildings have a contribution to make. In terms of construction urban buildings potentially use less materials as flats share foundations, roofs and party walls unlike detached dwellings. Against this must be set the need to use energy intensive materials such as steel in larger structures. However systems can be used, such as that proposed for the Millennium Village (see page 120), which have low embodied energy values and can also be dismantled and recycled. More significant in terms of energy used in construction is infrastructure. Urban development can make use of existing roads, services and facilities so avoiding the resources that would be required to provide them on green field sites. The higher density of urban development also reduces the length of roads and service runs required which has both cost and environmental benefits.

Urban house types are also potentially more energy efficient in use than detached and semidetached forms. Heat is lost through the roof, walls and floors of buildings. Since flats and terraced houses have less exposed wall area and, in the case of flats, often no heat-loss roof or floor they are far more energy efficient than detached

housing and focused on the main street and at or around nodes of activity to attract passing trade.

Public transport: The Sustainable Urban Neighbourhood should also be served by an efficient public transport system. In cities like Sheffield, Birmingham and Manchester this may be one of the new tram services; however in many cases it will be the bus. We may lament the decline in public transport and the effects of deregulation and reducing subsidy. However it must be recognised that the dispersal of development and the reduction of housing densities has also played its part. The Local Government Management Board[22] estimates that densities of 100 persons per hectare are required to support a viable bus service and 240 persons per hectare for a tram service, whereas the average density of new housing development is just 22 units to the hectare which, at an average household size, would accommodate around 50 people. Low-density districts will therefore struggle to maintain a bus service and where they exist people will be forced to walk long distances to stops increasing the incentive to use the car. The sustainable urban neighbourhood must counter this trend. It should be organised around public transport so that the maximum number of people can walk easily to stops which are safe and easily accessible. In this way the neighbourhood can tip the balance away from the car by giving people real public transport alternative.

dwellings given the same level of insulation. This is also true of mixed-use buildings where workspace and shops below housing will lose less heat than single-storey structures. Urban buildings are also more likely to be sheltered by surrounding buildings which is one of the factors taken into account when calculating domestic energy use[23]. With district heating or combined heat and power systems, terraced forms also mean that pipes can run within houses so minimising heat loss. It may not always be possible to maximise solar orientation to benefit from passive solar gain. However this accounts for just 15% of the heating needs in most houses and only rises to 25% in south-facing dwellings. With improved window designs which are both airtight and use low emissivity glass to reflect heat back into the home, windows will not lose significant amounts of heat even on north-facing walls so that housing is less sensitive to orientation. There is however much that we can learn from Tony Garnier and his high density housing in the Cité Industrielle. His urban housing on east-west streets along the contours of south-facing slopes maximised both densities and orientation.

Urban buildings are also more efficient in their reuse and refurbishment. Much of the urban housing that has been created over recent years has been in former commercial buildings such as historic mills or offices. This is indicative of the way that urban buildings are flexible enough to be converted to different uses so that the resources used in construction are recycled. Likewise new urban buildings can be designed with reuse in mind; which is one of the principles to guide the Crown Street redevelopment in Glasgow[24].

Power generation: The main source of energy use and CO_2 in a well-insulated building is not heating but lights and appliances which are reliant on electricity. The impact of reducing the electricity consumption of buildings, important as it is, will never have a huge impact because of the inefficiency of power generation which is only 30% efficient.

In the past power generation was locally based. Urban power stations run by councils or small companies would be located in the very heart of cities. While they may have caused problems in terms of pollution they were well suited to serve the needs of their local market and to respond to local peaks of demand. They also had the huge advantage that their waste heat could be used to heat local buildings. Indeed there is still a power station huddled within the warehouses of the Whitworth Street area of Manchester. This no longer produces electricity but is used as a district heating plant providing hot water through steaming pipes running along the canal to the surrounding buildings.

With the nationalisation of the electricity industry many of these urban power stations were seen as uneconomic, out of date and polluting. They were therefore replaced with huge stations such as Ferrybridge in Yorkshire, able to buy coal in bulk and capable of serving whole conurbations. While this may have made economic sense, in energy terms it reduced the efficiency of generation. Rather than being used for heating, waste heat is squandered through huge cooling towers while the large stations find it difficult to respond to peaks and troughs of demand, and losses also result from the transmission of electricity over long distances through the national grid. The waste implicit in this system substantially reduces the impact of electricity-saving in buildings. It means that electricity is the most environmentally damaging form of power, even when it is used in electric vehicles which have so many other environmental benefits.

An important prerequisite for efficient power generation is to bring it back to the local level so that it is more responsive to demand, distribution losses are minimised and waste heat can be put to good use. This is now starting to happen through the privatisation and deregulation of the electricity market. This means that a range of smaller companies and even individuals can generate electricity and sell the surplus back to the national grid. It is also being made possible by the switch to gas as the primary fuel for power generation. Unlike coal or oil which must be transported by road or rail, gas can be piped into the tightest urban locations through the existing distribution network. Improved pollution control also means that power stations can operate in urban areas with virtually no harmful emissions.

The benefits of local power generation can be seen in London where the Corporation of London in partnership with British Gas have built a 30 megawatt power station in the heart of Smithfield Market. This is able to supply the power needs of much of the city and also produces heat for the market and local buildings. This technology is known as Combined Heat and Power (CHP). This is growing rapidly and has recently received government backing[25]. At one extreme it includes the sort of local power station that has been built in London which provides heat. At the other it can involve the conversion of communal heating and hot water boilers, as in the St. Pancras Housing Association case study, to generate electricity. CHP systems convert up to 80% of the fuel energy into a usable form compared to just 30% for traditional power stations and so have the potential to make a major impact

on energy use and the environmental consequences of electricity.

This raises the prospect of the sustainable urban neighbourhood having its own locally controlled power station producing environmentally friendly cheap heat and electricity. This would be linked to a district heating system so doing away with the need for individual domestic boilers. One of the largest such systems is in Copenhagen which has a CHP community heating grid serving 65% of the buildings in the city. Unfortunately district heating systems still have something of a bad press in the UK because of the experience of the 1970s when they were widely used on council estates and regarded as unreliable and inefficient. One of the problems was lack of control and metering so that residents often had to keep their windows open even in winter to control the temperature of their homes. They also had little incentive to conserve energy because they paid a flat rate charge regardless of the amount of heat they used. These problems can now be overcome with improved thermostatic controls and heat meters which measure the difference between the temperature of water entering and leaving the home so that bills can reflect usage.

However problems remain with the viability of CHP. The cost of the plant along with heat distribution pipes and heat meters (which can cost as much as a small domestic boiler) compares unfavourably with individual heating systems. This is particularly true for well-insulated buildings were the heat load is so low that heating is hardly required. Presently the economics stack up where a district heating system already exists and a CHP system can be installed as part of the scheduled replacement of the central boiler. This was the basis of the St. Pancras scheme and has also been done on the Alexander Park estate in Moss Side, Manchester. However where a system is to be installed from scratch the costs remain high and the viability questionable without the public subsidy which has helped many of the schemes on the continent.

A further problem is that the heat and electricity requirements of neighbourhoods differ.

ST. PANCRAS HOUSING ASSOCIATION AND CHP

St. Richards House and Hillwood House are blocks managed by St. Pancras Housing Association near to Euston Station in London. The blocks include 95 flats plus an elderly person's community centre and ten commercial units. The building has a communal heating system originally serves by two boilers. When these boilers were due for renewal it was decided to replace them with 54 kWe CHP unit. This now provides heat and light to commercial and residential units. This has resulted in primary energy savings of 650 000 kWh/year, a 20% reduction in CO_2 emissions and a 25% cut in residents' energy bills. The system cost £268 000 compared to the cost or replacing the existing boilers of £80 000. This gave a payback period of 7 years although the scheme did benefit from the existence of an existing district heating system.

On a cold, dark winter's evening, electricity and heat are required in large quantities yet a system sized to serve this load would be very inefficient in the middle of a summer's day when electricity is still required but there is little demand for the heat. This is generally overcome by regulating the system according to the heat load of the area. The national grid is then used to 'store' electricity by selling surpluses to the grid and buying back electricity when the needs of the heat load are insufficient to meet electricity demand. The efficiency of systems can therefore be improved by evening out the annual heat load which is easier in mixed-use urban areas. The density of development can increase the market served by the plant without huge distribution distances. Indeed the CHP association has identified 'heat densities' as one of the most important factors influencing viability. A mixed-use area can also help to even out energy demand since commercial premises use energy in the daytime and housing largely in the evening. Efficiency is also improved because in urban development forms such as terraces and flats, distribution pipes are shorter and can run within buildings so that heat losses are reduced along with the need to insulate pipework buried underneath pavements.

Once the control of power generation has been wrested to the local level it also becomes possible to consider alternative forms of power supply to supplement CHP systems. One possibility is to link the CHP system to a domestic waste incinerator. There is already a system in Sheffield where the municipal waste incinerator is linked to a district heating system serving 3 500 flats, 64 city buildings and both universities. There are currently plans to link this to a CHP plant so that it also generates electricity. However domestic incinerators can be controversial because they can produce harmful emissions and are often fiercely resisted by residents. It is also questionable whether incineration is the best way of using domestic waste compared to recycling and reuse.

It is however possible to use renewable energy sources. Wind turbines have been used in urban areas. However in Energy World in Milton Keynes the turbine had to be switched off because

of the noise it generated. A better option is solar power which is readily available even in our overcast climate. This has been widely used in the past for water heating although this has the problem that the energy tends to be most available when there is least demand for heat. A better option might be photovoltaic technology which uses sunlight to generate electricity. This is more compatible with CHP systems because it generates electricity to fill the gap in capacity caused by low summer heat loads. The German and Japanese governments are currently investing heavily in photovoltaic technology and BP have made a far-sighted corporate decision to change the emphasis of their business from oil to solar power. This is likely to mean that the cost of photovoltaic panels will fall and it may even be possible to use them to replace traditional roofing and cladding materials. Options also exist to use methane from local sewage treatment to generate power as well as more radical technologies such as hydrogen storage with fuel cell generation. These use surplus solar heat in the summer for the electrolysis of water into hydrogen and oxygen for storage. The hydrogen can then either be burnt for heat and cooking or reacted with oxygen in a fuel cell to generate electricity when there is no sun. Using this technology a government-sponsored house in Freiburg, Germany, has been built which since 1992 has supplied all of its heating and electricity needs from solar power.

These technologies hold tremendous potential for the reduction of energy use and CO_2 emissions. The impact however will be limited if we focus only on the scale of individual buildings. Instead we must rethink the way that energy is used and supplied at the neighbourhood scale.

Urban recycling

A key issue if linear resource systems are to be made circular is the recycling of domestic and commercial waste. In the UK, unlike the continent and parts of North America, this has developed as little more than a middle-class concern yet even now the volume of material collected for recycling is sometimes outstripped the capacity of the recycling industry to cope with it. A recent visitor to Britain from Holland was amazed at the scarcity of recycling facilities. In Holland there are recycling bins on every street, never more than a hundred metres from any house. In a recent article for the SUN Initiative Keith Collins[26] describes the reaction of another foreign visitor who suggested that the British attitude to recycling was like raising a child, feeding it, clothing it, putting it through school and university only to say, when it left its first job that there were just two options – incineration or burial. At present most UK recycling takes place through public recycling points and recent research has suggested that the environmental benefits of recycling in the UK are cancelled out by the environmental impact of driving to recycling points.

KERBSIDE RECYCLING IN HOUNSLOW

The London Borough of Hounslow has been at the forefront of the introduction of recycling. The borough has set a recycling target of 25% of household waste and has recognised the limitations of communal recycling points. When waste collection contracts expired in 1996 the council introduces a self-financing kerbside collection service. Segregation collection is now in place serving 68 500 households including 1 500 low-rise and 200 high-rise flats. Each home is given a green box (below left) which is used to collect recyclable waste. This is then segregated by operatives into sacks on handcarts (below centre) which are then left at pick-up points for collection (below right). The contract was awarded to a not-for-profit company and assistance was provided with capital costs. The target for 25% recycling had been achieved by mid-contract.

In Chapter 5 we described the moves that are being made in London towards municipal segregated waste collection. Here our concern is to assess the affect of these systems on the form of urban areas. One of the problems in the past has been that the difficulty of segregated waste collection in busy urban areas has made it uneconomic. Keith Collins describes the 'road rage' which resulted from refuse vehicles waiting in busy narrow urban streets while waste was sorted into containers. Such was the frustration of the blocked traffic that the refuse vehicle often had to flee the scene leaving the street teams with nothing to do. As a result this form of segregated collection in London was around three times more expensive that it has proved to be in American suburban environments. However the breakthrough with the London system was to devise a system suitable to urban areas with electric hand carts to segregate the waste and pick up points for the sacks. This not only brought costs down to American levels, it also proved as cost effective as traditional forms of collection.

Such systems could transform the economics of urban recycling systems increasing the amount of waste that we collect from 5% to 25% as in Hounslow. They may mean that urban density actually become an advantage for recycling because the volume of waste collected is sufficient to support viable recycling systems. The

URBAN MINES

The Urban Mines sustainable growth park was established in 1995 and named after Jane Jacobs' idea that the waste of cities would be the 'mines' of the future. Its aim is to circulate waste as secondary raw materials back into the local economy. In addition to this the aim is to promote economic regeneration, local employment and to develop new markets for recycled products. Quoting from the Delors European white paper on employment they suggest that the current economic model is based on an excessive use of resources and an insufficient use of labour. The Urban Mines project intends to turn this around suggesting that a million tonnes of waste will produce 500 jobs if it is recycled compared to 150 jobs if it is incinerated and just 50 if it is dumped in a landfill site.

The Urban Mines park will include a Materials Recovery Facility (MRF) along with a reprocessing operation. Refuse from the local authority's waste collection system will be sorted and reprocessed into workable secondary raw materials. These materials will then be used by a range of companies in business units which are to be developed as part of the park. In addition to this the park will run educational activities and will provide technical advice and assistance to local companies. Laboratories will also work to develop new uses for recovered materials which can be developed into commercial markets. In the process it is anticipated to deal with 40 000 tonnes of waste a year and to create 300 jobs. The project has been supported by English Partnerships and the local TEC. It is important because it addresses one of the main weaknesses of the recycling industry, the market for its products. A good example of this is green glass from wine bottles which is collected in large quantities but not used by the UK glass industry. By developing a business making coloured glass tableware the park hopes to create a market for this product making it economic to recycle.

RAW MATERIAL EXTRACTION

PRIMARY PROCESSING

MANUFACTURING

CONSUMPTION

REDUCE WASTE

REUSE

RECYCLE

ENERGY RECOVERY

LANDFILL

fact that the waste is segregated by the collection operatives rather than householders also gets around many of the design problems. In the past segregated collection in home and business premises has meant up to six different bins in kitchens or refuse areas to collect organic waste, paper, glass, aluminium, steel and general waste. This can cause particular problems in blocks of flats where refuse chutes and communal waste stores would need to be redesigned. However the London system uses a recycling box into which householders put all recyclable waste. This is then collected and sorted onto the pavement hand carts minimising the hassle for residents. This is probably more realistic in Britain than the Dutch system which relies on committed residents carrying waste to local collection points.

Urban systems then need to be established to make use of this waste. Much of this is likely to take place on an industrial level or be undertaken by the council. Examples include paper mills set up to recycle newsprint which can also use substandard material to produce cardboard or even to ferment it to produce ethanol as a fuel. It includes the composting of household and garden waste to sell back to householders, or facilities such as the Urban Mines project in Yorkshire which is using recycling as a spur to economic development and employment creation.

However the recycling capacity of urban areas extends far beyond the formal recycling industry. Cities are great recyclers of materials as anyone will know if they have watched an urban skip for a few days. As soon as a skip is delivered to a street it starts to fill with rubbish – much to the consternation of the person who hired it – as people take the opportunity to off-load bulky items. However other people in the street will often claim some of this rubbish, finding a use for an old chair or table or reclaiming the wood to use in something else. Over the days the rubbish in the skip will constantly change as a result of this informal exchange of materials. This system has been formalised in the squatters' community of Christania where a compound is specifically set aside for this exchange of goods. This is a good example of a neighbourhood scale recycling activity, but there are many others such as local composting to feed gardens and allotments which in turn produce food for local people. It can also include community furniture projects which take cast-off furniture and refurbish it for sale to needy households, creating local employment.

On a larger scale this recycling of materials is an important part of urban economies. As Jane Jacobs points out[27] this is an area where cities have tremendous environmental and economic pot-

ential. She uses the metaphor of cities being the 'urban mines' of the future. She gives as an example an advert for a paper recycling company which used a picture of New York under the slogan 'our concrete forest'. Rather than extracting resources from finite natural sources she envisages a future where we will mine urban waste for many of the raw materials we need. This already happens to a much greater extent than one might imagine. In addition to the conventional recycling systems for paper, glass, aluminium etc. there are charity shops which recycle cast-off clothes, antiques shops, scrap yards, and architectural reclamation yards. Warmcell, a company in Wales makes domestic insulation from old newspapers, others recycle photocopier toner drums, manufacture concrete from power station fuel ash, or generate power from old tyres. These are all examples of economic activities based on mining the waste of cities. As Jane Jacobs points out, these activities are driven not by environmental consciousness but by commercial principles. As such they illustrate the potentially rich vein of economic activity which could do much to revive the flagging manufacturing base of urban areas.

Water and sewage

Water, like many of the resources used in urban areas, is drawn from a wide area. The city of Birmingham imports its water from Wales whilst Manchester draws its supplies from the Lake District. The purification and transport of this water is costly and consumes large amounts of energy as does the treatment and disposal of this water after it is used. This is a classic linear system and, as with other linear systems, there is the potential to close some of the loops to create circular systems at the local level. Yet most cities do not even make good use of the rain which falls on their roofs and streets only to be channelled directly into the sewers.

These systems can be closed at a number of levels. Herbert Girardet[28] recounts how in the middle of the last century two systems were considered for the disposal of London's sewage. One involved a system of sewers, like the spokes of a wheel, feeding the sewage out to composting

---

USING WATER WISELY - KOLDING IN DENMARK

As part of the renewal of an areas of 40 properties in three-and four-storey blocks containing 129 dwellings it was decided to explore a number of ecological measures. Some of the most radical measures related to water consumption.

Rainwater from roofs in the scheme is directed into a pond in the centre of the scheme. This is kept fresh by being circulated over a cascade and stream and is pumped to the flats for use in washing machines and toilets. However pride of place is given to the bioworks, a 13m high glass pyramid at the centre of the courtyard which treats all of the waste water on the site. Waste is first collected in tanks where sludge settles and it is treated with ultraviolet light and ozone. It is then fed through a series of tanks containing algae, plankton, and mussels/fish. The water is then used to provide nutrients to 15 000 flats as part of a commercial operation which covers all of the running costs. The bioworks is warm and humid and filled with plants and insects and therefore seen as an asset by the surrounding residents rather than as a local sewage works.

plants which would then be used on a ring of market gardens surrounding the city, the other (which was eventually chosen) involved the construction of sewage works and the disposal of treated effluent into the river. As a result the city consumes the fertility of agricultural land only to dump it into the sea rather than to replenish it with compost. However this circle can be closed. He describes a facility in Bristol which turns domestic sewage into pellets which can be used to fertilise and reclaim derelict land and will soon be available for agricultural use once they have devised a system to deal with the industrial pollutants in the waste.

These loops can also be closed at the neighbourhood level. It is possible to recycle water from baths and sinks for toilet flushing. This is known as grey water restoration and involves the collection of waste water which is then filtered and pumped into storage tanks. This was explored in some detail as part of the Homes for Change project that we describe in Chapter 13. In this case the capital costs of meeting the requirements of the local water board meant that it was not viable on a scheme of fifty flats. This was partly because of the fact that it doubled the amount of plumbing in the scheme. However the main reason was the structure of water charging which meant that savings for residents were minimal. As a result the capital costs would have translated into rent increases of £4 per week while the savings on water bills would have been no more than £2.50. However the situation is changing as the water companies seek to increase water charges and the diminution of water supplies becomes more of a problem. Grey water systems are now being marketed for individual homes for only a few thousand pounds. At the other end of the scale systems serving whole neighbourhoods could benefit from economies of scale.

Indeed as illustrated by the case study of Kolding in Denmark, such systems need not confine themselves to grey water but could even become local sewage treatment facilities. The traditional means of treating sewage in autonomous development has been to use reed beds. Notwithstanding the vertical reed beds in oil drums in Kreuzberg, this is not really practical in an urban setting. However the intensively managed bioworks system is ideal for urban areas resembling, as it does, a humid, verdent greenhouse rather than a traditional sewage works. The output water from the bioworks is of bathing, if not drinking quality and can be used either to supply grey water systems or, as in Kolding to support a horticultural business. An alternative would be to use composting toilets which could be used to fertilise urban agriculture. On a more simple level the use of water butts and permeable surfaces can reduce the need to use tap water for gardens.

Green space

There is a great deal of confusion about green space and sustainability. Part of this revolves around the idea that green spaces are the 'lungs of the city'. Yet as Robert and Brenda Vale[29] have pointed out, Milton Keynes may have a million trees but the layout which makes this possible generates levels of car use which produce vastly more CO_2 than the trees are able to absorb. Indeed Jane Jacobs ridicules the concept of green space being the 'lungs of the city' pointing out that three acres of woodland is required to absorb the CO_2 produced by just four people. This, of course, is not the only reason for green space in urban areas. Green lungs are important psychologically to city dwellers even if they are not of practical value as can be seen by New Yorkers' devotion to Central Park. Green space is also an important contributor to biodiversity encouraging flora and fauna.

However green space also has disadvantages. Too much of it can reduce the density of urban areas lessening the viability of public transport and increasing walking distances. Its maintenance can also be a drain on public resources and at night it can create personal safety problems. Urban green space therefore needs to be careful designed and planned to maximise its contribution to the environment of urban areas while minimising its negative aspects.

This is what we have failed to do in many of our cities. In Manchester, for example, it is estimated by the planning department that a third of the city's land area is open space and this does not include land which is vacant or derelict. Much of this open space is parks and playing fields which are rightly protected from development. However the majority of it is neither vacant nor parkland. It is the result of past planning dogma which has regarded open space as a good thing in its own right so that everything from shopping centres to housing estates have been marooned in great savannas of council-maintained grass land which contribute little or nothing to biodiversity. Many of the main roads in the city run through land-scaped corridors, some originally reserved for future road widening but most with no other function than to protect surrounding development from the road. This land is increasingly being seen as having development potential to accommodate projected levels of household growth. To some people this may represent an erosion of the environmental quality of cities. However if it is properly managed it need not reduce either the

psychological or biodiversity benefits of urban open space.

Sustainable urban areas are not necessarily those with the largest area of open space. It is quality not quantity which counts. The sustainable urban neighbourhood may not therefore have large areas of open space but it should nevertheless maximise the opportunities for wildlife and biodiversity. Indeed in Richard Register's vision of Ecocity Berkeley, the metropolis becomes a haven for wildlife and a net contributor to bio-diversity. This it can do through street trees, parks, squares, balconies, window boxes, courtyards, private gardens and even roof gardens. The Homes for Change scheme (see Chapter 12) includes 75 flats and 16 000 square feet of work-space on just 1.3 acres of land yet incorporates extensive planting in its courtyard, three roof gardens – some of which are used for food growing – and many of the flats have balconies. Thus despite the density of the scheme the opportunity for greenery is maximised. When

The urban park: Traditional urban parks and squares like Park Square in Leeds illustrate the characteristics of successful public open spaces. They tend to be defined and supervised by peripheral streets and fronted by buildings

URBAN OASIS

The Apple Tree Court Tenants' Association formed a management company in 1996 to take over the management of the tower block from Salford City Council. As part of the agreement the land around the block passed to the tenants who decided that it should be put to productive use both to grow food and to provide a focus of the community in the flats.

The land has been fenced and developed with organic gardening, an orchard, a pond, wild flower meadow and seating areas. It has used horticultural principles imported from the Middle East through a partnership with the Arid Lands Initiative and has been implemented by local people along with community service offenders. As a results the residents of the flats are almost self-sufficient in fruit and vegetables and there have been spin-off benefits in terms of the management of the block.

Future plans include the recycling of waste heat from the flats to heat polytunnels, the collection of rainwater to remove reliance on mains water and composting of domestic waste as well as a geodesic conservatory and a café.

The project has attracted national interest after it won the BT/WWF Partnership Award and is being established to provide a food crop for the wider inner city for the elderly and people in high-rise flats. A tree growing kit has been used in over 500 schools and an Urban Oasis pack is being produced to help people replicate the project elsewhere.

viewed on aerial photographs some of our older urban areas like Toxteth in Liverpool or Moseley in Birmingham are virtually obscured by tree cover and mature gardens. Such urban areas provide homes for all manner of wildlife from foxes and owls to birds, insects and wild plants, and yet often have very little designated public open space. This is the sort of environment that we should be creating in new urban areas and is not at all incompatible with high-density development.

Large areas of public open space are, of course, important in urban areas. These can include wilderness areas like Hampstead Heath but just as important are urban parks, play areas, and sports facilities. If these areas are to work as successful, safe public spaces they need to be designed along the same principles as successful streets. They need to be overlooked by surrounding buildings or supervised by activity. The early parks like Sefton Park in Liverpool were financed by the development of up-market housing around the periphery which benefited from the views over the park. This meant that the park was supervised and clearly part of the public realm. By contrast many modern public open spaces are bounded by the back gardens of houses and therefore become abandoned to gangs of dissolute youths. One of the parks that I (DR) use regularly illustrates the point. Alexander Park in Manchester is a large Victorian park which adjoins the most dangerous and notorious part of Moss Side. Yet the park is very well used and suffers from none of the problems of the surrounding area including lower levels of van-dalism than some of the parks in more prosperous parts of the city. This is because it is active throughout the day with dog walkers, fishermen, cyclists, children at play, people playing football, cricket or tennis and parents taking their children to the play centre in the middle of the park. It is surrounded by roads so that, while it may not be the most tranquil park in the city, no part of it feels isolated, despite its size. It is also bounded on two sides by large Victorian property much of it subdivided into flats. This, along with the resident park keeper, gives the impression that the park is overlooked even though the mature tree cover means that for most of the park this is not the case. There is much that we can learn from such Victorian parks about the way that green space and landscaping can be successfully incorporated into urban areas.

Open space can also be put to productive use through the use of gardens and allotments for food growing. Urban agriculture is a traditional part of urban areas and is actually increasing in scale. It is also an important use for recycled waste, be it composted organic household waste or the product of locally treated sewage. Urban food growing can reduce the transport costs associated with imported food, provide fresh produce for low income groups, and reduce travel to large supermarkets[30]. The Diggers self-build housing scheme in Brighton uses grass roofs to house beehives and the Springfield Community Garden in the heart of Bradford provides seven acres for organic food growing along with employment training, education and recycling workshops. In

New York encouragement by the municipality has helped to create over 700 such community gardens which together produce around $100 000 of fruit and vegetables a year[31]. Such projects can also be linked to permaculture initiatives as in Apple Tree Court in Salford where the Urban Oasis project has transformed the land around a tower block into an organic food-growing area.

In this chapter we have reviewed the factors which taken together have the potential to significantly reduce the environmental impact of the Sustainable Urban Neighbourhood. In doing this the neighbourhood could play an important role in the wider task of greening the city. Yet most of what we have suggested is based upon existing technology, is practical and could be easily implemented without major increases in costs. These principles may be based on the lessons from eco-communities but they are appropriate for the urban context. Indeed many require an urban context since they are based upon a density of people and activities to make systems viable. In the next chapter we discuss in more detail this urban context and the characteristics which lie behind successful urban areas.

CHAPTER 11
Urban building blocks

In the last chapter we described the impact of environmental sustainability on urban development. Here we explore the meaning of the word 'urban'. This is first and foremost a description of the location of development, the fact that it takes place within existing towns and cities. However it also relates to the character of the neighbourhood, its physical form and its relationship to urban traditions which have endured for thousands of years. In Britain and other parts of the world these traditions are being rediscovered. This is partly driven by environmental issues as we saw in the last chapter and the concern to promote urban areas based on walking rather than driving. However it is also based on the belief that traditional urban forms have stood the test of time and are more attractive, functional and less likely to fail than many of the other ways that we have devised for planning and designing cities in the recent past.

Over the last two hundred years British towns and cities have been transformed from the sort of dense urban settlements that we still admire on the continent to sprawling low-density conurbations. This has drained away the viability and vitality of many of our urban areas. It has created an outer ring of affluent suburbs, out-of-town shopping and business parks leaving an embattled town centre surrounded by inner city decay. We have in short largely destroyed our urban society in favour of a suburban society. In Britain this process is far from reaching its logical

conclusion for this we must look to America. Having exported the suburb to American, we have spent most of this century looking across the Atlantic for inspiration. We must now ask whether we are prepared for our cities and indeed our society to follow the American model? Do we want the centres of British towns and cities to become nothing but tourist attractions which draw only a fraction of retail spending? Are we prepared to abandon our inner cities as no-go areas with burgeoning crime and social breakdown? Do we want to live and work in isolated 'edge cities' where social contact is limited and no journey is possible without a car? This is not science fiction, it is the reality of many US cities. If it is to be avoided here our task is nothing less than to reinvent the British town and city.

We are not alone in recognising a need to reinvent urban areas. HRH Prince Charles, in his book *A Vision for Britain*[1] urged that we should learn from traditional urban areas. This is something that the urban design profession has been doing for years. Writers like Kevin Lynch, Francis Bacon, Gordon Cullen, Spiro Kostof, Francis Tibbalds, Ian Bentley and Harley Sherlock[2] have sought to distil from the Italian hill town, the renaissance city, Georgian Bath or Napoleonic Paris the principles of successful urban planning. These writers generally agree on what makes urban areas work and from their writings we can draw a set of principles to guide the development of the sustainable urban neighbourhood.

The importance of the street

A central feature of much of the new urban thinking is a rediscovery of the importance of the street as the central organising element of urban areas. The idea that urban areas should be based on streets seems self-evident. It is the way that traditional towns work and remains the way that most town centres are structured, at least where they avoided the redeveloping zeal of the postwar planners. Yet on the ground the notion of developing new housing and commercial uses along traditional streets is far from obvious to many people including developers and planning authorities. Better the cul-de-sac to remove through traffic and provide defensible space than the noisy dangerous old street that Le Corbusier so detested. Better the business or retail park with its secure perimeter fence and ample parking all in one ownership than the congested, diverse urban area with all its dangers and distractions.

We have lost faith in the traditional street just as we have lost faith in the city. Indeed before the days of high-rise council estates social problems manifested on street corners and in back streets. Ne'er-do-wells hung out on street corners, prostitutes were called streetwalkers, and gang violence was called street-fighting. The location was confused with the problem so that the street came to be seen as the cause of many urban evils and was swept away in slum clearance and redevelopment areas. However the streetless council estate has fared even less well than the terraced streets that survived redevelopment. Removing the arena of the street did not sweep away urban problems, it just pushed them into staircases, walkways and parking lots or into the generous areas of landscaping provided to 'humanise' new estates. Here the problems have proved much more difficult to control and much more threatening to the inhabitants of the area. Should we therefore

The traditional street: Roupell Street in Waterloo is now something of a rarity in our urban areas. It is tightly defined by its houses with a shop or pub on every corner. Yet such streets were once seen as at the root of many urban problems

reconsider our negative view of the street? Is it possible that streets are a civilising influence which ameliorate rather than exacerbate the problems of urban life? This is not the view of the developers and planners who are still replacing streetless high-rise estates with streetless low-rise suburban estates based on the cul-de-sac. It remains to be seen whether these areas will be any more successful than their high-rise predecessors.

To understand both the potential benefits of the street and why it has, and continues to be, so resisted we must understand a little more about its nature. The street brings together two quite different functions. It is both a route for movement through an area and a focus for a local community. These are functions that postwar planning has regarded as incompatible but which compliment each other to create the magic of successful streets. A cul-de-sac can provide a community focus but only its residents and their visitors have any reason to be there. A street by contrast will serve more than just its residents and will welcome and accommodate strangers. Yet for many years the stranger has been seen as the enemy in urban areas, someone who causes noise and disturbance and leads to crime and congestion. This is why since Parker and Unwin designed the first garden suburbs we have been so attracted to the cul-de-sac. However an area without strangers is an area which cannot support shops, which is deserted for large parts of the day and where there are few passers-by to deter the criminal. The cul-de-sac may be ideal for the leafy suburb where such things are less of a problem but it is less well suited to the town and city where one expects to find more vitality and where crime is a fact of life.

A street is more than a road since, as well as being a route from A to B, it is a place where people meet and interact and hence where the public life of the city is played out. It has become a feature of postwar planning that routes carrying anything but the most local of traffic need to be separated from residential and other types of development. Engineering guides contain hierarchies of distributor roads to be kept free of frontage development. This is partly out of concern that traffic noise will damage the amenity of

residents but mostly to avoid curtilage access to individual properties interrupting the free flow of traffic. As a result our towns and cities are blighted with roads and roundabouts bounded by green swathes of landscaping and shunned by the buildings which would traditionally have sustained them. The street by contrast can perform an equally important role as an artery for movement and a place defined and animated by its buildings. It is on streets such as this that the public life of the city is played out. There are still many unappreciated streets that throng with life throughout the day, that nourish lively communities and support diverse commercial activity. At their best they are the 'great streets' described by Allen Jacobs but at the more mundane level they are what makes all urban areas work.

It could be argued that the idealistic notion of streets as public meeting place and artery is no longer possible in the modern city. The car and bus have filled the once civilised street with their noise and fumes, undermining its role as community focus. What is more, the idea of urban places where local people and strangers mix in harmony is at odds with the reality of modern city life. Streets may be the stages on which the drama of urban life is played out but people no longer wish to be part of the play alongside the mugger and the drug dealer[3]. This however is a counsel of despair. We must tame and civilise the worst aspects of urban life if cities are to be repopulated. In this task the traditional street is likely to be our most potent weapon. Take for example the issue of traffic as we discussed in the last chapter. The road which is free of frontage development is designed to increase traffic capacity whereas the environmental impact of the car means that we should be doing just the opposite. Cars need to be discouraged from coming into towns so road capacities must be reduced and speeds checked, which is exactly what traditional streets do.

In terms of fear and crime, the street has also been wrongly accused. The flight of the middle classes may mean that the city today is more dangerous than it was between the wars. Yet is it more dangerous than the London described by

Dickens? Cities have always been dangerous places, yet in no other age has this caused people to abandon the concept of streets or indeed to abandon cities. The street is the way in which cities have dealt with crime and allowed civilised life to continue. Good urban streets create a robust delineation between the public and the private realm protecting the latter and ensuring the former is surveyed by windows and passers-by. Suburban forms lack both of these properties. This is largely because, in suburbs with their low levels of crime and emphasis on family life, it is possible to blur the distinctions between the public and the private. It would however be a mistake to believe that because the suburbs have less crime, suburban forms will reduce crime in the city, as many crime prevention officers would have us believe[4]. The use of the more robust traditional street may therefore be a prerequisite for attracting a broader range of people back into urban areas.

What then are the practical implications of building urban streets? If a street is to fulfil the role of a route from A to B it must clearly lead somewhere. This relates to the concept of **permeability** as described in the last chapter. This simple rule means that all streets connect at both ends to other streets. This is the first important characteristic of an urban street. The route need not always allow access for cars but pedestrians should normally be able to use the street as a route. Permeability is central both to the concept of a pedestrian-friendly neighbourhood and to its

urban character. It has the effect of reducing walking distances because it makes it possible to reach your destination without major detours. This also has the effect of increasing activity on streets to support a wider range of economic activity and to make the area feel safer. At first this may seen counter-intuitive since greater permeability should lead to a dissipation of pedestrian activity. However in impermeable urban areas, where large housing estates or business parks allow no through routes fewer journeys are possible on foot. Furthermore, trips by car are concentrated on a few main routes which become unbearable because of the volume of traffic. This approach to the street therefore creates the twin evils of congested high streets where life is impossible and deserted side streets which can sustain nothing but housing (see page 152). This further discourages walking creating a vicious circle of car dependency. Some evidence for this has been provided by Bill Hillier through his studies of urban syntax[5]. This has illustrated that areas with low levels of connectivity (another word for permeability) have low encounter rates (the frequency at which you meet other people) and also higher rates of domestic burglary.

Permeability does not mean, as many developers fear, that the cul-de-sac is outlawed. Urban areas have always included cul-de-sacs, or at least their urban equivalent the mews court. These are essential to open up sites within urban blocks or land along railway lines and rivers. However it is important that cul-de-sacs, where there are used, should be short and should not predominate so that ease of access through the area is maintained.

Permeability also relates to traffic which is where the dual role of the street as a route and a community focus is thrown into sharpest focus. One need only watch forty-tonne juggernauts lumbering through streets built when the horse was the main form of transport to understand the appeal of the bypass. It should however be remembered that the shops and facilities on these streets are there precisely because of the volume of traffic and passing trade. Excluding through traffic, or pedestrianising the street entirely runs the risk cutting off its commercial life blood in all but the

The urban mews court: Orchard Street in Bristol shows how 'cul-de-sacs' can have a place in urban areas

most central streets. It is noticeable travelling through Britain by car that you hardly ever pass through the centre of a British town. As you approach the outskirts of the town you are channelled onto a ring road or bypass, no doubt much to the relief of local people. In France by contrast you are almost always channelled directly through the heart of the town passing the main shopping streets and the town square. The highways engineer no doubt considers France to be a very backward country. Yet it is no coincidence that many French town centres prosper despite the rumbling juggernauts whereas their British equivalents stagnate or decline.

If this is true of major streets it is even more the case with streets further down the urban hierarchy. These streets depend for their success on a flow of activity to create a degree of vitality to provide surveillance and to support services. This can rarely be achieved outside town centres solely with pedestrian flows – traffic is important. However to a highway engineer this implies rat runs, pedestrian/vehicle conflict and a loss of control over where the traffic goes. It is therefore important to design streets to accommodate traffic. Major streets should be able to accommodate traffic without squeezing out pedestrian life or becoming urban motorways. In this way permeability can be maintained for both pedestrians and cars whilst not allowing the car to dominate.

A framework of streets

The simple rule that all streets should join at either end to other streets creates the second important characteristic of urban areas – that they are based on a framework of streets. This framework is far more than just a movement system, it is a central organising element of any urban area. This framework of streets is the trellis on which the vine of the city grows giving it its form and structure. It is also the central nervous system carrying movement and communications (from bus routes to services and telecommunications under the pavements).

Street frameworks can take many forms, however there is a clear difference between the planned and unplanned city (see pages 152 and

The magic of successful streets: A street in Romania which is a route for movement, a place to spend time and a focus for a local community

153). In the former the framework of streets is planned in advance and is generally geometric in form. This is most commonly an orthogonal grid as in Roman towns, New York, Barcelona or even more recently the 'super grid' of Milton Keynes. However planned towns can also be circular or hexagonal as in many medieval walled cities. The other type of street network, and the one which characterises most British cities, is the organic or unplanned grid. The organic grid is not planned but grows naturally over time and often resembles a spiders web. It is based on a series of radial routes which converge on a central square. Over time new roads are built to open up the land between these routes in a process described by Christopher Alexander in his book *A new theory of urban design*[6]. We will return to the importance of grids on the process of urban development in Chapter 14. One of the most damaging aspects of modern town planning has been its failure to recognise the importance of the framework of streets within

Street networks: Figure ground plans of continental and British towns illustrating how continental towns are based on a strong network of streets defined by buildings. This network can be organic or based upon a grid iron such as Turin (3), New York (6) and Glasgow (9). Many UK cities like London (7), Edinburgh (8) and Glasgow (9) retain a strong street network although in the case of Glasgow this has broken down around the edges as a result of the ring road. This is more pronounced in other UK cities such Barnsley (10) where a traditional structure has been undermined and Coventry and Bracknell (11 and 12) where comprehensive redevelopment or new town planning has meant that it has been entirely lost.

Full list: 1. Bordeaux, 2. Naples, 3. Turin, 4. Palma, 5. Dublin, 6. New York, 7. London, 8. Edinburgh Old Town, 9. Glasgow, 10. Barnsley, 11. Coventry, 12. Bracknell Numbers 1-8 courtesy MBLC Architects.

a town. This can be clearly seen by comparing the figure ground plans of British and continental towns (to the left). In the British examples the remnants of organic street plans can be seen with major streets converging on a central square (see for example plan 9). However the development of ring roads and the existence of a band of ill-defined development around the medieval core means that the grid soon breaks down. This is in sharp contrast to many continental towns where traffic has been accommodated within the original street framework rather than by abandoning it in favour of the ring road.

One important effect of a grid is to make it easy to find your way around an urban area, the concept of legibility which was also covered in the previous chapter. A New Yorker could be dropped anywhere in the city and know immediately from the shape of the city blocks and the numbering of the streets exactly where he or she was. The same is true of many traditional cities where orientation is possible because you know that all major streets lead to the centre.

Hierarchies

This leads to a further urban characteristic – hierarchies. The internal structure of all urban areas is based on an interconnected series of hierarchies. Uses, buildings and open space all have a hierarchy developed over time and reflecting the democratic organisation of the area. The most important of the hierarchies from which all others are derived is the hierarchy of streets. Street networks are never uniform, some streets are more important than others just as some areas are more important. In small cities there is a simple hierarchy with the most important area being the centre and the most important streets those leading to the centre. In larger cities the hierarchy is more complex as the centre is divided into a series of sub areas and complemented by a range of satellite centres. The most important streets are then both the radial routes and the streets linking the smaller centres. This creates a hierarchy of streets and this hierarchy determines the nature of development along each street. The street hierarchy is central to the structure of many urban design guides such as those produced by Andres Duany and Elizabeth Plater-Zyberk in America[7]. It was also used in the *Hulme Guide to Development*[8] (see Chapter 13) which has at its core a simple hierarchy of streets. These street hierarchies usually contain the following categories of street:

High streets: At the top of the hierarchy are high streets which are the busiest streets in any area and the most urban in character. They tend to be the original radial routes into the city, the routes linking sub-centres and the main shopping streets within each centre. In the heart of shopping centres the high street will often be pedestrianised but elsewhere it is an important route for through traffic, cars, pedestrians and public transport. The high street will thus be the shopfront of any city, since it will be the most visible street to the largest number of people. It will also be the focus for surrounding communities. In the past people would have gone 'up the high street' to do their shopping, to visit the bank, to meet other people and to worship. Unfortunately such high streets, in Britain at least, are increasingly rare. Many were lost in the redevelopments of the 1960s. Hulme in Manchester lost its High Street (Stretford Road) and in the process lost more than thirty pubs and almost a hundred shops. They were replaced with a shopping precinct, a new church, pub and

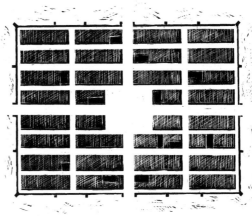

Street hierarchies: The standard form of many Roman towns with primary routes, converging on a central square surrounded by specific quarters with secondary and tertiary streets

health centre designed to serve the needs, and no more, of the planned population of the area. Thus was lost the magic that sustains a good high street which, because of passing trade, supports a far wider range of services and specialist shops than would be justified by the size of the local community. Such high streets often pass through deprived areas and play an important role in preventing the area becoming a ghetto as happened in Hulme when its high street was lost.

Even those high streets which came through the 1960s unscathed are not out of danger. Even today high streets are being destroyed

THE A6 CORRIDOR – MANCHESTER

We recently organised a series of workshops as part of a team developing a strategy for the A6 corridor (the Stockport Road) in Manchester. This is one of the city's great high streets passing through the district centres of Longsight and Levenshulme and is also an important transport route between the city and Stockport. It is the subject of a regeneration project which is promoting environmental improvements and economic development. Levenshulme in particular has declined as it has lost much of its retail role. The strategy aims to reconcile the regeneration of the centre with the needs of through traffic by promoting new uses such as the evening economy and antiques, creating a new public space, while slowing down traffic, creating bus lanes and providing short-term customer parking.

CREATING BOULEVARDS – BRACKNELL

As part of the development on an urban design guide in Bracknell (see page 41) we needed to reduce the impact of the town's two ring roads. We proposed that the inner 'ring' should be partly closed. However the outer ring road was an important primary distributor and carried most of the traffic passing through the town. The solution was to transform this route from a hostile dual carriageway into a boulevard by creating frontage development, planting avenues of trees, creating surface-level pedestrian crossings and introducing cycle lanes.

One of the best examples of this is the inner ring road in Birmingham which has been downgraded in recent years. This following the Highbury Initiative, a symposium in the late 1980s, where it was decided that the city needed to break its 'concrete collar'.

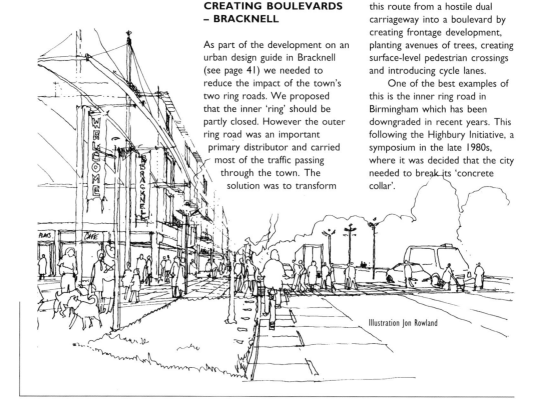

Illustration Jon Rowland

by road widening schemes and others are choked with traffic. In an effort to deal with this traffic local councils are removing on-street parking (such as the Red Routes in London), fencing in pedestrians on narrow pavements and restricting turning movements to and from side streets. The result is to ease traffic flow, for a time at least, but to undermine the viability of high street uses as their customers can no longer park or cross the road (other than at designated crossing points). The environment becomes even more dominated by moving traffic which can be much more intrusive than stationary congestion. Traditional functions such as shopping, leisure and even churches are therefore moving away from the high street which is left deserted and lined by empty and decaying buildings. In the past high streets were the main economic thoroughfares along which everyone in the city passed. They were lined with lively commercial frontages and often served to hide the adjacent slums from the eyes of passers-by. The opposite is often true of the modern high street where vacant, decaying commercial frontages can hide quite successful residential areas. The impression that this 'shopfront' to the city gives is that it is dirty and dangerous and closed for business. An important task in rebuilding urban areas is therefore to rediscover appropriate economic roles and design models for the high street.

Primary distributors: In the modern city we cannot escape the fact that there is another type of street at the top of the hierarchy, the primary distributor. They are a product of the motor age and would not have existed in tradition towns but, until major reform takes place in our car-based culture, they will remain important for the free flow of traffic. These are normally dual carriageways and are kept free of frontage development and they are therefore the least urban element of the hierarchy. It is however possible to give these primary distributors an urban character as demonstrated by the boulevards of Paris. The Champs Élysées, after all, has six lanes and accom-

modates a huge volume of traffic yet still operates as a street. This it does by providing very wide pavements and small feeder roads off the main carriageway to accommodate on-street parking and servicing. Two rows of trees then protect the buildings from the traffic noise allowing the pavements to accommodate street cafés and activity. This however only works because of the scale of the buildings which face onto the Champs Élysées which creates a strong sense of enclosure despite the width of the street. It is probably unrealistic to expect that we can recreate such great streets in modern urban areas but it is important that we recreate a modern version of the boulevard, as proposed in Bracknell, so that these main traffic routes do not undermine and isolate the character of urban neighbourhoods.

Secondary streets: There can be a number of rungs to the hierarchy below the high street. Secondary streets are similar, in many ways, to high streets. They provide the main circulation routes within, rather than between, neighbourhoods and generally include a mix of uses including local shopping parades, small businesses and services such as doctors etc. However the balance on these streets swings more towards a residential environment. In major cities secondary streets are characterised by specialist shops, cafés and other uses which thrive away from the hustle and bustle of the high street. However smaller towns and declining urban areas often find it difficult to sustain lively secondary streets. This

can be exacerbated by the efforts of highway engineers to prevent these streets being used as 'rat runs' which often leads to through traffic being blocked, further undermining their viability.

Residential or tertiary streets: Below this is the residential or tertiary street which accounts for the majority of streets in an urban area. These streets carry only a small amount of traffic and are therefore seen by few people other than those who live and work there. These tertiary streets serve as the focus for local communities. They also accommodate parked cars and local servicing as well as community activities and even children playing on the street. In traditional urban areas these minor streets tend to be narrower and more intensely urban in character. However because they are not seen by so many people it is also possible to relax the urban form in places to allow for different building types such as larger houses or workshops. It is however important to maintain the permeability of these areas and also to retain, where possible, their mixed-use nature.

The secondary street: Ayres Road in Stretford (above)

A residential street in Newcastle (below)

There can sometimes be levels of the urban hierarchy below the residential or tertiary street. In Georgian areas, such as the district around Hope Street in Liverpool, the main houses face onto the residential streets and to the rear they have stable blocks and servants' quarters facing onto back streets. These back streets can form a parallel street network allowing services such as refuse collections and deliveries to be kept off residential streets. On a smaller scale this is true of the back alleys which characterise areas of by-law terraces which were originally designed for the collection of 'night soil'. In Sunderland these back alleys are wide enough for a car and a refuse truck to pass and are therefore still used for refuse collection and parking. The modern equivalent might be the off-street parking area and there are occasions where there may still be a role for back streets.

This street hierarchy plays a central role in structuring urban areas. The frequency of high streets increases towards the centre and residential streets predominate on the periphery. It can also play an important role guiding urban regeneration. Traditionally urban areas expanded along radial routes and only later was the open land between

these routes built up, often for poor quality residential development. As a result people moving in and out of the city were unaware of the open land or poverty just behind the high street frontage. Yet urban regeneration often starts in the back lands where the worst problems exist whilst ignoring the high street. As a result, people passing in and out of the city see only the problems and are unaware of the improvements behind the decaying high street frontage or landscaped buffer zone.

The urban block

Having established the framework and hierarchy of streets we have also created the main building component of an urban area – the urban block. Today the street tends to be seen as a means of gaining access to a site whereas in traditional cities streets were the way in which the boundaries of sites were defined. Once a framework of streets has been established, and in many urban areas it already exists, the streets naturally define a series of development sites. In urban areas these sites are then developed with perimeter blocks in which the buildings are placed around the edge of the site facing onto the surrounding streets. This creates a clear distinction between the public realm of the street and the private domain to the rear of the buildings.

The urban perimeter block may conjure up an image of a continuous terrace of buildings such as blocks 3 and 4 on the plan to the left. The principle however is more fundamental than this and is equally appropriate for suburban and urban development as illustrated by block 6. Indeed if you look at early suburban layouts such as Welwyn Garden City (page 32) and Bentilee in Stoke-on-Trent page (page 109) they are largely based on the perimeter block principle. The housing faces outwards onto the streets and cul-de-sacs are used sparingly to open up large sites. In the context of existing urban development this can seem so obvious that it is hardly worth explaining. Yet it is entirely at odds with current practice, as illustrated by the plan to the right. This shows how development takes place at present for housing, commercial and industrial development. A

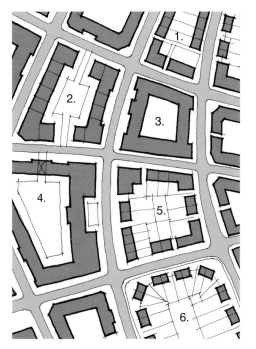

CROWN STREET – GLASGOW

The redevelopment of the Gorbals in Glasgow has been at the forefront of the development of a new approach to urban design in the UK. The nineteenth century Gorbals was characterised by closely packed tenements. It had once been a respectable mixed community but deteriorated into one of Britain's most notorious slums. Redevelopment in the 1960s with monumental blocks, some designed by Sir Basil Spence and Robert Mathew, did nothing to dispel this image.

A comprehensive redevelopment scheme has recently replaced all but two of the 1960s blocks with a series of three-and four-storey courtyard blocks covering forty acres. The concept was to return to the original tenement pattern although at lower densities. The population after redevelopment is forecast to be 20 000, a fifth of that of the original Gorbals.

A master plan was prepared for the development by Piers Gough following a nationwide urban design competition. This was not a blueprint, but enabled outline planning consent to be secured and provided the basis for infrastructure works and development phasing.

The master plan accommodated almost 1 000 new homes, a local shopping centre, hotel, student housing and a new local park. It is based on a grid of streets which then defined building plots to be developed with continuous frontage perimeter blocks. Storey heights are then varied along with front gardens, and 'necking' (a setback in the building line) to create variety and interest in the public realm.

Family maisonettes have been created on the ground floor of blocks with separate back gardens backing onto communal open space at the centre of each block. The flats above are accessed by communal staircases. The planners have insisted on higher levels of parking than current car ownership levels would suggest with negotiations only succeeding in reducing levels from 130% to 115%.

The project has sought a high level of investment in the external environment (said to account for 10 – 15% of development costs in Northern Europe but less than 1% in Scotland). Traffic calmed streets with on-street parking are helping to integrate the area with the outside world where it used to be cut off by heavy traffic routes and functionless open space.

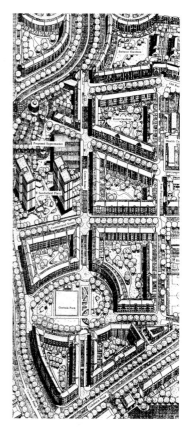

distributor road is kept free of frontage development and feeder roads open up each development site. These single access points then branch out into a series of cul-de-sacs serving small clusters of housing or individual buildings. As a result many of the houses back onto the main road which would normally be regarded as a high street in the local hierarchy. This type of suburban development is inevitable where there is no development framework. Individual developers have neither the reason nor indeed the ability to create a street network other than that required to service their own site. In existing urban areas a street network will often exist into which development can be accommodated. However even here and on larger brown field sites these suburban forms tend to be transplanted to urban areas. While the initial impetus for this type of built form probably stems from highways guidance and the desire to keep traffic routes free

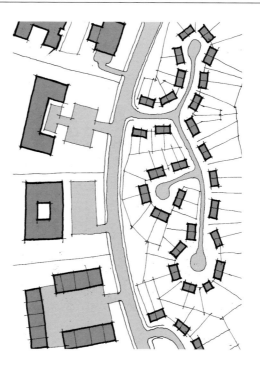

of curtilage access, it has become the accepted model for many developers. It gives the illusion of privacy and security and has proved popular with house-buyers and commercial developers. However the new roads within such areas play no role in a wider framework of streets and are thus deserted for most of the time while the distributor road is forced to carry all traffic and is therefore congested and dangerous. The orientation of the houses can also make them vulnerable to burglary and means that they present a blank frontage to the main streets which in turn makes it dangerous and unattractive to pedestrians.

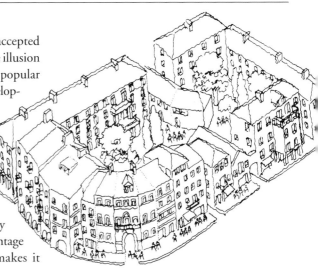

The plan on page 178 shows an alternative approach to the development of the same site. This has a similar mix of development, albeit at higher densities, and is based on the principle of perimeter blocks. It also shows how this form of development is appropriate for a variety of uses and can even accommodate semidetached housing.

The practicalities of development influence the size and shape of urban blocks. In order to maximise the development potential of land, buildings tend to back onto each other. With housing this means a minimum distance between the backs of the buildings of 20 – 25 metres. If the width of the buildings is added to this along with a setback from the street (which is not always necessary) it creates a minimum block depth of 40 – 50 metres. However blocks of this width

Perimeter blocks:
Above, an illustration from the Urban Villages Forum showing a traditional urban block. Below, A housing development by North British Housing Association showing the use of urban perimeter blocks

tend to consist of two parallel rows of housing and closing the end of the block can be difficult (see block 1 on the plan). Highway engineers will also often insist on at least 60 metres between junctions so that if the streets are to be traffic routes this determines the block width. It is therefore common for blocks to be slightly wider than the minimum with the space in the centre being used for larger gardens, communal space, parking, or even additional housing as in Poundbury.

The only limit on length of the block is the permeability of the area and the optimum is probably somewhere in the region of 70 – 90 metres. The ideal arrangement is for the shorter edge of the block to front onto a high street. This creates regular links from the main circulation route so maximising permeability. This however runs counter to the philosophy of the highways engineer who will generally seek to limit the number of roads joining a high street to minimise traffic conflicts. Indeed engineers may insist on at least 90 metres between junctions onto a main road which can only be achieved if some of the side roads are pedestrian only.

There are many variations on the urban block. In medieval cities block sizes tend to be much smaller. These however are almost impossible to develop to modern standards of daylight and overlooking distances. In cities where apartments rather than houses predominate there is more flexibility in block layout. In Barcelona the blocks are square and have the flexibility to accom-modate either courtyard blocks or individual buildings. In Paris, Berlin and Vienna the blocks are bounded by six-storey apartment buildings and often include other uses in the centre. Indeed in most older continental cities it is common for housing to be built around an internal courtyard within an urban block accessed through an arch-way, creating a secluded place off the busy street. Urban blocks are however more difficult to develop with the individual houses preferred by most UK developers. It is therefore important that we evolve techniques for building in this way and in particular that building types are developed which are able to 'close' the corners.

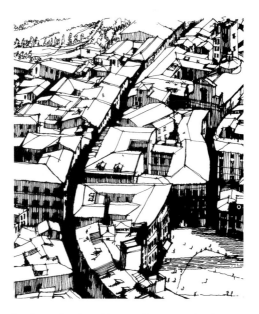

Urban grain: The scale of building plots is much smaller in traditional urban areas to create a fine grain of development

Urban grain

It is important not to confuse the urban block with the urban building plot. This is a mistake which has been made in many recent urban devel-opments in the UK. The nature of redevelopment in inner city areas means that it is often difficult to attract developers. This can be compounded if they are asked to build urban mixed-use schemes which the development industry regards as risky. This can mean that only large developers are willing to get involved and able to take on the risk or negotiate a grants package. Hulme, for example,

has been developed by just four main developers, two housing associations, a private housebuilder and a commercial developer. As a result each developer has taken on very large sites. Variety has been introduced by undertaking develop-ment in phases and using different architects for each phase. Yet even these phases have generally included a number of urban blocks with the result that the development has a feeling of uniformity or artificially introduced variety. This is one of the

---

URBAN DESIGN AND URBAN CAPACITY

The recent interest in urban capacity studies has created a new role for urban design. The design exercises below are from the urban capacity study undertaken by Llewelyn-Davies for the London Planning Advisory Committee. This identified potential development sites around public transport nodes (Ped Sheds) before assessing their capacity by applying a series of design scenarios. The first applied existing planning policies while the second and third progressively reduced parking provision to create a more urban development form. This had the result of doubling the capacity of the sites and also improved both their contribution to urban form and the value of the development.

A similar approach has been used in a handbook for the North West Regional Association to allow local authorities to assess housing capacity. The technique is important because it treats urban design not as an aesthetic side issue but as something of relevance to mainstream planning policy.

reasons why these developments have failed to capture the true character of traditional urban areas.

The grain of most urban areas is much finer than this. If you examine a typical urban block in a great city like London it is made up of a variety of buildings built at different times by different developers with different designers. There is value in the unity of Paris or Bath but it is variety which characterises most urban areas and this is created by a fine grain of development. However carefully an architect seeks to introduce variety into a large scheme it always tends to look artificial. True variety comes from the development of small plots and individual buildings by different developers and not by giving one developer and one architect an entire urban block.

The other aspect to urban grain is the size of urban blocks. In traditional cities blocks become smaller towards the centre. This means that streets become more frequent and permeability increases. This both accommodates and promotes a greater level of pedestrian activity and also means that the density of development and the mixture of uses increases towards the centre. However while this increase in grain through decreasing block sizes can be seen in most traditional towns it is rarely incorporated into new development.

Street Theatre: The Streets Ahead Festival in Stockport. The provide the backdrop to the drama of urban life

Places not spaces

So far we have said nothing about buildings yet, unlike a road, a street without buildings cannot exist. If a street is to play the dual function of a route and a focus for the community it must be framed by buildings and enriched by their activity and life. The street network of a city along with its squares, parks and other public spaces makes up the public realm of an urban area. This can be likened to a stage on which the public life of the city is acted out. Yet a stage is nothing without a back drop and in urban areas the back drop is made up of buildings. In this context the most important role of buildings is to frame and define the public realm. As Francis Tibbalds said in the first of his ten commandments for urban design, 'spaces are more important than buildings'[9]. The quality of spaces within urban areas is what determines their success yet too often this is ignored by planners, architects and engineers, concerned about buildings as objects.

In the medieval city only the cathedral would have been treated as an object to be viewed from all sides and even that would have very little space around it. Other buildings from the grandest merchant's palace to the lowliest hovel were joined to their neighbours and architectural expression was confined to the street façade. In the twentieth century the modern movement has taught us to view buildings as pieces of sculpture to be viewed from above, as in the architect's model or from the moving car rather than experienced as a pedestrian. Such buildings do little to enclose and enliven the public realm and are surrounded by space designed as a setting for the building which is, as a result, formless and lacking in human scale. Think of any great city and you bring to mind a few great buildings, the cathedral, town hall, perhaps a palace or a museum. However the majority of the buildings will be nondescript, and walking around its streets you probably do not even notice the upper floors. Yet these nondescript buildings do not detract from the quality of the urban space, they enhance it. Quality buildings provide landmarks and their value is increased by scarcity. A city made up of nothing but landmarks would be too rich a meal to digest.

It is therefore important to concentrate on the ordinary as well as the extraordinary when considering urban buildings and to focus on the space that buildings create as well as their design. The previous government's campaign *Quality in Town and Country*[10] has played an important role in raising awareness of design but there is an equal need to promote the good manners which should shape all urban buildings. These are ground rules which determine the position, height and form of buildings and if they are followed then even a poor building will not detract from the quality of the public realm. These rules are outlined on the following pages.

The building line: The first rule of urban etiquette is that buildings should follow a building line. This is the line created by the main frontage of the building, ignoring projections and setbacks as illustrated in the plan to the right. There has been a tendency in modern urban design to introduce variety in the position of buildings. However in most urban areas the building line is continuous even if it is not always straight. The distance between the building lines defines the width of the street far more than the carriageway or pavements. It therefore determines the scale, proportion and character of the street, characteristics which will soon be lost if the building line is broken or ignored. On most urban streets the building line is already well defined by existing buildings and planning authorities are usually careful to ensure that new development does not project forward of this line so as to interrupt views along the street. However the tendency with many modern development forms is to set buildings back from the building line to create space for car parking. This can be seen in housing developments where planners or developers insist on a driveway to park the car off the street. It is also the case with retail developers who like car parking to be visible to passing motorists. While it is possible for buildings to be set back from the building line if this is done too often the integrity of the street space can be undermined.

Enclosure: If a street is to work as a place it must be enclosed by its buildings. In simple terms this means that as you walk down a street or through a square you should not be able to see out other than into other defined spaces. Good urban space, like water, needs to be contained and if you leave a hole it soon drains away. In most urban areas this is achieved by using terraced building forms. Indeed in Dutch new towns one of the few ordinances regulating development is that all buildings should have party walls with those on either side. It is however also possible to contain urban space with detached and semidetached buildings provided that the gaps between buildings are small and do not leak space when you look along the street (see the plan below).

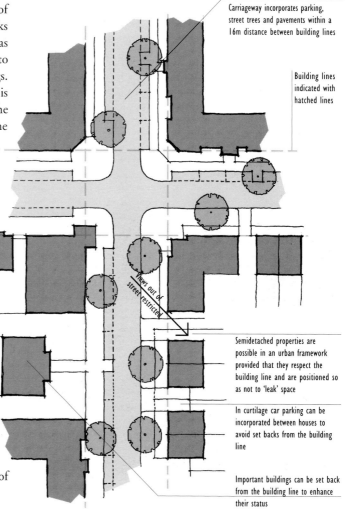

Carriageway incorporates parking, street trees and pavements within a 16m distance between building lines

Building lines indicated with hatched lines

Views out of street restricted

Semidetached properties are possible in an urban framework provided that they respect the building line and are positioned so as not to 'leak' space

In curtilage car parking can be incorporated between houses to avoid set backs from the building line

Important buildings can be set back from the building line to enhance their status

The junction between the building and the street:
In suburban layouts buildings stand within a landscape but in urban areas it is important to consider the way in which they address the street. Because of the proximity of urban buildings to the public life of the street it is important to create a transitional zone, however small, to protect the interior life of the building. In Victorian terraces this was often little more than a doorstep and recessed doorway. With larger buildings like the American brownstone tenement or the Georgian terrace, the main entrance is accessed via a flight of steps thus creating a type of moat and draw-bridge. The footpath is framed by railings behind which is a light well opening up a half-basement. In the early suburbs in Britain and in the suburbs of continental cities the relationship is even more complex with an avenue of street trees, a wide pavement and a significant boundary wall. However the character of an urban street is retained. While the houses are set back they follow a common building line and are of sufficient scale to relate to the street.

Scale and proportion: If buildings are to define the public realm they must be large enough to enclose the space. This is defined by the enclosure ratio of a street which measures the height of buildings against the width of the street (between the building lines). In a street with an enclosure ratio of 1:1 the buildings on either side are as high as the street is wide. In many medieval cities and the urban canyons of New York, or indeed Victorian Manchester, the enclosure ratios are far greater than 1:1 as indeed should generally be the case in central commercial and retail areas. However in residential areas it is often neither possible nor desirable to achieve such a high level of enclosure. In these areas enclosure ratios can drop to 1:3 on streets and as much as 1:10 around parks and along boulevards. With the exception of boulevards, enclosure ratios apply to all levels of the street hierarchy. A high street will be much wider than a residential street but its buildings should be correspondingly higher. A residential street which is 15 metres wide can adequately be enclosed by two-storey buildings whereas a high street, 30 metres across, will require buildings of at least four storeys.

There are two main problems today in achieving urban enclosure ratios. The first is the fact that modern buildings are much lower than those in the past, something which is obvious if you look at a modern house standing next to a Victorian property. Modern residential storey heights and level ground floor access mean that a

Addressing the street:
A cross section of Roslyn Place in Pittsburgh (above), the street described by Allen Jacobs on page 108. This shows an enclosure ratio of 1:2.5 and also the transition between the private life of the home and the public life of the street.
New urban housing in London (above left) which employs the traditional technique of steps up to the ground floor and a half basement. This however creates problems with disabled access. An alternative is to use small front gardens and street trees (bottom left)

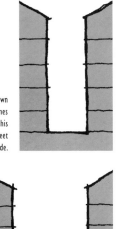

3:1 - The medieval street or downtown Manhattan. The buildings are three times higher than the street is wide. In this case five-storey buildings on a street which is 5m wide.

1:1 - The ratio of many Victorian commercial streets. In this case four-storey buildings on a street which is 10m wide.

1:2 - An urban residential street such as many of the terraced housing areas in Britain. With modern two-storey buildings this implies a street width of 10m which is too narrow in many cases to meet highway requirements.

1:3 - This is probably the optimum ratio possible while maintaining the char- acter of an urban street. With modern storey heights it

implies a street width of 15m for two-storey property, however the street could be wider if the height of buildings was increased

two-storey property is little more than five metres high to the eves. A Victorian property in contrast will often have a half basement and storey heights in excess of three metres so that a two-storey house is as high as a modern three-storey building. This means that a modern street needs to be 15 metres wide to achieve a 1:3 enclosure ratio whereas a Victorian street could be 22 metres wide and achieve the same level of enclosure. This leads to the second problem since the demands placed upon the street by the transport engineer have increased since Victorian times so that modern carriageway widths, footpaths and parking do not easily fit within a 15 metre street. Nor indeed does the planning requirement for privacy dist-

ances of up to 22 metres between facing properties. The tightness of the engineering of such streets is illustrated on the table below which is taken from the *Hulme Guide to Development* in Manchester [11]. Here the residential street width is set at 15.5 metres and the suggested eves height is increased to 5.8 metres to achieve a 1:2.5 enclosure ratio. The latter is achieved by raising the ground floors of properties slightly above ground level (providing ramps for disabled access) and also hiding the roof behind a parapet to increase the appearance of height. However even this leaves little scope for on-street parking. In reality what happens is that a strip is created between the footpath and the road which accommodates street trees, visibility splays at junctions and parked cars although if junctions are frequent parking can easily be squeezed out. This is illustrated on the plan on page 183 although this is based on an 18-metre street width.

Enclosure ratios: The character of urban streets in a function of the height of the buildings in relation to the width of the street (left)

The ground rules: The technical guidance from the Hulme Guide to Devel- opment which sets down some basic rules for street widths and enclosure.

	High Streets	Secondary Streets	Residential Streets
Recommended distance between building lines	21m(max)	17.5m(max)	15.5m(max)
Recommended building height to eves	9m	7.6m	5.8m
Number of storeys on footprints over 100m²	4-6	3-5	2-3
Carriageway width	10mmax	7m	6m
Minimum footway width	2.5m	1.8m	1.8m
Cycle lane where appropriate	2m	2m	Within carriageway
Additional margin for street trees	1.2m	1.2m	1.2m
Design speed limit	30mph	30mph	<20mph
Kerb radii	10m	6m	3m
Visibility splays	2.4x70m	2x60m	2x33m
Minimum distance between junctions	60m (same side) 30m (opp. side)	60m 30m	30m 15m
% of frontage complying with enclosure ratio	90%	80%	60%

Source: Guide to development, Hulme - Manchester City Council

Stroget in Copenhagen: One of the world's great streets

Active frontages: The final ground rule for urban buildings is that they should interact with the street rather than turn their back onto it. This is naturally achieved with mixed-use development where the ground floors are used for retail and commercial development. The frontage of the building is then made up of shop fronts interspersed with doors giving access to housing or offices on the upper floors. This is the predominant building type in most continental cities but, other than in Scotland, is less common in the rest of the UK where there is neither the demand to sustain ground floor retail uses (other than in town centres) or to live on the upper floors. There is however much that can be done with single-use buildings to ensure that they contribute to

development which minimise the number of widows to maximise usable floor area.

These ground rules create an envelope for buildings in urban areas. They define the position of the front wall, the orientation of the main entrance, the height of the building and its relationship to adjacent buildings. These parameters are set by the context that is the existing buildings surrounding a site and by the position of the street within the urban hierarchy. A good example of the use of such principles is the *Manchester Guide to Development* [12] or the recently revised *Essex Design Guide* [13], both of which establish a simple set of rules for urban development. To some these principles may seem to trespass onto territory which should rightfully be left to the developer and the architect. Yet they are ground rules which were once implicitly understood but have been forgotten in recent years. Indeed far from constraining the designer these ground rules should be seen as a liberation. If the rules are followed then there is less need to control the design of the building and to meddle in the detail as has become the habit of the development control planner. These rules are well illustrated by the illustration of Stroget in Copenhagen which is one of the finest medieval streets in the world. While the buildings that make up the street are not of great architectural merit they create a public space of the highest quality by following a defined building line, creating a well proportioned space, curving gently so that new vistas are constantly opened up and enlivening the street with active frontages. We find such great streets so difficult to recreate today because we have lost an understanding of the etiquette or good manners which should guide urban development.

The identity of urban areas

Whilst it is vital for buildings to follow these rules of urban etiquette, a city or neighbourhood is more than the sum of its parts. It also has an overall unity and identity which results from the layout of its streets and the cumulative impact of its buildings. To understand this we must discuss well-established urban design concepts such as landmarks, vistas and focal points. These are the

the life of the street. They should firstly face onto the street and take their main access from it, rather than from a car park to the rear. They should have windows which provide 'eyes onto the street' and along the street there should be entrances at regular intervals. Most important of all, they should not create dead frontages as so often happens with modern retailing and industrial

elements that allow you to locate yourself within an urban area, provide points of orientation, and linger in the memory when you leave. They can be found in both planned and unplanned cities suggesting that they need not be imposed by the city planner but are part of the natural organisation of urban areas.

Focal points in urban areas are established by the urban hierarchy. The main focal points are the centre and sub-centres and these are generally marked with public squares and landmarks. This can be seen most clearly in the medieval city with its market square in front of a cathedral which dominates the town's skyline. On a smaller scale centres can be marked with sculptures or fountains. In the medieval city the streets leading to the centre were generally curved so that there were few views into the main square increasing the sense of arrival on entering the square. However in planned cities it is common for vistas to be created which terminate in a landmark. Perhaps the grandest example of this is the Champs Élysées which provides visual links through the heart of Paris to the landmarks of the Place de la Concorde, the Arc de Triomphe, and more recently the grand Arche de la Defense. However city planners rarely

have the backing of an Emperor like Napoleon to make such grand vistas possible. It is however extraordinary how often the vista down an urban street is terminated by a landmark, be it a church spire or a tower. A fine example is Corn Street in Bristol (below) which has a tower at either end to terminate vistas along the street. This happens far too often for it to be pure chance even in cities which have not been planned. This suggests that the creation of landmarks and vistas is part of the urban etiquette that we have already discussed. When landmark buildings are planned they are placed so that they can be seen from a distance along a vista and are often associated with a public space. Alternatively when planning the develop-

The use of landmarks: Above, Blackburn where a modest commercial building creates a landmark terminating the vista of the street. Below, Corn Street which runs through the medieval heart of Bristol and is terminated by landmark towers at either end.

ment of an urban block certain points can be emphasised such as the corners and points which terminate the vista of adjacent streets as in the illustration of Blackburn. This has been well understood in the development of the Crown Street neighbourhood of Glasgow where detailed briefs [14] have been drawn up for each development site showing the position of buildings and the points to be emphasised with landmark features.

The importance of landmarks and vistas has also been used in the regeneration of Barcelona. Here a policy which roughly translates as 'point and line' [15] has been used to regenerate large areas around the edge of the city. The process starts with the identification of a series of focal points which are marked with public sculptures and landmarks. The streets (or lines) between these points are then improved creating a network of visible improvements which then permeate the surrounding areas. This also emphasises the importance of public art in giving identity to urban areas.

There are two further aspects to urban areas that we should discuss in this chapter, both of which are central to the concept of the walkable city, namely density and a mix of uses.

A critical mass of activity

As we discussed in the first part of this book, density has been a bugbear of planners and other urban professionals. Density has been associated with all manner of urban evils and used to justify clearance and redevelopment. The same is true today as witnessed by the fear that the development of more housing within urban areas will lead to 'town cramming'. This is an emotive phrase but we are yet to see a satisfactory definition of what it means. If town cramming means congested streets then most of our towns and cities are already crammed. If it means overcrowding the solution is to build more not less housing. If it means a loss of privacy and overshadowing then the answer lies in better design. As we suggested in Chapter 9, town cramming will only occur if we seek to introduce more housing into cities without rethinking the design of urban areas, if we do

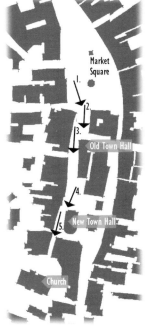

Serial vision: The use of landmarks and vistas can create the magic of urban areas as in this series of views of Devizes in Wiltshire. The series starts in the main market square with a glimpse of the old town hall. As this comes into full view the new town hall is seen and as this is approached the church starts to come into view.

nothing but pack the suburban semi more tightly or put more traffic onto streets without promoting a shift to walking and public transport.

The urban framework described so far in this chapter need not mean higher density development. If urban blocks are large, streets widely spaced and the predominant building form detached and semidetached then urban development can take place at relatively low densities. Indeed the early garden city developments like Hampstead Garden Suburb share many of the urban characteristics described so far in this chapter. However urban areas have the potential for much greater densities as illustrated by the

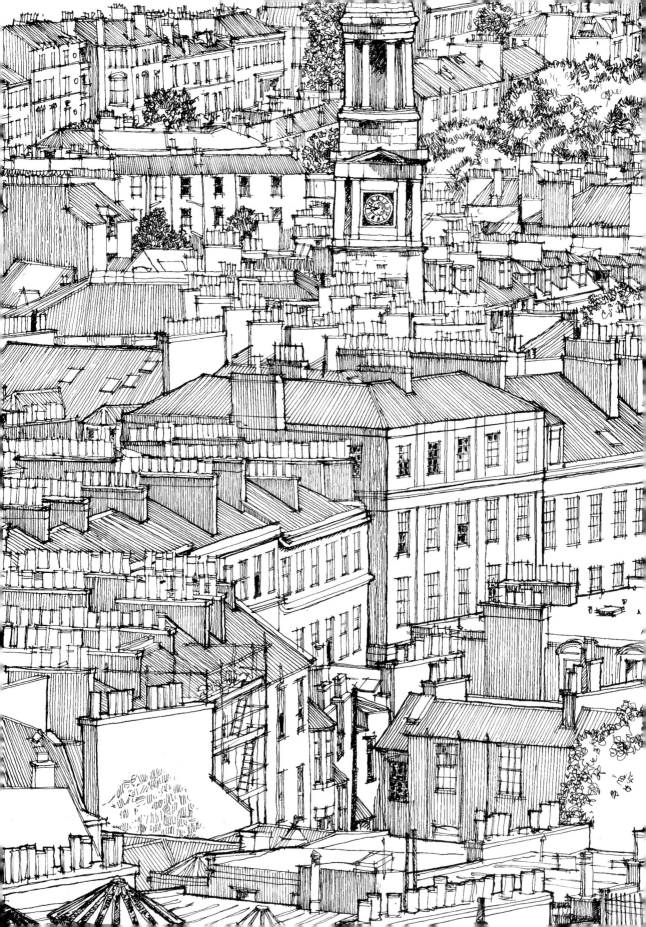

density gradient on page 142. Whereas suburban areas start to squeak if net densities rise much above 37 units to the hectare (fifteen to the acre), with urban layouts much higher densities are possible without undermining the quality of life. Jane Jacobs[16] refers to ideal urban densities of almost a thousand persons per hectare (more than 400 people to the acre) and that in areas which also contained a range of other uses. In Kowloon densities can rise as high as 1 250 dwellings to the hectare and yet still the city functions. It is therefore clear that the design and layout of urban areas will determine their ability to accommodate a higher density of population. As we suggested in Chapter 9, architects since the 1960s have known that three-and four-storey perimeter blocks around squares and open spaces are the optimum form to maximise density while protecting the amenity of residents. This is very similar to the terraced perimeter block with a mix of housing and flats on the corners that we have described in this chapter. This may not achieve Jane Jacobs' benchmarks for ideal urban densities but it should comfortably achieve densities of 60 – 120 dwellings to the hectare (25 – 50 to the acre).

But density is not a necessary evil in urban areas. It is essential to their social and economic life. If urban areas are not built to high densities they will not sustain a range of economic activity and shops, their streets will not be nourished by activity and public transport will not be sufficiently viable to provide an alternative to the car. In the low-density neighbourhood the streets will be congested with cars whilst the pavements are deserted whereas in the high density neighbourhood the streets may be equally congested (but no more so because of the limits set by highway capacity) and the pavements will bustle with life.

The importance of density can be illustrated by public transport. The Local Government Management Board's Manual on sustainable development[17] suggests net densities of 100 persons per hectare to sustain a good bus service. On the density gradient we have suggested that this corresponds to 25 dwellings to the hectare because we have used an average dwelling size of four bed spaces. However if we use instead current average household size in the UK we would need 40 – 50 dwellings per hectare to sustain a bus service. This is above what can be achieved with suburban development but would be quite comfortable with the urban development forms described in this chapter.

It should also be remembered that the figures that we quote here are net densities and relate only to the site where the housing has been built. The density across the whole neighbourhood is referred to as the gross density and can be substantially lower than the net densities if the neighbourhood includes large areas of open space or existing low-density development. It may therefore be that to achieve gross densities capable of sustaining and animating an area net densities will have to be further increased to compensate for existing low densities elsewhere.

Within urban areas densities are not even. Densities traditionally increase towards the centre and around local centres. This is a natural result of the street hierarchy which dictates that buildings should be taller on high streets and secondary streets. This increased density ensures that the centres remain lively and also sustains the public transport which runs along these arteries. This is similar to the model of a string of high density centres along public transport routes proposed by the American Pedestrian Pocket movement and indeed the Town and Country Planning Association.

A rich mix of uses

Our discussion of density has so far been confined to housing development. However an important characteristic of successful urban development is that it contains more than housing. If people are to walk to work, to school and to the shops, these uses must also be located within the neighbourhood, which leads us to the concept of mixed-use development.

Mixed-use development has become a much used concept in recent years partly because it has been so loosely defined. The huge city centre retail developments in Britain and America in the 1970s were called mixed-use schemes as indeed

Density but not crammed: Attractive neighbourhoods such as Edinburgh New town illustrate that high density areas can be attractive and need not feel crammed (facing page)

they were since they contained a mix of retailing, offices and often hotel and residential accommodation. More recently in the 1980s schemes like Canary Wharf and Chiswick Park have been referred to as mixed-use since they incorporated some other uses alongside the predominant office use. But is this really what we mean by mixed-use development? As Alan Rowley has pointed out [18] 'the term mixed-use development is in danger of degenerating into a slogan for a product that is a pale imitation of traditional mixed-use areas'. These schemes owe little to the European tradition of small-scale development with active ground floor uses and housing on the upper floors which is what many people bring to mind when thinking about mixed-use development.

These very different concepts of mixed-use development highlight the different roles that it can play. If our sole concern is the accommodation of different uses in proximity to each other to create activity throughout the day and to promote walking rather than car use, then the form of development matters little. As Andy Coupland [19] has pointed out most of these benefits can be achieved by mixing uses horizontally within streets, blocks or neighbourhoods. However if our concern is to create a building type which is appropriate for the urban streets that we have described in this chapter then we need to

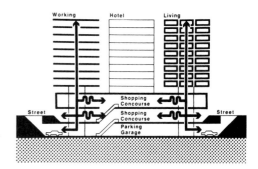

take the concept a stage further by mixing uses vertically within buildings. This is what developers find so difficult. Indeed good examples of new vertically mixed-use development are remarkably rare in the UK and schemes such as Deptford High Street in London and Gloucester Green in Oxford have been widely written about in the professional press despite the fact that they represent a form of development which would be bread and butter to continental developers.

The reason for this goes very deep and is the result of many of the trends that we described in Part 1 of this book. English people have largely rejected the flats and apartments which are an inevitable result of mixed-use development. The planning system has also sought to separate uses to avoid conflicts and therefore has tended to deter mixed-use development. These attitudes may be starting to change but we are still left with more fundamental barriers in the workings of the development industry. In the UK developers have become very specialised so that housebuilders do not build commercial property and commercial developers steer clear of housing. This is reinforced by the different way in which residential and commercial property markets operate. Houses are either built for sale or for rental with secure tenancies which means that the developer and investor loses control of the completed development. Commercial development, by contrast takes place on the basis of twenty year leases often with the intention that the building will be redeveloped or refurbished after that time. If this commercial space is beneath residential accommodation the options for the developers and investors are thus limited, making the develop-

TESCO/PEABODY – HAMMERSMITH

Large shops are a fact of life and they can be difficult to accommodate in urban areas. The Crown Street redevelopment team in Glasgow planned to develop a back of pavement supermarket with parking on the roof but have experienced resistance from operators. Another option is to wrap housing and other uses around the supermarket or to build on the roof. This has been done by Peabody in association with a Tesco supermarket in Hammersmith.

ment less attractive as an institutional investment. This is compounded by concerns about security, particularly from the tenants of social housing, and very practical issues such as what happens when someone lets their bath overflow and floods the commercial property below. However these problems can be overcome. The *Living over the Shop* project for example [20], has developed a mechanism by which the building owner gives a fixed term commercial lease to a housing association which safeguards the value of the property. The association then grants assured shorthold tenancies to its tenants. The practical problems are also soluble – in the Tesco/Peabody scheme, for example, there is a pitched roof over the supermarket above which is a concrete platform on which the housing has been built.

There remain however problems with the way that mixed-use property is valued which undermines its attractiveness to investors. The main exponents of this type of development have therefore tended to be small independent developer like Urban Splash or First Premise who are not reliant on institutional investors. However the success of these developers could persuade more mainstream developers to find ways around the problems. A good example is the partnership between the commercial developer Amec and Berkeley Homes who are creating a joint venture company to undertake mixed-use development with the investment and profits being split equally.

It is important that the problems of mixed-use buildings are overcome if we are to build the sustainable urban neighbourhood. While it is possible and important to mix uses horizontally across the neighbourhood, if we fail in the task of creating vertically mixed-use buildings we will not have a building type capable of creating the high streets and secondary streets that form the heart of the neighbourhood.

DEPTFORD HIGH STREET

Deptford High Street in East London is a busy market street. However like many streets of its kind, it has declined in recent years and many of its buildings are dilapidated and the upper floors are largely vacant. Over the last few years a small developer, First Premise has undertaken a series of four innovative mixed-use developments:

■ 164-168 Deptford High Street, which includes seven workshops and one studio on the ground floor totalling 3 829 sq ft with fifteen one and two bedroom flats on the upper floors.
■ 133 Deptford High Street includes six flats above a pair of shops, a large studio/workspace and a church hall. There is a courtyard behind the building with a staircase giving access to the flats from the High Street.

■ 210-212 Deptford High Street, which is a block of two shops with five one and two bedroom flats on the upper floors.
■ 46-50 Deptford High Street, a corner site which First Premise developed for another owner. This includes two blocks of flats around a small paved court at first floor level with two shops and a row of garages on the ground floor.

In total the four sites provide 50 flats along with just over 10 000 square feet of workspace and shops. The flats are all for private leasing and are funded with a combination of City Grant and private finance from the Unity Trust Bank. The residential and commercial property has been successfully let and the schemes have encouraged other development on the High Street.

In many respects, the most remarkable aspect of these schemes is the amount of attention that they have received. This is the sort of development that would be bread and butter to developers on the continent but in Britain is so rare that Deptford High Street is still being used as an exemplar of mixed-use development years after it was completed.

We have in this chapter described the importance of a framework of streets in giving structure to urban areas. We have discussed how this framework is ordered by a hierarchy of streets, how it defines urban blocks and how the buildings on these blocks are subject to an urban etiquette which ensures that they contribute to the public realm. We have explored how unity and a sense of place can be created on these urban streets and how a critical mass of development can be accommodated with a mix of uses to sustain the social and economic life of the city. In doing so we have described the characteristics of urban as opposed to suburban design. This is both a description of how cities were built in the past and a prescription for how they might be built in the future. If we are right that environmental pressures and social and demographic change will herald a rediscovery of the importance of urban living these techniques of city building must be rediscovered. But urban development will not, on its own, make a district into a neighbourhood. We therefore turn in the next chapter to the social context of the urban neighbourhood.

Wind Street in Swansea: A medieval street with many of the qualities of the Stroget in Copenhagen (page 186) but unfortunately dominated by cars and a number of important gap sites. Following recent work by URBED the street is being improved and development is being promoted on the most prominent gap site.

CHAPTER 12
The sociable neighbourhood

Environmental sustainability goes hand in hand with social sustainability. Towns and cities are first and foremost places where people live and work, not just as individuals but as communities. If urban areas do not provide civilised places for people to live and for communities to prosper then it will not matter how 'green' they are, they will not be sustainable. We must therefore widen our definition of the sustainable urban neighbourhood to include social as well as environmental concerns. We need to draw upon the concept of neighbourliness or being a good neighbour which is potentially far stronger than the more widely used term community.

It was Ruskin who said 'when we build let us think that we build forever'. This, on the whole, is what we have striven to do in the UK. The Japanese may treat buildings like automobiles, to be discarded when tastes change, but in Britain our intention at least has been to build to last. Yet we have failed lamentably in this task over the last half century. Many neighbourhoods built since the war have failed the most fundamental test of sustainability and have been demolished only a few decades after they were built. Their only legacy is the debt charges which will continue to burden the local tax payer for years to come. To this economic cost must be added the environmental cost of resources squandered and the social costs of communities uprooted and destroyed and people consigned to life on estates which rob them of their health and dignity.

It is the nightmare of any urban planner and architect that they are unwillingly repeating the mistakes of their predecessors. However persuasive the arguments may seem for one new model of development or another (like the sustainable urban neighbourhood) we can be sure that they are no more persuasive than were the argument for the deck-access estate or the tower block. Yet there are many neighbourhoods which have endured and it is from these that we must learn when planning new neighbourhoods.

In the early 1980s we would probably have agreed that the problem of failing estates was history, albeit very recent and rather uncomfortable history. We would have regarded the high-rise council estates of the 1960s and 70s as problems to be sorted out but would have been comforted by the fact that at least they would never be built again. They were an aberration and never again would we play fast and loose with architectural innovation and allow planning dogma to ruin the lives of vulnerable people. We would have agreed that we had learnt our lesson and would, in the future, build traditional buildings with traditional bricks. It may not be exciting but at least it would last. Innovation had become a dirty word and British housebuilding retreated into an arcadia of leafy suburbs and semidetached housing. Everything else that we had tried this century had failed. Better to stick to the housing forms that we are good at – Britain's only successful housing model, the suburban housing estate.

It is therefore all the more disturbing when new estates built to suburban designs fail as disastrously as their modernist forbears. As we quoted David Page as saying in Chapter 4; 'There is now evidence that the process of rapid decline of large social housing estates, which some had thought peculiar to council housing, can also apply to the stock of housing associations'[1]. These housing associations have not been building architectural flights of fancy, they have been building traditional suburban estates. They are indeed often located in the suburbs and built in partnership with private housebuilders using their standard house types. Estates of identical design serve the needs of the first-time buyer admirably but in the social housing sector decline has sometimes been swift and merciless. As Page points out, whereas deck-access council estates took more than twenty years to decline, some housing association estates built in the 1980s declined to the same extent in as little as four years. It is therefore an illusion to believe that the key to social and economic sustainability lies in bricks and mortar as opposed to concrete and steel. In our haste to condemn the despised housing of the 1960s we have overlooked some fundamental questions about social sustainability.

The immortal neighbourhood:
Ancient towns like Cirencester have existed since before Roman times. While there are few Roman buildings left in the town, its street patterns and neighbourhoods are the result of an unbroken chain of evolution and change since that time

The challenge of creating sustainable communities

The challenge of social sustainability is to build neighbourhoods which last not for twenty or even two hundred years but which are immortal. This, after all, is what sustainability means. This is not to say that the buildings or even the streets of the neighbourhood will last forever. It does however mean that change will take place naturally and gradually over time without the need for radical redevelopment. There are neighbourhoods in ancient cities which have lasted for more than a thousand years. Their function may have changed many times and their buildings will have been demolished and rebuilt time and time again but the neighbourhood has endured. In this respect successful neighbourhoods are like great forests which outlive even their most ancient trees. Like great forest, they develop naturally rather than being artificially planted, they are constantly renewed by new growth and they contain a rich variety of species. The buildings of a sustainable

Order and disorder:
The paradigm of problem high-rise estates and successful garden city estates does not always hold true as demonstrated by Roughy Gardens in Wyhenshawe and the Barbican

neighbourhood, like the trees of a forest, are not all of the same type or age. They will not all reach the end of their natural life at the same time or be decimated by some external change – be it Dutch elm disease in the case of the forest or the obsolescence of a particular industry in the case of the neighbourhood. These are some of the issues that we explore later in this chapter.

But social and economic sustainability is about more than mere survival. We should be aiming higher than this. We should be creating neighbourhoods which enhance the quality of social and economic life of their citizens, which are a joy to live in, to work in or to visit. This at its root is the key to a sustainable neighbourhood. Places that are popular will attract people and investment and will be constantly renewed. Unpopular neighbourhoods, by contrast, will be places from which people seek to escape, where people live and work out of necessity rather than choice and where, what is now called 'social exclusion', takes firm root. However to advocate popular neighbourhoods is one thing, to build them is quite another. Overcoming social exclusion is now seen by government as a key priority yet there is still considerable confusion about the best way to tackle it.

Sustainability in terms of the basic survival of neighbourhoods is something which largely relates to social housing. True there are private housing estates which have failed but these are rare. Owner-occupation gives people a vested interest or stake in the success of their neighbourhood – if it declines so does the value of their house. A few years ago the Joseph Rowntree Foundation held a conference to discuss failing council estates at the Barbican Centre in London[2].

The irony was not lost on many delegates that the concrete towers surrounding the conference hall bore a striking resemblance to the council estates that they were discussing. Yet the Barbican has not failed, it is one of the most desirable addresses in the City of London and the flats in its concrete towers change hands for hundreds of thousands of pounds.

Yet in social housing areas decline can sometimes be rapid and unforgiving. Some years ago we undertook work in an area of Wythenshawe on the southern edge of Manchester[3]. As described in Chapter 2, Wythenshawe was developed in the 1930s and designed by the garden city architect Barry Parker. It housed families decanted from slum clearance areas in the city and has over the years nurtured many strong communities. We however were asked to look at a close of fifty council houses which had literally been destroyed in less than six months. The problem had started when a small number of vacancies started to appear. These had been passed by the council to a housing association for refurbishment as short life property. There were delays in the work taking place, by which time other voids had appeared, these were also passed to the housing association. All of the properties on the close except for two were subsequently vandalised and gutted by fire, including those refurbished by the association, with the result that the area resembled a war zone. It transpired that the problems stemmed from two 'problem' families one of which lived in a council house and the other, which had been allocated to one of the refurbished properties, had systematically intimidated all of the other tenants out of the area. This may be an extreme example but it is not unique and cannot be put down to design since the close had survived more than sixty years without problems.

Such problems of social sustainability go to the heart of the sustainable urban neighbourhood. Why is it that the concrete towers of the Barbican prosper while good quality social housing fails? The breakdown of social structure in small areas like the part of Wythenshawe described above is an extreme example of the problems facing all social housing and also many of the inner city areas that we are seeking to repopulate. It is tempting to believe, as the Conservative government did in the 1980s, that the answer to these problems lies in home ownership. If social sustainability seems so much easier to create in private housing than in social housing then why put so much effort and resource into the latter? The 1980s therefore saw a huge increase in the level of owner-occupation which was extended to households which, never before, had been given the opportunity to own their own home. Right-to-buy policies in particular transformed many council estates as council tenants bought their homes and ploughed money into home improvements.

Putting aside for a moment the political issues about right-to-buy and the concerns about negative equity and repossession, it is clear that in many areas this policy has been very successful. There is little doubt that the magic of home ownership has contributed greatly to the sustainability of many council estates such as Kirkby in Liverpool. It has however focused the problems of social sustainability more sharply on the remnants of the social housing sector, the unpopular council estates and the new housing association estates. As the amount of social housing has declined it has been rationed to those in greatest need. It has therefore become welfare housing as in the United States so that a council or housing association tenancy and an inner city address have become a badge of disadvantage. The residualisation of social housing and the growth of home ownership has therefore stabilised the more successful council estates but it has made ghettos out of less successful areas. At its most extreme it has made instant ghettos out of brand new housing association estates let entirely to people from the homeless register.

It was not always thus. When Peabody and Guinness started building social housing in the middle of the last century and when council house building started in earnest in the 1920s it was let to the 'upper' sections of the working class[4]. The theory was that these new tenants would be responsible, could pay the higher rents and would release their previous homes so that poorer people could also improve their housing conditions creating a 'ladder of opportunity'. Today we shy away from such notions of 'deserving' and 'undeserving' poor but a politically correct policy which leads to social breakdown is of benefit to no one. In the 1920s a council or housing association home was a matter for pride whereas today it is a mark of failure which is no basis on which to build a sustainable community. As a result it has been suggested by a number of studies for the Joseph Rowntree Foundation[5] that new social housing should not be let to the most needy but rather to established tenants wishing to move and with the capacity to establish a new community. These tenants would then vacate property within established communities which would be let to those in greatest housing need.

In this book we have advocated the repopulation of urban areas by a wide cross section of people. Yet the residualisation of social housing and inner city areas is one of the factors driving the middle-class flight from the city. We must therefore overcome this stigmatisation if the lives of inner city residents are to be improved. More than anything else, it is attracting the middle classes and the upper sections of the working classes back to urban areas which will overcome this stigma. If this is to happen we must follow some basic principle of social sustainability.

Continuity

One of the most important factors in the creation of sustainable communities is time. Just as a derelict site, left for long enough, will become a haven for wildlife so people left to their own devices in urban areas will create communities. It sometimes seems that the recipe for a sustainable neighbourhood is to build whatever you want and leave to stand for a hundred years. Yet to build a community from scratch is almost impossible however carefully conceived. This has often been the tragedy of large-scale redevelopment over the last thirty or so years. The terraced communities swept away by the slum clearance of the 1960s did not survive being transplanted to the overspill estate and high-rise block. In these new and often hostile environments the communities took years to regenerate. But regenerate they did only to be swept away once more by the redevelopments of high-rise estates of the late 1980s and early 90s.

In the 1990s as in the 1960s the value of these communities, or even their very existence, is not recognised. Professionals may talk at length about the value of community but, as we described in Chapter 7, these rough edged urban communities rarely correspond to the cosy notion of community held by planners and architects. Yet they are the glue which holds urban areas together and, like listed buildings, they should be subject to preservation orders. When problems occur in urban areas, as they always will, we must resist the urge to wipe the slate clean and start again. We must instead tap the capacity of existing communities to address local problems. In extreme cases where redevelopment is inevitable communities can still be preserved. Their housing can be left standing until new housing is complete, they can be involved in the design and neighbours can be given the opportunity to move together. In this way we will, at least, not destroy what we have. But we must do more than this, we must strengthen communities and we must promote social sustainability where it does not exist.

Hidden communities: They may not be recognised but communities thrive in many problem housing estates and are as worthy of preservation as listed buildings

Balance

We must therefore analyse the nature of socially sustainable urban areas. To many professionals the key to sustainability is an arithmetic balance of tenures and social groups. Housing associations are now encouraged to incorporate private or shared equity homes in their estates and planning policy often requires private developments to include an element of 'affordable' housing. But what do we mean by balance? True the iconic village and urban communities described in Chapter 7 are socially mixed. However many communities thrive on shared rather than diverse interests. Communities work in miners' villages as they do in suburban closes because people like living with people like themselves. Mixing the two very different communities so that they become more 'balanced' would not be a recipe for strengthening either.

It may be part of the human condition to seek out people like yourself and to fear those who are different. At its most ugly this can manifest in the racist attacks on black families in white working-class areas. However it can also be seen in campaigns against gentrification (homes for yuppies) in working-class communities and against social housing in middle-class areas. These are powerful forces working against the creation of balanced communities and it is far from clear that they work in practice. The unspoken aim of those who advocate balanced communities seems to be that owner-occupiers will exert a civilising influence on social housing tenants and will prevent the area being stigmatised. This however will not happen if social divisions are simply redrawn at a more local level with protected enclaves of private housing built side by side with social housing. This can be seen in America where a large proportion of new private housing is being built as gated communities[6] protected by walls and security guards from the surrounding area. So while balance may have a role in overcoming stigmatisation it is not the whole answer and must be reflected in the design and layout of the area.

Neighbourhood-based development

One way of doing this is to think about development at the neighbourhood scale. The neighbourhood as a concept has fallen out of favour and today we deal in housing or industrial *estates* or business and retail *parks*. In a more confident age the neighbourhood was the natural unit for the planning or urban areas from Perry's plan for New York to Abercrombie's plan for London. But now we rarely think beyond the bounds of the site under development. Planners may claim that they no longer zone uses but the truth is that they do not have to. The development industry has become so specialised that different developers specialise in housing, commercial and retail development. Their interest is to seek out sites for single-use development and their normal practice is to develop these sites as estates. Like their distant relative, the country estate, these estates will be self-contained and inward-looking. They will have a single point of access and are likely to be surrounded by a high wall or fence. It is this form of development which makes balanced communities so difficult. Mixing tenures and uses within estates can lead to conflict whereas developing them as separate estates reinforces divisions.

The urban principles described in the last chapter imply a very different kind of development. Rather than being zoned into estates, uses and tenures are integrated into the urban fabric and linked by a common street network. Urban neighbourhoods tend to be fine grained and complex so that developments are small and different classes are accommodated within a shared framework for streets. This can still be seen in many traditional urban neighbourhoods like Chorlton in Manchester, Moseley in Birmingham, Hackney in London and even Toxteth (despite its reputation) in Liverpool. Such districts have found a point of balance between gentrification and decline and contain streets of desirable housing cheek by jowl with bedsits, council housing and new housing association development. Their residents can therefore relate to the neighbourhood that they share rather than the social housing estates with the stigma that it has come to imply. Social divisions will not of course be abolished. In even the most balanced neighbourhood, certain streets will acquire good or bad reputations. But these divisions will be blurred and ill defined on the ground. They will also be fluid as decline is followed by regeneration in a process which has always characterised urban areas. The proof of the effectiveness of neighbourhood-based development can be seen in areas like Hulme in Manchester and Crown Street in Glasgow where it has made it possible for regeneration agencies to attract private housebuilders for the first time in decades. It does however imply an urban approach to development, which is the next principle of social sustainability.

Robust urban development

Mixing uses and tenures at the neighbourhood scale will not work unless the design of the area is sufficiently robust. We hesitate to suggest that the design of urban areas has an important role to play in the creation of sustainable communities. There is a long and largely discredited tradition of designers who believed that communities could be created on drawing boards; they clearly cannot. However the design of an area must have an influence on the lives of its residents.

It is tempting to believe that suburban designs are the most effective at creating communities. This is partly based on the sustainability of suburban communities but also on the fact that many inner city residents express a preference for suburban design when consulted on new housing. However the success of the suburb is based on the intrinsic sustainability of home ownership and also its location in areas where crime and other social problems are less prevalent. In the city and in social housing areas, the benefits of suburban design are less clear-cut.

The reason for this is that suburban areas are sustained by a fragile framework of social and economic pressures which do not always exist in urban areas or in social housing. Freedom from the petty and sometime intrusive values of the middle-class suburb is, to many, one of the attractions of urban living. Yet in many respects it is these values which make the suburb work. They work as a check on antisocial behaviour and ensure that gardens and properties are well maintained. The criminologist Barry Poynter has pointed out[7] how in middle-class areas boundary fences are

maintained and houses are rarely left empty because people do not move out until their house is sold. This is not the case in social housing where maintenance is the responsibility of the landlord and there are inevitable delays in reletting property. Empty units can be vandalised and give access to the rear gardens of surrounding property. As in the Wythenshawe example this can lead to an escalation of problems and in the worst cases can undermine the sustainability of the area.

It is also questionable whether suburban designs can foster urban communities. We have long abandoned the idea that grouping housing into small courts creates communities but the suburban close still holds a powerful attraction. It can work as in the Old Eldonians Housing Co-operative in Liverpool where a strong urban community has been created in what is essentially a suburban estate in the heart of the city. It is however likely that the success of this community has more to do with the co-operative structure of its tenants rather than its design. Other examples such as Arkwright town in Derbyshire have been less successful[8]. Arkwright was a mining village of

Robust urban development: Social housing in Brixton creates a clear definition between the public realm of the street and the dwellings

some four hundred people based in tightly-packed terraced streets with a pub, post office, local shops, school and church. Due to the leakage of methane from mine workings British Coal agreed to rebuild the village in a safer location. Following extensive consultation the residents opted for a suburban design based around semidetached housing. Work by Gerda Speller, a research psychologist, has charted the effect that this has had on the residents. Despite a vast improvement in housing conditions people soon felt that the community had been lost. 'A lot of them asked for privacy but now they are finding that privacy isn't really how they want to live. They are keeping themselves to themselves and now they are isolated'. This illustrates the danger of uprooting communities but also suggests the importance of urban form. Urban communities are very different to suburban communities and demand a very different approach to design.

We therefore believe that in urban areas the design principles outlined in the last chapter have an important role to play in promoting social

SECURE BY DESIGN PRINCIPLES:

- Houses should be clustered in small groups and estates should have clearly defined boundaries.

- Rumble strips, pinch points or changes in road texture should be used at the entrance to the estate to give the impression that the estate is private.

- Public access should be restricted to as few routes as possible so as to avoid unnecessary public access.

- Communal areas such as playgrounds should be open and supervised by surrounding houses.

- Good lighting covering all parts of the estate will deter intruders and reduce fear of crime.

- House frontages should be open so that views are not obstructed by planting and high walls or fences.

- In-curtilage parking is preferred but if communal parking is required it should be in small groups open to view and well lit.

- Commercial development should create a defined perimeter to increase 'natural surveillance'.

Paraphrased from Secured by Design Guidelines published by the Home Office Prevention Centre 1994.

sustainability. The perimeter block with its clear delimitation between the public realm of the street and the private realm of the house and garden is far more robust than the suburb. The street expands opportunities for socialisation rather than confining them to the dozen or so houses on a suburban cul-de-sac. It makes civilised life possible in neighbourhoods where there will always be strangers and crime is an unfortunate fact of life. Indeed crime is one of the most important issues of urban sustainability and is dealt with below.

Secure places

There have always been two faces to the city, one associated with culture, civilisation and wealth, the other dark, dangerous and full of unseen threats. To some this may be part of the excitement of urban living but to the majority it is the most important reason for shunning cities[9]. If it is to succeed the sustainable urban neighbourhood must therefore tackle the issue of crime. Yet some of the most powerful arguments against the urban forms that we describe come from the police and institutional investors who believe that far from reducing crime, urban forms will make the problem worse[10]. It is clear that the widely promoted principles of Secure by Design (see insert) promote the type of estate-based suburban development that we believe undermines social sustainability in urban areas.

Much of the theoretical framework for Secure by Design is based upon the writings of academics like Oscar Newman[11] and Alice Coleman[12]. Newman for example, argued for the elimination of routes through residential blocks, something which has been adopted by Secure by Design and is used as an argument against permeability. He also developed the idea of defensible space which is used to justify a preference for estate-based layouts and cul-de-sacs. Yet Newman also argued for small urban blocks and was actually arguing for the type of fine-grained perimeter block that we described in the last chapter, something which is quite consistent with permeability. In a similar vein Coleman states 'as cul-de-sacs have multiplied so have deaths and serious injuries to child pedestrians... DICE recommends traditional street plans'. Those who argue from a Secure by Design perspective against urban layouts would therefore benefit from a rereading of the original sources.

One of the main critics of Secure by Design is Bill Hillier. This is based upon his space syntax studies[13] in which he correlates the extent to which streets are connected to other streets with the level of pedestrian activity or encounter fields. In his studies of modern housing estates he shows that 'the daytime encounter field in the estates turns out to be like the night time in ordinary urban streets. In terms of their naturally available encounter fields, people on these estates live in a kind of perpetual night'. Hillier goes on to demonstrate a correlation between encounter fields and domestic burglary and suggests that permeable layouts may help to reduce crime.

Research evidence for the effect of urban layouts on crime reduction is sparse and we would hesitate to suggest that urban layouts are the whole answer. However if we are to build sustainable urban areas as we must clearly move away from what the Safer Neighbourhoods Unit[14] have called 'a drawbridge strategy protecting the most stable and prosperous communities against the criminally inclined residents of poorer, less stable neighbourhoods.' To do this we must focus not only on the design of the neighbourhood but the attitudes of people living there. Having windows as 'eyes onto the streets' is of little value unless the people behind those windows feel some level of stewardship over the area and a willingness to get involved.

Community and stewardship

This leads to the final principle of social sustainability. The most important challenge of the sustainable urban neighbourhood is to engender in its residents a feeling that they belong, a pride in the area, and a sense of responsibility for it. In other words to create neighbourhoods where the word neighbour means something. This challenge is greatest in social housing and in inner city areas where the process of marginalisation and stigmatisation has corroded these community values.

BO 100 – MALMÖ, SWEDEN

One of the most striking examples of tenant involvement in the development of social housing can be found in Malmö. In 1987 the city commissioned

the architect Ivo Waldhör to undertake a radical experiment in social housing. An initial meeting brought together 70 tenants and a development company was established with a tenant majority on the board along with the city, the developer and the Swedish Architectural Institute. Ideas were developed through detailed interviews with tenants and a *boskolan* (living school) was established to teach tenants the basics of building and design with a view to each of them producing a 1:20 model of their ideal flat. At the same time the tenants learnt about the area's history, planning policy, and infrastructure to inform the development of the whole building.

Design and construction lasted four years with tenants moving in the summer of 1991. Of the thirty-nine households who moved in eighteen had been involved from the start and a further eight had been involved for more than two years.

The five-storey building which has resulted contains an enormous variety of flat types and detailing. Whilst some standardisation was introduced by the architects – the number of window types was reduced from 150 to 48 – tenants were able to change elements throughout the design and construction process both to individual flats and to the whole building following a vote at the general meeting. This resulted in party walls which do not line up with the walls below and kitchens and bathrooms which fail to line up for soil stacks and services. The scheme also includes communal facilities – unusual in Swedish social housing – such as a community room, a sauna and a guest room on the roof along with a hobby area in the basement.

The scheme cost some 25% more than comparable social housing. It has also been incredibly demanding on the time of everyone involved, not least tenants. However the participatory design process has produced a strong and characterful building occupied by a community which has been created through the process and is committed to both the building and to each other.

However it is possible to engender pride and stewardship through the way that housing is planned and managed as organisations such as the Priority Estates Project had demonstrated.

An important element is community involvement in design both of new housing and refurbishment schemes. For this to be effective residents need to be identified in advance and given the time and skills to work alongside planners and architects as in the BO 100 example in Sweden. Once the housing is complete there is also a role for resident involvement in management co-operatives. In this way local people are given both the responsibility and the power to address local problems, rather than regarding them as someone else's problem. Tenant involvement in design and management is coming back onto the agenda as a response to the problems experienced in recent social housing development. Yet the fact remains that most housing associations have limited experience of this field and are constrained by funding pressures and the fact that housing is generally not allocated to tenants until it is complete. We have a long way to go just to get back to the level of consultation that was in the council house building of the late 1970s and early 1980s following the Skeffington Report. One of the first major schemes to fully involve local people was Ralph Erskine's redevelopment of the Byker estate in Newcastle (see page 65). The success of Byker stands in stark contrast to many of the estates built at the same time or a few years earlier which have failed so disastrously. Yet even today there are few redevelopments which can claim the level of involvement achieved in Byker.

The involvement of residents in the design of housing can raise difficult issues about the design of housing. Indeed, as we have suggested, if most social housing tenants are asked what sort of housing they would like to live in, like the residents of Arkwright, they will opt for something that makes them look like an owner-

Communities taking control: Left an urban self-build scheme in Berlin where the building frame was erected by a contractors and fitted out by residents. Right the award-winning Diggers self-build scheme in Brighton using the Segal system

occupier. How do we square this with our advocacy of urban development forms? Rod Hackney [15] was prominent in the late 1980s as an advocate of community architecture which he saw as a means to puncture the pomposity of architects and designers who for years had inflicted their Utopian ideas on vulnerable people.

However community architecture does not mean that architects can abdicate responsibility for design. This is illustrated by the example of St. Wilfreds in Hulme, Manchester (see page 104). Unlike most parts of Hulme this area was home to a traditional ageing community many of whom had lived in the terraced housing which had been cleared in the 1960s. The area was redeveloped by North British Housing Association who put a great deal of effort into the involvement of local residents. At the same time the city council were developing a vision for the redevelopment of the area as an urban neighbourhood as we describe in the next chapter. The problem was that the plan which had been developed with strong community involvement was at odds with the council's vision for the area. Of most concern was the fact that, despite most of the housing being terraced, the estate had been designed with one access road and three cul-de-sacs. A local community architecture project led by Charlie Baker was therefore asked to work with tenants to redesign the plan that they had already agreed. The starting point was to show the tenants a series of slides of different types of urban development elsewhere from which they picked the ones that they liked. They then dug out old street plans of the terraced housing that many of them had lived in before the 1960s and discussed what it was that they liked and disliked about the old housing. It transpired that most of the negative points related to the interior of the home and most of the older residents had fond memories of the terraced streets while the younger tenants could relate to terraced housing areas which still stood in adjacent districts.

As a result of this process the tenants suggested that the new development should be based on the original street pattern which had existed in the area. This made a great deal of sense since many of the underground services still

followed the old street patterns. They then experimented with models to decide on the character and width of streets and developed a plan based upon perimeter blocks. The estate has since been completed and is very successful. It demonstrates that the key to successful community involvement in urban development is not to give the residents a blank sheet and to ask them what they want but to treat them as a designer would treat any client. This involves explaining to them the constraints on development, including the policy context, and giving them a full range of options of what is possible within this context. Similar techniques for community involvement alongside professions are becoming more common with the growth of techniques such as action planning.

If taken to its logical extreme community involvement can promote stewardship by empowering local people to take control of their neighbourhood though housing co-operatives, self-build groups, estate management boards or community-based housing associations. These are the exceptions to the rule that sustainable communities cannot be created from scratch. When groups of people commit years of their life to building and managing their own housing they are also building a community and have an incentive as strong as any owner-occupier to ensure that the community is successful. Within weeks of the completion of the Homes for Change scheme in Manchester (see Chapter 13) the community spirit was tangible. People felt able to leave their front doors open and populate the walkway outside their flats with plants. Yet in physical form, Homes for Change is very similar to the deck-access flats in Hulme which had never managed to generate this level of community spirit. The difference was not so much the design of the housing but the fact that through the co-operative the members of Homes for Change felt that the building belong to them, had been designed in partnership with them and was their responsibility.

Balanced incremental development

We have suggested in this chapter that sustainable communities, like good wine, need time to mature, that they should include a balance of tenures and uses and should be organised as neighbourhoods rather than estates. We have argued that they should be urban in character to promote community and to reduce crime and should engender in their residents a feeling of ownership and stewardship. These are the things that successful urban areas seem to achieve almost effortlessly and yet which constantly elude us when we try to build new urban areas. One of the reasons for this is that, like the forest that we described earlier in this chapter, urban neighbourhoods are almost never successfully built from scratch. They rather evolve naturally over time through the accretion of small-scale development and redevelopment.

This balanced incremental approach to development is something which we have been promoting in our urban regeneration work for many years and is also the key to successful urban development.

Comprehensive development or redevelopment is a risky business. It puts all your eggs in one basket and means that if mistakes are made they will be big ones. As we have seen with many system-built estates, a simple problem such as the wrong mix of concrete or a poorly specified construction detail can mean that hundreds of properties have to be consigned to the scrap heap or subjected to expensive remedial works. Balanced incremental development by contrast suggests a fine grain of development with large numbers of small sites being developed over time by different developers. When this is done the inevitable mistakes which are made will be small and easily fixed. If a particular development type fails it can be demolished or refurbished without the disruption of the whole area. Similarly when schemes prove to be successful they can be identified and replicated. It is also impossible to predict what will happen in the future in terms of demographic, social and economic change. Many deck-access estates were built for families with children in manual employment and were unable to adapt to a time when the manual employment had disappeared and the families were moved away. Contrast this to the traditional Georgian street which was originally built for well-to-do families with servants, subsequently was subdivided into flats and bedsits and is now being converted back into desirable homes for the urban middle classes. Fine-grained diverse urban areas can adapt to such change and in this way we can build neighbourhoods which will evolve and adapt over time rather than being cast in concrete and steel. This is the key to building the 'immortal' neighbourhood and will be the focus for the final chapter of this book. But we will first explore the implication of these ideas on a model neighbourhood in Manchester.

CHAPTER 13
A model neighbourhood?

There is no better place than Manchester to explore how cities might change in the future. The city described by Disraeli in 1844 as 'the most wonderful city of modern times' was, after all, the birthplace of a model for economic development which was to reverberate around the world. The Manchester School of 'laissez faire' economics provided the foundations for modern capitalism and the city is a textbook case of how the forces of industrialisation and economic growth have shaped urban areas ever since.

Back in Chapter 1 we described how the origins of suburbanisation in the UK can, in part, be traced back to the flight of the merchants of Manchester in the first half of the nineteenth century. In setting up the early suburbs, merchants like Samuel Brookes abandoned the polluted, overcrowded city and leapfrogged an area of low-lying marshy land to create suburbs like Whalley Range and Victoria Park. The marshy nature of the land that they crossed lives on in names like Moss Side, Rusholme and Hulme. Less than twenty years after these suburbs were established this low-lying land was also being developed, not for exclusive suburbs but for working-class housing. As wave after wave of suburbanisation swept out from the city these working-class areas declined into what was to become known as the inner city. This too has since expanded outwards to engulf the original exclusive suburbs. Thus was created in Manchester the classic 'doughnut' shape of the twentieth century western city.

Manchester along with Glasgow and Liverpool declined further and lost more population than any other UK cities. Manchester and Glasgow however have also led the way in showing how cities can reinvent themselves for the twenty-first century. It is, of course, too early to tell, but it is just possible that Manchester is once again leading the way in the transformation of British cities. Just as Whalley Range was a fundamental turning point in the 1830s so the neighbouring district of Hulme could come to be seen as equally significant in the future.

The Hulme area is one of the most important redevelopment projects in the UK. While flawed in many respects it does provide a model for the sustainable urban neighbourhood. In this chapter we therefore use the Hulme area as a test bed to illustrate how the sustainable urban neighbourhood might be developed.

The development of Hulme

As Manchester boomed in the middle of the nineteenth century the Hulme district, immediately to the south of the city centre, was one of the first districts to be developed in the 1850s. The housing in Hulme was of a poorer quality than the later bylaw development in Moss Side and had become a notorious slum by the end of the century. In 1923 there were 130 000 people living in Hulme. At a time when the average population density of Manchester was 34 people per acre, in Hulme it was 136 persons per acre

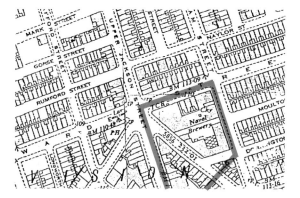

Stretford Road in the 1950s when it was one of the city's prime commercial routes (right)

Hulme pior to redevelopment: The Naval Brewery stands on the site which has been developed by Homes for Change (far right)

A brave new world: The Crescents under construction in 1970 (below)

rising to 196 persons per acre in the north of the area[1]. Hulme was declared Britain's largest clearance area in 1934.

However Hulme was also a vibrant urban area. Until its closure in 1965, Stretford Road which ran through the heart of Hulme contained the largest selection of shops outside the city centre including, a what was later to become, the Debenhams department store. The area contained churches designed by Pugin and Charles Barry as well the extraordinary St. Mary's Church by Crowther which still boasts the tallest spire in the city (the can be seen in the background of the

drawing on page 50). It included more than sixty pubs, three breweries and two music hall theatres. It was also a mixed-use areas with large factories such as the Dunlop rubber works and Gaythorn gas works as well as hundreds of small workshops, with specialities like gold beating and sign writing, including one where the engine for the first Rolls Royce was designed.

The clearance and redevelopment of Hulme took place in a piecemeal fashion from the 1930s onwards but it started in earnest in the 1960s. The housing was subject to compulsory purchase orders and was cleared. Eventually all

that was left was the Stretford Road which was closed in 1965 leaving only the churches by Pugin, Barry and Crowther and a handful of pubs. The redevelopment of the area was planned by the city architect incorporating many of the principles described in Part 1 of this book[2] (see the illustration on page 37). The area was dissected by a series of major roads designed as grade separated dual carriageways. These roads then marked out a series of neighbourhoods each to be served by a local shopping centre. Stretford Road was pedestrianised and its shops were replaced with a large covered shopping centre and a series of local centres. The housing was redeveloped with thirteen tower blocks and six deck-access housing estates, the last and most impressive of which was the Crescents designed by Wilson and Warmersley Architects. The Crescents were modelled on Georgian Bath and included four nine-storey deck-access blocks named after the architects Charles Barry, William Kent, Robert Adam and John Nash. By the early 1970s there were 5 000 properties in Hulme and its population had fallen from 130 000 to around 12 000.

This massive investment in slum clearance only served to make the problems of Hulme worse. When you talk to the older residents of the area it is clear, as in other similar areas, that there was a short honeymoon period in which they enjoyed their large comfortable flats with internal toilets and central heating. However it did not last long. Following an accident in the mid 1970s when a child fell to his death from an upper walkway the council resolved to move all families out of the area and its decline accelerated.

The reputation of the area rapidly deteriorated and it suffered all of the typical problems of urban decline: poverty, crime, drug use, and unemployment. However the easy availability of large flats in the area and its proximity to the University meant that Hulme became a magnet for young people many of whom would stay in the area for a few years before moving on. Over the years Hulme became a focus for Manchester's subculture. Many of its residents were squatters living as single people in flats designed for families and pressing spare bedrooms into service as offices,

workshops and even recording studios. There was at one point a publishing company which employed eight people from a flat in Hulme. A major government-sponsored report on the area in the late 1980s (The Hulme Study[3]) found that 30% of the population had higher education qualifications, more than Manchester's most affluent suburb. However another 30% of the population had no qualifications at all and unemployment

The hidden community: While the Crescents deteriorated into a notorious slum they were home to a strong if unconventional community. Their demolition was celebrated by a local performance group the Dogs of Heaven (below)

2 500 deck-access properties have since been demolished to be replaced by 1 026 housing association properties and a similar number of homes for sale. Stretford Road has been reopened and the covered shopping centre has been redeveloped with a new supermarket which is eventually to be part of a new high street and market. A range of other facilities has been created including workspace, local shops, community and cultural facilities and a new park. The City Challenge project came to an end in March 1997 although work will continue on the redevelopment of Hulme for many years to come.

The redevelopment has been undertaken by a handful of developers. The social housing has all been developed by two housing associations, North British and the Guinness Trust. A large part of this social housing has then been transferred to six local associations for management including a community-based association and a housing co-operative. The majority of the private housing is being developed by Bellway Urban Renewal and the shopping centre redevelopment is being undertaken by Amec in partnership with two further private housebuilders.

There is little doubt that Hulme has been transformed by this process. The first £100 000 home has recently been sold in an area where home ownership was, until recently, inconceivable. But not everyone is impressed. There has in recent months been an upsurge of protest from parts of the community who feel alienated from the increasingly commercial focus of development. Perhaps more damaging if Hulme really is to become a model for urban development was the critical reaction of Lord Roger's Urban Task Force following a recent visit to the area. Their reaction however was probably more disappointment that the Hulme redevelopment failed to live up to its reputation. The question in Hulme is whether it should be criticised for falling so far short of what it could have been or praised for being so much better that similar schemes elsewhere. In our view it is the latter and we believe that Hulme is a good starting point to explore the implications of the sustainable urban neighbourhood.

An aerial view:
A view of Hulme from the spire of St. Mary's Church looking across the area covered by the plan on pages 216 and 217. The numbers correspond to the index to the plan. Also shown are the last of the deck-access blocks prior to demolition and the City Centre in the distance (above).

Hulme III:
One of the phases of the Guinness Trust development in Hulme designed by OMI Architects (below).

rates were the highest in the city. Despite, or perhaps because of its reputation the young community which adopted Hulme thrived in the area and many fought hard to prevent the area being redeveloped.

Manchester City Council had quite different views about Hulme and had been working on redevelopment since the mid 1980s. The area had originally been planned as one of the first Housing Action Trusts, something which was fiercely resisted by local people in a campaign which was eventually successful. Following a further study by Price Waterhouse[4] in 1991, the Housing Corporation allocated funds for the redevelopment of two of the deck-access estates and the following year Hulme was designated as one of the first round City Challenge projects. The redevelopment plans were widened to include all six of the deck-access estates. Around

The great urban experiment

Traditionally cities in the UK have compared themselves to their nearest competitors. In the past Manchester would have to looked to cities like Birmingham, Leeds and Glasgow to gauge its success. However as the Hulme redevelopment was being planned Manchester was bidding to stage the Olympics and was therefore seeking to compete on an international rather than just a national stage. As part of the Olympic bidding process, senior politicians from Manchester spent time in Barcelona, host of the 1992 games. Manchester had always seen itself as one of Europe's great provincial cities alongside cities like Barcelona, Milan and Frankfurt yet the politicians were shocked by the contrast between Manchester and Barcelona. It was clear that while Manchester had been doing well enough in comparison to other British provincial cities it had fallen a long way behind its European counterparts in terms of their economy, culture and sheer urbanity. Manchester's leaders concluded that if Manchester was to take its place as a leading European city it would need to transform itself and a central part of this project was the transformation of its urban environment. Hulme was to be the test bed for this transformation.

The leader of the Council, Graham Stringer, pledged that Hulme would be redeveloped as a vibrant, mixed-use, urban quarter, although it must be said that few people in the city understood what this meant at the time. Initially a master plan was commissioned from a Canadian architect Joe Berridge, although this failed to live up to the politicians' expectations. Following this a local architect George Mills was commissioned to develop an urban code similar to those of Duany and Plater-Zyberk in the US. While George was to play a central role as urban design advisor to the council throughout the redevelopment the

Hulme V:
A development by North British Housing Association. The streets are well-proportioned but the area looks artificial since all the buildings are of the same design

A new urban vision: One of the illustrations from the Hulme Guide to development (above) and below the Hulme Arch, a major new landmark in the area

code proved difficult to understand and failed to overcome the resistance of many of the key players in the area. It was therefore decided to commission a written urban design guide[5] from a local designer and activist Charlie Baker who at the time was running the Hulme Community Architecture Project. This written guide which was eventually co-written with myself (DR) set out a series of principles for urban development and codified these into a set of simple rules covering:

- **Streets:** The development of streets which are more than traffic routes but which promote sociability, community and natural surveillance.
- **Integration:** The promotion of a rich variety of uses within an integrated pattern of streets.
- **Density:** The creation of sufficient density of people and activities to animate streets, to support public transport, and to sustain a wide range of shops and services.
- **Permeability:** The development of a neigh-

bourhood with strong links to surrounding areas, which is easy to move around.

- **Routes and transport:** The accommodation of the car without allowing it to dominate by reducing traffic speed.
- **Landmarks, vistas and focal points:** The use of existing and new buildings along with public art to create interest, excitement and character.
- **Definition of space:** The creation of an attractive well-proportioned public realm defined by appropriately scaled buildings.
- **Hierarchy:** The organisation of uses and buildings within a recognisable hierarchy of streets reflecting the organisation of the area.
- **Identity:** The encouragement of diversity in the design of buildings and spaces to create a strong sense of place.
- **Sustainability:** The promotion of development which is sustainable environmentally, socially and economically by encouraging energy efficiency, recycling, public transport and urban ecology and allowing the area to adapt to future change.

There was nothing particularly original about these principles. They were being promoted by the Urban Villages Forum[6] and had been part of the Crown Street development guide published the previous year in Glasgow[7]. However initially the Hulme guide was fiercely resisted. The housing developers said that it would make their housing expensive and unpopular. The Housing Associations complained that it could not be achieved within their regulatory framework or cost yardsticks. The police argued that it would increase crime, the traffic engineers that it would lead to accidents and the institutional investors that it would reduce the returns on their investment in an area which was already high risk. These objections were thrashed out in hours of negotiation with these different parties. The most difficult discussions were those to reconcile the guidance with the city's highways standards and the framework set by Design Bulletin 32[8]. It is difficult, after all, to pursue a principle when you are told that it will lead to road deaths.

The guide came through all of these discussions remarkably intact and was adopted by the Council in June 1994. The reason for its survival was the fact that it was being pushed not by professionals but politicians. A council sub-committee had been established to deal with all planning applications and land disposals in Hulme. This was chaired by the leader of the council and included the key politicians in the city. Because the committee had planning and land ownership powers it was able to exert a huge influence on development. Whereas a planning committee rarely spends more than a few minutes considering a planning application, the Hulme committee would spend several hours with pouring over the detail of applications and quizzing architects and developers even before the guide to development was adopted. Virtually none of the schemes in Hulme were approved at the first meeting as developers were sent away – much to their frustration given funding deadlines – to reconsider detailed elements. In the process the politicians became even more convinced that this was the way forward for the city and learnt a great deal about urban development. They increasingly began to question the professional advice from their own officers in departments such as planning and highway engineering leading to considerable internal tension within the council.

While many council officers welcomed what was happening in Hulme, others were very concerned and comforted themselves with the thought that at least these ideas were not being applied to the whole city. There was therefore consternation when a resolution was passed by the Council applying the Hulme guide to the whole city. It was rightly pointed out that many of the items in the guide were not enforceable through planning legislation and were of questionable relevance to the more suburban parts of the city. However the application of the Hulme guide to the whole of the city was only ever an interim measure and the Council set about developing a city-wide guide which could be adopted as supplementary planning guidance. Because there remained considerable concern about the willing-ness of parts of the Council to take on this new agenda an external panel was convened to develop the Manchester guide. We were privileged to take part in this panel alongside leading professionals from private practice in the city as well as developers and academics. It was serviced by the council officers responsible for the Hulme redevelopment. The Manchester guide revisited many of the same conflicts and negotiations that had been had in Hulme. While a large measure of agreement was reached quickly detailed concerns remained about highway engineering, crime, investment and its enforceability through the planning system.

A draft guide was published for consultation and elicited hundreds of responses both within the city and nationally. There was a particular problem with the police's architectural liaison officer which was only resolved after a meeting between the leader of the council and the Chief Constable. Articles also appeared in the property press[9] accusing Manchester of being irresponsible and risking the loss of inward investment into the city by insisting on permeable street layouts. These were sensitive issues since large parts of the city fall outside Manchester City Council's administrative area – Salford and Trafford councils actually adjoin parts of the city centre. It was not therefore that the city as a whole would lose investment but that it would slip over the border into neighbouring districts which were not promoting urban development thus undermining the impact on the city. These issues were brought into focus by a major application to

Urbanising the city: Mixed-use student housing developed by Manchester University illustrating the application of urban principles to other development in the city.

develop a large student hall of residence on the edge of Hulme. Manchester Metropolitan University was concerned that the perception of the city as a dangerous place was putting off parents who might otherwise send their children to the university. They had therefore proposed an inward-looking compound which involved the closure of part of the Stretford Road which the Council was putting so much effort into reopening. This went to the heart of the debate over permeability. The University argued that a permeable street layout would give criminals access to their accommodation, putting students at risk. The Council countered by contending that street life and activity created by a large student population would make the area safer. A compromise was agreed and the street was retained for pedestrian use. Elsewhere in the city the politicians made clear that they would stand firm on the urban principles, arguing that any negative impact on the city would be short-lived and outweighed by the long-term benefits.

The *Manchester Guide to Development* was completed in 1997 [10] and appended to the city's

unitary development plan as supplementary planning guidance. Despite all of the concerns expressed, once the guidelines were adopted they were largely accepted by the development industry and the results can already be seen in new developments in the city. Following the adoption of the guide a series of training sessions were organised for development control officers in the city to explore the impact on their work. Three recent redevelopments in the city, a housing scheme, a commercial development and a retail park were used to demonstrate how the approach to design would be altered by the new guidance. All of those involved in these sessions were shocked by how far-reaching the impact was. Guidelines which, in their written form, seemed innocuous or motherhood and apple pie actually involved a complete reversal of many of the principles which had guided the planners work for many years. The housing scheme which had been designed as an inward-looking cul-de-sac was turned inside-out as the houses were made to front the surrounding streets and the internal roads were driven through to link to the surrounding street network. The commercial development, rather than being an isolated block in the centre of a large area of landscape became a perimeter block with an internal courtyard and the retail scheme was moved from the back of the site to the front with parking to the rear. In fairness to the planners who took part the majority were very enthusiastic about these changes and their work to apply these principles is starting to have a significant positive impact on the city.

The enormity of the transformation being attempted in Manchester should not be underestimated. Through the Hulme redevelopment and the adoption of urban design guidance for the whole city an attempt is being made to reverse urban trends and planning theory which have held sway for more than a century. It is not surprising that mistakes have been made. However if Manchester is successful, the significance for other UK cities is enormous as are the implications for urban repopulation and the development of a new urban vision in Britain.

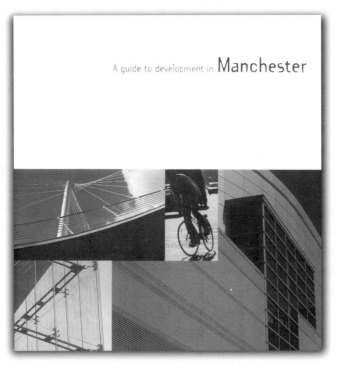

A guide to development in **Manchester**

A model neighbourhood?

The development of Hulme has not been without its problems. When the redevelopment started Hulme was seen as a huge risk for developers and investors so that only organisations with the financial muscle to take this risk were able to get involved. Development sites were parcelled up into very large chunks which only large developers could take on. The result is that the area looks artificial which is not entirely due to the fact that it is so new. This approach also shut out smaller developers and created a very course grain to development with little diversity. The scale of the area cleared for developed was huge as an attempt was made to develop a new urban neighbourhood from scratch. As we have already suggested this is almost impossible and most successful neighbourhoods tend to grow organically. This has also meant that at the end of the City Challenge process almost half of Hulme remained undeveloped leaving islands of high-density urban development marooned in a sea of future building sites. This has undermined the benefits of diversity, activity and safety that the high-density was designed to create. It will be many years before the urban vision for Hulme is fully realised and the hope is that the area will survive in the interim.

We have been fortunate to play a small role in the redevelopment of Hulme. This experience has informed this book and the development of the idea of the sustainable urban neighbourhood. However because Hulme has a number of weaknesses and is not yet complete we have hypothesised what the area might look like if it were completed along the lines that we are suggesting. The result is illustrated on the plan on the following pages[11]. This is based on the central part of Hulme. The plan includes the new developments that had been completed at the time that it was drawn as well as a number of existing buildings in the area. It does not however represent the plans that the Council is developing for the area some of which have since been completed. The intention was not to develop an alternative plan for this part of Hulme or indeed a critique of the development that is planned.

Rather we wanted to use the area as an example of a place where a sustainable urban neighbourhood would be appropriate and which was typical of many of the sites created by the redevelopment of council estates or indeed brownfield land formerly in industrial use. The result is an illustration of what the sustainable urban neighbourhood might look like.

In developing the plan we have sought to incorporate all of the principles described in Part 3 of this book. The aim has been to create a high quality urban environment with well proportioned buildings and attractive streets, squares and parks. The public realm is human in scale but urban in nature and designed to promote interaction and to accommodate the diversity of urban life. The plan is based on a clear framework of streets designed to serve both as routes and as public places supervised by the occupants of surrounding buildings. This street framework contain a density of different uses, buildings and tenures to create a balanced community, to reduce car travel, to animate streets and public places, to sustain shops and other public facilities and to foster activity and security throughout the day. The plan is also based on a high degree of permeability so that there is a choice of routes through the area. It also avoids the development of housing and workspace as defined estates but rather mixes them up and blurs the boundaries between them.

The plan covers an area of 45 hectares (112 acres) and includes up to 2 500 housing units, 45 000 m^2 of commercial space plus a 75 000 m^2 supermarket and could accommodate a population of 4-5 000 people. A wide range of uses have been incorporated into the plan including different types of housing, local shops as well as office accommodation and light industrial workspace.

The concept of the sustainable urban neighbourhood is based on the principle that neighbourhoods are more sustainable environmentally, economically and socially when they include a mix of uses and are built as part of a city to high densities, so contributing to the vitality and walkability of urban areas. But what are the implications of putting these ideas into practice?

Live/Work accommodation - Units which can be jointly used for living and business (see page 97)

Workshop units - One of the problems with much urban development is that it does not make provision for small scale manufacturing yet this is often more appropriate to the skills of urban communities

Student housing Student populations are increasing rapidly in many urban areas and represent an important source of demand for new urban housing

BUS ROUTE

BUS ROUTE

BUS ROUTE

Public facilities - Public facilities such as a health centre, library, pub, an existing church and local shops are located at the junction of the two high streets as an important activity node served by public transport.

Urban park - There is a tension in urban areas between the desire to create large amounts of open space and the need to maintain densities. Whilst urban communities will often fiercely resist development on land which has been landscaped, the reality is that these areas are a drain on resources, often a target for fly tipping and can be dangerous at night. A better solution is the more intensively used and overlooked urban park linked to a network of green spaces, including back gardens and green roofs, to support a range or urban flora and fauna.

High streets - Many important routes through urban areas were closed off in the 1960s or turned into formless dual carriageways. Here the high street has been recreated with existing landmark buildings supplemented by four and five storey development to recreate the character of an important street.

an edges - An important principle of the sustainable neighbourhood is to maximise the number of links between ~~b~~rough areas. Railways or motorways can make this difficult. ~~s~~olution is to treat the barrier as you would a river bank with ~~eq~~uivalent of an embankment street so that local traffic can ~~opera~~te without conflict with the main road traffic.

Combined heat and power plant and recycling point - The recycling point has been located on the edge of the area so that it can be accessed by lorries. The CHP plant is located away from housing because of the noise generated and to allay public concern about emissions. It is also linked to the recycling point to allow it to be powered by a waste incinerator. This would be linked to a district heating and a power distribution system serving the area.

Supermarket - Large shops are a fact of life and can be difficult to accom-modate in urban areas. One option is to wrap housing and other uses around the super-market or to build on the roof. This has been done by Peabody in association with a Tesco supermarket in Hammersmith (see page192). The plan shows a similar solution with a landscaped car park to the rear.

Shopping high street and market square - Many inner city shopping areas have declined as trade has been diverted to supermarkets. This can even happen around inner city supermarkets as shoppers travel to the supermarket by car and never leave its territory. By linking an urban supermarket to an outdoor market shoppers are offered a wider range of goods and can support a range of small shops.

Leisure and recreation facilities An attempt has been made to integrate leisure facilities into the local shopping centre. The main building is therefore brought to the back of pavement on the high street with outdoor activities to the rear.

BUS ROUTE

Bus routes - The bus routes are based on existing routes running through the area selected for this exercise. The white circles are 160m in diameter representing a 2 minute walk time (in a straight line). This illustrates that all buildings in the area will be within five minutes walk of a bus stop on one of these routes.

Existing buildings - Redevelopment areas generally contain a variety of existing buildings. Some like the old instutute illustrated here can be refurbished as landmarks. Others like the school and old people's home to the rear are of less architectural quality and contribute little to the urban fabric. These have been framed by more substantial buildings to create a boulevard with the lower buildings in the centre.

Educational facilities - Like business and retail uses there is a tendancy to develop educational facilities on campus. This illustrates how a university department of a college extension could be integrated into an urban area.

Dense mixed-use development One of the principles of urban areas is that the grain of development should increase around activity nodes. This means a greater density of mixed-use buildings and decrease in block size, as in the picture of Deptford High Street. (See page 193)

Main illustration by Jonathan Polley of Build for Change

RTH

There has been a significant backlash against many of these ideas. As we have already described it has been argued that compact development will lead to 'town cramming' and that cities have become such dirty, congested and dangerous places that people cannot be forced to live in them. Critics have also questioned the benefits of compact development, suggesting that it is impossible to increase densities to the level required for even a small reduction in energy use or car travel. These arguments turn on circumstances at the most local level. What sort of urban areas are created if we increase densities? What are the walking distances to facilities and to public transport? How viable is waste recycling and combined heat and power? These are questions that we have sought to answer through the hypothetical neighbourhood.

Density: One of the main bones of contention about urban development is density which, to its critics, is synonymous with overcrowding and town cramming. As the *UK Strategy for Sustainable Development* suggests, intensification should be a 'dynamic process, but the limits and thresholds must be understood… for the city to be sustainable' [12]. The hypothetical neighbourhood seeks to test these limits. It is based on net residential densities of 62 to 124 units per hectare (25 to 50 per acre). These densities are measured to the centre line of the surrounding streets and therefore equate to the standard density measure used by most local authorities. Indeed the densities are broadly comparable to the standard set in the *Hulme Guide to Development* which includes a density guideline of 86 units per hectare (35 to the acre).

The plan explores the implications of building at these densities. It is clear that 62 units to the hectare can be achieved with a mix of terraced housing and flats on the corners or above commercial premises (Site C). However to achieve 124 units per hectare requires the predominant use of flats as in sites A and B. It should also be noted that these sites also include a range of other uses which further increase the density of development and activity. The potential housing yield of the area has been calculated by applying these two density levels to the developable land in the area. This would produce 1 225 units at 62 to the hectare and 2 450 units at 124 to the acre. The quality of the residential environment created is a matter of personal taste. However we would suggest that the plan and indeed the completed developments within Hulme illustrate that densities of this level are consistent with a high quality residential environment, albeit not the sort of suburban environment that has come to be seen as the norm in recent years.

However plot densities have little meaning when considering issues such as walkability. We have therefore looked at the gross residential density of the neighbourhood. The area covered by the plan is 45 hectares so that the gross residential densities across the area would be between 27 and 54 units to the hectare which is less than half the net residential densities. This is a point which is often missed in the discussion about density. At net densities of 62 units to the hectare the gross residential density across a mixed-use urban neighbourhood can fall to the equivalent of a single-use suburban development. This clearly depends where the boundaries are drawn.

KEY TO PLAN ON PREVIOUS PAGE

1. The Hulme Arch – see photograph on page 212
2. Mixed-use development by North British Housing Association – see photograph on page 211
3. Princess Parkway – the main route out of Manchester to the south and the airport.
4. Homes for Change.
5. The Junction Pub, one of the handful of pubs to survive the redevelopment of the 1960s.
6. This area is currently being developed as Zion Square and Hulme Park, although not to this design.
7. The Zion Institute recently converted to an arts centre.
8. Royce Primary School
9. The Hulme Playhouse and Hippodrome – two listed music hall theatres. The Playhouse was converted to an Afro-Caribbean cultural centre which has recently closed
10. The Chichester Road housing scheme by Triangle Architects for North British Housing Association.
11. St. Mary's Church – see photograph on page 208
12. Loretto Sixth Form College.

habitable rooms. In an area of mixed houses and flats it is probably reasonable to assume four bedspaces per dwelling. This however will only translate into population density if all of the properties are fully occupied which is very unlikely. We have therefore also used a measure of people to the hectare based upon an average household size of 2.4 people. This was the average household size across the country in the 1991 census and while it is about right for much of the development in Hulme, the growth in single-person households may mean that it is an overestimate for new development.

It is also important to take into account employment uses since three of the sites that we looked at include significant commercial floorspace reducing the net residential density. Density guidelines generally do not take into account nonresidential uses and so are difficult to apply to

In the illustrated neighbourhood, for example, the area includes a park, a school and other institutional buildings. However the fall in gross density is also due to the area devoted to the street network (just over 17 hectares) and there may be value in increasing the size of blocks or reducing the width of streets to reduce the gap between net and gross densities. However at present if the housing in the area was built to traditional garden city densities of 30 units to the hectare (12 to the acre) the gross densities across the area would fall to just 12 units to the hectare (5 to the acre) and the yield to just 588 homes. This illustrates the danger of using net densities to assess urban land capacity and the viability of services such as public transport and recycling.

It is also important to realise that the number of units to the hectare is less important than the number of people. Indeed one of the problems with falling household size is that the population density of many urban areas is falling even though all of the housing remains fully occupied. The two measures generally used to estimate population density are bedspaces and

ANALYSIS OF DENSITIES AND HOUSING YIELDS

Neighbourhood area	112	45	
Developed area	69	28	Excluding roads
Area developed for housing	49	20	Excluding non-residential uses
DENSITIES			
Assumed net densities			
units/acre	12	25	50
units/hectare	30	62	124
Gross densities			
units/hectare	13	27	54
Bedspaces (net)			
per hectare	119	247	494
Bedspaces (gross)			
per hectare	52	108	216
Persons (net)			
per hectare	71	148	296
Persons (gross)			
per hectare	31	65	130
Housing Yield	588	1225	2450

ANALYSIS OF EMPLOYMENT DENSITY AND YIELDS

	Floor area m^2	m^2/job	Total jobs
Retail space	11,250	40	281
Supermarket	7,500	40	187
Workshops (B2)	11,250	50	225
Warehousing (B8)	6,750	80	84
Office space (B1)	15,750	25	630
Total	52,500		1,407
Employment density/hectare	31		

mixed-use schemes. Yet the density of people working in an area is just as significant when considering the viability of public transport and the vitality of areas. We have therefore estimated the number of people employed in the area. This is illustrated on the table above which shows a total of 52 500 m^2 of employment floorspace, a workforce population of 1 400 producing employment densities of 31 workers per hectare.

Urban transport: The most common justification for mixing uses and building to higher densities is the reduction of car use and the promotion of walking, cycling and public transport. Some commentators have questioned research[13] which suggests that people living and working in dense urban areas make less use of their car. However, as we have suggested, car use will inevitably be reduced by regulation, taxation or sheer congestion. The question is therefore not whether the design of urban areas will reduce car use but whether urban areas can be designed to accommodate a less car-intensive way of life. If this is to work it is vital that the alternatives to the car such as walking, cycling and public transport are available. It is therefore important to design urban areas which ensure that alternative forms of transport are practical, attractive and viable.

The viability of public transport and the walkability of urban areas both impact on urban form. The maximum distance that people are prepared to walk is generally considered to be around 2 000 metres although the optimum is 800 metres (a comfortable ten-minute walk)[14].

Indeed in shopping areas developers use 400 metres as the distance that people will walk with shopping. This means that, to promote walking, distances within the neighbourhood need to be short. The example neighbourhood is approximately 1 000 metres from north to south by 740 metres from east to west so it would take no more than fifteen minutes to walk from end to end and everywhere within the neighbourhood would be easily accessible on foot by all residents. Given that the neighbourhoods includes shops, schools, a park, significant employment and other public facilities it should therefore be possible to meet most of their daily needs without using a car.

The second criteria is public transport. The Local Government Management Board's sustainable settlements guide[15] suggests net densities of 100 persons per hectare to support a good bus service. As the table on the previous page shows, this could be achieved with suburban densities if the bedspaces measure is used. However it is also important to consider gross densities across the area and the likely occupancy levels of the housing. The table illustrates how easily this can fall well below 100 persons per hectare even with relatively high net densities.

Energy use: We have also used the neighbourhood to model energy use. Whilst buildings can be made energy efficient wherever they are built, there are some inherent advantages of building within urban areas. Urban terraces and flats have fewer external heat loss walls so that the heat loss for any given level of insulation is lower. They are also more likely to be sheltered by surrounding buildings. However against this should be set the possibility that they will be overshadowed and the fact that they are unlikely to optimise their aspect to maximise passive solar gain.

However the real advantages in terms of energy efficiency and emissions come with the introduction of Combined Heat and Power systems. We have therefore assumed that the neighbourhood will include a district heating system. This is likely to be more viable in dense urban areas which reduce the distances over which heat and power mains extend minimising thermodynamic losses and infrastructure costs. The mix of uses also helps to smooth out the demand profile over the day. Because there is just the one heat source for the neighbourhood, a district heating system would be more efficient than individual boilers in each building, particularly given improvements in heat metering.

However even greater savings could be made by linking the district heating to a Combined Heat and Power system. This would use gas to generate electricity and heat, increasing operating efficiencies to 80 – 90% so reducing bills to local residents and businesses. Assuming net densities of 62 units to the hectare the total annual energy requirement of the area would be just under 10 000 MWh for electricity and 18 000 MWh for space and water heating. The CHP plant would be sized to meet the electricity requirement and would therefore require additional boiler capacity to meet winter heat loads. The calculations on CHP undertaken as part of the Sustainable Urban Neighbourhood Initiative[16] show the virtual elimination of SO_2 emissions and a potential reduction in CO_2 emissions of around 40%.

It has been suggested that further savings could be made by linking the system to a waste incinerator so that a proportion of the heat is generated from locally-produced waste. However again the calculations that we have undertaken show that the calorific value of the waste generated by the housing in the neighbourhood would amount to little more than 2 000 MWh per year which is just 7% of the district heating requirement. Taking into account the fact that incineration carries the risk of pollution and dioxin emissions and is likely to encounter local resistance it appears that this is a less attractive option than the recycling of local waste.

Autonomous urban development

One of our concerns in the development of the sustainable urban neighbourhood is that too much emphasis has been devoted in recent years to the design and technical specification of individual buildings and not enough to planning at the neighbourhood scale. The model neighbourhood described above has therefore proved very useful in exploring issues such as density, transport and the economics of power use and CHP systems. However if it is to be built we must reconcile these neighbourhood issues with the practicalities of development. We have therefore explored a section of the plan in more detail as illustrated on the following pages. This examines the implications of sustainable urban development on the design of individual blocks. In doing so it starts to develop a new language for sustainable architecture as an alternative to the rural venacular which has characterised much green architecture to date. This is still work in progress and we are currently researching the technical implications, practicalities and viability of urban development with virtually no reliance on fossil fuels using this area as a model. Our hope is that, if the concepts prove to be viable, we will be able to actually develop of all or part of this area to build upon the Homes for Change scheme which is described later in this chapter and is shown as Block 1. We are also working with a number of other developers to apply the principles to other schemes. The main characteristics of the plan are described below:

Mixed-use development: The illustration shows a very broad mix of uses both within blocks and across the areas. Blocks 1, 2 and 4 which front main streets are vertically mixed-use with ground and first floor commercial or retail space below housing. Block 3 is then an attempt to incorporate manufacturing into urban areas. This is based upon a concern that much of the progress on mixed-use development has involved office-based uses where the jobs are not well suited to the skill-base of many inner city populations. The neighbourhood plan on pages 216 – 217 therefore suggested the incorporation into the area of manufacturing workshops and the plan on the following pages explores their physical form. The concept is to create an urban edge of well-proportioned offices which backs onto a series of workshops within the block. This concept has already attracted considerable interest and is likely to be the first part of the neighbourhood to actually be

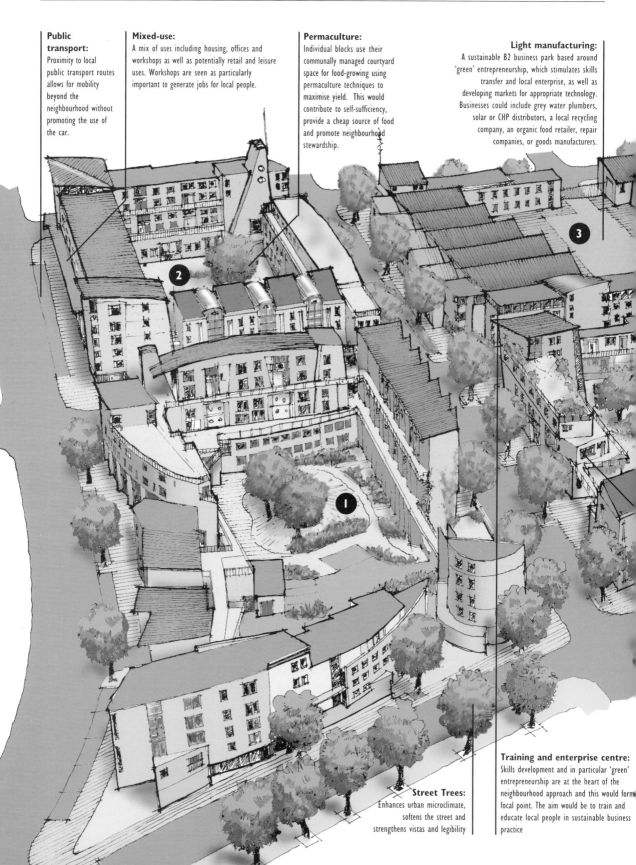

Public transport:
Proximity to local public transport routes allows for mobility beyond the neighbourhood without promoting the use of the car.

Mixed-use:
A mix of uses including housing, offices and workshops as well as potentially retail and leisure uses. Workshops are seen as particularly important to generate jobs for local people.

Permaculture:
Individual blocks use their communally managed courtyard space for food-growing using permaculture techniques to maximise yield. This would contribute to self-sufficiency, provide a cheap source of food and promote neighbourhood stewardship.

Light manufacturing:
A sustainable B2 business park based around 'green' entrepreneurship, which stimulates skills transfer and local enterprise, as well as developing markets for appropriate technology. Businesses could include grey water plumbers, solar or CHP distributors, a local recycling company, an organic food retailer, repair companies, or goods manufacturers.

Street Trees:
Enhances urban microclimate, softens the street and strengthens vistas and legibility

Training and enterprise centre:
Skills development and in particular 'green' entrepreneurship are at the heart of the neighbourhood approach and this would form focal point. The aim would be to train and educate local people in sustainable business practice

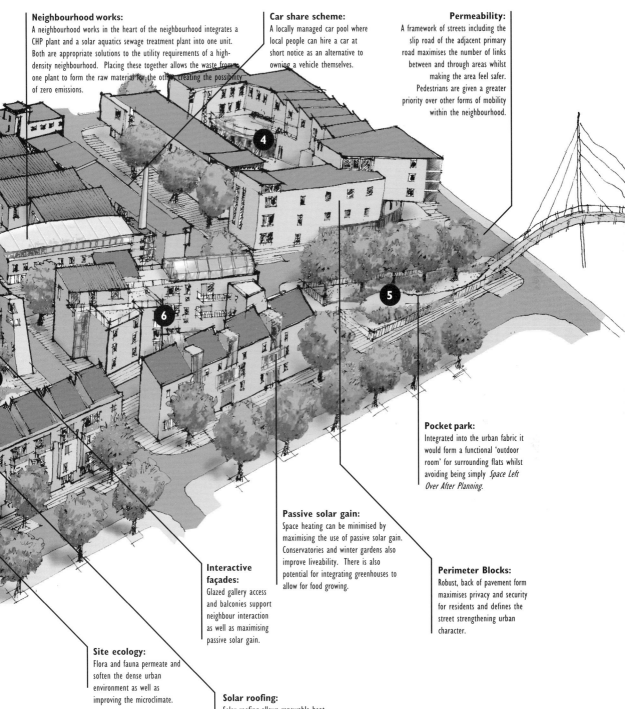

Neighbourhood works:
A neighbourhood works in the heart of the neighbourhood integrates a CHP plant and a solar aquatics sewage treatment plant into one unit. Both are appropriate solutions to the utility requirements of a high-density neighbourhood. Placing these together allows the waste from one plant to form the raw material for the other, creating the possibility of zero emissions.

Car share scheme:
A locally managed car pool where local people can hire a car at short notice as an alternative to owning a vehicle themselves.

Permeability:
A framework of streets including the slip road of the adjacent primary road maximises the number of links between and through areas whilst making the area feel safer. Pedestrians are given a greater priority over other forms of mobility within the neighbourhood.

Pocket park:
Integrated into the urban fabric it would form a functional 'outdoor room' for surrounding flats whilst avoiding being simply *Space Left Over After Planning*.

Passive solar gain:
Space heating can be minimised by maximising the use of passive solar gain. Conservatories and winter gardens also improve liveability. There is also potential for integrating greenhouses to allow for food growing.

Perimeter Blocks:
Robust, back of pavement form maximises privacy and security for residents and defines the street strengthening urban character.

Interactive façades:
Glazed gallery access and balconies support neighbour interaction as well as maximising passive solar gain.

Site ecology:
Flora and fauna permeate and soften the dense urban environment as well as improving the microclimate.

Solar roofing:
Solar roofing allows renewable heat and power to be integrated more cost effectively by reducing the capital cost of installation.

Design by Charlie Baker, Build for Change,
Illustration David Rudlin

developed after Homes for Change. The block also includes a training and enterprise area and a 'bioworks' as described below with the intention that it will be developed as a base for green businesses in areas like recycling and remanufacturing to tap the employment potential of sustainable development. Blocks 6 and 7 then also include an element of live/work accommodation as described on page 97.

Urban green space: One of the concerns expressed to us about the urban neighbourhood is that it will lack landscaping and urban green space. We have therefore used the plan to explore how vegetation and wildlife habitats can permeate the area. This includes a pocket park which is supervised by surrounding buildings and can provide an 'outdoor room' for residents and workers in the area. This however is only part of a wider network of green space which includes courtyards within each block and a variety of roof gardens at different levels as have been incorporated into the Homes for Change development. An important role is also played by street trees which are used throughout the area. A number of the blocks also include balconies, winter gardens and even roof-top greenhouses for cultivation and food growing.

Car use: The green space within the area has been achieved largely at the expense of car parking. We have opted not to go for an entirely car-free neighbourhood because of concerns about the viability of commercial space and also about the danger of pedestrianised streets in inner city areas such as this. However there is no off-street parking other than that which was required by the planners as part of the completed phase of the Homes for Change scheme and service access to the workshops. The plan also incorporates space for a car pool which would be locally managed and which would give residents and workers access to a hired vehicle as an alternative to owning their own.

Housing density: The incorporation of such a wide mix of uses and green space has an impact on the residential density across the area. The Homes for Change scheme achieves net densities

of 124 units per hectare as well as being mixed-use and the other residential blocks (2, 4, 6 and 7) aim to achieve broadly similar densities. However the incorporation of the workspace and the park reduce the overall residential density of the area. The area covered is just over 3.6 hectares and it is estimated that the housing yield should be around 300 properties which will give an overall density of 83 units, 200 people or 300 bedspaces to the hectare.

Eco-design: The most radical aspect of the neighbourhood is however its environmental design. This is still at the experimental stage and is being further developed at present. However it is based upon a series of targets, that the development should achieve a net balance of CO_2 emissions, that it should eliminate fossil fuel for heat and power, that it should have a closed water system without reliance on the mains or external sewage treatment and that all recyclable waste should be recycled. This is not quite autonomous urban development since the area would still rely upon and provide services to the wider urban area. However it would substantially reduce the area's environmental impact.

This is achieved by wresting control of resources and waste flows to the neighbourhood level as we suggested in Chapter 10. Rather than rely on large centralised systems for power generation, water supply and waste treatment the neighbourhood will be designed to provide these services at the local level. This has a number of advantages. It means firstly that full use can be made of natural resources such as solar energy and the rain falling on the site (which in Manchester could potentially provide the entire water needs of the development). Secondly it means that resource systems can be converted from linear to circular systems by using locally generated waste, such as heat, organic matter and domestic waste as resources to be used locally. Thirdly it means that the jobs and economic activity generated by resource consumption can be created locally rather than in distant power stations, or recycling plants and so are available to local people in areas of high unemployment.

At the heart of this local resource system is the combined bioworks and CHP plant illustrated in the centre of the scheme. These would be linked so that the waste from one would form the inputs to the other. This is similar to the system in Kolding in Denmark that we described on page 164. The bioworks is an intensively-managed, solar-aquatic local sewage works processing local waste through a series of controlled tanks in a greenhouse full of plants. It would be fuelled from the sun and also from the surplus heat from the CHP plant. The water from the bioworks can be used for food growing and it can also produce compost and harvest methane to fuel the CHP plant. The bioworks and CHP plant are linked to the workshop spaces which would then be let to businesses able to use the outputs of the plant as well as other waste generated locally. The car pool is also part of the block and it is possible that the CHP plant could be used off-peak to recharge electric vehicles.

In addition to this the neighbourhood incorporates a range of further environmental features. Many of the roofs are made up of photovoltaic panels to generate electricity, possibly linked to hydrogen storage and fuel cell generation. These panels would help to overcome one of the problems of CHP systems which is that the electricity demand in summer is far greater than the heat load. While the technology is currently expensive the trend in countries like Japan and Germany is that prices are falling rapidly and by using the panels to replace traditional roofing there is the potential to reduce the overall price by making savings elsewhere. The heat load is also reduced by ensuring that the buildings are highly insulated and by including features such as winter gardens and glazed access balconies on south-facing elevations. The closed water system is also made possible by grey water restoration linked to rainwater collection and we are also exploring the use of water storage tanks as heat stores.

Many of these suggestions are at an experimental stage and while initial calculations suggest that they are capable of achieving a net balance of CO_2 emissions, a non-reliance on fossil fuels and a closed water system, it is not yet clear whether they are affordable or viable in the development process. This is what we will be exploring over the coming year and the work will be published in a report for the Building Research Establishment in the UK.

SMITHFIELD – MANCHESTER

There as been a remarkable change in the last years or so. The ideas that we have advocated in this book were until recently regarded as radical yet they are now being accepted by mainstream developer. Nowhere is this more apparent than in the illustrated scheme proposed by Amec and Crosby Homes in Manchester.

This includes buildings by most of Manchester's leading architects including MBLC, Hodder Associates, and Stephenson Bell. The scheme accommodates almost 250 residential units at 60 units to the acre yet most of the ground and first-floor floorspace is in commercial use.

The specification for the scheme includes far-reaching environmental measures including a combined heat and power plant and grey water recycling.

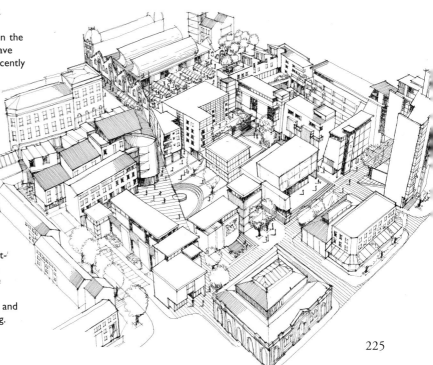

The sustainable urban block

We can be much more certain about one part of the neighbourhood because it has already been built. The first phase of the Homes for Change scheme (Block 1 on the plan) was completed in September 1996 and the second phase will be completed in 1999. This is one of very few mixed-use, high-density urban blocks developed recently in the UK and provides a living model of the sort of development that we are advocating. It is also a scheme that I (DR) know intimately since I was a founder member of the co-operative and its secretary for many years. It is also home to URBED's northern office from which the Sustainable Urban Neighbourhood Initiative is run.

The scheme was developed by the Homes for Change housing co-operative and a sister co-operative, Work for Change, which has developed the workspace. It is a product of its environment and a physical embodiment of the character of the Hulme community that created it. The building dominates the heart of Hulme and is to many a symbol of the area's rebirth. It is based

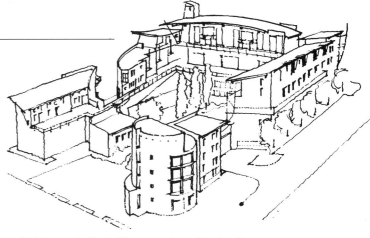

on a recognition that, whilst the Hulme built in the 1960s may have failed, it nevertheless nurtured a strong if unconventional community. This community quite liked the old Hulme, the proximity to the city centre, the size of the flats, the tolerance of the community and the close networks of neighbours. These are the positive aspects of urban living that we are promoting and existed even in the heart of what was considered to be one of the country's most notorious system-built housing estates. With the launch of the City Challenge funded redevelopment of Hulme, parts of the local community feared that these benefits might be lost and conceived Homes for Change as a lifeboat to preserve at least part of the local community. The co-op sought not to reject the past but to build upon it by rescuing the best points of the old estate. At the same time they used their very practical experience of its failings to ensure that these were not repeated in the new development. In doing this the co-operative has created a potential model for the regeneration of other British cities.

The relevance of the Homes for Change model is not so much the architecture of the building, striking as this is, but the process by which it was built. It illustrates that when local people are given a full and informed choice over their environment, the result need not be the blandness which has characterised so much community architecture. It has been suggested that the development is the result of a unique combination of circumstances and people. But the membership of Homes for Change is not untypical. They may be young and largely childless but so are 40% of UK households and more than 80% of the 4.4 million extra households predicted by the government. Given a choice such people may not create another Homes for Change but they are likely to opt for something very different to the current product of most mass housebuilders.

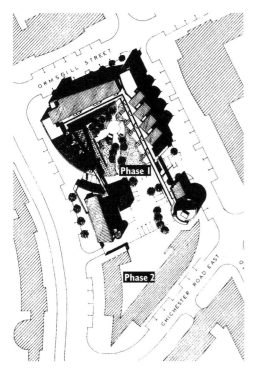

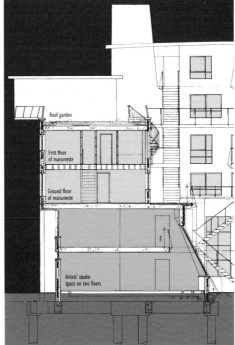

Homes for Change:
A site plan showing Phases 1 and 2 of the scheme making a perimeter urban block (left). A section through the building showing the two floors of workspace below the housing and roof garden (right)

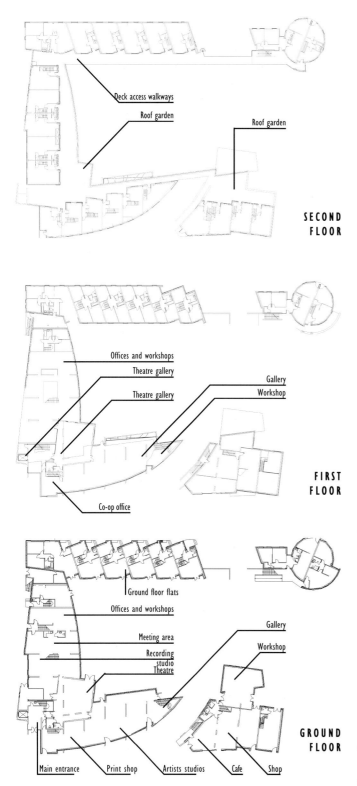

Deck access walkways
Roof garden
Roof garden

SECOND FLOOR

Offices and workshops
Theatre gallery
Theatre gallery
Gallery
Workshop

Co-op office

FIRST FLOOR

Ground floor flats
Offices and workshops
Gallery
Meeting area
Workshop
Recording studio
Theatre

Main entrance   Print shop   Artists studios   Cafe   Shop

GROUND FLOOR

The development of the scheme: The Homes for Change co-operative emerged from Hulme in the late 1980s. Its members spent almost five years working on a scheme to convert a former police station in Central Manchester. Whilst this project did not happen, it did give the co-op a huge amount of experience. Crucially the co-op was registered with the Housing Corporation, something which few new-build co-ops have achieved since 1988. When it was announced that Hulme was to be redeveloped through City Challenge, Homes for Change was able to turn its attention to its home territory as an already established and recognised co-operative.

Homes for Change was accepted as one of the social housing developers in Hulme and following lengthy negotiations was allocated funding for 75 flats and a site in the heart of the area. However the Housing Corporation as the main funder made it clear that an untried co-operative could not take on what was to become a £4 million development. The members therefore selected the Guinness Trust as development partners. Under the terms of the partnership agreement Guinness was to undertake the development for the co-op whilst co-op members were given the right to be involved in all decisions and to take on ownership on completion if they could raise the necessary finance. This arrangement led to inevitable tensions, however to Guinness's credit, they have given the co-op real control as witnessed by the fact that the building is radically different to anything that a mainstream housing association would normally have developed.

The impetus for mixed-use development: From the start the co-op's vision has been of an urban mixed-use building. This was entirely in line with the strategy for Hulme but was particularly important to co-op members, many of whom were used to working from home and had developed businesses in the space provided by the old Hulme flats. There was a risk that these businesses would be destroyed by redevelopment unless affordable workspace could be provided. Homes for Change therefore planned to incorporate 1 500 m² of workspace into the scheme and established a sister co-op, Work for Change, to develop and manage this space. Work for Change is organised like a housing co-operative and is run by its member businesses. It has developed a concept of 'self-managed workspace' so that businesses put time into managing the space in return for a reduction in service charges. A feasibility study for the workspace was commissioned from URBED, and funding was secured from City Challenge, the Moss Side and Hulme Task Force and the European Regional Development Fund. As with the housing, there was also a borrowing requirement which is provided by the Guinness Trust until Work for Change is able to raise its own finance. Because the tenants of Work for Change have been members of the group for some time, the workspace is almost unique in being virtually fully let the day it opened.

The design process: After Guinness, the most important appointment was the architects. Whilst the co-op wanted a building which was both 'green' and collectively designed, they took the unusual decision of appointing architects who were specialists in neither of these areas, and

indeed were not even recognised housing architects. The Manchester practice Mills Beaumont Levey Channon Architects were appointed for their design flair and because of their attitude to the co-op, not as a group to be consulted, but as a multi-headed client. The co-op were confident that they knew how they wanted to be involved and were concerned to find consultants who shared their vision and would not be constrained by conventional wisdom.

The design process which followed was one of the most participatory to have been undertaken in recent years. Day-long workshops took place every month for more than a year. In the early workshops members visited schemes around the country and plundered architectural journals to make up style sheets to illustrate the sort of building that they wanted. They made 1:50 Plasticine models of the scheme to explore building forms and worked with larger models to understand the space. The group even made up full-scale models of the flat interiors in a local church hall. Hours were spent pondering brick types, colour schemes, door handles and windows. Throughout there were disagreements; Guinness for example initially objected to the grass roofs and deck-access walkways both of which were subsequently incorporated into the scheme. These disagreements were, however, resolved through informed debate within the partnership which took account of costs and management implications. This meant that when members had to drop elements they understood the reasons and in most cases took the decision themselves.

Environmental design: Co-op members were concerned that the building should incorporate best practice in environmental design. The development became a demonstration project as part of URBED's *21st Century Homes* research for the Joseph Rowntree Foundation[17]. This provided funds to engage environmental consultants ECD, who worked with the group to draw up a range of environmental targets ranging from CO_2 emission to sustainable materials and waste recycling. These targets were monitored through the development process[18]. Seventeen of the targets were met in full and only two: embodied energy and water saving, were not achieved. As part of the development of the scheme a number of environmental features were considered which could not be incorporated into the scheme. These included a grey water restoration system which, because of the attitude of the local water board, would have added almost twice as much to rents as it saved in water charges. Similar problems were experienced with a passive stack ventilation system. The building is therefore 'green', certainly by the standards of the early 1990s when it was designed, but falls short of what many of the co-op members would like to have seen and what is possible today. This is why our current work on the eco-neighbourhood is seeking to substantially increase the environmental performance of this type of urban building.

The perils of innovation: The Homes for Change scheme innovates on many levels. It is innovative in its layout, design and structure, the co-operative way in which was built and is being managed, the mix of uses and its environmental specification. Innovation is always a risk and, when undertaken on this scale, is something that organisations with more experience probably would not attempt. There have indeed been problems the tenders to build the scheme came in well over budget and savings had to be made quickly by the co-op and

its architects. There was a range of problems on site and the scheme was completed over budget and behind schedule. There is always a cost to innovation and everyone involved has paid it heavily. To some this may reinforce the view that the scheme is a one-off. However innovation is only justified if it leads to lessons being learnt. If this is done, there is no reason why this building, and particularly the process by which it was built, could not provide a cost-effective model and an inspiration for urban communities elsewhere.

Much of this book has been about the theory of urban development. Those of us who have been involved in the practice of development know that theory is all well and good but is difficult to relate to practical decisions made on the ground within tight timescale and funding constraints. The experience in Manchester, as described in this chapter, illustrates this tension and there are many aspects both of the overall development of Hulme and of the Homes for Change scheme in particular which fall short of the principles that we have been advocating. This is why we have used design exercises to roll forward the redevelopment of the Hulme area and to illustrate the type of neighbourhood which could result from the work that has been set in train. The practical experience thus far does however show that while the principles that we have set out in Part 3 of this book can at times seem to be a statement of the obvious their impact on the ground can be very radical. They involve new ways of working and thinking about urban areas and run counter to many powerful professional ideologies and commercial orthodoxies. It is therefore not surprising that they have encountered resistance and that mistakes have been made. However the lessons are being learnt and the impact of these ideas on the future development of Manchester and hopefully other UK cities is likely to be very significant.

CHAPTER 14
The process
of urban generation and regeneration

We may believe passionately in the importance of cities. We may even be able to describe and analyse the characteristics of an urban neighbourhood that make it successful. This we have sought to do in the last part of this book. However putting this passion and knowledge into practice in the creation and recreation of successful urban neighbourhoods is quite another matter. As Elizabeth Plater-Zyberk has stated [1]: 'Our predicament is this; we admire one kind of place... but consistently build something very different'.

In this final chapter we therefore explore a process for the creation of successful urban neighbourhoods which can then become the building blocks for successful cities. This relies crucially upon an understanding of the economic and social forces outlined in Part 2 of this book and the principles and characteristics described in Part 3. However the genius of city building lies not solely in a vision of physical forms and space but in an understanding of the process by which they are created.

There is a view that the rediscovery of successful urban planning depends solely upon the recognition of the 'timeless principles which underlie successful communities' [2]. Prince Charles in his introduction to the Urban Villages report goes on to say that these principles are 'manifest good sense and must surely be plain to anyone' regardless of planning or architectural qualifications. There is an implied irritation in his words – it is easy, anyone can see it, why is it that pro-

fessionals cannot create it? This is like admiring a fine painting and bemoaning the fact that we have lost the ability to create such masterpieces. We can analyse the qualities that make it great, the composition, execution and symbolism, but this knowledge and understanding does not allow us to create a masterpiece. If it did all art critics would be great painters. The creation of greatness requires more than analysis, it requires an element of genius. If the genius of great painting is rare how much more unattainable is the genius of great city building? This is the creation of not just one mind but of hundreds and thousands and takes place not over days and weeks but over centuries.

Yet for thousands of years this mammoth act of collective genius has come naturally to the human race. People from all cultures have created cities and urban spaces of great beauty, complexity and functionality. What is more this has been achieved effortlessly, almost accidentally and often without the aid of planners and architects or even in some cases any coherent municipal government. The results could be seen as a happy accident if it were not for the fact that such 'accidents' can be found throughout the world and in most human cultures. Indeed many of their characteristics can still be seen in modern unplanned squatters' settlements. Such places can be chaotic and overcrowded with their narrow streets and tightly-packed buildings but where they have been mellowed by the passage of time as in the towns

of northern Italy or the medieval streets of York or Chester they remain some of our most enduring and popular urban environments. For many years planners and designers have analysed and plundered these historic cities and derived from them the principles of urban design. Yet as Elizabeth Plater-Zyberk points out it has proved almost impossible to apply these principles to modern cities. The reason, we believe, is that designers have concentrated on the physical form of these historic places and not the process by which they were created.

There are, of course, many very attractive towns and cities which have been shaped by the firm hand of state. The beauty of Rome and Paris owes much to the visionary plans of Pope Sixtus and Hausemann and cities as diverse as Bath, New York and Barcelona are based upon strong master plans. However even these cities have been shaped as much by the process of organic growth as they have by the hand of the master planner. The plan has provided little more than the trellis up which the vine of the city can grow. It gives form to the whole and this form can enhance the beauty, function and coherence of the city. But the trellis does not sustain the vine and many of the world's most beautiful cities have grown organically without such artificial support. The city planner may be able to guide and shape this process of

natural growth but cannot replace it. Where this has happened, as in modern planned cities such as new towns, the result has been to create artificial, soulless places which have not proved popular. It is this process of organic growth that we need to study if we are going to rediscover the art of creating successful urban neighbourhoods.

This natural process of urban development has shaped settlements throughout human history until, that is, the twentieth century. It is a sad indictment of twentieth century planning in Britain that whilst it has been able to protect the urban areas of the past it has been unable to create new urban areas of the same quality. In the twentieth century we have created many fine buildings and some fine spaces yet it is difficult to point to any urban neighbourhood created since the birth of town planning which is likely to merit conservation in the future. The dead hand of planning, in its quest to ameliorate the worst excesses of urban development, has sought to eliminate the very characteristics which result from organic urban growth and which make urban areas work. We have sought to tame the city and bring order and logic where once there was confusion. In doing this we have ignored the fact that conflict is part of the very nature of the city. The operation may have been successful but unfortunately the patient has died.

The natural process of urban growth

The author who has done most to analyse and describe the natural process of urban growth is Christopher Alexander[3]. Through his writings he has described how humans have developed a 'timeless way of building' which guides the natural process of creating beautiful places and buildings that we describe above. In his book *A pattern language* he describes the patterns which lie behind this process and in his book *A new theory of urban design* he applies them to the creation of urban areas. The overriding principle behind this natural process of urban development is that every action undertaken in an urban area should take place in such a way so as to heal the city and to make it whole. This wholeness – which can be experienced in urban areas when they feel 'right' – works at every level from the detailed design of buildings to the shape of the whole city. In order to achieve this Alexander suggests seven rules which are required to achieve 'wholeness in urban development':

Piecemeal growth: The whole is too complicated to be created in large chunks so that the grain of development and the time over which it takes place must allow room and time for wholeness to develop.

The growth of larger wholes: The creation of larger patterns and order from urban development develops slowly from the cumulative effect of local decisions rather than being imposed by a plan. When the process starts no one knows what the end result will be but gradually over time the process creates a natural form. Alexander is very uncertain about how this principle can be applied to new development but it is clearly the way that traditional settlements developed.

The timeless way of building:
An illustration from Christopher Alexander showing the results of a natural process of urban growth

Vision: Each individual action within an urban area is guided by an 'authentic' or 'heartfelt' impulse of vision which can be communicated to others. This is based not upon consumer surveys or economic returns and cannot be decided by committee. It is rather a sense of what feels right and is intricately tied up in people's experience of an urban area and what is required to make it more whole.

Positive urban space: In making these decisions the natural process of development considers space as a positive quantity rather than the area left over after a building is created. In other words when people create buildings they are thinking as much about the quality of the public realm that they are creating as they are about the design and planning of the structure. In this way the public realm is understood and shaped by the individual decisions of developers which is the opposite of modern development where the roads come first, the footpaths second and the buildings third.

The design and structure of buildings: Rules five and six govern the design, internal layout and structure of buildings so that they too contribute to the creation of the whole.

The formation of centres: The final rule then describes the character of centres and how a system and hierarchy of centres is created.

In *The Oregon experiment* and *A new theory of urban design* Alexander describes the application of these principles to the design process for a building and an urban area. In the San Francisco waterfront area a simulated design exercise was undertaken over a five-year period with students. The plan for the area was developed incrementally with individual decisions taken by students and mediated by Alexander based upon the principles outlined above. The result is an organic urban area which is remarkably similar to a medieval city and which has none of the artificiality of a single master plan. We were involved in something similar in the development of the Smithfield scheme described on page 225. This was designed by a group of six architecture practices. Rather than undertaking an initial masterplanning exercise each practice was given a portion of the site and told to liaise with the designers of adjacent sites to work out issues such as access and the relationship of one building to another. Models were produced for each building which were assembled on the plan of the whole site. Like unplanned development, the result was a scheme which was much denser than a masterplanner would have dared to create. It was also striking once the models had all been assembled that the scheme looked like a natural piece of the city rather than a masterplanned enclave. However, as Alexander admits, the process that he describes in *A new theory of urban design* can throw up many difficulties when applied to the planning and creation of new urban areas. It may be that the theory is more useful as a description of the way in which urban areas were developed in the past than as a practical tool for their creation in the future.

A new theory of urban design:
The plan of the completed design for the San Francisco waterfront site developed as part of a simulated design exercise over five years.

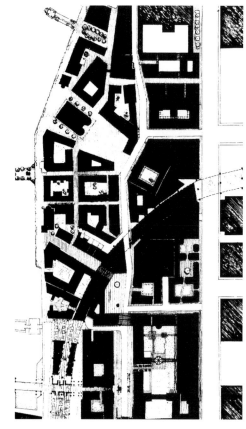

The reason is that Alexander describes a natural, organic process. Just as in ecology or medicine, our understanding of such processes does not mean that we can or should recreate them artificially. If this 'timeless way of building' is really the natural state of things, the priority should be to look at the barriers that prevent it from happening at present rather than to try and apply it to urban decision-making systems which are profoundly at odds with these natural processes.

What then does this natural process of urban development mean in practice? Alexander suggests that 'this feeling of "organicness" is not a vague feeling of relationship with biological forms. It is not an analogy. It is instead an accurate vision of a specific structural quality which these old towns had… and have. Namely each of these towns grew as a whole, under its own laws of wholeness… and we can feel this wholeness not only at the largest scale, but in every detail; in the restaurants; in the sidewalks; in the houses, shops, markets, roads, parks, gardens and walls'.

I find this easiest to understand by thinking about the French market town of Périgueux which is the home town of Hélène, my (DR's) wife. This is an exquisitely beautiful town about the size of Chester but unlike British towns seems still to be 'owned' by its people. Most of the shops are independently-owned and much of the development is financed and undertaken locally. Even the local council seems responsive to local people. This may have something to do with the fact that many of the influential people in the town live in the centre including elected officials and officers. In a British town when development takes place people tend to talk about it in terms of what 'they' are doing. Who 'they' are is never really specified but the word implies an external force beyond the control of local people. In Périgueux it is more common to hear conversations about what Monsieur X or Madam Y is doing. The development is personalised even when it is undertaken by the council where it is seen as the mayor's doing. It is likely that the person involved will be known locally as will his or her family. It is true that this perception of the town is more characteristic of Hélène's grandparents than her own generation and there is little doubt that it is dying out slowly. However if we imagine Alexander's principles being applied in this context they start to make much more sense.

It is clearly not the case that when development takes place in traditional towns like Périgueux the developer understands the principals set out above. They are expressed not as practical principles but as tradition, an understanding of the town, its people and its history and an empathy with the place. The developments will, of course, have to be viable and the developer will be concerned to make a profit but these will not be the only factors. One of the most powerful factors is peer pressure. Since developers are not faceless their buildings affect their reputation in the town. This might emphasise their importance and wealth but the opposite is also true if a scheme is built or designed badly. The effects of this process can be seen clearly in the design of shopfronts in Périgueux which are of the highest quality (to emphasise the status of the shopkeeper) and yet respect a series of unwritten but universally understood rules and are entirely in harmony with the character of the town. This contrasts sharply with the situation in similar UK towns where the rules are often very specific but the multiple stores with their corporate designs lack an understanding and empathy with the town so that their shopfronts jar and grate.

There was a time when this process applied to all development in towns and cities. It can be seen in the market towns of Britain and even in the Victorian cities where merchants would use local architects to build residences and warehouses for their own use to emphasise their status. The unwritten rules which guided this development were widely understood and rarely transgressed. They could be seen as the good manners and etiquette of urban development. It is ironic that the understanding of these rules was lost with the introduction of the planning system which took these decisions off the developers and vested them with remote bureaucrats that we now refer to as 'they'.

The natural process of urban development is also about incremental change as we

Périgueux where some elements of a natural process of urban development can still be seen

advocated in Chapter 12. Traditional urban areas are based upon a continuous cycle of development, demolition and redevelopment and at each stage the urban good manners are followed. They are also fine grained because development is locally controlled and no one, not even the council, has the capacity to buy up large parts of the town. This natural process of incremental change allows the town to evolve gradually in response to changing circumstances and economic conditions, so that it is constantly able to reshape itself to meet its needs while retaining a continuity of character.

This raises questions about our ability to conserve historic urban areas. We closely protect the environments which predate modern town planning, from medieval York to Georgian Liverpool and the Victorian splendour of Manchester lest our incomprehension of the principles which made them would destroy the very thing that we cherish. Yet the principles which shaped these areas are not static but fluid. They are (were) based upon this constant cycle of demolition and renewal, and our efforts to protect them by conserving everything or insisting that new buildings are an artificial pastiche of their historic neighbours runs the risk of atrophying these areas and turning them into museum pieces cut off from the forces which have historically shaped them. The same lack of understanding of process lies at the root of our inability to build successful new urban areas.

How we lost the art of city building

The first part of this book was devoted to the reasons why we lost the art of urban development. We described how in the pre-industrial city there was a natural tendency for people and activity to gravitate towards the centre of towns and cities and how this created a rich, dense and attractive urban form. We looked at how the pressures created by the industrial revolution placed intolerable pressures on this traditional form of city building and caused people to flee urban areas creating the engine of suburban sprawl. We also explored how many of the urban professions grew up to address the problems that the industrial revolution created in towns and cities, such as overcrowding, insanitary conditions, pollution and congestion. These gave birth to the two main philosophies that have shaped urban areas in the twentieth century, the garden city and modernist Utopias of people like Le Corbusier. All of these factors contribute to our inability to develop urban areas as we did in the past.

We have however argued that these trends are being reversed and that environmental, demographic and social pressures are leading us towards a rediscovery of the value and importance of urban living. We have also described the characteristics of sustainable urban neighbourhoods capable of responding to these trends and creating urban areas fit for people to return to. However we should not make the mistake of believing that there is one correct model for urban areas and that our troubles would be at an end if only we could discover it. The key is not to find the right physical model but to discover or rediscover the natural process of city building which enables a city to naturally work towards and to constantly reshape the physical model which best meets its needs. There are however many powerful barriers which block this natural process of urban development.

Planning policy: The first of these barriers results from the policies and attitudes which still live on in many parts of the planning system. As we have described in this book, while many of the Utopian models of twentieth century planning have been discredited their legacy lives on in the minutiae of planning policy. These include the reduction of densities, the promotion of public open space, the zoning of different uses and the creation of an efficient transport network. While taken individually these policies seem perfectly reasonable, their cumulative impact is to undermine the character of urban areas and to distort the natural process of urban growth.

A fragmented approach: As Rob Cowan has suggested[4] one of the reasons why these attitudes are perpetuated is the fragmentation of the development industry. Ever since the 'big bang' created by Ebenezer Howard and Patrick Geddes the participants in the urban regeneration industry have been 'flying away from each other at unimaginable speed'. He writes that 'from their distant planets they [architects, engineers, developers, planners and politicians] now beam messages to the rest of the universe in the strange language that they have evolved and wonder why there is no reply'. Each of these players is responsible for a small part of the urban fabric and has evolved a professional philosophy which optimises its performance from their perspective. But they have no responsibility for the whole and a poor understanding of the motivation of other players. Engineers are concerned to ease congestion and reduce accidents, housebuilders to cater for the aspirations of buyers, developers to maximise the return on their investment and planners to minimise the impact of this development. It is hardly surprising that this leads to conflict and makes it so difficult to develop a coherent approach to urban areas.

End-state plans: This is compounded by the way that we plan urban areas. There has long been a debate about the way that public policy should influence urban areas. There was a great deal of interest in the 1970s in the concept of cybernetics in which the process of planning and the process of urban development ran side by side with the former seeking to influence and guide the latter. However it is easier to think in terms of end-state plans be they a local plan adopted or a master plan drawn up for a development. Such end-state planning starts with a decision about how an area will be in the future and then works towards achieving this vision. If this master plan is confined to the trellis on which the city can grow, as Hausemann's Paris, or indeed Crown Street in Glasgow, it can be very positive particularly if it creates confidence and certainty. However plans tend to be more prescriptive than this and define not only the framework but the type of uses and the design of buildings to be developed as part of the plan. This works against the natural process of urban development and has one of two results. Either the plan is not completed and is undermined by later developments or it is completed and people wonder why it looks so artificial.

Negative planning: The final problem with the planning system is that it only really has the ability to say no. The planning system established by the 1947 Town and County Planning Act was based on the assumption that the majority of developments would be undertaken by the public sector. At the time four out of five new homes were being built by councils or in new towns. When the act created local planning authorities and required them to develop five-year plans for their area it was therefore assumed that they would also have the power to implement these plans directly[5]. At the same time development land rights were nationalised and private developers were required to apply to the local authority for permission to develop or change the use of land. The situation since then has changed radically and the vast majority of new development is now undertaken by the private sector. A system designed to deal with a small rump of non-public sector development has therefore become the main tool to shape the pattern of settlements.

The public and the development industry seems to regard planners as all powerful. While they do often wield considerable influence on the detail of development much of this influence is exerted through a process of persuasion and bluff using the threat of a refusal of planning permission to get the developer to comply. However when their bluff is called planners are exposed as having relatively limited powers of refusal because the risks of appeal means that only the very worst applications are refused. While the threat of refusal will persuade most small developers to comply with the planner's wishes this is less true of larger developers with the resources to take on the system. It also does not work in areas of decline where local authorities are keen to promote development and are therefore reluctant to refuse anything, particularly if it is seen to be creating jobs. Planning is therefore a very negative process designed to prevent the unacceptable rather than to promote the ideal. It is lamentably ill-equipped to deal with the issues of urban good manners described above.

We may by now have managed to irritated most of those involved in the planning and design of urban areas. But this is not an argument against planning or planning professionals. While the natural process of development that we have described could be seen as the product of capitalism unconstrained by planning law, we need look no further than the cities of the new industrialised nations like Taiwan to see that the commercial forces that created the medieval city or Victorian cities like Leeds and Manchester are now so strong that they dwarf the capacity of even the greatest cities to control and shape them. This is not a phenomenon confined to the Far East. Similar forces can be seen at work in the UK where relaxed planning controls in the Enterprise Zones of the 1980s in areas like London's docklands created not well mannered urban development but the excesses of Canary Wharf. The other side of this coin is the fact that commercial forces are abandoning large parts of our cities, something which the planning system finds difficult to deal with. Something has changed and we can no longer rely upon the natural forces of development to produce successful urban areas.

The developers, financial institutions and international companies who shape the modern city are very different to those who built the traditional city. They are rarely based in the city nor are the banks and financial institutions who provided the funds. Buildings are developed for occupation by others and, in a global market, international design styles rather than local character hold sway. It is not that the pace of change has accelerated because even today there is little to rival the explosive urban growth of the industrial revolution. What has changed is the view that developers take of the future. Whereas in the past developers built monuments to themselves which they expected to last forever, today investors are concerned with the investment return over ten or, at most, twenty years so that the building becomes a disposable commodity.

At the same time developers and investors are abandoning large parts of our cities. The problems here relate not to unconstrained growth but to decline which can be even more corrosive to the quality of the urban environment. This decline stems from the dispersal of activity to the suburbs that we have already described. Here the planning system lacks the capacity either to prevent the dispersal of activity or to promote development in the inner city. The planning system seems to be based on the assumption that there are an infinite number of developers willing to undertake any type of development on every site and all that is required is the designation of a use in the local plan to achieve development. However if there are no developers willing to undertake the development the site will remain vacant and conventional planning approaches are powerless to promote development.

A new planning approach

The twin problems of controlling development in areas of growth and promoting economic activity in areas of decline make it very difficult to recreate the natural process of urban development as Alexander suggested. The pressures are either so strong that they will overwhelm these natural processes or so weak that they will make development impossible on the scale required. A new approach to the planning of urban areas is needed if we are to secure the repopulation of cities and the promotion of sustainable urban neighbourhoods. In many urban areas all that is required is the reversal of detailed policies which currently prevent the development of urban form. However in some parts of the inner city an urban structure no longer exists. Here something more radical is required.

Simplified planning zones: One possibility is the reduction of planning control over areas where we want to promote development. If it is true that the introduction of planning controls has distorted the natural process of development then it may follow that a relaxation of these controls would allow it to emerge once more. To an extent this was tried through Enterprise Zones in the 1980s which were based upon the belief that the bureaucracy of planning was one of the impediments to inner city regeneration. This concern was never really justified. While the need for planning permission could often delay schemes, local authorities keen to promote development were already reluctant to refuse or even influence development for fear that the investment would be lost. It is also clear that the experience with Enterprise Zones did not lead to high quality urban development. The removal of planning controls alone is therefore not the answer.

It may however be possible to devise an alternative approach to development which does more naturally lead to the creation of urban form without relying on the planning system. We have postulated in the past that one of the ways of creating a dense mixed-use urban area would be to establish a street network, divide each of the urban blocks into small plots of say less than half an acre and to auction these blocks to developers while removing all requirements for planning permission. This would be interesting to undertake as an experiment although the results would be very difficult to predict. It is based upon the idea that the form of traditional places is not the result of controls but is quite tightly constrained by the circumstances of development. In a traditional town if sites are small and hemmed in by other buildings and land prices are high then there is little option but to build densely and to the back of pavement if development is to be viable. In new development if such circumstances were recreated artificially there may be less need for planning controls. The auction of a series of small sites within an existing street framework could do just this. The small size of sites would create a fine urban grain, would promote a variety of development and allow a range of smaller developers to participate. It would also create the robustness discussed in Chapter 12 since any mistakes that were made would be small and easily repaired. This would even be the case if developers were able to create larger sites by bidding for more than one plot or by buying up plots from other developers. This process of site trading could also create a land market in the area inflating land values and creating another of the conditions for urban development.

Something of this kind has been tried in the development of Dutch new towns. Here small plots have been sold off to developers with minimal planning controls in place. Developers are required to respect the building line and to join their building to those on adjacent sites but can otherwise build whatever they wish. It may be that in its purest form as described above, this system is unlikely to be implemented in the UK. However it may be possible through the use of a mechanism like a simplified planning zone to develop some of the ideas. In such a zone a set of planning policies would be set out in advance and any development which met these policies would be able to proceed without planning permission. This begs the question of what these policies should be. One possible answer is the urban design guide.

Small sites tend to promote high density development: The size of sites and the way that they are hemmed in by development in many traditional towns and cities makes urban development almost inevitable as in Mychull House near the Cathedral in Manchester

Design guides and codes: One approach to the promotion of the urban good manners that we have described above is the use of design guides. In the absence of the shared knowledge and understanding of these issues that existed in the past the adoption of a guide can be a powerful tool to transforming urban development.

We described the Hulme and Manchester design guides in the last chapter and the effect that they have had on the city. It is worth dwelling in a little more detail on the role of the *Hulme Guide to Development*[6] as a potential model for a new approach to planning. One of the most important aspects of the Hulme redevelopment was that it was decided not to have a master plan so that it avoided the pitfalls of end-state planning. Instead a framework of streets was established (the vine on which development could grow) but this still left the problem of how new development could made more urban in character. In existing urban areas the basic principles of development are implied by the buildings and public spaces which already surround a site. These will, for example, set the building line, position, height and massing of new development and thus its contribution to the public realm. However in an area like Hulme where no built context existed it was necessary to create it through a design guide.

The Hulme guide contains ten core principles which are developed into 53 guidelines. These are stated in simple but specific terms such as 'all streets should terminate in other streets' or 'doors onto streets should be at no more than 15 metre intervals'. The guide goes into far more detail than is possible through traditional planning control and could only be enforced because the council had land ownership and grant-making as well as planning powers. It was initially seen by many developers as over-prescriptive and thus a disincentive to development. However the experience of implementing it on the ground has been that this is not the case. The guide, for example, says nothing about the architecture of buildings, the materials used or their elevational treatment, all areas normally of concern to development control planners. It establishes instead an envelope into which buildings must fit in terms of their position, height and orientation. If this is done then developers, in fact, have more freedom of design and detailing than they would be given by traditional development control as testified by the very wide variety of traditional and modern buildings that have been developed in Hulme.

A similar approach has been adopted in many continental cities and by the new urbanists in the US through the work of Duany and Plater-Zyberk[7]. They have developed a system of urban ordinances and codes which have come very close to recreating traditional urban form. As they state: 'In a town built without the benefit of centuries or a diversity of founders, the codes encourage variety whilst ensuring the harmony required to give character to a community'. This method does involve the creation of a master plan but only to illustrate the way that the settlement might develop and to determine the location of the centre and sub-centres as well as the network of streets. The master plan is then developed into a street plan showing a hierarchy of different streets as well as the building plots which are small enough to ensure that buildings face onto the street. Each of the streets is then developed as a section showing the width between building lines and the character of each space. The next stage is to develop a regulating plan which designates each building

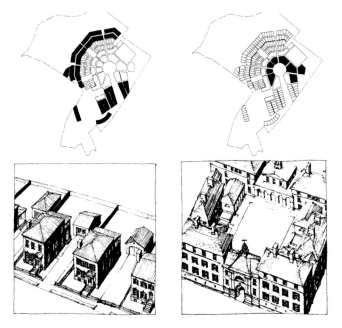

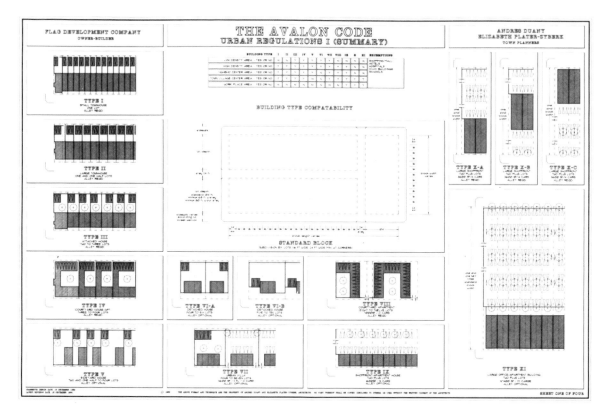

plot for a particular type of development. This does not refer to the land use of the site but to the form of development, its height and position. A series of detailed guidelines are then set out in a set of graphic codes which specify everything from the design of streets to the height, massing and position of buildings down to the detailed design and materials to be used. These codes are presented as matrices so that each street and building type can be related to the different areas designated on the regulating plan.

This is clearly a much more prescriptive process than the Hulme guide to development but it nevertheless very different to a traditional master plan, such as the plan by Ralph Erskine for the Millennium Village in Greenwich (see page 120). In the latter case we know from the plan what will be built where, when it will happen and how it will look. The Duany Plater-Zyberk approach by contrast creates a framework which can be developed gradually by a wide range of small developers over a number of years. This is on fact very similar to the traditional way in which

parts of Victorian London were developed as described on page 56. The only application of the Duany Plater-Zyberk approach in the UK was the development of Poundbury in Dorset (see page 156) where it was made easier because the land was owned by the Duchy of Cornwall. Its strength in the US has been that the plan and code is developed in close partnership with the local community through a week long *Charette*. This involves the establishment of a team of five to ten people on site who work closely with local architects, developers and other professions and run a series of intensive workshops with local people. In small town America this means that the whole community is able to influence the plan, can understand why it has been done and can sign up to the vision that it contains. Given that the community in these small towns will also include the local developers a consensus is created which overcomes local resistance.

The use of urban design guides could play an important role in creating a new role for planning. A number of places in the UK are

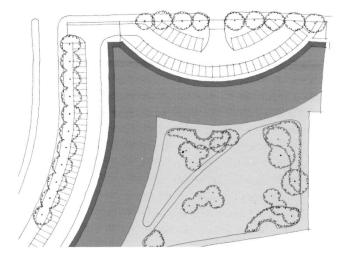

currently working on design guides or codes and English Partnerships have recently commissioned a guide to influence all of the schemes where they invest grant.

Development briefs and competitions: Design guides are not the only way to influence development. An alternative approach, particularly on individual sites is to use the traditional method of a planning brief linked to a competitive bidding process. This is something which local authorities have always done for important sites although many briefs have been confined to technical information such as underground services, access and highway or planning regulations. In many cases these technical requirements will determine the form of development. If, for example, only one access point is allowed the development will inevitably be serviced by a cul-de-sac.

It is however possible to use briefs much more creatively as has been done in Crown Street in Glasgow[8] (see page 179). Here again a master plan was commissioned although the role of this was to establish the street network and public spaces. Once this had been done the area was split into a series of building plots which, unlike Hulme, did not generally include entire urban blocks. Detailed briefs were then written for each of these development plots. The briefs indicated a strip down the front of the site where the front

wall of the building was to be positioned along with the positions of entrances and the points to be emphasised with landmarks. They also specified the height of the blocks and where parking was to be accommodated but otherwise said nothing about the design of the buildings. Like the Hulme guide this created an envelope for development without being prescriptive about design. The next stage was to hold a seminar with potential developers to explain to them the vision for the area. Then the sites were put out to competitive tender. Crucially this was on the basis of a fixed price and grant requirement. Hence the only factor determining which scheme was selected was therefore the quality of the development which gave the tenderers a real incentive to invest in design. While this may be a very artificial way of recreating the process of organic urban development the evidence of Glasgow is that it is capable of producing a high quality environment.

Planning for Real: It is not possible to discussing the reform of the planning process without dwelling on the role of the community. There has been a tendency over the last thirty or so years to suggest that the solution to urban ills is to wrest planning controls from the planners, politicians and architects and to vest them in the local community. It is local people, after all who have to live in the area and who know it best. Why should they not be the one who shape the way that it is planned and developed. We have indeed argued in this chapter that organic urban development and character grows from a rootedness in a locality. Is it not therefore more likely to emerge from the local community than from professionals?

For all of these reasons and more it is vital to create a central role for the community in the planning of urban areas. We should not however assume that this alone will create quality urban development. As we have described, many community groups given the choice will opt for suburban designs. Local people have limited knowledge of what is possible or of experience elsewhere and will fiercely resist certain types of socially valuable development (such as social housing). As Rob Cowan argues in his manifesto

The cities design forgot[9] the solution is not to abdicate responsibility by leaving everything to the community but to develop collaborative ways of working which include professionals, developers alongside the community. In recent years a number of techniques have been developed to make this collaboration a reality as documented by the Directory of Social Change[10]. These include Urban Design Action Teams (UDATs), planning weekends, Charettes, round table workshops and *Planning for Real* events. The latter, pioneered by Tony Gibson[11], uses very simple models to allow people to visualise and respond to their environment. These techniques used in conjunction with design guides and briefs have enormous potential to rehumanise the planning of urban areas and to reawake the natural process of urban development.

These approaches to urban development may start to address some of the failings of the planning system. They relate mainly to the recreation of urban fabric in areas where is does not exist or has been destroyed such as large brownfield sites, or redevelopment areas. They appear to have the potential to mimic if not to recreate the natural process of urban growth. However alone they are not enough. These techniques have the potential to shape development where there is pressure to build but they will not on their own promote development if that pressure does not exist. The regeneration of Crown Street and Hulme has as much to do with the availability of grants than the urban frameworks that have been created. The process of urban generation therefore needs to be combined with a coordinated approach to the process of urban regeneration if our towns and cities are to find a new lease of life.

New life for urban Britain

We have in this book argued that the settlement pattern in the UK is changing. After a century or more of dispersal and suburbanisation, forces are at work which could lead to the repopulation of British towns and cities and the rediscovery of new forms of urban development such as the sustainable urban neighbourhood. If this happens

then we will have gone a long way to accommodating household growth without building in large parts of the countryside and we will also have regenerated our cities. In suggesting this we are mixing prediction and advocacy. Strong as these forces may be they will not create a new life for urban Britain unless we create the conditions that make this possible.

One of the participants at the recent TCPA seminars on urban housing capacity[12] accepted that areas like Hulme illustrate that it was possible to attract a range of people back to inner city areas. He pointed out however that this has only been possible because of huge public investment through City Challenge to develop just a few thousand houses. Given that the targets for the accommodation of household growth in urban areas imply the development of up to three million such homes the question was asked whether the nation is willing or able to commit the resources necessary to make this possible. The answer is that it clearly is not. If urban repopulation is to succeed we must change the market for urban development so that values rise sufficiently to make it possible without relying on public subsidy. The process of urban regeneration is therefore not about ongoing public subsidy but about reversing the market trends towards the dispersal of UK settlements. What is required is an intensive effort over the coming decade to bring about an urban renaissance just as happened at the end of the last century with the garden city movement. If we succeed we will have changed the dynamic of urban development and should be able to considerably scale down the level of resources devoted to urban regeneration and repopulation. Many of the planks of this approach are already in place or are under consideration by government.

The accommodation of household growth: The predicted increase in households is a huge opportunity for the regeneration of urban areas. While it is not possible to force people to live within cities it is possible to frame policy to make it a far more attractive proposition. This issue is covered in detail in our report for Friends of the Earth[13] where we recommended that household allocations should not perpetuate past trends of dispersal. Instead regional housing allocations should underprovide for projected household growth in rural areas and compensate for this by increasing the allocation for urban areas. This is already implied by the government's new policy on household growth[14] which moves away from the 'predict and provide' approach to a system where growth is planned, monitored and managed. This regional approach should then be combined with a local mechanism to promote housebuilding within urban areas. At present local authorities are required to provide for a five-year supply of housing land but have no way of managing the release of this land so that all of the greenfield sites are developed first. We have suggested instead a system by which authorities can manage the release of land on an annual basis and can require that a certain proportion of urban sites are taken up before greenfield sites are released.

Changing the market: So far this is good old-fashioned planning policy designed to prevent greenfield development rather than to promote urban development. To achieve the latter we must address the market for urban housing. The most immediate way in which this can be done is through the use of grants to make development more attractive. However as we suggest above the scale of funding required over a period sufficient to bring about a change in the market may be beyond our capacity. This has led to a great deal of interest in the use of taxation to promote urban development. One option is the harmonisation of Value Added Tax rates on new-build and the conversion and improvement of existing buildings. At present VAT is not charged on new housing whereas it is on works to existing property creating a clear disincentive to do the later. However much of the debate has focused on the introduction of a new tax on greenfield development. There are a number of forms that this tax could take as described in our Friends of the Earth report. However the principle is that it should alter the financial balance between greenfield and urban development so making the latter more attractive

without denuding the pubic purse. It has also been suggested that the revenue from such a tax could be hypothecated to promote urban development so that the system as a whole would be self-funding.

Promoting urban development: Planning policy plus the use of fiscal measures have the potential to tip the balance in favour of urban development. But such measures will be deeply unpopular if they force people back to blighted and unpleasant urban areas against their will. They must therefore be combined with a concerted approach to the transformation of urban areas to make them attractive as places to live and work. To do this we must trespass on many areas of local and national government policy. Making urban areas more attractive is not just a matter of environmental improvements or even the promotion of urban development forms. It means addressing the quality of inner city schools, upgrading healthcare, reforming urban transport policy, improving shops, services and other facilities, combating urban crime and creating employment. At present many of these issues are being addressed by government. The recently announced Education Action Zones, for example, could play an important role in addressing the problems of inner city schools. The Transport White Paper addresses congestion and public transport and initiatives are also being taken on health and crime.

The challenge is to bring these initiatives together at a local level to achieve a transformation in urban areas. At the root of many of these problems is the fact that the inner city has been abandoned to those without the means to escape. This creates a ghetto mentality of social exclusion which contributes to educational underachievement, social problems and crime. If this cycle of decline is not broken people returning to cities will leave when their children reach school age or when they get burgled for the third time. Yet the presence of a broader range of people in cities is the only way to find solutions to these problems. We have therefore suggested the introduction of Urban Priority Areas where initiatives can be focused on local areas to bring about change.

Urban Priority Areas: The idea is based on the experience in Ireland of promoting urban regeneration in places such as Temple Bar in Dublin. Tax incentives, rather than grants, have been used to encourage urban regeneration and housebuilding by small developers. Tax relief on both capital investment and rent in designated areas has created a powerful market for urban development where it did not exist before. In Urban Priority Areas these measures could be combined with the new approaches to planning described above to create a powerful engine for regeneration. They would also be combined with initiatives to improve local schools, to create employment and to combat crime and social exclusion. The danger is that this will regenerate one area while displacing poverty to other parts of the city. However if the principles of social sustainability as described in Chapter 12 are followed, it should be possible to balance these different needs by focusing concerted action in these areas over a specified period to bring about a dramatic change. This in turn is likely to affect the wider dynamics of urban development so that over a ten-year period the dynamics of urban development could be reversed.

It is a hundred years since Ebenezer Howard published *Tomorrow: a peaceful path to real reform*. The impact of this work and the early garden cities that it inspired on the public and professional consciousness cannot be underestimated. Howard saw cities as 'ulcers on the face of our beautiful island' and for much of the intervening hundred years people in Britain have tended to agree with him. Howard's ideas struck a resonant chord in the times in which he lived, but times have changed. Since his time towns and cities in Britain have changed out of all recognition. They are less crowded, less polluted, greener and support a quality of life undreamed of at the end of the last century. However the changes have not all been positive. Urban areas have sprawled over the countryside rather than been integrated with it as Howard proposed. As cities have expanded congestion and environmental degradation have spread and while the quality of life for the many may have improved a significant minority have

been left behind. The urban evils of dirt, overcrowding and pollution may have been overcome but crime and poverty have proved more resilient to reform and new urban problems such as drug dependency, unemployment and economic collapse have emerged in the inner city. Howard was responding to the runaway growth of urban areas whereas our problems today are to stem their decline.

As we have shown in this book the ideas which lay behind the garden city continue to exert a powerful influence on the policies and professional attitudes which shape our cities today. However the world is changing and it is time for these attitudes and the way that we deal with our urban areas also to change. The garden city has served us well but we need new models if we are to build the twenty-first century home. In this book we have described how this could take place and how new models could emerge such as the sustainable urban neighbourhood to give a new lease of life to urban Britain.

Edinburgh Old Town: In the UK we can build urban areas of the highest quality. Can we create a new life for urban Britain so that similar areas can once more be built in the future?

Epilogue
Nicholas Falk

Realising the urban renaissance

When societies have made great leaps forward, it has frequently been through looking back and looking abroad. The rulers of Italian medieval cities looked back to the Golden Ages of the Greek and Roman civilisations. Ruskin in turn looked back to Venice in castigating what Victorian industry had done to our towns, and Morris to an idealised version of the Medieval English village. Olmstead looked to London's suburbs, and the Great Exhibition in replanning New York. The planners of Milton Keynes looked to Los Angeles. In European Urban Renaissance year in 1980 we looked to historic towns like York, and where do we look now?

Personal reflections

Inevitably our views are framed by personal experience, and just as David Rudlin has revealed the origins of his thinking, so too should I. My own values have been influenced by growing up in suburban Surrey and then living in everything from an Oxford college to an Essex council flat, as well as long periods in Palo Alto, Primrose Hill, Brixton, and now Hampstead Garden Suburb and Stroud. This illustrates one of the central propositions of this book, that the human life cycle requires different type of housing and location at different stages. It has also helped me understand why some areas thrive while others die, and the importance not only of the 'timeless qualities' of design that Christopher Alexander has identified, but also the impact of area management.

My views have also been shaped by an education that started with philosophy and economics, which was refined through an American business school, and a long period doing a doctoral thesis on planning at the London School of Economics, as well as subsequent studies in urban design. Formative influences have included Peter Hall (my external examiner and subsequent friend), Donald Olsen (through books such as *Town Planning in London*), Fritz Schumacher (and other advocates of libertarian socialism), and Howard Glennester at LSE, who helped me shift from my original focus on social services to a much more ambitious thesis on planning and development in London docklands, based on action research projects in Rotherhithe.

Courtyard blocks whether they be Oxford Colleges or Palo Alto blocks of apartments generate a sense of community

However it is learning by doing that really shapes a mind. My interest in how to manage change took me first to Ford Motor Company, where for three years I worked on the marketing and development of new and successful ranges of commercial vehicles. After Stanford, three years at McKinsey and Company provided a first-class grounding in consultancy and problem-solving skills, and enabled me to develop my interests in planning through work for some top public sector organisations. It also gave me the confidence to set up URBED in 1976, after David, now Lord Sainsbury, had read my Fabian pamphlet *Inner City, Local government and economic renewal* (with Haris Martinos), and provided the initial funding for the Urban and Economic Development Group through his charitable foundation.

The role of URBED

At URBED, we have sought to push forward thinking through applied research, while encouraging and promoting new initiatives to demonstrate practical solutions to the problems of regenerating rundown urban areas and local economic development. Initially our work focused on changing attitudes towards small business, including the ideas of reusing redundant buildings, undertaking environmental improvements to boost confidence, and enabling urban change through social entrepreneurs and the use of development trusts, and other forms of partnership.

Our interest in housing originally came about at as a solution to the problem of reusing derelict land. As well as helping to plan, and even promote a new village (Tircoed on the edge of Swansea), I drew on the experience of Primrose Hill and the writings of Herbert Gans, to advocate the idea of urban villages, originally through an article in *Built Environment* in 1978 called *New Life for Wasteland*. In a speech the Prince of Wales gave to the Institute of Directors in 1985, and in a study tour I subsequently organised for him, the message was that instead of allowing our cities to 'leak away', we should use good urban design to create an urban renaissance, starting with under-utilised assets like water or historic buildings, derelict land, and local communities.

The opportunity to develop these ideas further came in 1994 when Richard Best at the Joseph Rowntree Foundation provided funds to investigate the principles that should govern the development of new housing. This enabled David Rudlin and myself to develop the twenty-first Century Homes project, which evolved into the Sustainable Urban Neighbourhood Initiative, with support from the Department of the Environment and another charitable foundation. When our innovative project in Milton Keynes's Future World Midsummer Cottages aroused little press coverage, it made us realise that it was the 'neighbourhood', rather than the individual house or street, that should form the building block for sustainable communities. There is little point in minimising energy consumption in an individual life style, if the surrounding development is basically unsustainable or wasteful. And few want to live in an architectural zoo.

By 1995 we realised that the urban battlefield had shifted from former industrial sites or inner cities, to the very hearts of our towns and cities. URBED's consultancy work on town and city centres, and our influential report *Vital* and *Viable Town Centres: Meeting the Challenge*, brought home the huge number of opportunities to reverse the polarities in Ebenezer Howard's magnet. David's report on urban housing capacity for Friends of the Earth, *Tomorrow: a peaceful path to urban reform*, showed that the physical space was there, provided attitudes could be changed. Shortly afterwards Peter Hall and Colin Ward's book *The Sociable City* suggested that Howard's basic concept can apply just as strongly to regenerating existing areas, using good public transport to tie different settlements together. However, the sought-after urban renaissance requires action on a number of fronts simultaneously. Conventional physical planning, as Howard actually realised, is simply not enough. Organisational and financial mechanisms are needed to enable small and voluntary enterprise to compete on a level playing field with corporate giants.

In my doctoral thesis, and subsequent publications, I have put forward three principles as a test for what makes a good plan or project. These principles of social justice, natural balance, and the minimisation of waste can not be achieved through conventional planning. We need a paradigm shift. Instead of the mechanical model that dominated nineteenth century thinking, symbolised by steam pumping engines, or the electronic networks that shaped twentieth century thinking, symbolised by television, the model for the twenty-first century is surely an organic or ecological model, symbolised by a garden or an orchard. In other words, successful places, like gardens, are made and maintained by continual small improvements, or what Roberta Gratz calls 'urban husbandry'. Such a process crosses professional boundaries. The practice of urban regeneration is as much an art as a science.

Alternative scenarios

In this book we have argued for radically altering the way that we see our towns and cities. The loss of faith in grand plans, and general scepticism about changing the course of our towns and cities may make some doubt that the ideas put forward in this book can be implemented successfully. Yet there is enough experience to show that they can all be achieved, given the will.

Our current situation seems unsustainable. What Galbraith called 'private affluence and public squalor' has polarised society. Inequalities widened over the Thatcher years, while industrial capacity continued to shrink. The

Urban Husbandry: A series of images from URBED's early work using the transformation of a derelict site into a productive orchard as a metaphor for urban regeneration

Urban housing: Continental cities like Rotterdam show how good urban housing can bring rundown places back to life

promised leisure revolution ended up with private consumption of videos and take away meals and packaged holidays abroad. Those with jobs ended up working ever harder to stay in the same place. Spare time has gone into commuting. Britain has one of the lowest housebuilding rates in Europe yet still builds mean little boxes. Instead of an urban renaissance, consumers have generally rejected the idea of living in urban areas, and voted with their cars for sprawl. The trends of dispersal have drained town centres of life, and created high levels of property vacancy, in centres which seem dead much of the time. Concerns about security and education cause those who can to flee and leave behind those with time but no money to spend. The vicious circle of urban decay, which was graphically spelt out in my 1976 Fabian pamphlet, is more powerful than ever and has spread from the largest cities to the smallest town. With weak urban economies, plugging the leaks means that little is left over for improving the quality of life. Local authorities have seen their powers, self-confidence and resources whittled away. With a hole in the heart of much of urban Britain, the visions put forward for creating an 'urban renaissance', for example through cultural strategies or public art, can easily sound unrealistic and irrelevant.

Yet successful rebuilding of European cities after the destruction of the Second World War, ranging from small historic Italian cities like Padua and Verona, to the giants of Hamburg and Berlin, shows how good urban housing can bring rundown places back to life. Even the impoverished city centres of Central Europe, such as Bucharest, are sustainable because they combine high density living with reliable public transport, combined heat and power systems, and popular open spaces. Cities are a little like leaking ships, headed for the rocks, and slow to respond to instructions. Once the leaks that cause people to leave are plugged, they are much more responsive. Then the real priority is to know what course the city should be taking.

20:20 Vision: The regeneration of an area like Edinburgh Old Town has taken at least twenty years

New urban models

As the Chinese say, the best time to plant a tree is ten years ago. Our research has shown that regeneration takes far longer to produce the desired results than expected. Case studies of success stories as different as Baltimore Inner Harbour and Edinburgh Old Town show that at least 20 years is required to turn an area round to the point that regeneration becomes self-sustaining and the market can take over. Before reliance can be placed on the planning system, the negative factors must be neutralised and the right incentives provided. Also the methods used to assess projects and evaluate success are inadequate. They are based on an over-simplistic model of inputs and outputs rather than a more holistic framework. At the millennium, instead of the utopian scenario like *News from Nowhere*, or the nightmares of science fiction films like *Bladerunner*, we need 20:20 vision. This means looking both backwards and forwards, learning from other places, (which is the way most successful innovation occurs) and pursuing great ideas, rather than grand projects over a twenty year time span.

Street-life: Streets like Wind Street in Swansea are being brought back to life as pavement cafes take off even in the rainbelts of Swansea and Manchester

Great ideas can now be seen everywhere and it is no longer essential to go to the States or the Continent for inspiration; the way in which derelict sites end up covered in wild flowers and then bushes provides a metaphor for an organic approach to regeneration or rebirth. Over the last twenty years some encouraging changes have also taken place. While traditional industry has declined, there has been a resurgence in small enterprises in many parts of the country. The recycling of old mills and factories into business centres, managed workspace and 'working communities' provides an excellent model of how more sustainable forms of development can be achieved. While leisure time may not have increased for those of working age, there has been a revolution in eating and drinking habits; the numbers eating out for Sunday lunch has gone up by 40% in just the last two years and Indian food is now seen as part of our national cuisine. Ideas like eating outside, and pavement cafes are taking off, even in the rainbelts of Swansea and Manchester.

The environment too has changed. The air feels cleaner, thanks to the Clean Air Act. People have switched to lead-free petrol, due to tax incentives that made it cheaper, as well as concerns to be good citizens. Smoking in public places has been largely curtailed. As far as housing is concerned, people are changing the way they live; half of all flats have been built in the last twenty years; new concepts like loft apartments promoted by entrepreneurial developers have enabled the shock troops of urban renewal, the young urban professionals, to capture the pages of the Sunday colour supplements. As forgotten areas take off, they influence the hearts and minds of the wider population as well as gradually changing the attitudes of developers and investors. The idea 'seeing is believing' means that the new urban models emerging all over the country could create an urban renaissance over the next twenty years. Here are three examples:

Adaptive reuse: twenty years ago, many local authorities in the North of England were arguing that no use could be found for the upper floors of Victorian industrial buildings. Public funds were used to demolish what were seen as outmoded symbols of exploitation (as happened with Georgian Dublin up till recently). The success of well-publicised projects like Dean Clough Mills in Halifax, and

Adaptive reuse: The Chubb Lock factory in Wolverhampton was converted by URBED to creative workspace thereby saving a historic building and generating jobs and local economic activity

the many smaller projects up and down the country, see for example URBED's guide produced for the Department of the Environment in 1986 on *Reusing Redundant Buildings,* have helped to create a kind of movement (now given the name Regeneration Through Heritage). The resulting spaces have not only provided missing rungs on the 'premises ladder', but have helped colonise abandoned areas with new sources of employment. Perhaps the most dramatic example is the Cultural Industries Quarter in Sheffield.

Waterside revival: Areas like The Calls in Leeds have been transformed from a backwater into a fashionable district

Waterside revival: twenty years ago, most urban canals and docks were seen as dangerous places, and local authorities like Swansea in order to create its Maritime Quarter even had to dig out a dock which had started to fill in. Today there is widespread recognition that views over water add some 18% to the value of houses. Though development has often been protracted and difficult, waterfronts have once again become attractive places to visit. While it is wrong to transplant ideas and neglect the context (as with the misguided attempt to redevelop Cardiff Docks on the model of Baltimore), examples such as Bristol Docks, The Calls in Leeds, Exeter Riverside, Birmingham's Brindley Place and Newcastle Quayside are providing inspiration to other places.

Town centre revitalisation: the final and most difficult change to accomplish successfully is to bring the hearts of town and cities back to life. Yet again, despite the general gloom, there are many examples where towns have diversified their attractions and created living or softer centres. The success of historic towns like York or Worcester are taken for granted, but both suffered for many years from industrial decline, and were not revived without fights. More surprising are developments like Wolverhampton's Entertainment Quarter, with its flagship project of a media centre in the old Chubb Building, or the Merchant City in Glasgow, which is now a byword for smart living, a far cry from the picture of Glasgow drawn from statistics alone. While such developments can be criticised for being skin deep (and too often environmental improvements simply put cosmetics on a corpse), they help to boost confidence, and to turn the tide. Edinburgh, which is one of the few British city centres to be given World Heritage Site status, provides an important model for the integration of mixed uses and high density living. Similarly while twenty years ago, festivals were rare events, today they are common place. The magic of a fireworks display or outdoor performance can change the image of an area to its own people as well as the outside world[1].

Tools for Regeneration

Successful regeneration is not just a matter of economics or architecture. The good urban gardener respects the context, pays attention to maintenance and achieving a balance, and uses the right tool for the job. As some people find it hard to see how to get from the vision to results, or become obsessed with one solution or technique, here is URBED's 'seven level' model with some examples from our experience and research, together with recommendations for making these tools even more effective.

1. Devising a shared vision: the starting point in successful regeneration is getting people to see things differently. Our survey of waterside development in 1989 for the Royal Town Planning Institute identified

(1) URBED's handbook *New Life for Smaller Towns* contains over fifty case studies and thirty types of initiatives under five broad themes, and shows that revitalisation is not confined to city centres.

that the major obstacle to progress was securing agreement. Without a clear and shared vision, areas either stay derelict or end up, like much of the docklands, as isolated blocks that do little to regenerate the surrounding or improve the lives of the existing community. People often misunderstand what is needed, producing over-elaborate proposals which fail to convince the sceptics; community planning can end up with unbuildable drawings, and an even more divided community. The phrase 'Action Planning' was coined to describe a different approach, which we first used to generate a new vision for the centre of Birmingham in 1988. Bringing together key people in creative ways, and then adding the catalyst of outside experts, can set a fresh agenda and overturn outmoded ideas. The Highbury Initiative led Birmingham to seeing the centre as a series of distinct quarters linked by a high quality public realm that broke through the concrete collar of the ringroad. The process has been adapted into a half-day Round Table Conference format that has helped places as diverse as the city of Leeds, down to the centres of small towns in Powys and West Wiltshire, to frame new visions. Entrenched attitudes can be changed by finding common ground, and government can help by spreading good practice.

New vision: Techniques like our Round Table workshops can help people see areas in different ways

2. Establishing the impetus for change: to break the mould there is not only a need for people who want to create better places, but also an overwhelming reason for change. Sometimes this can be an opportunity, like putting together a lottery bid, but more often it is the recognition of a real threat. In the case of Birmingham, for example, the leading officers and politicians realised that the city centre had lost its traditional economic base, and needed to find a new role (as a meeting place). There were also some middle-ranking officers willing to take criticism and learn from the best practice elsewhere. Innovation typically comes from outsiders who have experienced alternatives, and who are not bound by their position in the hierarchy. Urban areas can establish the necessary catalyst for change by appointing outsiders to key positions, by taking part in networks or study tours to share experience, but also by using consultants to undertake health checks and audits. Government can help by properly funding the process of drawing up strategies, and by producing indicators of performance so that areas can compare themselves. Instead of a league table showing the best and the worst, it is equally important to identify areas 'at risk', and then catch them before they go over the tipping point.

3. Promoting a balance of projects: the sheer complexity of urban areas, and the need to take action over many years, has been too much for the conventional planning process. The constant pressure of dealing with unwanted applications has taken time and resources away from forward planning. Challenge funding such as the Single Regeneration Budget has encouraged the creation of partnerships; it has also brought a crop of policies, plans, programmes and projects. But too often the so-called partnerships are better described as conspiracies; and the plans are just bundles of ideas that happened to be on the shelf. Physical master plans are not the answer as they soon become out of date. Instead local authorities need to use well-researched planning briefs, coupled with urban design guides to secure the right combination of ingredients without being over specific about their precise location or floor areas. By publishing the brief as an adjunct to the local plan, and then pump-priming the initial projects, the local authority, or better still a partnership with the landowners, can create the confidence to attract property. A good example is the redevelopment of Shenley Hospital in Hertfordshire as a new village. It has proved possible there to apply the principles of social justice and natural balance, without wasting resources. The community has ended up with a 45 acre park, run by a trust, as well as a good mix of housing. Rather like a good cook book, a planning brief needs to recognise the ingredients available and for whom the meal is intended and government could insist that these are prepared for all major sites (like the Building Plans in Germany).

Planning briefs: The redevelopment of Shenley hospital in Hertfordshire illustrates the value of planning briefs

4. Having the guts to innovate: going from vision to results also means knowing when to take direct action. Almost all the success stories have involved someone taking risks, and going against the tide. Some have been led by community groups. Others have been led by former professionals, such as architects or planners, who have set up their own development companies. Project management is an under-appreciated set of skills, and should form part of the planner's training and tool-kit. As Sir Oscar Lewis said of development planning in the Third World, the only way to learn to play the violin is to start playing. Unfortunately the training required is not readily available. We could learn from American business schools and from postgraduate education on the Continent. Case study based masters degrees, should develop interpersonal skills and be interprofessional. Capacity can also be built by short courses run by people who have actually 'done it'. Another way is to use periods of secondment supplemented by networks and 'action learning' groups. The growing number of partnerships that bring different organisations together are breaking down sectoral and professional divides. However the professional system still fails to recognise the importance of urban design and urban economics. As Lord Roger's Urban Task Force seems to be suggesting, we need more 'urbanists' and 'social entrepreneurs', not planners and surveyors, if we are to turn liabilities into assets. This can be encouraged through changes in the professional system, for example to recognise those who have demonstrated experience.

5. Generating enough yield: projects depend on finance, and there needs to be an adequate payoff for all the investors. Yet the initial costs and risks of brown field sites deter private funders. Grants appeal to bureaucrats, not entrepreneurs, who are powerless on their own to deal with areas that are 'sinking ships'. Relying on lottery and other challenge funding bids can turn communities into beggars, and is no basis for long-term regeneration. Instead new mechanisms are needed to provide the necessary incentives for sustainable development. The fiscal system is far more effective than planning in changing behaviour, and we need a more intelligent tax system if development is to become more sustainable. Changes to VAT and to the Uniform Business Rate would enable urban areas to compete with green field sites for investment on more equal terms. Compulsory Purchase powers should be used to assemble sites where owners have unrealistic expectations (as the costs of holding on to derelict land take no account of the social or environmental costs). Mechanisms like Enterprise Zones, or the Priority Areas used in the Irish Republic could unleash the energy of small businesses through tax incentives. In turn this creates useful jobs for local people, without displacing what already exists – a virtuous circle of regeneration. Other ways of packaging the necessary resources include the use of job creation and training schemes (of which the latest is the Environmental Task Force) and the new Regional Development Agencies which will focus efforts on areas 'at risk'. The government is taking an interest in Town Centre Partnerships, and the scope for using supplementary or special rates to fund programmes that win business approval. Town Improvement Zones (influenced by the American Business Improvement Districts) could tap property owners for the extra funds to provide higher levels of cleansing and security, and hence remove an important deterrent to people moving back into town centres. Bonds could be used to fund capital projects, as in US cities, and by some housing associations. A few local authorities are beginning to use the Private Finance Initiative to apply more creative approaches to funding but many lack the skills, while businesses lack the motivation. The trick is packaging funds for complex projects from all the potential beneficiaries, short and longer term. This means decentralising funding decisions, and releasing the dead hand of the Treasury.

6. Organising for concerted action: while funding is indispensable, projects often fail because there is insufficient management capacity to use the funds effectively, or because action was not taken on a broad enough front. Projects that are funded from a single source are often over simple – a monoculture – which is why so many local authority developments feel sterile. Over the last twenty years there has been a new enthusiasm for the idea of working in partnership, and a variety of new organisations have sprung up. Just as limited companies and national banks were as important as technology to the growth of nineteenth century cities, so new structures like Development Trusts and Networks hold the key to the twenty-first century. The challenge is how to combine the energy and single-minded commitment of the developer or business with the wider public concerns of government. In looking for a 'third way' between the public and the private sectors many have looked to the voluntary sector. However, our six country study of *Voluntary Work and the Environment* for the European Foundation discovered voluntary organisations go through

The guts to innovate:
Birmingham is a city which has transformed its vision of the centre and has implemented a wide range of improvements over the last ten years

a common life cycle which makes them unsuited to managing longer-term developments, such as the regeneration of a large urban area. Yet local authorities have other calls on their resources, and public funding sources, such as the Single Regeneration Budget, have too short a time span. One answer lies in the French idea of the 'Contract de Ville', through which a range of organisations deliver programmes within an agreed regeneration strategy and action plan in targeted areas. Such programmes can also be used to develop what the French call the 'social economy', tapping into local concerns for self-development and mutual aid, so that local people develop their potential by being involved in regeneration projects. Britain has little to compare with the professionalism of organisations in the USA such as LISC, (the Local Initiatives Support Corporation) or the Main Street Programme. The housing association movement that might provide the leadership is still for the most part focused on relatively narrow goals. Now that a proportion of public project funding is at last being allocated to capacity building, there is a need to review how to encourage the spread of best practice to avoid 'reinventing the wheel'. Our report in 1987 for the Department of the Environment, *Managing Urban Change: the training need of project managers,* advocated support for networks, publicising demonstration projects, and more training. European priorities are switching from physical to human resource development, and a national award system needs to be used to share experience on how to put successful projects together, backed up by properly funded networks.

7. **Monitoring results**: the final level is producing lasting improvements on the ground. Performance needs to be monitored and evaluated within a wider perspective. As the impact is on social and economic, as well as physical objectives, regeneration projects need to be considered holistically. While this can seem daunting, performance can be monitored by using a few key indicators, and then evaluated against benchmarks drawn from comparable places, using area profiles. In reaching a judgement, it is essential to go beyond the crude and narrow concepts such as 'leverage' that were imported from America under the Thatcher years. The three fundamental principles should be social justice (now rechristened social exclusion), natural balance (now known as sustainable development), and the minimisation of waste (or economic efficiency). However monitoring needs to be properly resourced to avoid projects relying on their own 'hype'. What matters most is that there are changes in the attitudes of local people as well as investors, and other stakeholders. Opinion surveys have a crucial role to play in the management of urban change, just as they do in the decisions of large companies. Market research could do a great deal to refine the crude thinking based on projecting trends, and the 'predict and provide' philosophy that has governed the past twenty years. It is surely inequitable for major retailers to have so much information on what people buy and where, while public authorities depend on outdated census data and information from housing waiting lists to plan the future shape of urban conurbations. The techniques now exist to give communities up to date profiles of how places are changing,

using Geographic Information Systems (GIS), sample surveys, and information collected for government departments. Both cities and areas within them can be profiled, and the results used to help assess priorities. The idea of 'Urban Observatories' to monitor change has been promoted by the European Union. Some cities have set up 'Architecture Centres' to publicise new schemes. Local shop-front offices for project teams backed up by the Internet should also be essential and may come to replace the nineteenth century Town Hall as a symbol of twenty-first century urban identity, along with periodic 'Round Table' conferences and forum meetings.

Resourcing a renaissance

Most of the tools or techniques for regenerating urban areas we recommend have already been used somewhere. These include round table conferences and visioning events; area audits and health checks; planning briefs and design guides, demonstration projects; urbanists and social entrepreneurs; intelligent tax systems and local funding packages; partnership agreements; development trusts and capacity building; urban profiles, indicators and architecture centres.

Yet the process of rebuilding our towns and cities to meet the needs of the twenty-first century still seems daunting. A handful of Millennium villages and a few 'grand projects', like the Dome, are not enough. With over a thousand town centres that are large enough to interest national multiples, we should be encouraging 'a thousand flowers to bloom'! Lyndon Johnson drew on the analogy of the Vietnam War to call for 'a war on poverty'. As the enemy is often concealed, we need a good battle plan or strategy, and one that will mobilise resources, as well as engage the hearts and minds of all those in the front lines up and down Britain, not just in London. It must not be stalled by the reservations of a Treasury that has presided over urban as well as industrial decline for the last 150 years.

If, as we have argued, it is now imperative to change what, where and how we build to meet the likely demands of the twenty-first century, the obvious question is how we can turn the tide. For the trends have been towards dispersal not concentration, and the underlying objectives have been towards quantity, not quality. The 'global economy' and 'information superhighway' seem to make urban living redundant. The new Labour Government has not yet felt able to allow local authorities to tax private parking let alone provide the resources needed to make alternatives to the car more appealing. People are no longer moving to find their dreams but to escape their nightmares. But what may make sense for the individual is collective madness. The Third Way, described by Joshua Rifkin in *The End of Work*, involves expanding local services that will make our neighbourhoods more sustainable, as we can no longer rely on the labour market to provide enough jobs. This means looking at people as resources, not just costs.

The resources are there to be tapped, given the will. The real

Innovative financing: Priority Areas have been used in the Irish Republic to give tax incentives for development in areas like Temple Bar, Dublin

challenge is changing the way decisions are made to reflect wider and longer term considerations. Someone once wrote 'The reason why cities are ugly and bare, is that the people who decide live somewhere elsewhere'. Resources are not distributed through competition, but through forms of oligopoly, and by large organisations following crude rules. Thus private investors follow their 'acid test' of whether equity exceeds debt, and are wary of backing new ventures. The Treasury follows its 'golden rule' of keeping current expenditure below tax receipts, and uses the Public Spending Borrowing Requirement as an excuse for centralising expenditure decisions. The individual invests in their own house rather than the neighbourhood, and sees the price of property as the measure of achievement. It is as though we were trying to drive a car using only the accelerator and the speedometer.

While it is understandable that the concepts of environmental capital and capacity are too complex for the layman to understand and use, it should be possible to make planning more holistic by applying the principles of Balanced Incremental Development, and the three 'green rules' that ensure long-term success and survival. In our report *Vital and Viable Town Centres*, we first used the idea of 'health checks' and 'environmental audits' to identify strengths and weaknesses in a reasonably systematic way. The three 'As' of attractions, accessibility and amenity provide a convenient way of thinking of a centre in a multidimensional way. Our seven level 'vision to results' model shows how to achieve action by using some basic human attributes. All this needs to be encompassed within a world view that gives equal weight to some higher level principles. Though the precise terms change over time, with social justice now being reinterpreted as social exclusion, the principles of the minimisation of waste, natural balance, and social justice can be used to set objectives and assess options in ways that go beyond a narrow concern of how much a project will cost or what grants are available.

Just as the roots of the Italian renaissance can be traced to a combination of merchant banking, a rediscovery of Greek and Roman culture and a healthy competition between different towns, the much overdue renaissance of British towns and cities needs to be led by a reawakening of civic pride. Our strategy is quite simple, and involves attacking three separate targets. The first is to use the excuse of the Millennium, as well as widespread concerns about employment, the environment, and health, to launch a major housing drive, to put right the neglect of the last twenty years, over the coming two decades. The second target is to do so in ways that will utilise neglected property, with a target of 75% of new houses built on brown field sites, using compulsory purchase with deferred payment to provide enough sites. The third target is to use the financial resources locked up in banks and building societies to secure more sustainable urban neighbourhoods, as a means of countering recession and unemployment, using new financial instrument.

The government can use the tax system to produce the necessary shift in attitudes (as it has already done in the cases of smoking and the use of lead free petrol). Financial incentives would be provided for building or refurbishing houses in urban areas that achieve specific sustainability targets, for example by providing larger mortgages at lower rates of interest. The confidence provided by 5–10 years regeneration 'contracts', managed by well-trained and committed people will provide the security needed to launch urban bonds for upgrading the infrastructure.

Conclusion

Though the twentieth century started off with the optimism of building new communities, it ended up confused and depressed and living in suburbia. Yet we are at a turning point. In little over two decades, urban renewal has given way first to regeneration, and adaptive reuse, then revitalisation. Urban renaissance may not be far behind. We are beginning to look to mainland Europe and not just America for inspiration. We now have many more models than Ruskin knew, when he wrote 'when we build let us think that we build for ever'. The challenge is no longer to criticise the present or to visualise utopia, but to mend what we have inherited and to make what we add truly sustainable. The central issue is not how we spend money, but how we use resources. The test of success may no longer be how long people live, or how much they earn, but how well they spend their time. The examples we have illustrated in this book show one can live well without consuming the earth. The twenty-first century will rediscover that towns and cities are not only mankind's greatest invention and cultural achievement, but that sustainable urban neighbourhoods will give us back the time and balance we have lost.

Index

Notes and references

INTRODUCTION
1. **Department of the Environment** –
Projections of Households in England to 2016,
London HMSO, 1995
2. **Alan Holmans** – Housing demand and need
in England to 1991-2011, Joseph Rowntree
Foundation, 1995
3. **Who says we have to slum it?** – Peter
Hall – The Guardian – 5th February 1997
4. **Robert Fishman** – Bourgeois Utopia: The
rise and fall of suburbia, Basic Books, 1987
5. **John Burnett** – A Social History of Housing
1815–1985, Methuen, 1986
6. **Will Hutton** – The state we're in – Vintage
Books – 1995

CHAPTER 1
1. See **Spiro Kostof** – The City Shaped and
The City Assembled, Thames and Hudson, 1991
as well as **Jane Jacobs** – The Economy of Cities,
Vintage Books, 1969
2. **Michael Breheny** – Urban Densities and
Sustainable Development, Paper to the Institute
of Geographers, January 1995
3. **Commission of the European Communities** – Green Paper on the Urban Environment,
1990
4. **David Morris** – The Return Of The City
State, Resurgence Journal Issue 167 page 4,
Nov/Dec. 1994
5. **W.G. Hoskins** – The Making of the English
Landscape, Pelican, 1955
6. **Robert and Brenda Vale** – Green
Architecture, Thames & Hudson, 1991
7. See Introduction note 4
8. **Peter Hall** – Urban & Regional Planning,
Pelican, 1975
9. **Stefan Muthesius** – The English Terraced
House, Yale University Press, 1982
10. See for example **Mulholland Research
Associates** - Towns or leafier environments; a
survey of family homebuying choices –
Housebuilders Federation, Dec. 1995
11. There have been various reviews of urban
depopulation. One of the best reviews is **Tony
Champion** (ed.) – Counterurbanisation: The
changing pace and nature of population
deconcentration, London, Edward Arnold, 1989
12. **Martin Mogridge** – The Rejuvenation of
Inner London, London Transport Planners,
1997
13. **URBED** – Vital and Viable Town Centres:
Meeting the Challenge, HMSO, 1994
14. **Nicholas Falk & Haris Martinos** – Inner
City; Local government and economic renewal,

Fabian Society, London, 1975
15. **Brian Robson** – Inner City Research
Programme: Assessing the Impact of Urban
Policy, HMSO, 1994
16. **Joel Garreau** – Edge Cities, Doubleday,
1992
17. Details of American initiatives described in
the Historic Preservation Journal – National
Trust for Historic Preservation – Sept/Oct.
1995
18. **Felson** – Routine activities and crime
prevention in the developing metropolis,
Criminology 25,4,911-931, 1987
19. **Donald J. Olsen** – The City As A Work Of
Art, Yale University Press, 1986
20. **Necdet Teymur, Thomas A. Markus,
Tom Wooley** - Rehumanising Housing –
Butterworths, 1988
21. **Jane Jacobs** – The Economy of Cities,
Vintage Books, 1969

CHAPTER 2
1. The material in this chapter draws on a
number of sources, the best two being: **Ian
Colquhoun & Peter Fauset** – Housing Design
in Practice, Longman Scientific and Technical,
1991, **Sim Van der Ryn & Peter Calthorpe**
– Sustainable Communities: A new design
synthesis for Cities, Suburbs and Towns, Sierra
Club Books, 1989
2. **Ebenezer Howard** – Tomorrow: A peaceful
path to real reform, 1898 (republished 1902 as
Garden Cities of Tomorrow)
3. **Raymond Unwin** – The Art of Building a
Home and Town Planning in Practice, 1909
4. **Peter Hall** – Urban & Regional Planning,
Pelican, 1975
5. Consultancy work in Benchill North,
Wythenshawe by URBED for Manchester City
Council, 1994, Unpublished
6. **Tony Garnier** – Une Cité Industrielle, 1917
7. **L'Office Public Communautaire D'HLM
De Lyon** – Musee Urbain Tony Garnier,
November 1991
8. **Le Corbusier** – The City of Tomorrow,
1922 La Ville Radieuse, 1933
9. **Marilyn Taylor** – Unleashing The Potential:
A review of the Action on Estates Programme,
The Joseph Rowntree Foundation, 1995
10. **Hans M. Wingler** – The Bauhaus, MIT
Press, 7th edition 1986
11. **Ludwig Hilberseimer** – The minimal home
in a stairless house, From the journal 'Bauhaus'
(Dessau), January 1931

CHAPTER 3
1. **Congres International de l'Architecture
Moderne** – Charter of Athens, 1933
2. **Conference proceedings** – The Heart of
the City, CIAM, 1952
3. **Clarence Perry** – New York Regional Plan,
1923
4. **Lewis Mumford** – The Culture of Cities,
1938
5. **Sir H Alker Tripp** – Town Planning and
Traffic, 1942
6. **Sir Colin Buchanan** – Traffic in Towns,
HMSO, 1963
7. **DOE/DOT** – Design Bulletin 32: Residential
Roads and Footpaths; Layout considerations,
HMSO, 2nd Edition 1992
8. **DETR** – Places Streets and Movement: A
Companion guide to Design Bulletin 32 -
Residential Roads and Footpaths, prepared by
Alan Baxter Associates, September 1998
9. **Raymond Unwin** – Nothing gained by
overcrowding, 1912
10. **Sir John Tudor Walters** (committee chair)
– Dwellings for the working classes, 1918
11. **J.B. Calhoun** – A Behavioural Sink: Roots of
behaviour, Harper, New York, 1962
12. **Alice Coleman** – Utopia on Trial: Vision
and reality in planned housing, Hilary Shipman
London, 2nd issue 1990
13. **Jane Jacobs** – Death and Life of Great
American Cities, Randon House 1961
14. **Patrick Abercombie** with **J.H.Forshaw**
the chief architect for London County Council,
published in 1943 and as a Penguin special
edited by **Arno Goldfinger**
15. **Manchester City Council** – Plan for
Manchester, 1949
16. **Jane Jacobs** – The Economy of Cities,
Vintage Books, 1969
17. Report to develop a cultural strategy for
Milton Keynes (unpublished)

CHAPTER 4
1. **Peter Gaskell** – Manufacturing Population
of England, 1833, reprinted 1972
2. **John Burnett** – A Social History of Housing
1815-1985, Methuen, 2nd. Edition 1986
3. **Freidrich Engels** – The condition of the
working class in England 1844, reprinted 1952
4. **Stefan Muthesius** – The English Terraced
House, Yale University Press, 1982
5. **Donald Olsen** – The City As a Work of Art :
London, Paris, Vienna, Yale, 1986
6. **Donald Olsen** – Town Planning in London:
The Eighteenth and Nineteenth Centuries, Yale

University Press, 2nd edition 1982
7. **H.J. Dyos** – Victorian Suburb: A study of the growth of Camberwell, 1961
8. **Gillian Tyndall** – The fields beneath, Granada Publishing, London, 1980
9. **Linda Clarke** – Building Capitalism, London, 1991
10. **H.J. Dyos and D.A. Reeder** – Slums and suburbs in the Victorian City; Images and Realities, Volume 1, 1973
11. **John Burnett** – A Social History of Housing 1815-1985, Methuen, 2nd. Edition 1986
12. **Stefan Muthesius** – The English Terraced House, Yale University Press, 1982
13. **Sir John Tudor Walters** (committee chair) – Dwellings for the working classes, 1918
14. **Local Government Management Board** – Manual on the preparation of state-aided housing schemes, 1919
15. **Peter Hall** – Urban & Regional Planning, Pelican, 1975
16. **Earl of Dudley** – The Design of Dwellings, Report of the Design of Dwellings Subcommittee of the Ministry of Health Central Housing Advisory Committee, 1944
17. **Parker Morris** – Homes for Today and Tomorrow, Department of the Environment, 1961
18. **The RIBA/Institute of Housing** – Homes of for the Future Group, 1983
19. **Valerie Karn** – British Housing Standards : Time for a new approach? Joseph Rowntree Foundation Enquiry into housing standards – 1994
20. **Tim Mars** – The good the bad and the ugly: Housing in Liverpool 8, Roof, Sept/Oct 1981
21. **Peter Bibby and John Shepherd** – Urbanisation in England: Projections 1991-2016, London, HMSO, 1995
22. **Martin Richardson** – Tower Block: Modern public housing in England, 1994
23. **Christopher Booker** – Writing in Building Design 15th April 1994
24. **Necdet Teymur, Thomas A. Markus, Tom Wooley** - Rehumanising Housing – Butterworths, 1988, Chapter 5, **Bill Hillier** – Against enclosure
25. **Oscar Newman** – Defensible space: People and design in the violent city, Architectural Press, 1972
26. **Ian Colquhoun and Peter Fauset** – Housing Design in Practice, Longman Scientific and Technical, 1991
27. **John Burnett** – A Social History of Housing

1815-1985, Methuen, 2nd. Edition 1986
28. RIBA Client Focus; Housing – RIBA Journal November 1994
29. **Tom Barron** – The challenge for the UK housing industry in the 1980s and the planning system, Construction management and Economics 1983
30. **Mark Stephens** – Housing policy in a European Perspective, Centre for Housing Research, Joseph Rowntree Foundation, 1994
31. **John Wrigglesworth** – Housing and Planning Review, February/March 1994
32. **Duncan MacLennan** – A Competitive UK Economy: The challenges for housing, Joseph Rowntree Foundation, 1994
33. **John Stewart** - Writing in the Housebuilder 1994
34. **John Wrigglesworth** – Housing and Planning Review, February/March 1994
35. **Savills** – Quarterly Residential Research Bulletin, FPD Savills Residential Research, Sept 1995
36. **Adrian Coles** – Paper to NFHA Conference 1994
37. Salford Builds 200 at 25% grant – Inside Housing news story 23rd Sept 1994
38. **Valerie Karn and Linda Sheridan** – New homes in the 1990s: A study of space and amenity in housing association and private sector production, Joseph Rowntree Foundation, 1994
39. **David Page** – Building for Communities: A study of new housing association estates, Joseph Rowntree Foundation, 1993
40. **Hamish McRae** – Writing in the Independent 24th March, 1994

CHAPTER 5
1. **Elizabeth Wilson** – The Precautionary Principle and the Compact City, Chapter in **M. Jenkins, E. Burton & K. Williams** (Eds) – Compact City: A Sustainable Urban Form? p217-330, F & FN Spon, 1996
2. **Jane Jacobs** – The Economy of Cities, Vintage Books, 1969
3. **Rachel Carson** – A Silent Spring and **The Club of Rome** – The Limits to Growth
4. **Ulrich Beck** – Ecological politics in an age of risk, Policy Press, Cambridge, 1995
5. **Commission of the European Communities** – Green Paper on the Urban Environment, 1990
6. **Tony Aldous** – Urban Villages: A Concept for creating mixed use urban developments on a sustainable scale, Urban Villages Forum, 1992

7. **Peter Calthorpe** – The Next American Metropolis, Princeton Architectural Press, 1993
8. **Gro Harlem Brundtland** (Chair) – Our common future, World Commission on Environment and Development – NY Oxford University Press 1987
9. **DOE** – White Paper This Common Inheritance, HMSO, 1990
10. **Commission of the European Communities** – 5th Environmental Action Plan, Towards Sustainability, Commission of the European Communities, 1993
11. **J.T. Houghton, B.A. Callender, S.K. Varney** (Eds.) – Climate Change 1992: Supplementary report to the IPCC's Scientific Assessment, Cambridge University Press, 1992
12. **UK Climate Change Impacts Review Group** – Review of the Potential Effects of Climate Change in the UK, HMSO, 1996
13. **Friends of the Earth** – Getting out of the greenhouse, FoE, 1992
14. **Agenda 21** – Action plan for the next century, UNCED NY, 1992
15. **UK Government** – Climate Change: The UK programme, HMSO, 1994
16. **UK Climate Change Impacts Review Group** – Review of the Potential Effects of Climate Change in the UK, HMSO, 1996
17. **Robert J. Lowe and Malcolm Bell** – Towards sustainable housing : building regulation for the 21st century (draft), Leeds Metropolitan University for the Joseph Rowntree Foundation, Dec. 1997
18. **David Malin Poodman** – Getting the Signals Right: Tax reform to protect the environment and the economy, Worldwatch Paper 134 – http://www.worldwatch.org/pubs/paper/134a.html
19. **Sustainable London Trust** – Creating A Sustainable London, Sustainable London Trust, 1996
20. **Robin Murray** – Towards a London Waste Strategy, LPAC, 1997
21. **Royal Commission on Environmental pollution** – 12th Report, Best Practicable Environmental Option, HMSO, 1988
22. **Savills** – The market for residential developments in the 1990s, Savills Residential Research, 1992
23. **DETR** – Developing an integrated transport policy, DETR, 1997
24. **CBI** – Moving forward: A business strategy for transport, CBI, 1995
25. **DOE/DOT** – Planning Policy Guidance: Transport, PPG 13, HMSO, 1994 and **DETR** –

Developing an integrated transport policy, DETR, 1997
26. **Hugh Barton, Geoff Davis, Richard Guise** – Sustainable settlements; A guide for planners, designers and developers, Local Government Management Board, April 1995
27. **Jorge Wilheim** – Fax messages from a near future, Earthscan, 1996

CHAPTER 6
1. **Office for National Satistics** – Regional Trends 32, the Stationary Office, 1997
2. **Mulholland Research Associates** - Towns or leafier environments; a survey of family homebuying choices – Housebuilders Federation, Dec. 1995
3. **Robson, Bradford and Deas** – The Impact of Urban Development Corporations in Leeds, Bristol and Central Manchester, DETR 1998
4. **John Burnett** – A Social History of Housing 1815-1985, Methuen, 2nd. Edition 1986
5. **Office of Population Censuses and Surveys** – Department of the Environment, The Scottish Office Environment Department, General Register Office (Scotland) Edition: 25 Published 1995
6. **Andres Duany** – Paper given to the Connected City Conference, Liverpool Architecture and Design Institute, 1997
7. **Brian Lewis** – A Home for Life, Search 14, Joseph Rowntree Foundation, Dec. 1992
8. **The Joseph Rowntree Foundation** – Building Lifetime Homes, Joseph Rowntree Foundation Feb. 1997
9. **John Burnett** – A Social History of Housing 1815-1985, Methuen, 2nd. Edition 1986
10. **DOE** – Projections of Households in England to 2016, London HMSO, 1995
11. **Central Statistical Office** – Social Trends 1970-1995, ONS CD-ROM, 1996
12. **Alan Holman** – Housing Demand and Need in England 1991 - 2011: The National Picture, The People - Will where they go? TCPA, Jan. 1996
13. **Central Statistical Office** – Social Trends 1970-1995, ONS CD-ROM, 1996
14. **Henley Centre** report described by **Ian Wray** – Can women save the city? Town & Country Planning Vol. 66 No 2 page 34, Feb. 1997
15. **Will Hutton** – The state we're in – Vintage Books – 1995
16. **Michael Breheny and Peter Hall** – So where will they go? Summary of TCPA Enquiry, Town & Country Planning July/Aug. 1996 Vol. 65 No 2, July / Aug. 1996
17. **Department of Employment** – Labour force survey, HMSO 1994
18. **V. Huws** – Teleworking in Britain, Analytica, Employment Department, 1993
19. **S. Graham and S. Marvin** – Telecommunication and the City: Electronic Places, Urban Spaces, Routledge London, 1996

CHAPTER 7
1. **David Page** – Building for Communities: A study of new housing association estates, Joseph Rowntree Foundation, 1993
2. **David Rudlin** – Valuing the value added: The role of Housing Plus in creating sustainable

communities, Report by URBED, The Housing Corporation 1998
3. **Ian Taylor** – Private Homes & Public Others, British Journal of Criminology Vol. 35 No 2, Spring 1995
4. **Jane Jacobs** – Death and Life of Great American Cities, Randon House 1961
5. **Michael Breheny** – Centerist, Decenterists and Compromisers, Chapter in **M. Jenkins, E. Burton & K. Williams** (Eds) – The Compact City: A Sustainable Urban Form?, E & FN Spon, 1996
6. **Allen Jacobs** – Great Streets, MIT Press
7. **David Popenoe** – The Suburban Environment: Sweden and the United States, University of Chicago Press, 1977
8. **Sheila Hayman** – Two-dimensional Living: Celebration, The Independent, 30th June 1996

CHAPTER 8
1. **Sir Michael Latham** – Constructing the Team, Final report of the Government/Industry Review team on procurement and contractual arrangements in the construction industry, HMSO 1998
2. **David Olivier** – Energy efficiency and renewables: Recent experience on mainland Europe, Energy Advisory Associates, 1992
3. **Valerie Karn** – British Housing Standards : Time for a new approach? Joseph Rowntree Foundation Enquiry into housing standards – 1994
4. **John Wrigglesworth** – Housing and Planning Review, February/March 1994
5. **Colin Ward** – Grays Inn Road and its marble halls - T&CP August/September 1998 - Quoting from **John McKean** – Learning from Segal and from BBC Radio 4 on 13th August 1997
6. **Savills** – The market for residential developments in the 1990s, Savills Residential Research, 1992
7. **John Willoughby** – NHER Training Course, Energy Advisory Associates, 1993
8. RIBA Client Focus; Housing – RIBA Journal November 1994
9. From consultancy work by URBED work for the Threshold Tennant Trust in London
10. **Valerie Karn and Linda Sheridan** – New homes in the 1990s: A study of space and amenity in housing association and private sector production, Joseph Rowntree Foundation, 1994
11. **David Rudlin** – Valuing the value added: The role of Housing Plus in creating sustainable communities, Report by URBED, The Housing Corporation, 1998
12. **Conran Roche, Davis Langdon and Everest, Aston University** – Cost of Residential Development on Green Field Sites, DOE, 1991
13. **David Rudlin and Nicholas Falk** – Building to Last: 21st Century Homes, The Joseph Rowntree Foundation, 1995
14. **Tia Cymru** – Technical Standards, Volume one: Development - The design and siting of housing, Tia Cymru, 1994
15. **Michael Ball** – Housing and Construction: A troubled relationship, Joseph Rowntree Foundation, 1996

16. **Jane Jacobs** – The Economy of Cities, Vintage Books, 1969
17. Better ways to build homes - Japanese Industrialised Housing, Agenda Housing Magazine, May 1997

CHAPTER 9
1. **Champion** (ed) – Counterurbanisation: The changing pace and nature of population deconcentration, London, Edward Arnold, 1989
2. **Peter Bibby and John Shepherd** – Urbanisation in Britain: Projections 1991-2016, London, HMSO, 1995
3. **Commission of the European Communities** – Green Paper on the Urban Environment, 1990
4. **DOE** – Sustainable Development: The UK Strategy, HMSO, 1994
5. **UK Round Table on Sustainable Development** – Housing and urban capacity, Feb. 1997
6. **Breheny, Gent and Lock** – Alternative Development Patterns: New settlements, Department of the Environment, 1994
7. **DOE/DOT** – Planning Policy Guidance: Transport, PPG 13, HMSO, 1994
8. **Department of the Environment** – Projections of Households in England to 2016, London HMSO, 1995
9. **UK Government** – Our future homes: Opportunity, choice, responsibility, DOE, London HMSO, 1995
10. **UK Government** – Household Growth - Where Shall we Live?, DOE, London HMSO, 1997
11. **DOE** – Land use change in England – No. 11 Ruislip, Government Statistical Office, 1996
12. **Nick Raynsford** – Quality, Sustainability, Suitability, Town and Country Planning , Vol. 66, No. 3, March 1997
13. **Richard Cabon** – Interview on the Radio 4 Today programme, Autumn 1997
14. **UK Government** – Planning for the communities of the future, DETR, London HMSO, 1998
15. **David Rudlin** – Tomorrow: A peaceful path to urban reform, Friends of the Earth, 1998
16. **Commission of the European Communities** – Green Paper on the Urban Environment, 1990
17. **Newman and Kenworthy** – Gasoline consumption and cities: A comparison of US cities with a global survey, Journal of the American Planning Association 55, 24-37, 1989
18. **Gordon and Richardson** – Gasoline consumption and cities: A reply, Journal of the American Planning Association 55, 342/5, 1989 plus **Gomez-Ibanez** – A global view of automobile dependence - Cities and automobile dependence: A source book, Journal of the American Planning Association 57 376/9, 1991
19. **ECOTEC** – Reducing transport emissions through planning, for the Department of the Environment, London HMSO, 1993
20. **Michael Breheny** – The compact city and transport energy consumption, Institute of British Geographers NS 20 81-101, 1995
21. **P. Headicar & C. Curtis** – Strategic housing location and travel behaviour, Oxford

Brookes University, 1995
22. **Andres Duany** – Paper given to the Connected City Conference, Liverpool Architecture and Design Institute, 1997
23. **Henley Centre** report described by **Ian Wray** – Can women save the city? Town & Country Planning Vol. 66 No 2 page 34, Feb. 1997
24. **Tony Burton** – Urban Footprints, CPRE, 1996
25. **Peter Bibby and John Shepherd** – Urbanisation in England: Projections 1991-2016, London, HMSO, 1995
26. **UK Round Table on Sustainable Development** – Housing and urban capacity, Feb. 1997
27. **Housebuilder Federation** – The People: Where will they go? Contribution to TCPA enquiry, Feb. 1996
28. **TCPA** – A series of papers were published as part of the national enquiry The People – Where will they go?' 1996
29. **TCPA** – Urban housing capacity and the sustainable city, A series of reports and a summary report published by the TCPA, 1998
30. **Michael Breheny and Peter Hall** – So where is it? Summary of TCPA Enquiry, Town & Country Planning July/Aug. 1996 Vol. 65 No 2, July / Aug. 1996
31. **Tony Champion** – Migration between metropolitan and non-metropolitan areas in Britain, Newcastle University, H507255132, 1996
32. **David Rudlin** – Tomorrow: A peaceful path to urban reform, Friends of the Earth, 1998
33. **Michael Breheny** – Urban housing capacity and the sustainable city (Appendix 1 - Success in using urban land) TCPA/Joseph Rowntree Foundation, Dec. 1997
34. **DOE** – Survey of derelict land in England, London HMSO, 1993
35. **John Shepherd and Andris Abakuks** – The national survey of vacant land in the urban areas of England - 1990, Planning research programme, London HMSO, 1992
36. **David Hall** – Housing capacity, how much and where is it? Town and Country Planning Vol. 66, No. 9, p230, Sept. 1997
37 **James Barlow** – Offices into flats: Flexible design and flexible planning, Policy Studies Institute, March 1994
38. **Herring Baker Harris Research** – Behind the facade, London, 1992
39. **Urban Initiatives & Chestertons** – Hertfordshire: Dwelling provision through planned regeneration – Hertfordshire County Council, 1995
40. **Empty Homes Agency** – Press release: England's empty homes, Feb. 1998
41. **DOE** – The English House Condition Survey, DOE, London HMSO, 1991
42. **Llewelyn-Davies** – Providing more Homes in Urban Areas, for the Joseph Rowntree Foundation published by the Policy Press, 1994, also **Llewelyn-Davies** – Sustainable residential quality: new approaches to urban living, LPAC, January 1998
43. **Office for National Statistics** – Regional Trends 32, the Stationary Office, 1997
44. Quoted by **Kate Williams, Elizabeth**

Burton and Mike Jenks – Achieving the compact city through intensification, Chapter in **M. Jenkins, E. Burton & K. Williams** (Eds) – Compact City: A Sustainable Urban Form? F & FN Spon, 1996
45. **Alan Hooper** – Housing Requirements and Housing Provision: The Strategic Issues, Background paper for The People: Where will they go? TCPA, Jan. 1996
46. **Brenda Vale and Ernie Scoffam** – How compact is sustainable, how sustainable is compact, Chapter in **M. Jenkins, E. Burton & K. Williams** (Eds) – Compact City: A Sustainable Urban Form? F & FN Spon, 1996
47. **Alice Coleman** – Utopia on Trial: Vision and reality in planned housing, Hilary Shipman London, 2nd issue 1990
48. **Harley Sherlock** – Cities are good for us, Paladin, 1994
49. **Michael Breheny** – Centerist, Decenterists and Compromisers, Chapter in **M. Jenkins, E. Burton & K. Williams** (Eds) – The Compact City: A Sustainable Urban Form?, E & FN Spon, 1996
50. **Jane Jacobs** – The Economy of Cities, Vintage Books, 1969

CHAPTER 10

1. **Robert and Brenda Vale** – The Autonomous House: Design and planning for self-sufficiency, Thames & Hudson London, 1975
2. **Robert and Brenda Vale** – Housing development at Cresswell Road Sheffield for North Sheffield Housing Association
3. **Eco-Village Foundation** – Proposal prepared by the Gaia Trust, May 1994
4. **Koen Steemers** – Project ZED: towards Zero Emission urban Development, The Martin Centre for Architectural and Urban Studies, Cambridge, 1998
5. **Robert and Brenda Vale** – Green Architecture, Thames & Hudson Ltd. 1991
6. **Mathis Wackernagel & William Rees** – Our Ecological Footprint - reducing human impact on the earth, New Society Publishers, 1996
7. **Herbert Girardet** – From Mobilization to Civilization, Resurgence Journal, Issue 167, page 6, Nov/Dec 1994
8. **Herbert Girardet** – The Gaia Atlas of Cities, Gaia Books, 1992
9. **ECOTEC** – Reducing transport emissions through planning, for the Department of the Environment, London HMSO, 1993
10. **Roger Levett** – The Green City – What might it be? Planning Exchange Conference; Green Housing - Housing, planning, building and the environment, Feb. 1991
11. **Joe Ravetz** – Manchester 2020 - A Sustainable City Region Project, CER for the Town and Country Planning Association, Sept. 1995
12. **DOE** – Making Waste Work, Dept of the Environment, HMSO, Dec. 1995
13. **Tony Aldous** – Urban Villages - A Concept for creating mixed use urban developments on a sustainable scale, Urban Villages Forum, 1992
14. **Peter Calthorpe** – The Pedestrian Pocket Book - A New Suburban Design Strategy, Princeton Architectural Press, 1994

15. **Richard Register** – Ecocity Berkeley, North Atlantic Books, 1994
16. **Robert and Brenda Vale** – Green architecture, Thames & Hudson Ltd. 1991
17. **Environmental and Transport Planning** – Streets as living space for the DETR, HMSO, 1997
18. **Colin Davis** – Improving Design In The High Street, Royal Fine Arts Commission, DOE, Land Securities and Marks & Spencer, 1997
19. **Alan Baxter Associates** – Master Plan for Poundbury, Dorset, Dutchy of Cornwall, 1994
20. **David Rudlin and Nick Dodd** – Managing Gridlock: A sustainable transport policy, SUN Dial 5, URBED, Autumn 1997
21. **Francis Tibbalds** – Making People-Friendly Towns: Improving the public environment in towns and cities, Longman, 1992
22. **Hugh Barton, Geoff Davis, Richard Guise** – Sustainable settlements; A guide for planners, designers and developers, Local Government Management Board, April 1995
23. **John Willoughby** – NHER Training Manual, Energy Advisory Associates, 1993
24. **Elsbeth Wills, Mike Galloway, Piers Gough** – Crown Street Regeneration Project, Glasgow Development Agency, 1993
25. **Michael King** – The role of community heating in the sustainable urban neighbourhood, SUN Dial 2, URBED, Autumn 1996
26. **Keith Collins** – Recycling: No longer just a middle-class fad, SUN Dial 5, URBED, Spring 1998
27. **Jane Jacobs** – The Economy of Cities, Vintage Books, 1969
28. **Jane Jacobs** – The Economy of Cities, Vintage Books, 1969
29. **Robert and Brenda Vale** – Green Architecture, Thames & Hudson Ltd. 1991
30. **Tara Garnett** – Harvesting The Cities, Town and Country Planning, Vol. 65, No. 10, Oct 1995
31. **Levitt Berstein Associates** – Building Homes as if Tomorrow Mattered, The RIBA exhibition, Levitt Berstein Associates, June 1997

CHAPTER 11

1. **Prince Charles** - A Vision of Britain : A Personal View of Architecture, Doubleday,1989
2. **Kevin Lynch** – Image of the City, MIT Press, 1975. **Francis Bacon** – Design Of Cities, Thames & Hudson, 1975. **Gordon Cullen** – Townscapes, Architectural Press 1961. **Spiro Kostof** – The City Shaped, Thames and Hudson, 1991. **Francis Tibbalds** – Making People-Friendly Towns: Improving the public environment in towns and cities, Longman, 1992. **Ian Bentley** – Responsive Environments - A manual for designers, The Architectural Press, 1985. **Harley Sherlock** – Harley Sherlock – Cities are good for us, Paladin, 1994
3. **Richard Sennett** – Uses of Disorder: Personal identity and city life, Faber and Faber, 1996
4. **Home Office Crime Prevention Unit** – Secured by design, Home Office, 1994
5. **Bill Hillier** – Against Enclosure, Chapter in: **Necdet Teymur, Thomas A. Markus, Tom Wooley** - Rehumanising Housing – Butterworths, 1988

6. **Chistopher Alexander** – A New Theory of Urban Design, Oxford University Press, 1987
7. **Andres Duany and Elizabeth Plater-Zyberk** – Town and Town-making Principles, Rizzoli International Publications Inc. 1991
8. **Charlie Baker & David Rudlin** – Rebuilding The City : The Hulme Guide To Development, Manchester City Council, June 1994
9. **Francis Tibbalds** – Making People-Friendly Towns: Improving the public environment in towns and cities, Longman, 1992.
10. **DOE** – Quality in Town and Country, DOE, 1994
11. **Charlie Baker & David Rudlin** – Rebuilding The City : The Hulme Guide To Development, Manchester City Council, June 1994
12. **Manchester City Council** – A Guide to Development in Manchester, Manchester City Council, 1997
13. **Essex County Council** – A guide for residential and mixed-use areas, Essex County Council, 1998
14. **Elspeth Wills, Mike Galloway, Piers Gough** – Crown Street Regeneration Project, Glasgow Development Agency, 1993
15. **Ajuntament de Barcelona** – Barcelona, Posa't Guapa, Ajuntament de Barcelona, 1992
16. **Jane Jacobs** – Death and Life of Great American Cities, Randon House 1961
17. **Hugh Barton, Geoff Davis, Richard Guise** – Sustainable settlements; A guide for planners, designers and developers, Local Government Management Board, April 1995
18. **Alan Rowley** – Mixed use development: Concepts and realities, RICS Books, 1996
19. **Andy Coupland** (ed.) – Rebuilding the city: Mixed Use Development, F & FN Spon, 1997
20. **Ann Petherick** – Living over the Shop, SUN Dial 5, URBED, Autumn 1997

CHAPTER 12
1. **David Page** – Building for Communities: A study of new housing association estates, Joseph Rowntree Foundation, 1993
2. **Marylin Taylor** – Unleashing the potential: A review of the Action on Estates Programme, Joseph Rowntree Foundation
3. **David Rudlin** – Roughey Gardens, for North Cheshire Housing Association, Unpublished
4. **John Burnett** – A Social History of Housing 1815–1985, Methuen, 1986
5. **Chris Bazlinton** – Mixed Blessings, Search 26 - the journal of the Joseph Rowntree Foundation, Winter 1996
6. **Sheila Hayman** – Two-dimensional Living: Celebration, The Independent, 30th June 1996
7. **Barry Poynter** – Paper to SUN Seminar, URBED, Unpublished, 1996
8. **Michael Simmons** – Out with the old, in with new, The Guardian, 3 Jan 1996
9. **Mulholland Research Associates** - Towns or leafier environments; a survey of family homebuying choices – Housebuilders Federation, Dec. 1995
10. **David Thame** – Fear is the Key - Manchester City Development Guide, Property Week, 21st Aug 1995
11. **Oscar Newman** – Defensible Space: People and design in the violent city, Architectural Press, 1972

12. **Alice Coleman** – Utopia on Trial: Vision and reality in planned housing, Hilary Shipman London, 2nd issue 1990
13. **Necdet Teymur, Thomas A. Markus, Tom Wooley** - Rehumanising Housing – Butterworths, 1988, Chapter 5, **Bill Hillier** – Against enclosure
14. **Steve Osbourn & Henry Shaftoe** – Safer Neighbourhoods: Successes and failures in crime prevention, Safer Neighbourhoods Unit , Joseph Rowntree Foundation, 1995
15. **Rod Hackney** – The Good, the Bad and the Ugly: Cities in Crisis, Frederick Muller, 1990

CHAPTER 13
1. **Peter Marcus** – Lessons from Hulme - Hsg. Summary 5, Joseph Rowntree Foundation, Sept 1994
2. **City Planning Department** – A new community: The redevelopment of Hulme, Manchester City Council, 1966
3. **Capita Consultants** – The Hulme Study, Commissioned by DOE and Manchester City Council, 1989
4. **Price Waterhouse** – Consultancy Study of Hulme which led to the establishment of City Challenge for Manchester City Council and the Housing Corporation, 1991
5. **Charlie Baker & David Rudlin** – Rebuilding The City : The Hulme Guide To Development, Manchester City Council, June 1994
6. **Tony Aldous** – Urban Villages: A Concept for creating mixed use urban developments on a sustainable scale, Urban Villages Forum, 1992
7. **Elspeth Wills, Mike Galloway, Piers Gough** – Crown Street Regeneration Project, Glasgow Development Agency, 1993
8. **DOE/DOT** – Design Bulletin 32: Residential Roads and Footpaths; Layout considerations, HMSO, 2nd Edition 1992
9. **David Thame** – Fear is the Key - Manchester City Development Guide, Property Week, 21st Aug 1995
10. **Manchester City Council** – A Guide to Development in Manchester, Manchester City Council, 1997
11. Illustrations first published in SUN Dial 4, SUN Dial 4, URBED, Spring/Summer 1997
12. **DOE** – Sustainable Development: The UK Strategy, HMSO, 1994
13. **ECOTEC** – Reducing transport emissions through planning, for the Department of the Environment, London HMSO, 1993. **Michael Breheny** – Urban Densities and Sustainable Development, Paper to the Institute of Geographers, January 1995
14. **Charles Fulford** – The Compact City and the Market, Chapter in **M. Jenkins, E. Burton & K. Williams** (Eds) – Compact City: A Sustainable Urban Form? p217-330, F & FN Spon, 1996
15. **Hugh Barton, Geoff Davis, Richard Guise** – Sustainable settlements; A guide for planners, designers and developers, Local Government Management Board, April 1995
16. **Nick Dodd and David Rudlin** – The Model Sustainable Urban Neighbourhood, SUN Dial 4, URBED, Spring/Summer 1997
17. **David Rudlin and Nicholas Falk** – Building to Last: 21st Century Homes, The Joseph

Rowntree Foundation, 1995
18. **David Rudlin** – Homes for Change, SUN Dial 2, URBED, 1996

CHAPTER 14
1. **Andres Duany and Elizabeth Plater-Zyberk** – Town and Town-making Principles, Rizzoli International Publications Inc. 1991
2. **Prince Charles** – Introduction to: Urban Villages: A Concept for creating mixed use urban developments on a sustainable scale, Urban Villages Forum, 1992
3. **Christopher Alexander** – A Pattern Language, 1977. The Timeless Way Of Building, 1979. A New Theory of Urban Design, 1987, All Oxford University Press
4. **Rob Cowan** – The Connected City, Urban Initiatives, 1997
5. **Peter Hall** – Urban & Regional Planning, Pelican, 1975
6. Charlie **Baker & David Rudlin** – Rebuilding The City : The Hulme Guide To Development, Manchester City Council, June 1994 and **Manchester City Council** – A Guide to Development in Manchester, Manchester City Council, 1997
7. **Andres Duany and Elizabeth Plater-Zyberk** – Town and Town-making Principles, Rizzoli International Publications Inc. 1991
8. **Elspeth Wills, Mike Galloway, Piers Gough** – Crown Street Regeneration Project, Glasgow Development Agency, 1993
9. **Rob Cowan** – The Cities design forgot, Urban Initiatives, March 1995
10. **Ed Mayo, Stephen Thake, Tony Gibson** – Taking power: an agenda for community economic renewal, New Economics Foundation, 1997
11. **Tony Gibson** – The power in our hands, Jon Carpenter, 1996
12. **Comments by Ted Kitchen at the TCPA seminar** Urban housing capacity and the sustainable city held in Manchester 1998
13. **David Rudlin** – Tomorrow: A peaceful path to urban reform, Friends of the Earth, 1998
14. **UK Government** – Planning for the Communities of the future, London HMSO, 1998

Images and Illustrations